Tikal: Dynasties, F
& Affairs of State

M000275097

Publication of the Advanced Seminar Series
is made possible by generous support from
The Brown Foundation, Inc., of Houston, Texas.

The Advanced Seminar upon which this volume is based
was supported by a generous grant from John Bourne.

**School of American Research
Advanced Seminar Series**

Richard M. Leventhal
General Editor

Tikal: Dynasties, Foreigners, & Affairs of State

Contributors

Marshall Joseph Becker
Department of Anthropology, West Chester University

T. Patrick Culbert
Department of Anthropology, University of Arizona

Robert E. Fry
Department of Sociology and Anthropology, Purdue University

Peter D. Harrison
Maxwell Museum of Anthropology, University of New Mexico
MARI, Tulane University
American Division, University of Pennsylvania Museum

William A. Haviland
Profesor Emeritus, University of Vermont

Christopher Jones
American Division, University of Pennsylvania Museum

Juan Pedro Laporte
Department of Archaeology, Universidad de San Carlos de Guatemala

H. Stanley Loten
School of Architecture, Carleton University, Ottawa

Simon Martin
Institute of Archaeology, University College London

Hattula Moholy-Nagy
American Section, University of Pennsylvania Museum

Jeremy A. Sabloff
University of Pennsylvania Museum of Archaeology and Anthropology

Robert J. Sharer
University of Pennsylvania Museum

Tikal: Dynasties, Foreigners, & Affairs of State

Advancing Maya Archaeology

Edited by Jeremy A. Sabloff

School of American Research Press
Santa Fe

James Currey
Oxford

School of American Research Press

Post Office Box 2188
Santa Fe, New Mexico 87504-2188

James Currey Ltd

73 Botley Road
Oxford OX2 0BS

Director: James F. Brooks
Editor: Sarah Nestor
Designer: Cynthia Welch
Indexer: Catherine Fox
Printer: Maple-Vail Book Group

Library of Congress Cataloging-in-Publication Data:
Tikal : dynasties, foreigners & affairs of state : advancing Maya archaeology / edited by
Jeremy A. Sabloff.
    p. cm. — (School of American Research advanced seminar series)
    Includes bibliographical references and index.
    ISBN 1-930618-21-2 (alk. paper) — ISBN 1-930618-22-0 (pbk. : alk paper)
    1. Tikal Site (Guatemala) 2. Mayas—Kings and rulers. 3. Mayas—Urban residence.
4. Mayas—Commerce 5. Heads of state—Succession—Guatemala—Tikal Site. 6. City planning—
Guatemala—Tikal Site. 7. Inscriptions, Mayan—Guatemala—Tikal Site. 8. Guatemala—
Antiquities. I. Sabloff, Jeremy A. II. Series

F1435.1.T5 T524 2003
972.81'2—dc21   2002042750

British Library Cataloguing in Publication Data:
Tikal : dynasties, foreigners & affairs of state : advancing Maya archaeology. — (School of
American Research advanced seminar series)
1. Mayas—Guatemala—Tikal—Antiquities 2. Mayas—Guatemala—Tikal—Social life and
customs 3. Tikal Site (Guatemala)—Antiquities
I. Sabloff, Jeremy A., 1944– II. School of American Research 972.8'1016

ISBN 0-85255-934-8 (James Currey cloth)
ISBN 0-85255-939-9 (James Currey paper)

Contents

Figures and Tables

Figures

Tables

Preface

It has been more than three decades since the University of Pennsylvania Museum of Archaeology and Anthropology, in cooperation with the government of Guatemala, completed its field research at the great Maya site of Tikal. As relatively short a period of time as the 30 years represents, for Maya studies it is like an eternity. Scholarly understanding of ancient Maya civilization has changed significantly during this period—in part stimulated by the research of the Tikal Project—and so, clearly, has the context for the ongoing analyses and publications of the Tikal Project data. Moreover, continuing research at Tikal has amplified our knowledge of the site as well as providing a new momentum for the completion of write-ups of the Tikal Project research.

The 1999 School of American Research advanced seminar "Changing Perspectives on Tikal and the Development of Maya Civilization" examined the potential contributions and impact that the unique and impressive Tikal database and the current writings on aspects of this database can make to scholarly perspectives on the nature of ancient Maya civilization. The seminar also assessed the ways in which growing insights into ancient Maya civilization affect the interpretations emerging from ongoing Tikal analyses. One of the principal goals of the seminar—and of this book—was to act as a bridge between the numerous Tikal Project publications published over the past 30 years and the many reports currently being readied for the press. This volume can be seen as a checkpoint in the midst of the ongoing analyses and manuscript preparations. Moreover, the intellectual excitement that the animated interchanges at the seminar provided the participants not only has led to the strong contributions reflected in the chapters in this book but also has stimulated many of the authors to complete or restart the manuscripts of the final Tikal reports for which they are responsible. Scholars of the ancient Maya will be pleased to know that the University of Pennsylvania Museum will publish these reports—it is to be hoped at a rapid rate—in the coming years.

The advanced seminar participants included eight scholars, each with a particular area of interest, who had worked at Tikal during the 1950s and 1960s: Marshall Joseph Becker (ancient Tikal social structure), T. Patrick Culbert (ceramics and environment), Robert E. Fry (ceramics from Tikal's sustaining area), Peter D. Harrison (excavations in the Central Acropolis and West Plaza), William A. Haviland (urban demography and human skeletal material), Christopher Jones (stratigraphy), H. Stanley Loten (architecture), and Hattula Moholy-Nagy (artifacts). Four other scholars—Juan Pedro Laporte, Simon Martin, Robert J. Sharer, and I—provided a broader context through additional presentations or general discussions.

Of particular value to the participants was the sharing of new information about Tikal that has emerged since the close of the University of Pennsylvania Museum research there. For example Juan Pedro Laporte, who has supervised a series of important research projects at Tikal, especially at the Mundo Perdido (or "Lost World") complex, was able to provide details on a variety of topics, including the major impact that the great Central Mexican city of Teotihuacan had on Tikal. Simon Martin, one of the leading Maya epigraphers in the world today, shared some of the insights he has gained about the Tikal royal dynasty, especially in relation to its beginnings. Robert Sharer provided comparisons between Tikal and Copan and discussed the growing evidence for a link between Tikal and the founding of Copan. The possible involvement of Teotihuacan in this founding was also pointed out.

The University of Pennsylvania Museum's Tikal Project, under the direction of Edwin M. Shook and, subsequently, William R. Coe, provided or stimulated a number of key breakthroughs in scholarly understanding of the ancient Maya in the 1960s and 1970s, which contributed heavily to the demise of the "traditional model" of Maya civilization. These new perspectives included: clear evidence for the rise of complexity in the Maya Lowlands more than 500 years before the beginning of the Classic period (A.D. 300); elimination of the old "vacant center" view of Maya sites in favor of a true urban model; support for a model of greater agricultural complexity than previously believed; strong evidence for conflict and warfare during the Classic period as opposed to the traditional view of the peaceful Maya; new light on political history during Classic times; and the overthrow of

Edwin M. Shook (courtesy University of Pennsylvania Museum).

the traditional contention that the ancient Maya were isolated from social, political, and economic developments throughout Mesoamerica. These important understandings were disseminated in a wide variety of scholarly publications.

As significant as the contributions of the research at Tikal have been to date in building scholarly knowledge of the rise of Maya civilization, its Classic flowering, and its subsequent collapse, the reports that are currently being prepared by the Tikal researchers promise to have just as an important impact on the field in the first decade of the 21st century. Robert Sharer's statement that the University of Pennsylvania Museum's Tikal Project underlined "the central importance of Tikal for understanding the overall development of lowland Maya civilization" is certainly as applicable today as it was years ago.

William R. Coe (courtesy University of Pennsylvania Museum).

Though the advanced seminar discussions were wide-ranging and varied, several historical and topical cultural questions emerged time and again in these discussions. One important question concerned the timing of the foundation of the Tikal dynasty (now dated perhaps as early as A.D. 100, if not before) and the initial indications of sociopolitical complexity (which clearly had emerged by 300 B.C. or earlier), as discussed in the chapters by Simon Martin, T. Patrick Culbert, Hattula Moholy-Nagy, William Haviland, Robert Fry, and Stanley Loten. A second question concerned the reality of the often discussed sixth–seventh century hiatus in monument erection at the site, which—as discussed in Simon Martin's chapter—does not appear to be as great a gap as has been argued in the past. A third and closely related question was the nature of the reassertion of central authority at Tikal around A.D. 700, after the hiatus with the political and military triumphs of Jasaw Chan K'awiil. This revival was also reflected in changes in ceramics (the transition from Ik to Imix), artifacts, settlement, and architecture, as discussed in most of the chapters in the book. Finally, the question of the rapidity of changes at Tikal during the onset of Terminal Classic times was answered by the growing evidence for

Edwin M. Shook and William R. Coe at Tikal in 1957 (courtesy University of Pennsylvania Museum).

relatively sudden collapse and depopulation during the ninth century, which is discussed in many chapters, including those by T. Patrick Culbert, Hattula Moholy-Nagy, William Haviland, and, especially, Christopher Jones.

In addition, data indicating that foreigners (possibly connected to Central Mexico) resided in the city; that there was a thriving marketplace in the center of Tikal; that ceramic shapes and forms can be good indicators of the function of structures at the site; that architectural form can be more important than size in assessing sociopolitical functions of residential groups; and that differences in tomb form and contents between the Early and Late Classic periods can shed useful light on the changing fortunes of Tikal's rulers are just a few examples of new or better information that the ongoing analyses of the Tikal excavations and surveys are revealing and that are detailed in this book.

Of all of the topics discussed, the ones related to the political underpinnings of the Classic flowering have particular resonance for current controversies in Maya archaeology. As noted in Simon Martin's chapter, one of the most important consequences of the epigraphic revolution in Maya studies has been the new insight into the complexity of Classic intercity political competition. More specifically, the rivalry between Tikal and the city of Calakmul to the northwest is shown to have structured much of these interactions between different polities. While the empirical evidence for the role of Teotihuacan in such political machinations in the Maya Lowlands in general and specifically at Tikal still remains unclear, the Simon Martin, Juan Pedro Laporte, and Robert Sharer chapters, among others, reveal that its role was far greater than most scholars have previously thought. Laporte, however, is still more cautious than the others about the strength of Teotihuacan's role.

Despite tremendous advances in the decipherment of Tikal texts and important new archaeological knowledge of the site (summarized in part by Laporte), which have provided important new insights into these political and (almost certainly) economic questions, the relationship between the epigraphic and archaeological data still remains problematic in regards to our understanding of the Classic period occupation of Tikal. As is frequently the case, the amalgam of the two data sets has raised many more questions than answers, but—as is demonstrated in several of the chapters—the earlier historical darkness is now better illuminated and the paths to stronger understandings are clearer.

The general chronology that follows this preface offers a nice example of this problematic relationship. The chronology illustrates the key periods used by the authors in the book, focusing on three sets of terms: general Lowland periods, Culbert's ceramic-complex names, and Martin's groupings of the 30+ rulers' times of ascendancy. It is intended to help the reader compare the terms as they are used in various chapters. While there are some intriguing correspondences between the ceramic and epigraphic sequences, especially in the Late Classic, there are also some clear differences, where changes in ceramic styles do not appear to relate at all to inferred political changes. Obviously, scholars will carefully explore these similarities and differences in the coming years, both in the Tikal reports and elsewhere. Moreover, As Simon Martin frequently reminded the seminar participants, the ongoing decipherments of Maya inscriptions remain tentative in many cases, and therefore the dynastic interpretations he presents in the first chapter must clearly be considered a work in progress.

While this book differs from other Maya volumes in the SAR Advanced Seminar Series in that it focuses on a particular site rather than a topic (such as ancient Maya settlement patterns), time period (Classic to Postclassic transition), or event (Classic Maya collapse), the discussions in the various chapters nevertheless focus in one way or another on most of the key questions regarding the rise, development, and decline of Classic Maya civilization in the southern Lowlands that have been raised in previous SAR volumes on the ancient Maya. The authors and I hope that this book will prove as useful as the earlier ones.

The authors are grateful to John Bourne, whose generosity made this advanced seminar possible. We also thank the staff of the School of American Research for their famous hospitality and support and to Douglas Schwartz for initiating and fostering the planning that led to the advanced seminar and to this book. Matthew Johnson prepared the combined references, while Bernard Ortiz de Montellano translated Juan Pedro Laporte's chapter from Spanish to English. We also appreciate the helpful comments of two anonymous reviewers of this volume and the assistance of the SAR Press staff.

Jeremy A. Sabloff

Tikal Chronology

A.D.	Lowland Maya Periods		Ceramic Complexes	Dynastic Periods
1200		POSTCLASSIC	Caban	
1100				
1000				A.D.
900	Terminal	CLASSIC	Eznab	889 — Terminal Descent (Rulers 30 to end)
800	Late		Imix	794 — Restored Fortunes (Rulers 26–29)
700				692 —
600	Intermediate		Ik	Dynastic Umbra (Rulers 20–25)
500	Early		Manik	562 — Complex Times (Rulers 19–21) / 508 — New Order (Rulers 15–18)
400				378 —
300				Early Dynasty (Rulers 1–14)
200	Terminal	PRECLASSIC	Cimi	
100			Cauac	100 —
1	Late			
100			Chuen	
200				
300				
400			Tzec	
500	Middle			
600			Eb	
700				
800				
B.C.				

Tikal: Dynasties, Foreigners, & Affairs of State

1

In Line of the Founder

A View of Dynastic Politics at Tikal

Simon Martin

Dynastic chronologies, like their ceramic and architectural counterparts, play a key role in our understanding of Classic Maya cities.
Inscriptions created to celebrate the lives and achievements of individual rulers not only provide us with an invaluable framework of absolute
dates; they reveal realms of sociopolitical culture irrecoverable by other
means. Through them we gain some perspective, however hazy, on the
personalities that once dominated the governmental process while also
receiving clues to a wider context—to the shifting fortunes of the state,
which had a telling impact on the lives of its citizens and the fabric of
the city itself.

As the last three decades have seen significant advances in epigraphic research, this is a stimulating area in which to review developments at Tikal. We have a wealth of new data on the political activities
of the polity and the biographies of its ruling elite, allowing us to paint
a more detailed picture of Tikal's ancient existence. For the purposes
of this study I have divided Tikal history into six thematic sections: The
Early Dynasty (c. A.D. 100–378), The New Order (378–508), Complex
Times (508–562), Dynastic Umbra (562–692), Restored Fortunes

3

(692–794), and Terminal Descent (794–889). Following a discussion of Tikal history in a particular period, each section presents a brief discussion of themes of broader relevance to Maya culture and society. Within this framework I have focused particular attention on new and/or problematic areas of Tikal epigraphy. Fresh insights bring with them fresh interpretative challenges, which are at their most acute where the relevant texts are few in number and preservation is poor. Very often, advances bring not clarity but only access to more complex historiographical problems.

A decipherment of immediate relevance concerns Tikal's ancient name. Independent work by Christian Prager and David Stuart in 1992 indicates that the kingdom was known as *mutul* or *mutal*. The same term stands for the city itself, though here with the additional prefix *yax,* an adjective of wide meaning including "first/new," "beautiful," and "green-blue." While the root term *mut* refers to the tied knot of hair depicted in the famous "bundle" hieroglyph T569, its deeper meaning as a place-name is currently lost to us.[1]

Following a consensus among seminar participants, I use the best available readings of Maya royal names, although traditional nicknames are noted at first appearance and a full concordance is provided at the end of the chapter in table 1.1.[2] All monuments and structures to which I refer are those of Tikal unless otherwise stated. A number of unprovenanced materials are included where they are informative, though they need not necessarily have originated at Tikal. Clearly, this chapter owes a tremendous debt to the Tikal Project and Proyecto Nacional Tikal for recording and publishing the site's inscriptions and to those authors who have worked on these endeavors, both formally and informally. Tikal Report 33A (C. Jones and Satterthwaite 1982) remains the cornerstone of epigraphic research at the city, while studies by Coggins (1975) and C. Jones (1977) stand out as important contributions to our modern understanding. For a fuller discussion of the macro-political context touched on in this chapter, see S. Martin and Grube (2000).

THE EARLY DYNASTY: C. A.D. 100–378

An issue of abiding importance in Maya studies is the Preclassic-Classic transition, the perceived shift from one social and political order to another. It would be premature to dub the Preclassic as truly "predynastic," but there is little question that the Classic placed an emphasis on dynastic rule that was either absent or weakly articulated in earlier times. The emergence of historical texts and personal portraits as well as changes in the style and use of monumental architecture—in particular its enhanced funerary function—reflect profound shifts in political rhetoric and ideology.

Evidence for an emic distinction, that the Maya themselves saw these changes as meaningful, emerges from their royal "successor titles" (Mathews 1975; Riese 1984). The numbering of rulers in sequence serves notice not only of a dynastic consciousness but a finite origin. While counts at some sites reach back into deep antiquity—potentially mythical in character—most are modest, seldom reaching back to the beginnings of major architecture or other evidence for an organized elite. The subsequent identification of the "founders" who initiated these lines has unmasked the very individuals to whom the Maya ascribed the "Classic" movement (Stuart and Schele 1986; Grube 1988; Schele 1992).

The stated progenitor of the Tikal dynasty was Yax Ehb' Xook(?) "First Step Shark(?)" (Schele 1986, 1992; Grube 1988; Stuart 1999) (fig. 1.1a–c).[3] His name appears in titular formulas used by his successors—as in "xth set in the count/line of Yax Ehb' Xook"—and as a secondary name carried by many of them.[4] Unfortunately, no dates for his rule have survived, and estimates rely on calculating average reign lengths and applying them to the numbered sequence. Previous estimates have produced ranges of A.D. 170–235 (C. Jones 1991:109) and 219–238 (Mathews 1985:31). Both of these, however, were predicated on fixing the end of the 9th ruler's reign at the year 378. There is now good reason to believe that this ruler was actually the 14th in line, with clear implications for early royal chronology (Grube 1998).[5] Grube's key revision places Tikal's dynastic foundation somewhere between A.D. 63 and 138, with 100 an acceptable mean.[6]

There is the potential here for an improved "fit" between epigraphic and archaeological data. Excavation of the North Acropolis revealed a certain sophistication surrounding Burial 85, which was richer than previous interments and subsequently encased by larger and more elaborate architecture. The precise dating of its nascent

FIGURE 1.1

The Tikal "founder," Yax Ehb' Xook, (a) *from an unprovenanced vessel,* (b) *detail of a headdress crest on Stela 31, and* (c) *Stela 5, A6. (All drawings by the author unless otherwise indicated. Inscriptions from Tikal after William R. Coe or field sketches by the author.)*

'Classic style' is unclear, but current judgment places it around A.D. 75 (W. R. Coe and McGinn 1963; W. R. Coe 1990; C. Jones 1991:106–107). Elsewhere, specifically at Copan, dynastic origins described in the inscriptions have had excellent archaeological corroboration (Sharer et al. 1999; Sharer, this volume). While we are unlikely ever to know if Burial 85 contained the remains of Yax Ehb' Xook himself, some connection to Tikal's count of kings is worth considering.[7]

Little evidence of Yax Ehb' Xook's immediate successors has come to light, and it is unclear when a monument program began at Tikal. One carved fragment, MS.69, has been dated stratigraphically to around A.D. 200, while other stones—such as Stela 36 from the Santa Fe group, 3.5 km. northeast of the site core—have been judged as particularly early on stylistic grounds (C. Jones 1991:108). The lengthy text of Stela 31 supplies the most important retrospective source for this period. The first ruler it cites is Foliated Jaguar, a name probably to be read as Huun B'alam, although his accompanying date falls on the missing stela butt and cannot be reconstructed (fig. 1.2a).[8] Interestingly, an identical name appears on a greenstone celt found in Costa Rica (Reents-Budet and Fields 1988) (fig. 1.2b). Suitably early in style, it could well represent the same person. A further appearance comes on an unprovenanced stela now in Cologne (Mayer 1978:pl.42), where it forms a frontal belt ornament (fig. 1.2c).

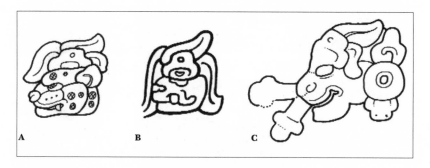

FIGURE 1.2

Foliated Jaguar, (a) *Stela 31, C5,* (b) *Jadeite Celt found in Costa Rica (after a drawing by Dorie Reents-Budet), and* (c) *Belt head from an unprovenanced stela (from a photo in Mayer 1978:pl.42).*

Such motifs are strongly linked to "ancestral" names (Houston and Stuart 1998:85; S. Martin 2002:59–60), and this may well be a sign that this fine early carving came from the Tikal region. Foliated Jaguar has been linked to the ruler depicted on Stela 29, dated to 292 (Mathews 1985), though the iconographic argument in this case is questionable. More compelling evidence from the imagery can be seen in the ancestral figure that floats above the king's head. This character is identified by a glyphic headdress in precisely the same manner as we see in the father's portrait on the front of Stela 31. Although damaged, it seems to bear all the elements of the Chak Tok Ich'aak name, referring presumably to a pre-292 king of this recurring nominal.

A little-studied monument from El Encanto, 11.5 km. from Tikal, has previously been assigned the date 9.8.4.9.1, falling in 598 (Morley 1937–38 II:2–7). However, the style of its battered portrait and text as well as certain aspects of its surviving date are much more consistent with a place in the 8th Cycle or early part of the 9th.[9] The subject of the opening phrase is named by a pair of glyphs, the first the well-known Stormy Sky glyph now read as Siyaj Chan K'awiil ("Sky-born K'awiil"), the second seemingly Chak Ich'aak ("Great Claw") (fig. 1.3a).[10] There is some reason to believe that this is the human protagonist of the preceding "conjuring" ritual; though it clearly bears some relationship to mention of the same paired names on Stela 26, which may concern ancestral invocation (fig. 1.3b). The dedicatory date of this

FIGURE 1.3

Early forms of the name Siyaj Chan K'awiil, (a) El Encanto Stela 1, A10–B10, (b) Stela 26, zA4–zB4, and (c) Siyaj Chan K'awiil I as the 11th Tikal ruler on the Tikal Dynastic Vase (see fig. 1.4).

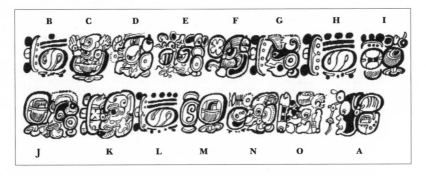

FIGURE 1.4

"Tikal Dynastic Vase," an unprovenanced vessel listing the 11th, 13th, and 14th rulers (after a photo by Justin Kerr, K4679).

particular monument remains uncertain, but it plausibly refers to an earlier namesake of the famous Stormy Sky (S. Martin 2000a). The very damaged right side has a concluding parentage statement, listing two characters otherwise unknown in Tikal history. The father, whom we can dub Animal Headdress, carries a version of the Ehb' "step" name of the founder and may also have been a Tikal king or other member of the dynasty. Most importantly, the existence of an early Siyaj Chan

8

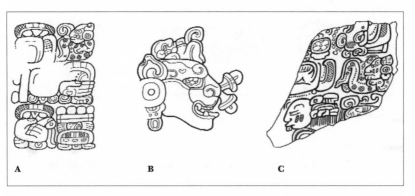

FIGURE 1.5

The Baby Jaguar, (a) *as the celebrant of the 8.14.0.0.0* (A.D. *317) Period Ending, Stela 31, C8–D10,* (b) *name spelled out in the form of an "ancestral" belt ornament, Stela 31, and* (c) *sherd from the Mundo Perdido (after Garcia Campillo et al.1990).*

K'awiil finds solid support in the text of an unprovenanced Late Classic vase that lists the 11th, 13th, and 14th monarchs in order, the first position given to someone of this name (Robicsek and Hales 1981:159, 234; Grube 1998) (fig. 1.3c, 1.4).[11]

No 12th in line is listed on the vase text, but we learn of a new ruler on Stela 31. The 8.14.0.0.0 Period Ending of 317 has previously been ascribed to the 14th king, Chak Tok Ich'aak I (Jaguar Paw), but it is now syntactically clear that the celebrant is named as the Baby Jaguar (Grube 1998) (fig. 1.5a). This reclining character appears in other historical contexts such as "ancestral" belt ornaments (fig 1.5b) but is clearly a name derived from that of an important deity at Tikal—one featured among a list of patron gods on Stela 26 and in a less clear context on an inscribed sherd excavated by the Proyecto Nacional Tikal (Garcia Campillo et al. 1990) (fig. 1.5c). The phonetic reading of the name was evidently *unen b'alam,* literally "baby/infant jaguar" (S. Martin 2002:61–64).[12] In Maya mythology this character had close connections to the infant Maize God and accompanying themes of sacrificial death and rebirth. The sexual ambiguity of some Maize God iconography initially suggested a female gender for this ruler (for example, S. Martin and Grube 2000)—an interpretation that seems more questionable today.

At this point in the Tikal sequence the finely worked Leiden

FIGURE 1.6

K'inich Muwaan Jol, the 13th in line, (a) unprovenanced vessel, K, (b) Stela 39, Bz5
(after Gonzalez Cano), and (c) Corozal Stela 1, A3.

Plaque is often cited, with its accession date in 320 and its protagonist "Moon Zero Bird." Damaged glyphs on Altar 13 and 19 resemble this form (the latter in a nominal context) (Fahsen 1987:48), but the only clear example, on Stela 31, represents the name of an altar or throne (Stuart and Houston 1994:49). Elsewhere in the Maya world this combination serves as a mythical location. The affiliation of the Leiden Plaque lord with Tikal is still very uncertain.

The 13th ruler on the dynastic vase has been dubbed Bird Skull, a name that most likely reads K'inich Muwaan Jol "Great-Sun Hawk Head" (fig. 1.4 above, 1.6a).[13] He is named in an apparent parentage statement on Stela 39 as well as appearing in an iconic array of rulers on Stela 28 (Stuart in Schele and Grube 1994a:7) (fig. 1.6b). He is also named on a stela at Corozal, some 5 km. from Tikal, probably in a reference to his death (fig. 1.6c, S. Martin 2000a).[14]

K'inich Muwaan Jol was succeeded by his son Chak Tok Ich'aak I. According to an apparent "regnum insert" (an accounting of his reign length) on Stela 31, his inauguration took place on 8.16.3.10.2 (360) (Nikolai Grube, pers. comm. 1998). In addition to his citation on the Corozal monument, which he presumably commissioned, Chak Tok Ich'aak dedicated Stela 39 on 8.17.0.0.0 (376), the lower half of which was recovered from Str. 5D-86-7 in the Mundo Perdido complex (Ayala 1987; Laporte and Fialko 1990:42–45). It is possible that Stela 26, found cached in Temple 34 of the North Acropolis, also carries his nominal.[15] Finally, the expanded name of Chak Tok Ich'aak appears on the shoulder cartouches of the unique Hombre de Tikal, and this portly figure could have been a personal portrait reworked in later times (Fahsen 1988; S. Martin 2000a).

It is widely believed that Tikal acted as a crucible for the development of Classic civilization in the Lowlands, and the latest data only serve to reinforce that assessment. The redating of Tikal's dynastic genesis puts it in line with the energetic but ultimately short-lived developments in the Highlands and Pacific Coast. Contacts between these areas and the Petén have been posited on ceramic grounds (Coggins 1975:52–85), with the appearance of the "stela cult" in the Lowlands interpreted as a direct import.[16] The traditional designation of Late Preclassic that is given to these southern societies obscures the fact that they fulfill most definitions of Early Classic civilization.

A foundation date of c. 100 has implications for the Preclassic chronology of the Petén, leading one to question whether Classic-style dynasties arose in a sudden political vacuum, overlapped with an existing order, or directly supplanted such an order. The paucity of very early monuments at Tikal may arise from their deliberate destruction, the vagaries of archaeological recovery, or a change in media (that is, a change from more perishable materials to stone) or in form (perhaps from portable carved celts to monolithic stelae, see Porter 1992). Alternatively, "Classic" features may have accumulated over time, making for a more evolutionary than revolutionary development.

Without contemporary inscriptions our knowledge of the earliest periods will always be especially feeble. Deeply retrospective texts such as that found on the facade of Temple VI (which begins its narrative in 1143 B.C.) offer tantalizing glimpses of the past, but differentiating history from legend and myth may prove impossible in such cases (C. Jones 1977). What recent finds have achieved is some fleshing out of the sequence through the fourth century, establishing a degree of continuity between the era of the once-isolated Stela 29 and later, better-documented periods.

THE NEW ORDER: A.D. 378–508

Few topics are more central to an understanding of Classic Mesoamerica as an interactive whole than the nature of Teotihuacan's influence in the Maya Lowlands. The Maya, for all their originality, adopted Mexican traits to a significant degree, reflecting both the enormous prestige of Teotihuacan and some tangible cultural contact. The existence of a glyphic record at Tikal allows a unique view of this phenomenon.

It has long been apparent that the date 8.17.1.4.12 (378) held a special importance for both Tikal and nearby Uaxactun. Tatiana Proskouriakoff (1993) was forthright in linking this date to the appearance of Teotihuacan-style iconography on both monuments and artifacts. The nature of the core event has been discussed by a number of authors, with varying emphasis on the degree of contact with Central Mexico, the introduction of military ideology and technology, and conflict between Tikal and Uaxactun (for example, Coggins 1975, 1979; Mathews 1985; Schele and Freidel 1990). More recently, David Stuart has taken the lead among epigraphers in illuminating some of the relevant glyphic passages (Stuart 2000).

Three of the accounts (the Tikal Marcador and Uaxactun Stela 5 and Stela 22) describe the 378 event as the *hul* "arrival here" of Siyaj K'ak' or "Fire-born" (Smoking Frog) (fig. 1.7a). On Stela 31 a less well-understood phrase that supplies additional information is connected (by a term that links two successive and related events to the presumed death of Chak Tok Ich'aak, described as his *och ha'* "water-entering" (fig. 1.7b). Though it is expressed in delicate terms, there is apparent cause and effect here—the arrival coincides with the incumbent king's death to the very day. Whatever the exact circumstances, it marks the end of the existing royal line and its replacement by lords with overt Mexican connections. Stuart has noted that Siyaj K'ak' is mentioned on a monument at El Perú just eight days earlier, implying an approach from the west along the Río San Pedro Martir. We have no direct evidence for Teotihuacan's ability to launch an invasion at such a distance, but the degree to which its wide-ranging cultural impact is associated with martial symbolism certainly implies an awesome military reputation (for example, Taube 1992b; S. Martin 2001a).

The dramatic upsurge in Teotihuacanoid traits, not only at Tikal but elsewhere in the Petén, reflects the introduction of some "New Order" (to borrow a term from Coggins 1979). Emerging epigraphic data link this phenomenon to the "incomers" at Tikal. Siyaj K'ak' is mentioned at Uaxactun in 378 and 396, at Bejucal around 381, and probably at Río Azul in 393—all in contexts that either imply his superordinate position over local lords or contain a direct statement to that

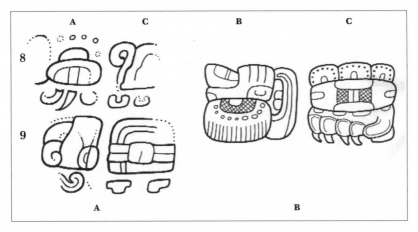

FIGURE 1.7

The "arrival" of Siyaj K'ak' and the "death" of Chak Tok Ich'aak on 8.17.1.4.12 (A.D. 378), (a) Uaxactun Stela 5, B8–C9 and (b) Stela 31, C23–24.

effect.[17] Although Uaxactun Stela 5 shows such a lord in full Mexican attire, the ethnic identity of these characters remains unclear. Where their names are known, they seem—like that of Siyaj K'ak' himself—to be Mayan in form.[18]

Another person of special importance to the New Order was Spearthrower Owl, the father of the next Tikal king. Given that his patriline was to rule Tikal for some 183 years, the precise identity of Spearthrower Owl is a crucial question. His name-glyph includes the *atlatl* spear-thrower of Mexican design and often takes the form of the "owl with shield and darts," a recurring motif in the art of Teotihuacan.[19] Its use as both an emblematic device and a personal name at Tikal can be seen on the splendid Marcador, an object with a close analogue at Teotihuacan (Fialko 1987a). Both Stuart and I have concluded that a major topic of the Marcador's text is the accession of Spearthrower Owl to *ajaw*-ship in 374 (S. Martin and Grube 2000:31; Stuart 2000:483) (fig. 1.8). More controversially, Spearthrower Owl's overt iconographic connections to Teotihuacan raise the possibility that he rose to a position of power, even rulership, at the great highland city itself (Stuart 2000:481–87). In any case his political role as another "overlord" of the Petén is clear (S. Martin and Grube 2000:30–31) (fig. 1.9a, b). His death in 439, apparently at an

FIGURE 1.8

Accession of Spearthrower Owl on 8.16.19.9.0 (A.D. 374), Marcador, E2–5.

FIGURE 1.9

Spearthrower Owl as an "overlord" in the Maya area (the first compound in both cases is yajaw *"the lord of"), (a) unprovenanced vessel and (b) unprovenanced jade earflare.*

advanced age, is recorded on both Stela 31 and El Zapote Stela 5.[20]

There seems to be another effect that we can link to the emergence of the New Order—the fate of Tikal's dynastic records prior to 378. No whole monuments at the city predate the *entrada*, while even a cursory examination of the carved fragments retrieved from construction fill shows almost every one to be very early in style (C. Jones and Satterthwaite 1982:figs.63–68). While the establishment of the New Order meant destruction for many monuments of the ancien régime, some pre-378 monuments—Stela 36, Corozal Stela 1, and probably El Encanto Stela 1—survived in peripheral locations and may even have been moved from the city center (Jones and Orrego 1987:129; S. Martin 2000a). The El Encanto stela was found without its butt, as if lightened for easier transporting, while the other two were set in enclosed rooms, a feature of reset monuments elsewhere.

Although Siyaj K'ak' was now in possession of Tikal, he did not take the throne for himself but rather installed Spearthrower Owl's son, Yax Nuun Ayiin I (Curl Snout), in 379.[21] Portraits of the new ruler on Stela 4 and on the sides of the later Stela 31 show him in full Teotihuacano dress, and most observers have taken him to be a foreigner or someone deeply acculturated in Mexican traditions. On both Stela 4 and Stela 18 he is described as the *yajaw* or "vassal" of Siyaj K'ak', who clearly remained the dominant authority in the New Order scheme. It has long been assumed, though without specific evidence, that the wife taken by Yax Nuun Ayiin was connected to the traditional Tikal ruling group (Coggins 1975:186). Certainly, the reign of his son Siyaj Chan K'awiil II (Stormy Sky) shows an explicit return to Maya modes and the reconstitution of an "orthodox" Maya kingship.

Integral to this program was Siyaj Chan K'awiil's claim to close connection with Yax Ehb' Xook, whose name he wears in his headdress on Stela 31, while he identifies himself as 16th in his line on two unprovenanced vessels (fig. 1.10a, b). Siyaj Chan K'awiil designed Stela 31 as an evocation of both the recent and the distant past, manipulating a variety of themes in support of his right to rule. The importance of the matriline to him is emphasized by another costume element, his front-facing belt ornament providing a spelling of his mother's name. (Its companion on the back of the belt spells the name of Baby Jaguar, the ruler he picks out for particular mention in the text of Stela 31.)

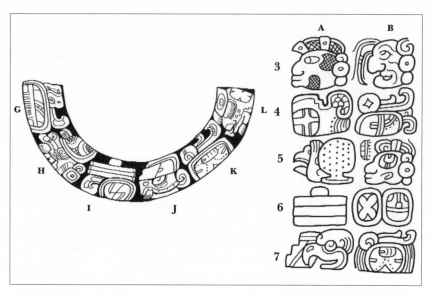

FIGURE 1.10

Siyaj Chan K'awiil II as the "16th in line" of Yax Ehb' Xook, (a) *lid of unprovenanced vessel, G–L 9 (detail after Lin Crocker) and* (b) *unprovenanced vessel, A3–B7 (after Lin Crocker).*

Apart from his close ties to the site of El Zapote, some 25 km. to the south (Schele, Fahsen, and Grube 1992), there are few clues to the extent of Siyaj Chan K'awiil II's political domain. However, one ceramic text is significant in that it places him in some kind of relationship to Ucanal, 51 km. to the southeast—as either an overlord or a relative to its ruler (S. Martin 2000a) (fig. 1.10b).

Little was known about Siyaj Chan K'awiil II's son and successor K'an Chitam(?) (Kan Boar) until the discovery of Stela 40 (Valdés, Fahsen, and Muñoz 1997).[22] Very traditional in style, combining features of both Stela 29 and Stela 31, it too includes iconography drawn from Teotihuacan, this time in the form of a plated Mexican-style headdress held by the king (S. Martin and Grube 2000:37). Stela 40's long rear text is effaced in places, but it establishes K'an Chitam's accession on 9.1.2.17.17 (458). His death date is unknown but probably fell close to 486. This year saw a *ch'ak* "axe" attack against the unidentified polity of Maasal (a one-time client of Spearthrower Owl) at 9.2.11.7.8 (486).[23]

Recorded retrospectively on Stela 10, the attack is among the earliest conflicts described in a Maya text.

A few months later, Stela 10 recounts a sacrificial rite performed by K'an Chitam's son Chak Tok Ich'aak II (Jaguar Paw Skull). Most likely this served as some prelude to his succession, and he was certainly in office by the time he erected Stela 3 in 488. An interesting development has been the recognition of a death statement for him on an altar recently uncovered at Tonina (David Stuart, pers. comm. 1999). This places Chak Tok Ich'aak's demise at 9.3.13.12.5 (508), only 14 days before one of his vassals was captured by tiny Yaxchilan (S. Martin and Grube 2000:37). Conceivably, the loss of its king exposed Tikal or one of its allies to opportunist attack, but we cannot discount the possibility of a wider military context.

While the precise nature of Teotihuacan's intervention in the Maya Lowlands will continue to be debated, recent epigraphic discoveries broadly support long-held ideas for a physical intrusion, even a political takeover in 378. This may serve as a precedent for similar phenomena at Kaminaljuyu and elsewhere in Mesoamerica. The wider appearance of Teotihuacan traits in the Petén is also reflected in the inscriptions, with evidence suggesting that the New Order established a political domain extending well beyond Tikal. Yet within a generation its more overt Mexican characteristics had disappeared and traditional Maya styles had reasserted themselves. Continuity through the matriline was probably instrumental in converting these "incomers" into Maya rulers with at least some claim to local legitimacy and connection to the founder, although evidence for this is currently lacking.

An unbroken line of kings through the fifth century saw Tikal reach its Early Classic "peak." Yet the emergence of warfare as a topic in the texts by the end of the century may signal growing challenges to its preeminence. The maturing landscape of numerous polities and their "holy" rulers—some of which may have been established under the tutelage of Tikal and its Teotihuacan mentors, as Copan seems to have been—reflects a deeply engrained Maya pattern of small, theoretically autonomous political territories. Tikal may well have exercised a wide-ranging hegemonic power, but there is no sign that it was forged into anything more formal and cohesive.

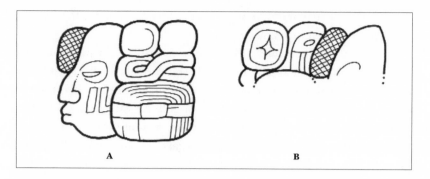

A   B

FIGURE 1.11

The Lady of Tikal in "birth" and "accession" statements, (a) Stela 23, C4 and (b) Stela 23, B6.

COMPLEX TIMES: A.D. 508–562

The so-called "Middle Classic," covering about 50 years of the sixth century, is an era in which many scholars have detected dynastic disturbance, most obviously reflected in the deliberate damage and displacement of monuments (for example, Coggins 1975; Haviland 1977, 1992b; C. Jones 1991; Proskouriakoff 1993). These records are now some of the most fragmentary and eroded at Tikal, presenting tremendous obstacles to the investigator.

The first of the Middle Classic monuments, Stela 23, was found broken, defaced, and reset in Group 7F-30, well away from the ceremonial core. Although the gender of the frontal portrait has been questioned by some, elements of its surviving dress are consistent with a female figure (Coggins 1975:219). This is strongly supported by the rear text, which chronicles the birth of the "Lady of Tikal" in 504. Although the text is damaged, the next event is seen to be an accession to *ajaw*-ship (Schele and Freidel 1990:167), while traces of the subject's name leave little room for doubt that it is the Lady of Tikal herself, acceding at the age of just six years (S. Martin 1998a) (fig. 1.11a, b).[24] This isolated reference has long made her a problematic figure. Were she a ruling queen, we might expect to find evidence for her tenure on other monuments of this time.

The next, Stela 6, commemorates the 9.4.0.0.0 mark of 514. The monument is badly shattered, but a portion of surviving text from the top right side includes the celebrant's name within a four-glyph phrase

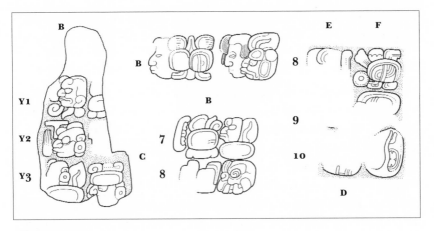

FIGURE 1.12

The 9.4.0.0.0 ruler of Tikal, (a) *Stela 6, By1–Cy3,* (b) *Stela 12, B5–B6,* (c) *Stela 8,*
B7–8, and (d) *Stela 10, E8–F10.*

on the right side (By2–Cy3) (fig. 1.12a). This begins with a god name
restricted to female nominals at Tikal, a supernatural character whose
insignia can be identified on the scant remains of Stela 5's frontal portrait.[25] The following sign is destroyed, but the next marries a portrait
head with a vegetal, podlike glyph over another, now effaced sign.[26]
Completing this section is a battered but recognizable spelling of
(u)naab'nal k'inich, "Pool Place of the Sun God," a name or title that
usually appears directly after the personal names of Tikal rulers.[27]

Stela 25 was the next erected at the city, at 9.4.3.0.0 (517), but due
to damage, little in the way of concrete data can be extracted from it
today. Stela 12, from 9.4.13.0.0 (527), is in better condition. Here the
rear text records the appropriate Period Ending ceremonies, together
with their protagonist. The first of the nominal compounds is obscure,
but the second is the title *kaloomte',* here prefixed by a human head in a
form only otherwise attested as the feminized *ix kaloomte'* or Lady
'Batab' (fig. 1.12b). (Prior to the Late Classic this designation as often
precedes as follows personal names.) Significantly in this regard, the
third element is another showing the pod sign encountered on Stela 6.
Here it is joined by a human head, quite probably the female agentive
ix in this context, and a deity portrait.[28] A "child of father" statement
follows, although the parent's name is now lost on the missing stela

butt. If we turn to the still undated Stela 8, we find an especially close match for the Stela 6 name at B7b (fig. 1.12c). Here it is extended to include a full Yax Ehb' Xook appellative (B7a–b), a formula carried by no less than seven rulers at Tikal.

Taking these various pointers together, it seems highly likely that a royal woman conducted the Period Ending ceremonies of 514 and 527. Was she the same woman as the Lady of Tikal? Stela 23 contains a partial count forward leading to a "round" date, for which 9.4.0.0.0 (514) is the earliest candidate (C. Jones and Satterthwaite 1982:51). The Stela 6 name does not appear on the extant portion of Stela 23, but the mere four-year gap between the two monuments could suggest that it was an alternative appellative, perhaps one she acquired at her elevation to office. A caveat here is that we also need to consider the partially preserved accession phrase on Stela 10, which includes a similar-looking but probably distinct podlike sign (Werner Nahm, pers. comm. 2000) (fig. 1.12d above).[29] The date of this event is mostly destroyed but does not correspond to the one on Stela 23. The parentage statement on Stela 12 once expressed this woman's principal claim to legitimacy. Presumably she was the progeny of either K'an Chitam or Chak Tok Ich'aak II (the latter if she was indeed the Lady of Tikal).

But there is further complexity to this period. The front of Stela 12 bears a male rather than a female portrait. A text on the left side gives a two-glyph name phrase for the stela's "owner": the first, the plain title *kaloomte'* (mirroring what we see in the queen's name); the second, a jaguar head combined with the head of a square-eyed deity with a nose ornament (fig. 1.13a). There is every sign that this a distinct male character. We can only nickname him "Kaloomte' B'alam" in the hope of a proper reading in the future. He is said to be the "19th in line" and thus a full king and successor to Chak Tok Ich'aak, Tikal's 18th king.[30] Probable references to him can be identified in two other contexts. On Stela 10, the twin of Stela 12, we see the jaguar and square-eyed deity heads separated (at C7–D7), while another spelling—this time with *kaloomte'*—can be seen in an apparent join between two fragments of MT.11, an incised vessel from Problematic Deposit 22 from the North Acropolis (Culbert 1993:fig. 125) (fig. 1.13b). It has been suggested that this cache is the cleared-out remains of a major burial once deposited in Temple 33-2nd (W. R. Coe 1990:326).

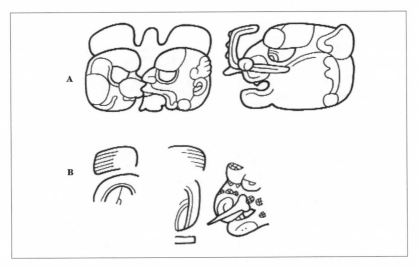

FIGURE 1.13

Kaloomte' B'alam, the 19th in line, (a) Stela 12, D4–5 and (b) MT.11, two fragments from a ceramic vessel, wA and yA.

The aforementioned Stela 8 presents a situation similar to that of Stela 10: a male portrait, which the text identifies as another bearer of the *(u)naab'nal k'inich* name/title, currently known only as Bird Claw. At the end of the inscription he is placed in some type of relationship with the Stela 6 woman, though unfortunately the term concerned, seen at B7a, is as yet undeciphered.[31]

Can we make sense of this complex—not to say confusing—picture? A division of ceremonial activity between two individuals, a male and a female, is not unknown in Maya history, where it constitutes a form of co-rulership.[32] Stela 10 links Kaloomte' B'alam to the attack on Maasal in 486, indicating that he was a mature, even elderly figure by the time the stela was commissioned in or around 527. Though he was perhaps of royal blood, he may have been a military specialist who rose to office through his marriage to, or guardianship of, this woman. Bird Claw remains an especially obscure figure. Aside from the problematic date of Stela 8—which is legible but difficult to place in the Long Count—there is its early style, which most resembles the stelae of Chak Tok Ich'aak II. He is certainly some associate of the Stela 6 woman and may have succeeded Kaloomte' B'alam as Tikal's 20th king.

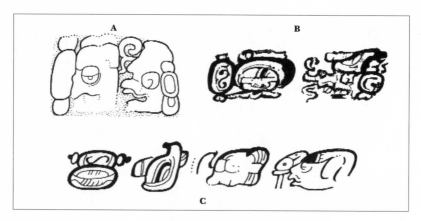

FIGURE 1.14

Wak Chan K'awiil, the 21st in line, (a) Stela 17, C1–D1, (b) unprovenanced plate E–F (after a photo by Justin Kerr, K8121), and (c) unprovenanced plate (after Houston and Taube 1987:fig.4k).

FIGURE 1.15

Text recording the Period Endings 9.6.0.0.0 (A.D. 557) of Wak Chan K'awiil (E–F) and 9.3.0.0.0 (A.D. 495) of Chak Tok Ich'aak II (N). Unprovenanced plate (after a photo by Justin Kerr, K8121).

We come next to the reign of the 21st ruler, long known by the nickname Double Bird.[33] His name phrase is long and complex. Though he seems at times to be ascribed a variant of the founder's name, the most consistent part of his nominal phrase is Wak Chan K'awiil (S. Martin 2001b) (fig. 1.14a–c).[34] His only surviving monument, Stela 17, was found abandoned by the side of the Maler Causeway, broken and deliberately defaced (C. Jones 1991:117). Significantly, it tells us that his father was Chak Tok Ich'aak II. This connection is reiterated on an unprovenanced plate that compares Wak Chan K'awiil's celebration of the 9.6.0.0.0 (554) Period Ending with the 9.3.0.0.0 (495) ceremony performed by his father (fig. 1.15).[35] Wak Chan K'awiil's name phrase here includes the *ochk'in kaloomte'* (West 'Batab') title seemingly associated with Mexican-derived legitimacy and links, fictive or real, with Teotihuacan. As a lineal descendent of Spearthrower Owl, his great-great-great-grandson in fact, he would have had a direct connection to the New Order of the fourth century.

Stela 17 was erected in 557 at the 1-K'atun anniversary of an event that took place on 9.5.3.9.15 in 537.[36] The attached phrase—generally assumed to be his inauguration—is now badly damaged but involves *yax mutal,* the place-name of Tikal. Statements of this kind commonly describe an "arrival" or associated events and, interestingly enough, the preceding event on the right side seems to be a form of *ihuli* "then he arrived here," attached to a prior date.[37] Some precedent for this kind of sequence exists in the inscriptions of Naranjo, where it forms part of a rite of dynastic "re-foundation" (Schele and Freidel 1990:185–86).[38] The length of Stela 17's text, minimally 108 glyph-blocks, is unusual and rather reminiscent of Stela 31, with its extended justification of local legitimacy.[39]

Although Wak Chan K'awiil evidently enjoyed significant power— he was a patron to the distant Caracol kingdom, supervising the accession of its ruler in 553 (Grube 1994:106)—Tikal's fortunes were on the wane. In 562 it was defeated in "star war," an event that elsewhere is synonomous with conquest or sacking (Houston 1987:93, 1991:40). Despite the appearance of this record on Caracol Altar 21, with the resulting assumption that this polity was the victor (for example, A. F. Chase and D. Z. Chase 1987:60–61; Schele and Freidel 1990:171–74), the scant remains of the triumphant king's name do not support this conclusion, and the kingdom of Calakmul emerges as the more likely culprit (S. Martin and Grube 2000:89–90). Subsequent phrases on the shattered Altar 21 make further mention of Tikal, but none of the actors can be identified.

New information has given us a better, if still far from satisfactory, understanding of the Middle Classic and its long-suspected dynastic disturbance. The renumeration of the Tikal sequence has removed the glut of six rulers once thought to have reigned between 508 and 537 (Mathews 1985), leaving only two, or more probably three, characters. Each can only be viewed through a fog of poor preservation, and even basic issues of their identity are often less than secure. Current evidence supports the notion that Tikal had a ruling queen, albeit one who shared authority with one or more male figures. There is no sign that she had a place in the numbered sequence of Tikal rulers, a feature that seems to be mirrored in female reigns elsewhere (S. Martin and Grube 2000:168). This scenario would imply internal intrigues, not least since her elevation would have been in preference to a son of the preceding king. The unusual narrative of this son's sole surviving monument raises similar suspicions about irregularities at this time.

Although the Tikal polity seems to have maintained its integrity and independence throughout the Middle Classic, the period ends in defeat and eclipse. Whatever the sequence of events, it is hard to see this as unconnected to the rise of a new rival for political dominance in the central southern Lowlands, Calakmul, the kingdom of the "snake." We know little about its early history and composition—or even whether Calakmul was truly the capital of the Early Classic "snake" kingdom—but by 542 its growing strength comes into view as it sponsors the accession of the Naranjo king (S. Martin and Grube 2000:72, 104).

DYNASTIC UMBRA: A.D. 562–692

The hiatus in monument dedications at Tikal has had a signal influence on thinking about Maya history and cultural development. Together with a perceived downturn elsewhere, it has been used to postulate a "little collapse" in the Lowlands and has been linked to wider events in Mesoamerica, such as the fall of Teotihuacan (Proskouriakoff 1950; Willey 1974). However, more recent data from a number of sites cast doubt on such a pan-Maya phenomenon, pointing instead to a more particularistic shift in political fortunes across the central region (see A. F. Chase and D. Z. Chase 1987:60).

An absence of data presents obvious difficulties. We cannot be sure that monuments did not exist at one time or, if they were later removed or destroyed, know exactly when or why this occurred. The only epigraphic data for this era that are available at Tikal itself come from Burial 195—the tomb of the 22nd ruler, Animal Skull—set deep within Temple 32 of the North Acropolis (W. R Coe 1990:565–68). Meticulously recovered casts of decayed wooden boards provide the date 9.8.0.0.0 (593), a mark repeated on an accompanying plate (although partially obscured beneath a later repainting) (Coggins 1975:352). Additional information comes from the sizable number of unprovenanced vessels that carry Animal Skull's name. In these painted texts his mother is accorded lengthy nominal phrases, but his father only appears once and in a very abbreviated, title-less form.[40] The name of this father never appears in the long sequence of Wak Chan K'awiil, and we can take this as a sign that some deviation or break in the patriline has occurred. The prominence given to Animal Skull's mother makes it clear that she served as his major claim to legitimacy (C. Jones 1991:116–17).

The grand—if not especially wealthy—burial afforded Animal Skull suggests that there was an orderly transfer of power at his death, while the long-term maintenance of his memorial temple argues that he was regarded as a legitimate king by later generations.[41] His immediate successors, the 23rd and 24th rulers, have not been identified, though during one seminar session it was suggested that they might be the two lords interred in Temple 33-1st, in Burials 23 and 24 respectively.[42]

It is around this time that Dos Pilas first emerges into Maya history. This small site in the Petexbatun region, 112 km. to the south, with an emblem glyph identical to that of Tikal but with a separate dynasty, has long presented a considerable puzzle. However, analysis of its rich collection of inscriptions, including notable recent additions, now offers key insights into its story. The most important sources are two hieroglyphic stairways (HS.2 and HS.4), together with two panels associated with the former, all commissioned by the first ruler of Dos Pilas, B'alaj Chan K'awiil. These describe a complex series of interactions between

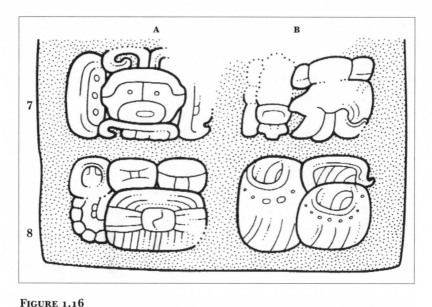

FIGURE 1.16

The parentage of B'alaj Chan K'awiil, Dos Pilas Panel 6, A7–B8 (drawings by Stephen D. Houston).

Dos Pilas, Tikal, and Calakmul, covering several decades of the seventh century (Houston 1993; S. Martin and Grube 2000; Fahsen 2002).

B'alaj Chan K'awiil's genealogical claim to the *mutal* title evidently once appeared on Dos Pilas Panel 6 (Houston 1993:fig. 4.7) (fig. 1.16). Although his own name is now effaced, it contains a parentage statement that is presumably his own and names his father as a Tikal ruler. Although this name resembles that of Animal Skull (Houston et al. 1992), there is some cause to doubt the association. If it is accurate, the "3 K'atun Ajaw" statement given on the wooden boards would make Animal Skull minimally 73 years old at the birth of B'alaj Chan K'awiil in 625. Moreover, the father's name glyph displays the feathery mouth of the Muwaan Bird—only otherwise seen at Tikal in the name of K'inich Muwaan Jol. This person could instead be the missing 23rd or 24th ruler. It has been further suggested that the Muwaan Jol name also appears on the sherd MT. 25 from Tikal, where it names the father of the contemporary Tikal king Nuun Ujol Chaak (Shield Skull) (S. Guenter, pers. comm. 2000). If so, this could identify Nuun Ujol Chaak and B'alaj Chan K'awiil as brothers and could support earlier speculation about

FIGURE 1.17

The subordination of B'alaj Chan K'awiil of Dos Pilas to the king of Calakmul. Dos Pilas
HS.4, Step IV, II–N2 (after Stephen D. Houston, abbreviated for the sake of clarity).

a fraternal conflict (Houston et al. 1992).

The first significant and fully legible episodes in the Dos Pilas narrative—shared between both stairways—occurs on a single day in 648. They seem to mark a particular pivot, involving the death of a notable lord or ruler holding the *mutal* title—most probably Tikal itself here—and B'alaj Chan K'awiil's first credited military victories. The full meaning of these events remains unclear, but it is certainly possible that they reflect internicene conflict within the Tikal dynasty (Fahsen 2002). It is at the end of one of these phrases that the vassal status of B'alaj Chan K'awiil in relation to the contemporary king of Calakmul is made clear (Houston et al. 1992; S. Martin and Grube 1994, 2000) (fig. 1.17). It quickly becomes apparent that the Tikal dynasty is indeed divided against itself and that the group at Dos Pilas, now acting under the protection of Calakmul, has established a rival *mutal* state.

Chronologically, the next recorded event is a "star war" attack that Calakmul staged against Dos Pilas, most likely in 650.[43] It is possible that this defeat is what brings about the submission of Dos Pilas to Calakmul, with the prior attachment of this relationship to the year 648 simply a rhetorical device. The result is B'alaj Chan K'awiil's flight from the city, with reason to think that he seeks refuge at the nearby site of Aguateca.[44] In 657 we receive first mention of the incumbent Tikal ruler Nuun Ujol Chaak (Shield Skull). This year marks a Calakmul attack on Tikal, resulting in Nuun Ujol Chaak's flight from the city (Houston et al. 1992; Houston 1993; Schele and Grube 1994b:21–23; S. Martin and Grube 2000:42, 57).[45] Three years later, in 659, a character of the same name "arrives" at Palenque (Schele 1994), a city that had itself suffered two major assaults at the hands of Calakmul (S. Martin 1997:861–62, 2000b:107–10). Despite the apparent connection, it is now clear that this appearance is coincidental. This Nuun Ujol Chaak is a different individual, a native of the so-called Wa-Bird kingdom, which can now be placed with some confidence to the site of Santa Elena in Tabasco, Mexico (D. Stuart, pers. comm. 2000).[46]

We next hear of Tikal's Nuun Ujol Chaak in 672, when he attacks and seizes Dos Pilas, ejecting B'alaj Chan K'awiil. The Dos Pilas king this time flees to the previously unknown location of Chaak Naah (Fahsen 2002). During an intense period in 673 Nuun Ujol Chaak burns two centers, one possibly Dos Pilas itself, and then attacks what is probably Chaak Naah. B'alaj Chan K'awiil evidently now removes himself to the site of Hix Witz. But once again, it is the involvement of Calakmul as the protector of Dos Pilas that will be decisive in the years ahead. Nuun Ujol Chaak is defeated by Calakmul again in 677, an event that leads directly to B'alaj Chan K'awiil's return to Dos Pilas (Nahm in Schele and Grube 1994b:23). Two years later B'alaj Chan K'awiil claims a major success over Nuun Ujol Chaak, though we might wonder if Calakmul is closely involved here too. Although this defeat has been linked to the death of Nuun Ujol Chaak by some, this is not explicit in the record. A reference to the battle is followed by a formulaic description of its consequences: *naahb'aj uch'ich'(?)el wihtzaj u-jolil* "(their) blood pooled, (their) heads piled-up" (David Stuart, pers. comm.

2001). The subject, which is described only as *oxlajuun tzuk* "Thirteen Provinces(?)," could be plural here but also appears as a singular title carried by Nuun Ujol Chaak and by another lord called Nuun B'alam, shown as a crouching prisoner beneath the feet of B'alaj Chan K'wiil on Dos Pilas Stela 9. Even if he survived the battle, Nuun Ujol Chaak did not live for too long. His demise must have come before 682, the year he was succeeded by his son Jasaw Chan K'awiil I (Ruler A) (C. Jones 1977). The traditional end of the Hiatus era comes with the erection of his first monument, Stela 30, in 692.

The latest evidence lifts some of the thick veil cloaking the Tikal Hiatus, revealing a complex period in which the absence of a surviving record at the city in no way reflects a moribund political situation. Military defeat was evidently the initial spark, with every sign that this coincided with some form of dynastic rupture. Both the origins and the relative autonomy of the succeeding king, Animal Skull, remain open questions. Virtually all of his surviving records appear on painted ceramics, several of which carry the kind of information normally found on stelae. We might wonder whether the lack of public monuments stems from a deliberate proscription imposed by Tikal's conquerors—a feature that could be relevant to hiatus periods elsewhere. Animal Skull's use of the designation "22nd in line" emphasizes that such reckonings represent simple sequences of officeholders and do not, in themselves, denote any lineal descent.

By their very nature, dynastic aristocracies foster internal competition. Often focused on a disputed succession, at their most severe they can result in a fissioning of the ruling group. Schisms of this kind are especially hard to detect in the "winners' history" of monumental inscriptions, but the emergence of Dos Pilas as a rival Tikal state provides evidence for just such a factional conflict. We cannot be sure exactly how this possibly fraternal dispute developed, but a crucial factor was the wider context of Tikal-Calakmul competition. Tikal's misfortunes throughout the Hiatus episode were inversely paralleled by Calakmul, which would now enjoy its greatest era of power. At least part of Calakmul's strategy against a resurgent Tikal was to support the breakaway group at Dos Pilas. The prestige of the exiles was sufficient for B'alaj Chan K'awiil's daughter Lady Six Sky to be used to 're-seed' the dynasty of Naranjo (Houston and Mathews 1985:14)—presumably at the behest of Calakmul, which is soon after said to be Naranjo's over-lord (Martin and Grube 1994, 2000:75–76).

RESTORED FORTUNES: A.D. 692–794

While the later stages of the Hiatus had seen the return of a militarily aggressive Tikal, it was only under Jasaw Chan K'awiil (Ruler A) that this revival was consolidated. The turning point can best be placed at Tikal's 695 victory over the Calakmul king Yich'aak K'ak' or "Claw of Fire" (Jaguar Paw Smoke) (J. Miller 1974; Schele and Freidel 1990:205–207; Martin and Grube 2000:45–46, 110–11). Calakmul's foreign mentions and evidence of hegemonic influence fall away markedly in the years that follow, and it seems never to have recovered its former status (S. Martin 1996a, 2000b).

This revival in Tikal fortunes was manifested, as several authors have noted, in a renewed emphasis on Teotihuacanoid symbolism. We can well imagine that Jasaw saw himself as restoring the New Order and the Early Classic glories that accompanied it. One of several construction projects dedicated to this end was Str. 5D-57 in the Central Acropolis, whose decorative program commemorates the success of 695. Surviving sections twice show Jasaw Chan K'awiil in full Mexican dress, in one holding a tethered captive said to be *nawaj,* or dressed for sacrifice, 13 days after the battle. This victim's title of *aj sa* may link him to the Naranjo polity. Yich'aak K'ak' is connected to the Tikal king in another caption, but damage leaves its full significance unclear.[47]

Jasaw Chan K'awiil is said to be the "overking" of a Motul de San José ruler in 711, and in the same year he participated in a joint ritual with the ruler of Maasal, as depicted on Altar 5. Given that this one-time enemy otherwise shows links to Calakmul, this may express an expanded Tikal hegemony to the north.[48] However, Jasaw lost one of his lieutenents in a battle with Dos Pilas in 705, and he had already had another captured by Naranjo in early 695 (Houston 1993:108, 111). The Tikal of this time was still surrounded by a hostile encirclement of Calakmul clients and affiliates (Schele and Freidel 1990:211).

The accession of Jasaw's son Ruler B in 734 brought an equally combative king to the throne, who set about breaking this long-established pattern.[49] Success came early, since Altar 9, from 736 or thereabouts, records his capture of a Calakmul lord or ruler. In 743 and

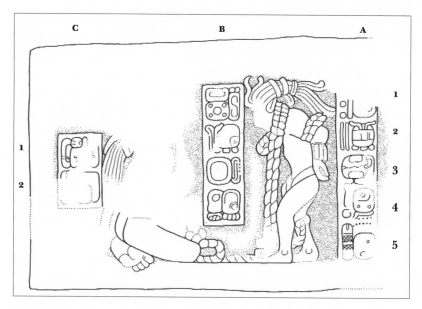

Figure 1.18

Tikal rock sculpture (provisional drawing based on drawing by Antonio Tejeda, with details from photographs in the Tikal Project archives and field sketches by the author).

744 he completed a pair of victories against the Calakmul clients of El Perú and Naranjo, celebrated in triumphant fashion on the wooden lintels of Temple IV (S. Martin 1996b, 2000b:113–22). The first involved the conquest of Yaxa', a site said to be "east of El Perú," which possibly resulted in the capture of the El Perú king Jaguar Throne. Only 191 days later Ruler B attacked Wak Kab'nal, seemingly the Naranjo capital, which led to the seizure of its king, Yax Mayuy Chan Chaak. Archaeologically, we know that this spell of military success correlates with the peak of Tikal's Late Classic construction boom, which is especially evident in the building or remodeling of many "palace" structures (C. Jones 1991:120; S. Martin 1996b:233, 2000c:186).

Twin Pyramid Group P in the North Zone, dating to 751, contains Stela 20 and Altar 8. Neither can be firmly tied to Ruler B, though examination of the headdress of Stela 20's portrait reveals a spelling of *chan k'awiil,* a key part of his name. Altar 8 records the sacrifice of a lord called Wilan Chak Tok Wayib' on 9.15.17.10.4 (748). Close inspection of the little-studied Rock Sculpture on the Maler Causeway, leading to the North Zone, reveals that the same lord is mentioned there, too (fig. 1.18). This roughly hewn and now much-damaged stone, the second largest extant Maya monument, records his *bakwaj* "capture" just two days earlier (S. Martin 2000b:111–13).[50] The *wuk tzuk* "Seven Provinces (?)" title he bears on Altar 8 and Column Altar 1 links him to the Naranjo–Yaxha region and suggests further campaigning in this area.

The 28th ruler of Tikal, a son of Ruler B, remains poorly known. Damage to the great glyphic facade of Temple VI, his only known monumental addition, even robs us of a clear view of his name. The only two dates we have for him both fall in 766. The 28th ruler was succeeded by his brother Yax Nuun Ayiin II (Ruler C) in 768 (this reading provided by D. Stuart in Harrison 1999). His position as "29th in line" of the founder is the last legible accounting of the Tikal dynastic sequence. His two Twin Pyramid Groups, Q and R, celebrate the K'atun endings of 771 and 791, their scale outstripping all previous efforts of this kind. Yax Nuun Ayiin's reign appears to have continued until at least 794. This seems to be the date indicated by a Calendar Round painted on a polychrome vase excavated from Str. 5D-46, which shows a palace scene with a lord sporting an *ayiin* "caiman" in his headdress. Given that he is the only character on the vase not otherwise named by caption, the headdress should identify this late Tikal king.

The contest for regional ascendancy between Tikal and Calakmul continued in the eighth century, though the balance of power now shifted substantially in Tikal's favor. The return of monument erection to the city (a feature mirrored at Uaxactun, where the previously misdated Stela 14 from 702 ends a 145-year hiatus) reflected a period of stability and success. While Jasaw Chan K'awiil initiated this era, there is little sign that he restored any "imperial" sphere, an objective only achieved under his son Ruler B. Although Ruler B achieved a measure of success against Calakmul, it was his victories over El Perú and Naranjo that seem the more decisive. Both cities experienced severe disruption in monument erections in later years. In the absence of a strong epigraphic record for Ruler B's son Yax Nuun Ayiin II, we might infer Tikal's continued strength and security from the scale of his construction projects. Yet the return of monumental programs at El Perú and Naranjo, in 775 and 780 respectively, could well suggest a decline of its regional dominance by that time.

FIGURE 1.19

A bone inscribed with the name Dark Sun (from a photo in Orrego and Larios 1983:pl.24a).

TERMINAL DESCENT: A.D. 794–889

The later rulers of Tikal are poorly known, and damage to a few key texts hampers any real understanding of them. Temple III is the locus of the two most important records of this era—a wooden lintel set high in its upper sanctuary and Stela 24, found at the base of its stairway. The former, once a magnificent carving, is now badly decayed, and the name of its protagonist does not survive. However, a clear parentage statement provides us with the name of his father, the otherwise unknown king Nuun Ujol K'inich or "?-headed Sun God." We might place him as a short-reigning figure between 794 and 810, but he could also be a candidate for the missing 28th Ruler. Stela 24, dated to 9.19.0.0.0 (810) but now badly smashed, mentions the king Dark Sun on three occasions (frags. 13, 29, and 30). He also appears on a bone excavated in Group G, the only other evidence for his reign (see Orrego and Larios 1983:pl.24a; Nikolai Grube, pers. comm. 1997) (fig. 1.19).

33

It is probable that Dark Sun was the character celebrated on the lintel, the last monarch in anything like dynastic continuity who can be firmly placed at the city.

The next great chronological event, the 10.0.0.0.0 Bak'tun ending of 830, has no surviving record at Tikal. A monument was raised at Uaxactun, however, while a large altar recently uncovered at the site of Zacpeten, south of Tikal, alludes to the same date (D. S. Rice, Rice, and Pugh 1998). It includes mention of Ruler B (as confirmed by the inclusion of one of his secondary names), here as the father of the lord memorialized by this stone.[51]

In 849 we are told that a Tikal king called Jewel K'awiil visited Seibal to "witness" the Period Ending 10.1.0.0.0 (Stuart in Houston 1992:66). At face value this submissive visit would seem to point to a radical shift in regional power, turning the political status quo of six centuries on its head. But with Tikal itself now silent, we might question whether the status of Jewel K'awiil matched his lofty title; he may simply have been a lesser potentate aspiring to a once-great kingship. Within a decade we see such figures proliferate at former satellites such as Ixlu and Jimbal, which produce their own monumental programs, both featuring "kings" using the full *k'uhul mutal ajaw* "Holy Lord of Tikal" title.

The restoration of some kind of royal power to Tikal came by 10.2.0.0.0 (869), when Stela 11 was erected. This ruler's name, Jasaw Chan K'awiil II, harks back to better times, but the city's precipitous fall in population was already underway, and it was not long before squatters moved into its once exclusive palaces (Culbert et al. 1990:table 5.1; Harrison 1970, this volume) (fig. 1.20a). Uaxactun's last monument, Stela 12 from 889, carries the same Jasaw Chan K'awiil name, though if this is the same ruler, he lacks a clear identifying title (Nahm in Schele and Grube 1994a:1) (fig. 1.20b).

The decline of Tikal mirrors that experienced by most of its contemporaries. The lack of any surviving monument commemorating the B'aktun Ending of 830 suggests that central authority had faltered by that time. While it has long been popular to see the collapse in the southern Lowlands as a process of extended decline over a century or so—a slow retreat from the margins of the Maya world to its Petén heartland, a gradual shift of power from old capitals to their satellites—it is clear that the falls of the most important Classic dynasties were

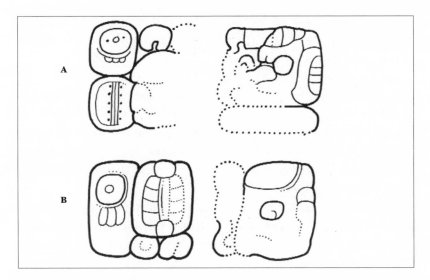

FIGURE 1.20

Late appearances of the name Jasaw Chan K'awiil, (a) *Stela 11, D15–C16, and* (b) *Uaxactun Stela 12, B2–A3.*

closely spaced in time. While some centers did persevere for a while, and some former outliers took up kingly traditions, these were very much the shell-shocked survivors of an earlier cataclysm, stalwarts desperately clinging to a social order whose time was past.

CONCLUSION

The rulers who counted themselves in line of Yax Ehb' Xook presided over Tikal for more than 700 years, a sequence unmatched in the Maya world for its combination of length and biographical detail. Tikal, like all Classic Maya kingdoms, presents us with idealized images of majesty and power, using text to fuse mortal lives within an immortal frame. Yet within these messages of pomp and circumstance we can still glimpse subtexts and perceive the political realities that impinged upon the lives of both the humble and the high and mighty. Despite some innovative aspects, the latest available information has more enriched than revolutionized our understanding of Tikal's story. The resulting picture is one that emphasizes the similarities rather than the differences it had with its rivals and contemporaries. It suffered the same highs and lows, triumphs and disasters as any of them.

The "wealth" of information now available from the epigraphic record is, of course, a relative term. Were we to have but a fraction of the archival codices that once existed, our understanding would be incomparably greater. As it is, we must work with thematically restricted and randomly preserved texts, which—even when perfectly legible—are often imperfectly understood. Damage and erosion are sufficiently severe in many cases to ensure that conclusions may never progress beyond a tentative status. Yet the contribution is real enough, and we are immensely fortunate to have ancient voices that answer at least some of our questions.

I have only lightly touched upon the opportunities for correlating archaeological and textual data. Epigraphy provides a particular kind of narrative, one comparatively rich in chronological, ritual, and political data but impoverished in many other realms of interest to the historian. Very often we can only understand its message in relation to an archaeological context, and a comprehensive narrative can only emerge from a combination of sources and disciplines. Yet in doing so we must be as ready to confront ambiguities in the archaeological record as in the textual one. There are various ways in which we might seek to test the inscriptions, but the great majority of topics they describe have left no physical vestige with which they might be compared or assessed, while cause and effect in history often has more twists and turns that we can safely predict.

It is significant that much of the most important new data comes from outside the city. In regard to foreign sites, Dos Pilas and Caracol have supplied invaluable material for events to which Tikal itself contributes little or nothing. Herein lies a wider message. The comparison and combination of data from many kingdoms allow us to go beyond the singular narrative of any particular one and toward a more synthetic history for the Classic period.

TABLE 1.1

The Tikal Dynasty

	Current Reading	*Nickname*	*Dates* (A.D.)
1st	Yax Ehb' Xook(?)	Yax Moch Xok	ca. 100
?	Huun B'alam	Foliated Jaguar	?
11th	Siyaj Chan K'awiil I		ca. 300
12th?	Unen B'alam	Baby Jaguar	>317>
13th	K'inich Muwaan Jol	Bird Skull	?–359?
14th	Chak Tok Ich'aak I	Great/Jaguar Paw	360?–378
15th	Yax Nuun Ayiin I	Curl Snout/Nose	378–404?
16th	Siyaj Chan K'awiil II	Stormy Sky	411–456
17th	K'an Chitam(?)	Kan Boar	458–486?
18th	Chak Tok Ich'aak II	Jaguar Paw Skull	486?–508
		Lady of Tikal/	
		Stela 6 Ruler	511?–527?
19th		"Kaloomte' B'alam"	?–527>
20th			?
21st?	Wak Chan K'awiil	Double Bird	537?–562
22nd		Animal Skull	?–628?
23rd		?	
24th		?	
25th	Nuun Ujol Chaak	Shield Skull	>657–679>
26th	Jasaw Chan K'awiil I	Ruler A	682–733
27th	Yik'in(?) Chan K'awiil	Ruler B	734>
28th		28th Ruler	>766>
29th	Yax Nuun Ayiin II	Ruler C	768–794>
30th?	Nuun Ujol K'inich		c.800?
31st?		Dark Sun	>810>
?		Jewel K'awiil	>849>
?	Jasaw Chan K'awiil II	Stela 11 Ruler	>869>

Notes

1. For the discovery of glyphic toponyms, see Stuart and Houston (1994). The basis of this particular reading is the phonetic prefix **mu** seen on La Amelia Panel 2 at A9 (Houston 1993:fig.3.21) and the suffix *tu* on Yaxchilan Lintel 17 at F (Graham and Von Euw 1977:43). The word **mut** appears in the Yucatecan Vienna Dictionary in the form *mut pol* "rodete hacer la mujer de sus cabellos (plait a woman makes of her hair)" (see Barrera Vásquez 1980:542), a fair description of the tied bundle represented by T569 and pictured graphically as hair in head variant forms of this sign (for example, Stela 5, D6) (glyph designations in this study follow those of J. E. S. Thompson 1962).

2. Transliterations in this study reflect the discovery of "complex" vowels and the disharmonic principle (see Houston, Stuart, and Robertson 1998). At present it is not possible to fully distinguish between long, glottalized and *h*-infixed vowels in the script, and this study has assumed the presence of long vowels, represented by doubled letters, as a default where lexical or historio-linguistic data are absent or uncertain.

3. The Ehb' "step" element, which appears both as a tied ladder T193 and a platform step sign T843, has recently been deciphered by David Stuart (1999). The Xook "shark" reading for T1012 remains unconfirmed (though see T. Jones 1996). The common appearance of shark motifs in Preclassic iconography, especially as earflare emblems, suggests that sharks had a special role within royal and mythic identity and may evoke ancestral creation myths. (My thanks go to Dicey Taylor for sending me the image redrawn as fig. 1.1a.)

4. These counts combine an ordinal number with **TZ'AK-b'u-IL** *tz'akb'uil* (long known as the "hel" glyph), a positional verb with a *-b'u* causative suffix (Stuart et al. 1999:32). This root appears in Yucatec as *ts'akab* "ancestry, caste, lineage, or generation" (Barrera Vásquez 1980:873), though its origin may be better reflected in *-ts'ak* "step or count of steps of parentage" (Michelon 1976:455) (see Houston 1998:356–57). It is this sense of counting that is active in its appearance as the Distance Number Introductory Glyph. At Tikal dynastic counts appear on Stela 5 (A5–6), Stela 12 (D6), Stela 17 (G1–H2), Stela 22 (A5–6), and MT.217 from Burial 195 (H–J) and on two unprovenanced ceramics (see fig. 1.10a, b). The appellative usage, with Yax Ehb' Xook or simply Ehb' Xook, follows the names of Tikal rulers on Stela 3 (D8), Stela 17 (D2), Stela 22 (B4), Stela 39 (Bz2), Stela 40 (D15, F10), and the Temple VI Facade (J3, O4).

5. The basis of this revision is an unprovenanced tripod vase lid that names the ruler Siyaj Chan K'awiil II (Stormy Sky) as 16th in line of the founder (see

fig. 1.10a). This clarifies a number of other references and links to the early sequence, not least the Tikal Dynastic Vase (see fig. 1.4). The former association of Chak Tok Ich'aak I (Jaguar Paw) with the 9th successor was based on a misunderstanding of the **9-TZ'AK-b'u-AJAW** "Many set in line lord" title, which is unrelated to the true dynastic count.

6. A figure of 22.5 years is used as the mean average reign (S. Martin 1997:853–54). If applied to the accession of the 29th king in 768 (counting 28 previous intervals), a figure of A.D. 138 is reached, although a calculation drawn from the end of the 14th reign in 378 gives A.D. 63 as a starting point. An average drawn from seven fixed points throughout the Tikal sequence comes to about A.D. 90.

7. The idea that Burial 85 was that of the Tikal "founder" was first posited by Freidel and Suhler (1995).

8. His name combines the three-leafed crest of the Jester God with the head of a jaguar *b'alam*. This crest appears as part of an accession event on Stela 4 (B4a), a context in which we find substitutions with T60, T522, the head of the Jester God T1030o, and the paired syllables **hu-na.** Noting the complex vowel indicated by disharmony, all of these logograms must therefore read **HUUN, HU'UN,** or **HU'N,** the ancient name of this Olmec-derived supernatural.

9. The Bak'tun value is missing, but examination of the rubber mold held by the Tikal Project indicates that the K'atun coefficient is 8 or, more probably, 13. Significantly, the Haab (here apparently 6 K'ayab) and the Tzolk'in appear to be reversed in order, a feature of dates before about 8.14.0.0.0 (317) (S. Martin 2000a).

10. The Stormy Sky name was first read as Siyaj Chan K'awiil by David Stuart (in Houston and Stuart 1996:295). The date of the El Encanto stela may be retrospective but cannot, it seems, fall within the tenure of the Siyaj Chan K'awiil we know as Stormy Sky. The damaged verbal event here (at B8) seems to be a *tzaak* "conjuring" ritual.

11. This count employs simple ordinal numbers in the form **u-#-TAL-la.** A comparison of glyphic handwriting strongly suggests that the painter of this vase, K4679, also executed K772 (Kerr 1989:46, 1994:584). The latter dates to the reign of Animal Skull, indicating that this dynastic list was created sometime around A.D. 600.

12. Initially *une'* rather than *unen* seemed the value in question (S. Martin and Grube 2000:27, 77), although it became increasingly clear that this was contradicted by two spellings in similar, if not identical, contexts (both of which

include the "doubler" diacritic [see Stuart and Houston 1994:46] that indicates an -*n* ending). Confirmation of this came with Marc Zendler's identification of the phonetic spelling of the deity GII at Comalcalco, where the relevant term is clearly rendered **u-ne**[2] in the same "infant" context (Zender, Armijo, and Gallegos-Gomora 2000).

13. The main part of this name is a human skull with feathers and birds' feet emerging from its mouth. Since this combination appears in no other context, it is reasonable to view it as a conflation between two common signs: **JOL** "head" (David Stuart, pers. comm. 1999) and the bird-eating **MUWA:N** "hawk" (Nikolai Grube, pers. comm. 1997). It is not possible to define their reading order with certainty at present.

14. The date here could well be 8.16.2.6.0 11 Ajaw 13 Pop (359). An alternate position has been offered by Stefanie Teufel of 8.17.1.10.19 11 Muluk 7 Pop (378) (in Vidal, Teufel, and Fialko 1998). See C. Jones and Orrego 1987 for excavation data.

15. In addition, a stela found at El Temblor, 18 km. to the south of Tikal, shows a possible example of his name (Stuart 2000:471). The partially preserved accession date clearly differs from that implied on Stela 31, and he could thus have been a namesake.

16. Stuart (1999) has noted a version of the Ehb' Xook name on a bone from Kaminaljuyu, which may be significant in regards to Tikal's connections to the highlands.

17. For Río Azul Stela 1 (B12) mention, see Adams 1998:fig.63, first noted by Nikolai Grube and Federico Fahsen (Nikolai Grube, pers. comm. 1998). Siyaj K'ak's name followed by an *ajaw* title can be seen at Palenque (see Maudslay 1889–1902:pl.34), though the full context of the text is uncertain.

18. It is possible that texts on the sides of Stela 31 refer to Siyaj K'ak' with other, potentially non-Mayan names.

19. For the substitution patterns in this name, see Grube and Schele (1994) and Stuart (2000).

20. The death phrase on El Zapote Stela 5 gives the phonetic rendering of Spearthrower Owl's name at D16 (Nikolai Grube, pers. comm. 1997), identified by both David Stuart and me on the Tikal Marcador (E3-F3) as **ja-?-ma ku?.**

21. The reading order in this name is still debated. Its original proposer, David Stuart, favors Nuun Yax Ayiin, while Stanley Guenter and Marc Zender argue for the sequence used here (pers. comm. 2000).

22. The father of K'an Chitam was first identified as Siyaj Chan K'awiil on

Stela 13 (A3–4) (Schele and Grube 1994a:7). His mother's personal name is seen on Stela 13 (A7) and Stela 40 (D9), within the headdress of her portrait on Stela 40, and perhaps as a rear belt ornament on Stela 2. It combines the female agentive head with the jaw and snout of the caiman *ayiin* and other, godlike attributes. A very similar name appears in the headdress of an ancestral figure on the left side of Stela 1.

23. Nikolai Grube (pers. comm. 1999) has visited the ruins of Naachtun and reports seeing a damaged emblem of **ma-x-AJAW** that may be that of Maasal. The protagonist of the attack is named as a *mutal ajaw,* with what could be a secondary name of K'an Chitam seen elsewhere (for example, Stela 40, D15).

24. The birth of the Lady of Tikal fell on 9.3.9.13.3 (504), where her name resembles the royal female title *ix mutal ajaw* but also includes the 'twisted cord' T98 seen in the name of a Tikal patron deity on Stela 26 (zB9). The next event on Stela 23, at B6a, takes place on 9.3.16.8.4 (511) and replicates the accession formula seen on Stela 31 at E10. The name of the subject begins at B6b. Although only a small part of it survives today, it does include a crossed-hatched forelock matching that seen in the queen's female agentive at C4.

25. The name of this god precedes female personal names on Stela 3 (D5), Stela 31 (A24–B24), and the Marcador (G8) as well as on the Palenque Oval Palace Tablet (A). One example might follow a female name on Stela 17 (G7).

26. The podlike sign suffers from erosion and is hard to identify. It resembles the syllabogram T115/651 **yo** and its logographic parent **YOP** "leaf" (the latter value posited by David Stuart, pers. comm. 1999), but its orientation favors a form of T370 **TZUH/tzu** "gourd," T559/696 **UNIW** "avocado," or less probably T547 **TA:K** (the same pod sign but with a *k'in* infix) that in some cases serves as a plural suffix (David Stuart, pers. comm. 1998). The front of Stela 6 may include this same name combination incised as part of an identifying caption or as the patron in a sculptor's signature.

27. The *(u)naab'nal k'inich* term appears directly after Tikal personal names on Stela 1 (Bz3), Stela 3 (C2), Stela 4 (A6), Stela 8 (A5, B3b), Stela 13 (B6), Stela 17 (H9), Stela 22 (B7), and Temple III Lintel 2 (D18) and after other royal titles on Stela 5 (A7), Stela 16 (C2), and Temple IV Lintel 3 (G1) (see also fig. 1.10a at K–L). In a few cases on ceramics it precedes the name, as it does on Stela 39 at Bz1 (Laporte and Fialko 1990:fig.10b). The version on Stela 6, a conflation with the head of the Sun God, appears on Stela 8 (A5) and less clearly in a number of examples on the Temple VI Facade (for example, A11, E19) (C. Jones 1977:figs.9, 18). In all later cases the T86 **NAL** "place of" sign is combined

with the water-lily pad T324 **NAAB'** "pool" (reading in this context emphasized by Stanley Guenter [pers. comm. 2001]). The initial possessive pronoun only appears in the earliest examples and was later omitted (for an especially clear case, see Berjonneau and Sonnery 1985:fig.355, at glyph G).

28. Although slightly elaborated, the human head is within the stylistic bounds of the Early Classic female agentive. David Stuart (1998:386) has shown that this head reads **IX** in the western Maya region. To its right we see a compressed version of the pod sign on top of a deity portrait, perhaps the Sun God *k'in* or *k'inich*. Note the latter's elongated infix, which is conceivably used as an abbreviation in the names on Stela 6 (By3) and Stela 8 (B7b).

29. The podlike sign in this case is clearly T567 **TA:K.** The Haab here is a "color month" of Ch'en, Keh, Sak, or Yax. Interestingly, a possible accession date on the right side of Stela 25 (E1–F4) similarly features one of these months. The subject is in some way connected to K'an Chitam, whose name appears at E4.

30. At D6 on Stela 12 the coefficient 19 is attached to the "K'in-Ak'bal" logogram for **TZ'AK** (see note 4). Beneath this is seen an animal head that would appear to represent a rare form of inflectional suffix. The name Curl Head, applied by Linda Schele to the 19th king, appears on the rear of Stela 12, where it actually seems to be a name or title borne by the queen.

31. The nickname Bird Claw arose from a misidentification of the name on Stela 8 at B6b. The true personal name, seen at both A4 and B3a, shows him to have been a close namesake of the later Animal Skull (Schele and Grube 1994a:5–6). In fact, Stanley Guenter (pers. comm. 2001) has suggested that Stela 8 is a monument from Animal Skull's reign executed in a deliberately archaicizing style and dated to the Period Ending 9.7.0.0.0 (although with an error to the Haab coefficient, which is written as *8* but should be *3*). The relationship at B7a is expressed by a possessed noun, perhaps *u-ti' hu'un*. This appears in a number of contexts, from Glyph F of the Supplementary Series to a title borne by subordinate lords in the western Maya region. There are several possible translations, but no indication as to which of them is the correct one here (T128 as logographic **TI'** "mouth, edge" has been suggested by David Stuart [pers. comm. 1998]).

32. We see something similar at Naranjo, where Lady Six Sky shares monumental portraits, royal titles, and the performance of calendrical ceremonies with her young son K'ak' Tiliw Chan Chaak (Smoking Squirrel) (Closs 1985:73).

33. The term *hun k'al/winik* "one twenty" can refer either to the number "twenty" or to "twenty-one," so the dynastic position of Wak Chan K'awiil is not

absolutely secure (Nikolai Grube, pers. comm. 1996).

34. This Wak Chan K'awiil name appears on Stela 17 at C1–D1 and F6–E7. Among those on ceramics we might add the one on the vessel K5452 at J–K (Kerr 1997:803), though no Tikal affiliation is stated here. The opening sign T367 routinely substitutes for the numeral 6, which is *wäk=* in Proto-Ch'olan (Kaufman and Norman 1984:161) and is a root reflected in virtually all Mayan languages. The "Double Bird" element is simply the poorly preserved name/title *(u)wuk chapaat-?* (this form read by Erik Boot, pers. comm. 1998) (S. Martin 2001b).

35. In the CR marking 9.6.0.0.0, a tiny dot at glyph A serves to 'correct' 8 to 9 Ajaw, while the month position is given as 3 Wayeb, here in the variant form *kol ajaw* (perhaps preferred at this Period Ending to lessen the "unlucky" associations of the year end). The 9.3.0.0.0 mark is indicated by a lone 2 Ajaw (S. Martin 2001b).

36. The reading order, contrary to its published labeling, seems to begin on the right side (at I1), progresses to the back (from E1), and then goes to the left (from A1). The first side most likely contained the early life events of Wak Chan K'awiil, perhaps beginning with the date 9.3.13.2.10 (A.D. 508), implied by a DN of 2.10.7.5 that counts back from 9.6.3.9.10 (A.D. 557), the final LC date on the left side.

37. A DN of 1.?.15.? on the back side counts forward to a verb consisting of a hand sign, which examination indicates is not a damaged form of T218a **TZUTZ** "to finish/end" but the "pointing hand" T713b. This sign is usually fused with the "moon" glyph T181 to form a single logograph reading **HUL** "to arrive here" (Macleod 1990:339–40; Stephen Houston, pers. comm. 1999). On a few occasions, however, T181 is omitted (see Naranjo Stela 8 [C5] and Stela 13 [E6] in Graham 1975). The following CR date is too badly damaged to identify.

38. Here Lady Six Sky first arrives from Dos Pilas in 682 and three days later dedicates or rededicates some important dynastic temple, a phrase in which the Naranjo emblem main sign features prominently. This marks the beginning of her tenure as de facto Naranjo ruler.

39. In this context it is interesting that Stela 17 makes mention of an apparent Xultun king called Upakal K'inich "Shield of the Sun God." For reasons that are still unexplained, the *mutal* toponym of Tikal appears on Xultun Stela 6 on a date that may fall in 511 (see Von Euw 1985).

40. A potential cause of confusion is the fact that Animal Skull carries a fuller spelling of his father's name in his own nominal sequence. Compare the

father's name on MT.217 (at A) (Culbert 1993:fig.50) with the unprovenanced plate K1261 (at I–K) (M. D. Coe and Kerr 1982:81).

41. A very similar nominal sequence to that of Animal Skull has been noted on Altar de Sacrificíos Stela 8, dated to 628 (David Stuart in Houston et al. 1992). If this was the same character, and a contemporary mention, he must have lived to a ripe old age. Interestingly, MT.218, a painted stucco text in Burial 195, includes the title Kan Ajaw "Snake Lord," though whether this is a reference to Calakmul or some other usage is unclear.

42. William Haviland made this suggestion.

43. Stanley Guenter (pers. comm. 2002) first suggested the date 9.10.18.2.19 (650) for this attack.

44. See Fahsen (2002) for fuller details of Dos Pilas Hieroglyphic Stairway 2 and additions to it discovered in 2001. Nikolai Grube first noted the collocation **K'INICH-pa-a-WITZ** *k'inich pa' witz* as a phonetic spelling of Aguateca's name (in Fahsen 2002).

45. Nuun Ujol Chaak (as Shield Skull) was first identified at Dos Pilas by Coggins (1975:379). Stanley Guenter has pointed out to me that a passage on Dos Pilas HS.2 (East, C4–D6) could well describe B'alaj Chan K'awiil and Nuun Ujol Chaak as joint participants in some action performed by Yich'aak K'ak' of Calakmul at one of the sites called Yaxa', dated between 657 and 662 (pers. comm. 2000).

46. The coincidence is even more marked when one considers that the arrival of Nuun Ujol Chaak of Santa Elena at Palenque is placed at 9.11.6.16.17 (659), precisely one K'atun before Nuun Ujol Chaak of Tikal was defeated by Dos Pilas on 9.12.6.16.17 (679) (Schele 1994:3–4). The ancient name of Santa Elena (the so-called "Wa-Bird" sign) is composed of three elements: the signs for **wa, k'a,** and a bird-head that may well conform to the syllabogram deciphered by David Stuart (pers. comm. 1999) as **be** (usually conflated with the **k'a** sign). A previously unrecognized appearance in a damaged text referring to Nuun Ujol Chaak on an inscribed *incensario* stand from Palenque (D7–C9) (Schele and Mathews 1979:no.281) links it to the same form already identified on Yaxchilan Lintel 16 (Graham and Von Euw 1977:41).

47. My thanks go to Peter Harrison, who supplied the field sketches that confirmed this idea (pers. comm. 1994).

48. Maasal lords use the names/titles *sak wayis* and *chatan winik*, linked to the Calakmul sphere, while a reference to Maasal appears in a recently excavated text at Calakmul (S. Martin 1998b). A stucco-painted vessel from Jasaw's

Burial 116 (MT.67) shows a presentation of gifts to an enthroned lord—presumably the king himself—before an assemblage of dignitaries (Culbert 1993:fig.68). A Maasal noble seems to be mentioned at A4, while one standing lord is captioned at wA1–3 with the foremost title of Yaxchilan's Shield Jaguar the Great and may be this well-known character (Guenter and Zender 1999).

49. The name of Ruler B includes T545, a verbal form of the word for "night" or "darkness" (the verbal suffix -ya appears on MT.176 from Burial 196). On Yaxchilan Stela 18 this sign, which introduces a nighttime event, seems to be spelled yik'in, literally "blackness of the sun" or "old sun." But the selfsame sign, where it is part of the G9 compound, is prefixed by the syllabogram cha, perhaps "darkened sun" (MacLeod 1991:5).

50. Additional passages on this stone are difficult to interpret. The block at the extreme left, C1–2, resembles the name of the Naranjo ruler Yax Mayuy Chan Chaak, captured by Ruler B in 744 (S. Martin 1996b). There is no visible name phrase for a Tikal king, and it possible that this scene featured two captives bound together.

51. David Stuart has identified the relevant passage as the supernatural rebirth of a son of Ruler B (pers. comm. to Nikolai Grube 1999). Ruler B's secondary, perhaps preinaugural name, takes the form **AJ-CHAK-?-TE'**. It appears on both MT.176 (vN–vA) and MT.180 (A2) from Burial 196 (for the former, see Culbert 1993:fig.84).

2

The Ceramics of Tikal

T. Patrick Culbert

More than 40 years of archaeological research at Tikal have produced an enormous quantity of ceramics that have been studied by a variety of investigators (Coggins 1975; Culbert 1963, 1973, 1977, 1979, 1993; Fry 1969, 1979; Fry and Cox 1974; Hermes 1984a; Iglesias 1987, 1988; Laporte and Fialko 1987, 1993; Laporte et al. 1992; Laporte and Iglesias 1992; Laporte, this volume). It could be argued that the ceramics of Tikal are better known than those from any other Maya site. The contexts represented by the ceramic collections are extremely varied, as are the formation processes to which they were subjected both in Maya times and since the site was abandoned.

This chapter will report primarily on the ceramics recovered by the University of Pennsylvania Tikal Project between 1956 and 1970. The information available from this analysis has been significantly clarified and expanded by later research, especially that of the Proyecto Nacional Tikal (Hermes 1984a; Iglesias 1987, 1988; Laporte and Fialko 1987, 1993; Laporte et al. 1992; Laporte and Iglesias 1992; Laporte, this volume). I will make reference to some of the results of these later studies but will not attempt an overall synthesis—something that must await a full-scale conference involving all of those who have worked with Tikal ceramics.

Primary goals of my analysis of Tikal ceramics were to develop a ceramic sequence and to provide chronological information for researchers. Although a ceramic sequence was already available from the neighboring site of Uaxactun (R. E. Smith 1955), the importance of Tikal and the scale of the project there dictated that the Tikal sequence should be developed independently, without reliance on the Uaxactun material. The results of this independence were to demonstrate that the sequences at the two sites were nearly identical and to provide confidence in the accuracy of both analyses.

This chapter will begin with a consideration of the methods used in the Tikal analyses and an outline of the resulting sequence. I will then examine the information that ceramics provide about the economic system, social status, and ritual practices of the ancient Maya.

KINDS OF DEPOSITS

Meaningful archaeological analysis is impossible without a careful consideration of a set of factors that provide or limit possibilities for various types of analyses. (See Moholy-Nagy 1997 for a separate but parallel consideration of these same issues.) Such considerations are especially true for a lengthy project at a very large site, where a huge variety of different situations will be encountered. Far too often, archaeologists tend to consider only certain deposits useful for analysis. This is particularly true for the claim that only "primary" deposits are useful, which frequently ignores the formation processes to which deposits have been subjected.

Several factors are important in determining the utility of deposits for providing specific kinds of information: the nature (for example, size, preservation, quantity) of the artifactual material; the amount of time represented by the deposit; the stratigraphic situation involved; and the formation processes, both cultural and natural, that have affected the material. Taking these factors into account, I classify deposits into several types.

1. *"Mixed grab bag."* This is a term I use for the typical deposit encountered at Tikal, especially in association with small structures. A mixed grab bag includes a mixture of artifacts from all periods during

which people engaged in activity at a location. There is no stratigraphic order to the deposits. Why such randomness should be typical becomes clear if one considers the cultural and natural processes to which refuse deposits were subjected after discard. The Maya were accustomed to use refuse as fill for new structures. In the process they moved material from one location to another and disturbed things that might have been left in place. For centuries after abandonment, the deposits were subjected to such natural processes as erosion, animal burrowing, and, especially, tree falls. When a dead tree is blown over in the forest, its roots remove soil and artifacts and strip an area clear down to bedrock. Eventually, the roots decay, and the soil and artifacts are released, slowly washing back into the hole in random order. The effect is like that of a giant mixing machine. Information contained in such mixed deposits is mostly chronological. The excavator may be able to make sense of the relative amounts of material from different periods of occupation. Most of the demographic history of Tikal (Culbert et al. 1990), in fact, was derived from such deposits.

2. *Middens.* If one defines a midden as an archaeological deposit left untouched by cultural or natural processes after being discarded by the ancient inhabitants of a site, such deposits are rare at Tikal or any other major Maya site. Stratified middens—deposits in which middens accumulate stratigraphically over long intervals of time—are almost unknown. The closest thing to true middens at Tikal were the often large accumulations of material left within rooms by the Terminal Classic inhabitants of range structures. In addition, some deposits found in chultuns seem to represent rapid dumping episodes that approach true midden status. Some deposits found outside small structures also represent relatively short periods of deposit, although it can be presumed that they have been somewhat mixed by the processes noted above.

3. *Fill deposits.* Often disdained by archaeologists, fill deposits were among the most useful in the Tikal ceramic analysis. Deposits from structure fill are critical for excavators to date construction. When fill is sealed, it is obvious that the structure can have been built no earlier than the latest sherd it contains. Large fill samples provide some security that the construction date is actually represented by the latest sherd; small samples may be problematic. For information in

addition to date of construction, other data become important factors to consider. These include the size of the structure involved, the group to which it pertains, and the number of reconstructions at the location.

Fill from Small Structure Groups provides an excellent source of information. Sherd fits between structure fill and refuse materials from outside other structures in the same group make it clear that the Maya moved accumulated refuse into platforms that were being constructed or remodeled. Such fill often represents a relatively unmixed sample from a short time interval, probably because contemporary refuse deposits within the group were readily available and provided enough material for filling operations.

Fill from large structures is another matter. Large construction usually involved dismantling of earlier structures at the same location, resulting in a constant "upwelling" of early material into later constructions that makes unmixed samples rare. Sealed fill from large structures, however, can provide important opportunities. Preservation of sherd surfaces is usually much better than it is in small structures, allowing description and analysis of decorated types. In addition, sequences of construction involving large quantities of sealed fill related to architectural stratigraphy can provide exceedingly precise information about the points at which ceramic features were introduced. The Preclassic levels in the North Acropolis (W. R. Coe 1990) are an outstanding example of this phenomenon. Level upon level of construction there provided huge samples of ceramics in an excellent state of preservation. The exact point in the sequence when a new ceramic element made its appearance can be documented. After being introduced, most elements showed a trend of increase followed by a decline in typical battleship-curve fashion. The curves, however, are not as well defined as in less mixed deposits, and once they are introduced, elements continue to appear in the deposits for centuries with no clear indication as to when they ceased to be produced.

4. *Special deposits.* The utility of burial and cache artifacts (including ceramics) for providing information about chronology, social status, and ritual practices is well known. These data, including a significant amount of published Tikal data, have been used by Krejci and Culbert (1995) for a consideration of social status and change over

time during the Preclassic and Early Classic periods in the Maya Lowlands. In addition, the Early Classic burials 10, 22, and 48 provide an excellent source of information about the impact of Teotihuacan on the Maya elite of Tikal and Kaminaljuyu (Reents and Culbert n.d.). Problematical deposits at Tikal, however, represent such a mixed group of situations and contents (as they were appropriately designed to do) that they cannot be considered a single category for analysis. Some types of problematical deposits are rich and varied in their ceramic contents and provide important collections for ceramic analysis.

CONSTRUCTION OF THE TIKAL CERAMIC SEQUENCE

Not all types of deposits were equally available for all time periods at Tikal. Consequently, different methods had to be used in the construction of the ceramic sequence. The two earliest complexes, Eb and Tzec, were defined on the basis of limited numbers of large, well-preserved collections with only enough stratigraphic evidence to indicate their relative placements in time. For the remainder of the Preclassic (the Chuen, Cauac, and Cimi complexes), the superb North Acropolis stratigraphy made possible the subdivision of what had been an undifferentiated Chicanel complex at Uaxactun (R. E. Smith 1955).

The Early Classic Manik-complex collections, although abundant and from a variety of locations throughout the site, lacked stratigraphy and quantity comparable to that of the North Acropolis and failed to seriate in a well-defined fashion. Consequently, no subdivisions of the complex were attempted. The research of the Proyecto Nacional Tikal (Iglesias 1987; Laporte and Fialko 1987; Laporte et al. 1992; Laporte and Iglesias 1992), however, provided detailed information that clarified this section of the Tikal sequence.

For the Late Classic (Ik and Imix complexes), the excellent architectural stratigraphy of the central core of the site did not include large enough samples to define ceramic change. As a result, the change between Ik and Imix was based upon a seriation of a large number of relatively unmixed samples that were mostly not in stratigraphic association with each other, supported by data from burials. The Terminal Classic Eznab complex was defined on the basis of very large collections left by Eznab occupation of range-structure groups.

CLASSIFICATION

Three different and independent systems of classification were used in the analysis of Tikal ceramics. The first was a traditional type/variety analysis (R. E. Smith, Willey, and Gifford 1960), the second was a classification of vessel shapes, and the last was a classification of pastes. In many type/variety analyses, a hierarchical sorting has been used, with vessel shapes and pastes treated under each type. This fails to give proper attention to the fact that surface treatment, paste, and shape are independent variables that may or may not correlate. The degree to which they correlate or fail to do so is a matter for investigation and an important source of information.

The type/variety analysis at Tikal was quite traditional, using names already established in the literature wherever possible. In the many collections where surface preservation was nonexistent, type/variety analysis proved impossible.

In general, the analysis of vessel shapes was more useful than that of types. Not only was shape classification possible for collections in which surface preservation was minimal, but also shapes usually provided greater diversity than types and changed more rapidly through time. In the classification of shapes, I developed an analytical system of two levels: shape classes and shapes. *Shape classes* are major divisions based on size, body proportions, and nature of orifice. They are likely to have been strongly correlated with vessel use. *Shapes* are subdivisions of shape classes, based on differences in wall or neck shape, modifications such as flanges and ridges, and so forth. Shapes changed more rapidly through time than shape classes and were often useful in establishing the distinctions between different ceramic complexes. In addition, shapes were probably less tied to the uses of vessels than were shape classes. As an example, the *shape class* "Medium Plates" occurs throughout the Late and Terminal Classic complexes. The basic dimensions remained consistent, as probably did the uses of the vessels. But the *shapes* of medium plates are one of the best diagnostics for distinguishing the Ik, Imix, and Eznab complexes. In the Ik complex, medium plates have lateral flanges or ridges. In the Imix complex, no flanges or ridges occur, but a characteristic beveled lip marks the Imix member of the shape class (the Tripod Plate with Beveled Lip). In the Eznab complex, the Tripod Plate with Beveled Lip continues to occur, but a flangelike modification appears again in the Notched Z-angle Tripod Plate.

Finally, as a device for quantification, I used a breakdown into four major "shape categories": wide-mouth jars, narrow-mouth jars, large-capacity bowls, and serving vessels. The first three categories are each single-shape classes, while the serving vessel category includes a number of shape classes. This unruly system simplifies quantification. Many lots were so small that if one were to quantify by shape classes, the serving vessels would be so split among their multiple shape classes that the results would be dubious. Also, I would argue that the jar and large bowl categories would almost always have had everyday domestic uses, while serving vessels were probably used for serving food, but also for ritual purposes and a variety of other uses.

The analysis of pastes at Tikal was based entirely upon visual inspection, with no attempts to deal with the chemistry or petrography of the inclusions noted except for a limited trial of x-ray florescence, which I will describe below. Such identifications as "shiny black particles" are technically unsophisticated but sometimes correlated with either types or shapes and, in a few cases, were temporally diagnostic. It is clear that far more information could be gained by technical analyses of Tikal pastes, but such analyses exceeded both the time available and my technical expertise.

THE CERAMIC SEQUENCE: THE PRECLASSIC

The ceramic sequence at Uaxactun (R. E. Smith 1955), the previous standard for central Petén ceramics, managed to achieve only the two-part division of Mamom and Chicanel for the Preclassic. The much more voluminous collections and superb stratigraphy at Tikal, especially in the North Acropolis, made possible the separation of five sequent complexes: Eb, Tzec, Chuen, Cauac, and Cimi (table 2.1).

The Eb Complex

Two temporal facets were defined for the Eb complex. Early Eb was the first pre-Mamom horizon material recognized in the central Petén. Since the definition of Early Eb at Tikal, significant quantities were also recovered by Prudence Rice (1979a) at Yaxha, the Proyecto Nacional Tikal in the Mundo Perdido complex (Hermes 1984a;

TABLE 2.1

Tikal Ceramic Complexes

Period	Ceramic Complex	Approximate Date
Postclassic	Caban	A.D. 950–1200(?)
Terminal Classic	Eznab	A.D. 850–950
Late Classic	Imix	A.D. 700–850
Intermediate Classic	Ik	A.D. 550–700
Early Classic	Manik	A.D. 200–550
Terminal Preclassic	Cimi	A.D. 150–200
Late Preclassic	Cauac	A.D. 1–150
Late Preclassic	Chuen	350 B.C.–A.D. 1
Middle Preclassic	Tzec	600–350 B.C.
Middle Preclassic	Eb	800–600 B.C.

Laporte and Fialko 1993), and David Cheetham (1998) in Belize. In the Pennsylvania collections, Early Eb ceramics occurred in quantity in only two locations, a pit in bedrock underlying the North Acropolis and Chultun 5G-15, 1.5 km. east of the site center. The deposit underneath the North Acropolis establishes the temporal priority of Early Eb.

Early Eb ceramics include a number of types and shapes that distinguish them from later Mamom horizon material. Although there are contemporary ceramic complexes known from both the Pasion River (Adams 1971; Sabloff 1975) and Belize (Gifford 1976; Hammond 1980, 1986; Kosakowsky 1987), as well as from neighboring areas outside the Maya Lowlands, these other complexes show relatively little relationship to Early Eb or to each other. The great diversity of the earliest ceramics from different regions of the Maya Lowlands has long been recognized (Culbert 1977) as suggesting that the initial populations moved into the Lowlands from several different directions, but no collections from surrounding areas seem similar enough to Early Eb to suggest a specific area of origin.

Late Eb ceramics came mostly from the tunnel excavated by the University of Pennsylvania Project into Str. 5C–54, the great pyramid in the Mundo Perdido complex. Many of the unique characteristics of

Early Eb continue to appear, but with a greater percentage of ceramics that characterize the Mamom horizon. In a sense, then, Late Eb is transitional between Early Eb and Mamom. Because the sample on which Late Eb is based was fill from a large structure, it is also possible that it represents at least some mixture between what might have been purer Eb and Tzec assemblages.

The Tzec Complex

The Tzec complex also shows a transitional character, this time between the Mamom and Chicanel ceramic horizons. The complex was sparsely represented in the Tikal collections. Only one location (a quarry pit underlying structures 5F-17 and 5F-18 about 1 km. east of site center) provided an unmixed Tzec sample that could be analyzed quantitatively. The collections from this location, however, were large and the deposits deep enough to demonstrate ceramic change within the Tzec complex and a gradual transition to the succeeding Chuen complex that overlay it. Like the Mamom complex at Uaxactun (R. E. Smith 1955), a principal defining characteristic of Tzec was a huge abundance of plates. This characteristic, also shared with the Mamom-equivalent San Felix complex at Altar de Sacrificios (Adams 1971), is difficult to explain in a functional sense. Whatever activity was represented by the use of plates, it was shared across the southern Maya Lowlands.

The Chuen Complex

The Chuen complex represents the beginning of the Late Preclassic (Chicanel horizon) complexes at Tikal. The archaeological evidence for the complex is much more complete than that for the Eb and Tzec complexes. The Chuen samples represent increased contextual variety, a greater number of locations, more samples per location, and an increased total quantity of sherds. It is also the point at which the North Acropolis floor sequence that seals large quantities of ceramics begins.

Typologically, Tzec and Chuen ceramics are relatively easy to distinguish, but with the beginning of the Chuen complex, Tikal ceramics entered a long period of typological stability during which the types that composed the bulk of the collections changed very little for a period of 600 years. During the time of the Chicanel horizon there was a strong similarity in ceramics across the Maya Lowlands, and even outside, to such areas as the Central Depression of Chiapas (Willey et al. 1967).

The Cauac Complex

The Cauac complex is the best defined of the Late Preclassic complexes at Tikal, both because more diagnostic shapes mark the complex and because the ceramic collections are more abundant. Typologically, there was little change between the Chuen and Cauac complexes in either the types represented or the frequency of these types. The only change worthy of mention is the appearance of the first types with Usulutan decoration. That such decoration had its home to the south of the Maya Lowlands in El Salvador (Demarest and Sharer 1982) seems clear, its introduction representing cultural contact. I consider it important, however, to make a distinction between what I term "Usulutan Style" and "Usulutan Ware." Usulutan *Style* consists of a multiple parallel wavy-lines decoration, usually made with a multipronged instrument. Usulutan *Ware* was made by a resist technique in which sections of the first slip were covered with something like wax before a second slip was added. Although resist techniques were used at Tikal in other types in the Tzec and Chuen complexes, resist pieces in Usulutan style were rare at the site, and most were probably trade items. Usulutan Style vessels in the entire Petén and Belize were usually decorated using a "wipe-off" technique, in which a second slip was added over the first and then removed, while still wet, with a multipronged instrument to reveal sections of the underlying first slip. There are also some pieces in which a second slip is positively painted with a multipronged instrument. In effect, then, the Maya of the Lowlands copied the stylistic approach of Usulutan, but they produced it with their own techniques.

Despite the small amount of typological change between Chuen and Cauac, the separation of collections of the two complexes is made relatively easy by the fact that quite distinctive changes in shapes occur in vessels that are common in the collections. Of these, the appearance of medial-flange dishes is the most obvious.

The Cimi Complex

The last of the Preclassic ceramic complexes of the Tikal sequence is the Cimi complex. The Cimi complex is both controversial (Laporte, this volume) and the most difficult to recognize of the Tikal complexes. Therefore, it is necessary to consider in some detail the basis on which it was defined, its content, and its position in relation to the Tikal sequence and to other sequences in the Maya area.

The Cimi complex was based primarily on the North Acropolis stratigraphy and associated ceramics that showed minor but significant additions to the preceding Cauac complex. Collections included all lots sealed by the seventh, eighth, and ninth floors from the top of the Acropolis (W. R. Coe 1990). This was an important interval of time in the Acropolis. A massive raising of the overall North Acropolis platform took place at some time, probably close to the beginning of the Cimi time span. The rebuilding associated with the new platform set a basic pattern of structures that would persist for centuries. The only chamber burial (Bu. 125) that occurred in this interval involved a very large chamber that was empty except for the remains of an elderly man. At the end of the Cimi complex but clearly before the start of the Manik complex, the entire approach to the Acropolis from the Great Plaza was changed by completion of a single frontal stairway that replaced what had previously been two separate stairways. Probably more than a century later and well into Manik times, a pit was dug through the fifth floor of the Acropolis sequence and filled with PD 87, a collection of Cimi ceramics and human bones that Coe (1990:831) suggests may have been a redeposited Cimi burial. If so (the ceramics seem appropriate for a burial), it would indicate that major chamber burials were still being made in the North Acropolis in Cimi times.

The Cimi ceramic samples were large and included 8,026 sherds counted for types and 1,548 rims counted for shapes. The differentiation between Cauac and Cimi is minimal, consisting mostly of the addition of new Usulutan varieties produced using a very liquid black slip that is easily given to jagged patterns and of tetrapodal vessels with mammiform feet. A few types and shapes that are more characteristic of the Manik complex also occurred in sealed Cimi levels. The Cimi markers never occur in frequencies greater than 5 percent. Consequently, their absence in small collections is not significant.

The Usulutan varieties that identify Cimi also appear at sites in Belize (Willey et al. 1965; Gifford 1976) and on the Pasión River

(Adams 1971; Sabloff 1975) in ceramic complexes that have traditionally been termed "Protoclassic." Like Laporte (this volume), I refuse to
use the term "Protoclassic" and call the time of the Cimi complex
"Terminal Preclassic." "Protoclassic" has been used in such a variety of
ways that almost every recent use results in generating endless verbiage
about the ways in which it has been used previously, usually followed by
a new definition (Brady et al. 1998). The continued use of the term
seems to me to simply compound the confusion.

It is also important to stress that the Cimi complex is clearly
Preclassic, although it includes a low frequency of types and shapes that
mark the Early Classic. Aguila Orange, the characteristic monochrome
type of the Early Classic, appeared in low frequencies well back in Cimi
levels in the North Acropolis sequence and increased gradually over
time. It was accompanied by a few sharp z-angle bowls and annular
bases, shapes that are more characteristic of Manik 1 and 2. In decoration, however, not a single polychrome sherd occurred in the huge
sealed lots of Cimi complex date. Instead, the decorative message was
carried by Usulutan types and a few dichrome decorations with simple
designs. In addition, there was not a single example of either a basal
flange bowl or a scutate lid, shapes that were strongly associated with
polychromes in Manik.

It is no surprise that a transition between complexes might occur
gradually, with different elements appearing at different times. A
ceramic complex is a heuristic device that summarizes the major characteristics of ceramics during a given time interval; it is not a closed box
that replaces the box of a previous complex overnight. Often, however,
our collections are not adequate to demonstrate the details of changes,
as will be apparent when I discuss the transition between the Early and
Late Classic, as reflected in the Pennsylvania data.

The fact that the Cimi complex has been considered to date
between a.d. 150 and 250 (Culbert 1993) does not constitute a problem. When the decision was made (I believe at the ceramic conference
in Guatemala City [Willey et al. 1967]) to change the date for the start
of the Early Classic from A.D. 300 to A.D. 250, there was little reason for
choosing 250 except to allow the recently discovered Stela 29 of Tikal
to fall within the Classic. Laporte (this volume) begins the Early Classic
at 200 A.D. I would have no problem adjusting the Cimi dates to fit his

chronology. Absolute dates were a question that unfortunately was not considered during the Santa Fe seminar.

THE EARLY CLASSIC

The Manik Complex

Although University of Pennsylvania Project collections for the Early Classic Manik complex at Tikal were abundant, they did not give sufficient information for subdividing the complex. A major problem was that the large collections of ceramics from sequent architectural levels that were so critical in defining the Preclassic sequence did not occur in the Classic architectural levels. I was unwilling, based on the hints of temporal differentiation that could not be treated quantitatively, to propose facets for Manik, but Coggins (1975), focusing on decorated vessels, achieved a three-part sequence (Manik 1, 2, and 3) that was successful as a preliminary effort.

The situation has been greatly clarified by the detailed analysis of Manik materials made possible by the excavations of the Proyecto Nacional Tikal, especially in the Mundo Perdido complex (Laporte and Fialko 1987, 1990, 1995). In the Proyecto Nacional material, an excellent sequence of Manik 1, 2, 3a, and 3b has been defined. The combination of that material with the North Acropolis data through the time of Cimi provides us with a superb understanding of the ceramic transition between the Late Preclassic and Early Classic. The changes are profound, representing a replacement of all types and shapes, both utilitarian and decorated. The replacement occurred gradually, however, with the addition of many "Early Classic" characteristics in the Preclassic.

The elaborate burials discovered in the Mundo Perdido Group by the Proyecto Nacional Tikal (Laporte and Fialko 1987) provide a rich picture of Manik 2. In those burials, polychromes were abundant, mostly on sharp z-angle bowls, although a few basal flange bowls occurred. Scutate lids were added to the repertoire, often with elaborate polychrome decoration and modeled handles. None of the Usulutan types occurred. Large mammiform feet, which characterized Cimi, continued to appear in the Manik 1-2 burials.

A sharp transition in serving vessels took place at the beginning of

Manik 3 (Coggins 1975: Krejci and Culbert 1995). Sharp z-angle bowls and scutate lids disappeared, the polychrome tradition continued but became less important in burial offerings, and the cylindrical tripod— often of decorated-incised and gouged-incised types—became a key feature, especially in chamber burials. The influences from Teotihuacan that mark Bus. 10 and 48 typify the transition. Krejci and Culbert (1995) note that in addition to ceramics, other very significant changes occur in burials and caches, which they relate to the dynastic change from Jaguar Paw (Chak Tok Ich'aak I) to Curl Nose (Nuun Yax Ayiin I). In the Tikal sherd collections the cylindrical tripod is not confined to ceremonial-elite contexts at the site center but occurs as a significant component of refuse in small mound groups. The ceramics of Yaxha, which are otherwise very similar to those of Tikal, offer a striking contrast in this regard. In Yaxha, cylindrical tripod vessels are almost totally lacking in the collections (Hermes, pers. comm.), although it must be stressed that no elaborate Early Classic burials have been discovered at the site.

THE INTERMEDIATE AND LATE CLASSIC

The appearance of Late Classic ceramics represents another drastic change in which all types and shapes were replaced, with the single exception of unslipped and striated large-mouth jars. How abrupt was this change? Unlike the Preclassic/Early Classic transition, in which the North Acropolis sequence showed the early introduction of some Early Classic markers, there was no key to the pace of change at this boundary in the Pennsylvania data. In the research of the Proyecto Nacional Tikal and the Proyecto Templo V (Laporte, this volume), however, several special deposits indicate a transitional period between a.d. 550 and 600 in which the majority of the ceramics were still Early Classic but Late Classic types and shapes had begun to appear. It would seem, then, that the Early Classic/Late Classic transition was also a gradual one.

For the Late Classic, the derivation of the ceramic sequence was based primarily on a seriation of lots, most of which came from the abundant collections provided by excavation of Small Structure Groups. Because these collections were poorly preserved, most of the information available concerned vessel shapes. A description of decorated types was possible, however, because of a few large and well-preserved collections from the fills of large structures (such as Str. 5D-33, 1st). Burials, of course, provided critical information on changes in decorated vessels (Coggins 1975).

Within the Late Classic there was great continuity in all categories except serving vessels. Unslipped and monochrome types are undifferentiable between Late Classic complexes. So are basic shapes of jars and large bowls, although quantitative changes in such minor modes as lip shapes provide clues differentiating complexes. But the shapes of serving vessels, which were almost entirely polychrome until the Terminal Classic Eznab complex, changed sharply, serving as an unmistakable key to the separation of the Ik, Imix, and Eznab complexes.

The Ik Complex

The Ik complex marked the appearance of almost all the types and shapes that distinguish the Late Classic from the Early Classic. Unslipped types and the wide-mouth jars produced from them changed very little from the Early Classic, but Tinaja Red became the dominant monochrome type, and the shapes of small-mouth jars and large-capacity bowls were quite different from those of the Early Classic. Decorated material was almost entirely of the Saxche Polychrome Group, with medial-flange or -ridge plates, barrels, and round- and straight-side dishes the most characteristic shapes.

The Imix Complex

Only minor changes in such modes as lip shape and the decoration of large-capacity bowls (for example, incised lines, fingernail punctations) separate Imix-complex utilitarian vessels from those of the Ik complex. The Palmar Polychrome Group replaced the Saxche Group as the primary decorated ceramic. The two groups are easy to distinguish because types of the Palmar Group were produced by starting with an initial coat of white pigment that underlay all further painting. In addition, there are differences between the two groups in shades of color and in pastes. To make the differences between Ik and Imix decorated serving vessels even more distinctive, beveled-lip plates replaced the medial-flange or medial-ridge plates of Ik, and barrels became much less common, while cylinders increased in frequency. The changes in serving-vessel shapes are so striking and the shapes are so common even in small structures that the two complexes can hardly be confused.

THE TERMINAL CLASSIC

The Eznab Complex

The definition of the Eznab complex was made easy by the abundant surface debris found in palace groups, especially in the Central Acropolis. Made in the last phase of occupation, these deposits remained largely undisturbed thereafter. With the beginning of the Terminal Classic Eznab complex, a set of changes even more obvious than those that separated the Ik and Imix complexes took place. An Eznab sample of even modest size can hardly fail to be identified. Typologically, unslipped and monochrome types remained the same as they had been earlier, except that the use of black slip became considerably more common for some types of serving vessels. Polychromes diminished greatly in frequency. Polychromes represented 30–40 percent of vessels in Imix and rarely more than 1–3 percent in Eznab. In addition, many of the polychromes that continued to be produced were off-color and poorly painted in comparison with those of Imix. A few Fine Orange vessels and local imitations of Fine Orange were added to the typological inventory. Among vessel shapes, such characteristic Imix shapes as beveled-lip plates and cylinders continued to be common but were now almost invariably red-slipped, which would never have been the case in Imix times. In addition, a whole series of new serving-vessel shapes were added to the inventory, including insloping-side and composite-silhouette tripod dishes, barrels with a pedestal base, and notched, z-angle tripod plates. It must be stressed, however, that the tradition of ceramic production was continuous from that of earlier complexes. There is absolutely no indication that the Eznab inhabitants of the site were anything other than descendants of earlier Tikaleños.

THE EARLY POSTCLASSIC

The Caban Complex

A final Early Postclassic occupation in a very few locations at Tikal is represented by the Caban complex. Collections are sparse, and the complex cannot be completely described. It seems quite certain, however, that the complex represents reoccupation by a few settlers with totally new ceramics closely related to the Early Postclassic complexes encountered along the lakes of the central zone of the Petén (P. Rice 1979b).

CULTURAL IMPLICATIONS OF TIKAL CERAMICS

I will next examine the information that ceramic analysis provides regarding the cultural system of the ancient Maya. First, I will examine data about the production and distribution systems for ceramics at Tikal. In the next section I will consider differential use of ceramics by various social groups. Finally, I will turn to the patterns of ceramics in caches and burials and consider what those patterns may tell us about social and ritual systems of the ancient Tikaleños.

PRODUCTION AND DISTRIBUTION SYSTEMS

Almost all Mayanists will agree that, at least throughout the Classic, pottery was produced in specialized centers. Because very few actual production centers have been located, this conclusion is based on the degree of standardization of vessels and indications that paste formulae differed slightly from one area to another (Fry 1980, 1981; Culbert and Schwalbe 1987). I believe that pottery production at Tikal was specialized at least from the Late Preclassic through the Terminal Classic. If one accepts that there was specialization in ceramic production, there are important questions to be asked. How many production centers were there? Did each center make all the various classes of pottery, or was there subspecialization? Was distribution of ceramics centralized— perhaps even under state control, was a market system in operation, or were most ceramics distributed locally through neighborhood barter?

Locating pottery-production centers in the Maya Lowlands on the basis of direct archaeological evidence is extremely difficult. The Maya did not use kilns or discard large quantities of sherd wasters. Only a few probable production centers have been identified in Tikal and its peripheries. The most certain is a center discovered by Becker (1973a; 1999) in Group 4H-1. At this location there were large quantities of such rarely used items as wall inserts, figurines and figurine molds, and whistles, as well as large quantities of more common ceramics.

Fry (1981; Fry and Cox 1974) suggests the presence of two possible production centers at and beyond the earthworks north of site center. One consisted of large quantities of a limited number of serving-vessel shapes of the Ik complex in a carbon-rich soil within the ditch of the northern earthworks adjacent to a causeway. As an alternative to the possibility that the remains imply a production center nearby, he also suggests that the deposit might have resulted from the breakage of several loads of ceramics being transported across the earthworks. Fry also suggests a production center using a highly micaceous paste 7 to 9 km. north of site center. In addition to these centers, Culbert and Schwalbe (1987) have identified the existence of a production center for a variant of the Late Classic type Tinaja Red. The location of the center is unknown but was probably outside Tikal.

In the mid-1980s Larry A. Schwalbe of the Los Alamos National Laboratories and I used x-ray fluorescence to analyze a set of elements in a sample of 362 Tikal sherds from the Manik, Ik, Imix, and Eznab complexes (Culbert and Schwalbe 1987). A sample of polychrome sherds was available from all complexes; red/orange and unslipped were available from the Manik, Imix, and Eznab complexes; and black sherds were available only from the Manik complex. The hope was that the analysis might separate groups that would indicate different centers of production. With the exceptions noted below, that hope was disappointed, not an unanticipated result, considering the geological uniformity of the Tikal area.

Based on our analysis, it was immediately obvious that there was a strong difference between sherds that included calcite and those that did not. For all except the Manik complex, this separated unslipped large-mouth jars with heavy calcite tempering from slipped vessels, a distinction that has long been obvious. The fact that large jars are uniformly calcite tempered suggests that the tempering may relate to properties desirable for their use.

Comparison of red/orange, polychrome, and (for Manik) black noncalcite sherds shows that there are far less obvious, but still statistically significant, distinctions between the pastes used with different color classes. That is, "it would appear that paste compositions of the various non-calcite groups of pottery followed slightly different traditions" (Culbert and Schwalbe 1987:642). By themselves, these results tell us nothing about centers of production or means of ceramic distribution. The differences are probably due to intentionally added temper that might be as likely to indicate traditions for different color classes shared by all potters as production of different colors in different workshops.

Inspection of clusters appearing in the plots of canonical variables, however, suggested that the tightness of clusters might provide other useful information. To approach this statistically, Schwalbe (Schwalbe and Culbert 1988) devised a set of statistical measures of degree of variability of different groups of sherds. We tested samples from several different proveniences within Tikal for degree of variability, in hopes that the results might provide a hint of production centers. These hopes were disappointed except in two cases.

One case was the ceramic production center in Group 4H-1 (Becker 1973a, 1999). When a sample of 19 polychrome sherds from this location was compared to a sample of 19 polychromes from a variety of other locations in Tikal, it was concluded that

> The group centroid of the 4H-1 is displaced a slight but significant amount from that of the other set. More importantly, the analysis of intra-group variation for the two samples shows the sherds from Group 4H-1 to be strikingly less variable than the composite sample from other locations. This clearly suggests that the paste formula for pottery from a specific production centre was quite tightly standardized. (Culbert and Schwalbe 1987:648–50)

These results confirm that the potters in Group 4H-1 produced polychrome pottery as well as specialty items. In addition, inspection of the clusters shows that some sherds from other locations fall within the tight 4H-1 cluster and were probably made at the 4H-1 center. That such a wide range of locations turned to Group 4H-1 for pottery implies some broader method of distribution than neighborhood barter. Other sherds are widely scattered in the plots, suggesting that they were produced at more than one other center.

The second case involves a production center whose chemical signature has been identified but whose location remains unknown.

During the Tikal ceramic analysis, a paste variant of the Late Classic monochrome type Tinaja Red had been identified that has a pinkish paste rather than the orange paste that characterizes most examples of the type. This "tinaja pink" variant, which was confined to the Imix complex, was relatively rare but was not localized and occurred throughout Tikal, as well as in Fialko's intersite survey between Yaxha and Nakum. Because of its distinctive appearance and relative scarcity, the conclusion had been reached well before the x-ray fluorescence analysis that "Tinaja pink" represents the production of a single center. When "Tinaja pink" sherds were compared by x-ray fluorescence with other Tinaja Red and polychrome sherds of the Imix complex, the "Tinaja pink" sample proved to have a strikingly different chemical composition. Furthermore, the sample showed the typically low degree of variation that marked the sherds from the 4H-1 production center: "Again, there is a clear demonstration that when the products of a single manufacturing centre can be separated they prove to have a very low degree of variability" (Culbert and Schwalbe 1987:648–50).

There is considerable potential for future studies of Tikal ceramics that might clarify questions of production and distribution. The study of considerably larger samples of sherds by x-ray fluorescence or neutron activation might define additional production centers. The same study would also indicate the distribution of vessels produced by the known center in Group 4H-1 or any other center discovered. A quantitative study of polychrome sherds focusing on such features as the motifs used, the ways in which they are combined, the location of designs in different design fields, and so forth, might well provide information that would make the identification of workshops (or even individual painters) possible. Once the patterns were identified, distributions would provide information on mechanisms of pottery distribution. Masses of data on designs have already been gathered and only await the lengthy analyses that are necessary.

In summary, what can we say about production and distribution of ceramics in the Tikal region during the Classic Period (the only period in which there is sufficient evidence to reach even tentative conclusions)? Both technological and stylistic evidence support the conclusion that ceramic production was, indeed, specialized. Fry's (1980, 1981) analyses suggest that both polychrome and monochrome pottery was produced at the same centers. Unslipped pottery may have been produced at a greater number of centers, some or all of which may have produced no other kind of pottery.

Fry's distributional studies of peripheral Tikal pottery show that frequencies of monochrome and polychrome vessels began to fall off sharply at 8 to 10 km. from a production center. Unslipped pottery, on the other hand, was rarely distributed more than 4–5 km. from its sources. Even within the "core area" of a center, however, significant quantities of vessels (greater than half the serving vessels and 40 percent of slipped jars and basins) were brought in from other centers. The data from the polychrome production in Group 4H-1 in central Tikal suggest a similar pattern. Group 4H-1 was only one of several production centers whose products were intermixed in consumer locations.

These patterns suggest both to Fry and to me that pottery was likely distributed through a system of local markets, although it is possible that the unslipped jars were procured directly from the production centers themselves.

DIFFERENTIAL USE OF CERAMICS

Differential uses of ceramics by various segments of a population can provide information about social organization. Among the Maya of Tikal, such differences tended to be quantitative rather than qualitative. Only a few kinds of ceramics were restricted to particular types of activities or to specific social classes. The most obvious kind of limited-use ceramics are the cache vessels of the Classic period. The cylindrical cache vessels of the Manik complex and flanged cache cylinders and rectangular cache vessels of the Ik and Imix complexes never occurred in general ceramic collections, and only the Manik cache cylinders also occurred in burials. Because all these vessels were poorly shaped and finished, it seems unlikely that they were too expensive for other uses. Perhaps the opposite was true—that they were regarded as cheap disposables for once-only use, simply to provide a container for offerings. The only kind of ceramic that seems to have been restricted to elite use is the type of Imix-complex figural polychromes that show humans or gods. These polychromes almost never occurred in contexts outside the site center and, even there, were mostly confined to burials. Interestingly, occasional figural polychromes occurred in the refuse

Table 2.2

Vessel Category Frequencies in Ops. 20 and 22Q

Op.	% Serving Vessels	% Small-Mouth Jars	% Large Bowls	% Wide-Mouth Jars
20	25–45%	10–25%	15–25%	15–25%
22Q	60–75%	15–20%	5–15%	3–9%

from small sites in the Bajo la Justa where I am currently working (Culbert et al. 1999). We do not have burials from these sites, so we have no information as to whether such polychromes were used in burials there.

Several analyses were done comparing sherd collections from structure groups of varying sizes. There is a quantitative difference between groups of different size in the use of the four major categories of shapes: wide-mouth jars, narrow-mouth jars, large-capacity bowls, and serving vessels. The first three categories were almost surely for domestic use. The serving-vessel category includes a variety of shapes, many of which were probably multifunctional and served both for household uses such as food serving and containers and for ritual purposes. The percentage of serving vessels correlated directly with the size of group: the larger the group, the greater the frequency of serving vessels.

Table 2.2 illustrates the quantitative differences by comparing samples from two locations. Operation 20 was the excavation of small mound groups 4F-1 and 4F-2 (Haviland 1985). Operation 22Q (C. Jones 1996) was from a large refuse deposit just north of the East Plaza, which may have been debris from the nearby market but might equally well have been from anywhere within the site core. Each location provided several quantified lots, so table 2.2 indicates the range of percentages for each location.

Operation 22Q had a far greater number of serving vessels, considerably fewer large bowls and wide-mouth jars, and about the same number of small-mouth jars as the small mound groups excavated in Operation 20. One could think of a variety of explanations for the equivalent percentages of small-mouth jars, but none of them stands out clearly as the best.

Fry's (1969, this volume) comparison of the same vessel categories between mound groups ranked by size in the peripheral area shows very similar results. None of his groups have as high a percentage of serving vessels as Operation 22O, but the large-mound groups in the peripheries rank closest to those figures, while those in Small Structure Groups compare closely to those in Operation 20. The key point in Fry's study is that occupants in the peripheries of Tikal did not differ significantly from occupants of small-mound groups in the site center in their access to the fancier vessels.

In the late 1960s Joseph Lischka and David Adam (Lischka 1968, 1970) conducted a factor analysis of ceramic distributions that was quantitatively more sophisticated (for its time) than the simple comparison of frequencies between Operations 20 and 22O. Their study used a large sample of Ik and Imix locations and included as variables the four major shape categories, as well as a subdivision of the serving vessel category. The results are similar to those from the simple comparison of Operations 20 and 22O described above. The first two factors contrasted serving vessel sets and the various utilitarian categories in different ways, demonstrating a strong association of elite/ceremonial locations with serving vessels and of utilitarian vessels with Small Structure Groups. In addition, the large number of samples from small structures was completely consistent in showing vessel frequencies within the standard range for small-mound groups. A few of the samples from construction fill in large groups, however, showed frequencies typical of those for small groups. These results support the conclusion that fill samples from small groups were obtained locally but that sometimes samples needed in large construction efforts were imported from more distant locations.

The conclusion one reaches from all the analyses of vessel distributions is that elite Maya used more fancy pottery. This is hardly a striking revelation, but it is at least a quantitative demonstration of the expectable.

It should be noted, however, that even the occupants of small-mound groups in Late Classic Tikal and its peripheries had numbers of polychrome vessels that accounted for one-quarter to one-third or more of their total vessel assemblage. It seems clear that—at least in the sense of access to specialist-produced painted pottery—even the lower-class inhabitants of Tikal had a high standard of living.

VESSELS FROM SPECIAL DEPOSITS

It must be noted at the outset that although consideration of ceramics from special deposits supplies important information, considerably more sophisticated results could be derived from a complete study of all the contents of such deposits. This analysis, however, should involve all those who have participated in both excavation and the analysis of different kinds of artifactual material.

CACHES

Preclassic

Few Preclassic caches were located at Tikal, and all were relatively impoverished in terms of ceramics. Large bowls were a favorite among the vessels, and no jars were included. All the vessels that occurred are of types and shapes common in general collections.

Manik

In the Early Classic, caches changed dramatically at a time that Krejci and Culbert (1995) believe corresponded with the change from the rule of Jaguar Paw (Chak Tok Ich'aak I) to that of Curl Nose (Nuun Yax Ayiin I). Vessels became abundant in caches, but the great majority were either cylindrical cache vessels with covers or outflaring-side cache vessels, usually placed in pairs, lip to lip. The cylindrical cache vessels (as distinguished from cylindrical tripods) were largely confined to caches (and some very elite burials) and rarely occurred in other contexts. The outflaring-side vessels occurred more broadly in general collections. A few jars were placed in caches, but there were no examples of such common shapes as basal-flange or sharp z-angle bowls or cylindrical tripods. Aside from the carved cache cylinder in Cache 198 (Jones and Sattherthwaite 1982:126; Culbert 1993:fig.108; Harrison, this volume) that names Jaguar Paw (Chak Tok Ich'aak I), no decorated vessel occurred. The vessel assemblage that was found with Manik caches was very specialized and quite distinct from either burial or general collections of the complex.

Late Classic

The vessels that marked caches of the Manik complex were no

longer used in the Late Classic. The cylindrical cache vessel of Manik was replaced by the flanged cache cylinder of the same general size and proportions. But unlike the Manik cache cylinder, which almost invariably had a cover, only one of the flanged cache cylinders of the Late Classic had a cover, even though the flange distinctly gives the impression of having been designed to support one. The rectangular cache vessel also appeared for the first time in the Late Classic. Both this vessel and the flanged cache cylinder occurred only in caches. The assemblage in caches in the Late Classic was broader than that of the Early Classic, containing some vessels such as cylinders and outcurving-side bowls that were important in general collections. Some of these were polychromes, but none were sufficiently preserved to show designs. On the other hand, jars, large bowls, and tripod plates were completely absent from Late Classic caches.

BURIALS

Preclassic
The three Tzec and Chuen burials contained the standard serving vessels and decorated types typical of their complexes. Chuen Bu. 164 also included two slipped jars.

Of the five Cauac-complex burials, three were the important Bus. 85, 166, and 167 (W. R. Coe 1990) from the North Acropolis, which included fine ceramics. Two shapes, the urn jar and urn bowl, were confined to burial collections. Otherwise, a full range of serving-vessel shapes and slipped jars was included, and even unslipped jars occurred in Bus. 85 and 167. Decoration focused on Usulutan-style types plus black incised vessels that were probably imports from the Guatemalan Highlands.

Manik Complex
A total of 24 Tikal burials contained ceramics of the Manik complex. The extremely complex and elegant ceramics included in Bus. 10, 22, and 48 (W. R. Coe 1990) are the centerpiece of the material, both for variety and the cultural information provided (Coggins 1975; Reents and Culbert n.d.). Bu. 22 is transitional, falling between Manik 2 and 3. It maintained the focus on polychrome decoration to be found

on basal-flange bowls and scutate lids that appeared in the Manik 2 burials in Mundo Perdido but also included a set of cylindrical tripods, one of which was stuccoed and painted with a hieroglyphic inscription. Bu. 10, that of Curl Nose (Nuun Yax Ayiin I), shows the deemphasis on polychromes and the focus on cylindrical tripods that marks Manik 3. It also demonstrates the peak of Teotihuacan influence and other external contact. Some of the round-side bowls with annular base are almost certainly Thin Orange pieces imported from Central Mexico, but all those who have considered the very overt Teotihuacan symbolism with which they were painted are convinced that the stucco and painting were almost surely done after the vessels had reached the Maya area (Coggins 1975; Reents and Culbert n.d.). Stormy Sky's (Siyaj Chan K'awiil II's) Bu. 48 shows less overt Mexican symbolism but also contained several elegant gouged-incised vessels that may have been imported.

In comparison to these impressive burials, the rest of the Manik-complex burials are ceramically disappointing. Bu. 177, from the edge of the Great Plaza in front of the Central Acropolis, had a nicely decorated cylindrical tripod that may have been a trade vessel and two polychrome basal-flange dishes among its five vessels. Bu. 160 from Group 7F-1, which Haviland (1981) suggests is that of a possible deposed ruler, had a collection of ceramics that might best be described as drab, although other contents were rich. The two cylindrical tripods from the burial were undecorated and without covers. In addition, the burial, produced two polychromes and several small monochrome vessels, including two unusual small jars with lids.

There seems to be little pattern in other burials except that unslipped jars and large-capacity bowls were absent. Unusual urns with appliquéd designs occurred in Bu. 162 from Group 7F-1 and Bu. 31 from Group 4F-1. Single cylindrical tripods without covers were found in two Small Structure Groups (Bus. 169 and 197). In other burials, polychrome basal-flange bowls and monochrome jars were common offerings, as were a variety of small bowls and dishes.

Ik Complex

The decorated vessels from Late Classic burials are described in such splendid detail by Coggins (1975) that they need only brief consideration here. Twenty-one Ik-complex burials were discovered at Tikal, although four of these were of less than certain temporal assignment. Ceramics from the most elite Ik-complex burials in the North Acropolis (Bus. 23, 24, and 195), although they contain some exquisite pieces, lack the quantity and variety of ceramics from comparable burials of the Manik and Imix complexes. In other burials, however, decorated ceramics, even from some small structures, were splendid. The range of vessel shapes included was quite narrow. In the entire Ik sample, there is only one jar (Bu. 195) and one large-capacity bowl. The great majority of vessels belong to only four shapes: those of cylinders, barrels, round-side bowls (which overlap with barrels in general shape), and lateral-flange or lateral-ridge tripod plates. These vessels were almost invariably polychrome.

Bu. 23 had the largest number of vessels (12), including nine cylinders, eight of them fluted, and three tripod plates with Ahau glyphs that may well be indicative of influence from Caracol. Bu. 24 had six vessels: two tripod plates, a cylinder, a barrel, and two round-side bowls. Bu. 195, that of the ruler Animal Skull, had only six vessels: two tripod plates, one with an inscription painted on stucco naming Animal Skull, the second also stuccoed and painted with an inscription; two round-side bowls; a cylinder; and the only jar in the Ik burial assemblage. Vessels from two burials in small structures are of unusual merit. Bu. 72 from the small Str. 5G-8 contained a barrel with an inscription that mentions the ruler of Naranjo. Bu. 81 from Str. 4G-9 provided a splendid incised pot showing a scene of herons and a plate with a dancing figure on the interior base.

The frequency of vessels with hieroglyphic inscriptions is worth noting. In the three major chamber burials, only the stuccoed vessels from Bu. 195 had what seem to be meaningful inscriptions. On the other hand, inscriptions occurred in four burials that seem to have been of lesser status. The same pattern of a wide distribution of inscriptions from groups of all sizes was mirrored in the sherd collections.

In sum, the Ik-complex burial vessels suggest a society in which there was a less profound gulf between social classes than in other Classic complexes. The burials from the most honored locations in the North Acropolis, including one that was surely that of a ruler, were ceramically less elaborate than those of the Manik and Imix complexes.

Burials in smaller groups, however, included a larger number of vessels of great artistic merit and frequently included meaningful hieroglyphic inscriptions. This mirrors the suggestion of Moholy-Nagy (this volume) that a similarly decreased social spread characterized artifact assemblages at the time of the Ik complex.

Imix Complex

There were more burials with vessels (71) for the Imix complex than for any other complex in the Tikal sequence. Large burial samples were located in Groups 4F-1 and 4F-2 (Haviland 1985), in Haviland's excavations of small-mound groups without shrines (n.d.a), and in Becker's (1999) investigation of groups with shrines.

The two richest burials (Bus. 116 and 196) contained the huge quantity and variety of ceramics found in the most elite chamber burials of the Manik complex. Other burials showed the same limitation in range of types and shapes that characterized Ik burials. No unslipped jars or large-capacity bowls occurred in the large sample of vessels, and the only slipped jar (represented by just the neck) may have been an accidental inclusion. The overwhelming majority of vessels were cylinders, beveled-lip tripod plates, and slightly outcurving-side bowls and dishes. Although preservation in many burials was too poor to permit determination of type, the examples that are preserved and evidence from sherd collections indicate that all of these vessels belonged to dichrome or polychrome types.

In discussing Imix burials, it is necessary to reemphasize the distinction between figural and "everyday" polychromes. Figural polychromes show human or deity figures usually accompanied by hieroglyphic inscriptions that often refer to historic persons or events. Paintings on figural polychromes were the products of highly trained and specialized artists who sometimes even signed their work. Figural polychromes were almost entirely confined to upper-level elite burials and are rare in sherd collections—even collections that come from the site center. "Everyday" polychromes were widely available and composed 30–40 percent of Imix vessels even in small mound groups. Although glyphic signs were among the repertoire of motifs used in decoration, they never appeared as full inscriptions.

Cylinders predominate in the two major chamber burials of the

Imix complex (Bus. 116 and 196). The ceramic centerpiece in the burial of Ruler A (Jasaw Chan K'awiil) (Bu. 116) is a set of ten painted cylinders that show scenes of individuals seated on thrones. Attendants, usually kneeling before the throne, appear on five of these cylinders; on the remainder, the person on the throne appears alone. The striking thing about these cylinders is the poor quality of much of the work. None of the scenes could be called great masterpieces, and some are amateurish. It seems clear that the painting was not done by highly skilled artisans. Coggins (1975) and I independently came to the conclusion that the vessels may have been painted by other rulers or their emissaries as a special mark of respect for Ruler A (Jasaw Chan K'awiil). Also in Bu. 116 was an additional cylinder on which a throne scene was painted after the vessel had been stuccoed (an exceedingly rare process for Imix). This scene is, indeed, a splendid piece of art. In addition, there was a carved cylinder portraying the head of a long-nosed god—a theme that reappeared in Bu. 196. The rest of the decorated vessels in Bu. 116 are nonfigural: an unusual tripod plate in the shape of a half conch shell, which may have served for holding paints and has a glyph in its central base relating to the act of painting (Simon Martin, pers. comm. 2000); three tripod plates; a straight-side bowl decorated with Muwaan Bird feathers, a symbol of death (Coggins 1975); a slightly outcurving-side bowl decorated with Mexican year signs and Ahau glyphs; and a simple, banded black-on-red cylinder.

Bu. 196 was considerably richer in ceramics, both in quantity and variety, than Bu. 116. Of the 48 vessels in the burial, 25 are cylinders. Three superb painted cylinders show a ruler on a throne accompanied by attendants. One, the "Hummingbird Pot," mentions the name of Ruler B (Yik'in' Chan K'awiil). Thirteen carved cylinders featuring the head of a long-nosed god show the same huge range in execution and talent as the throne scenes in Bu. 116 and can also be posited as the work of nonartists. A set of nine cylinders, seven fluted, completes the list of cylinders. There are ten tripod plates that feature Muwaan Bird feathers as a theme but differ considerably in other details. Ten small bowls and dishes of considerable variety, two unslipped bowls, and an unusual jar complete the inventory. One of the unslipped bowls and the jar are almost surely imports.

The paucity of meaningful inscriptions in Imix burials is striking.

The stuccoed vessel from Bu. 116 has an important, although largely illegible, text. Most of the seeming texts on the throne-scene vessels in the burial, however, are glyphoid rather than meaningful (Simon Martin, pers. comm. 2000). In Bu. 196, the Hummingbird pot has a text, and the throne scene with the dancing figure has captions that probably identify the individuals involved. Otherwise, only two additional burials (Bus. 78 and 190) have texts. It seems quite clear to me that the many looted cylinders with Primary Standard Sequence texts that have appeared in collections in recent years did not come from Tikal.

Eznab Complex

Six Eznab-complex burials were located in Tikal. Four contained only a single vessel; two contained two vessels. Two of the burials with a single vessel contained Zacatel Cream Polychrome tripod plates, both decorated with the Muwaan Bird Feather motif, the dominant motif in Eznab polychromes. Two burials with single vessels included Achote Black tripod bowl/dishes, a characteristic Eznab type and shape. The two burials with two vessels each included one Achote Black tripod vessel. One combined this with a red round-side tripod bowl; the other included a Pabellon Modeled carved barrel. All vessels fit in the serving vessel category and are typical of the complex.

Caban Complex

The single Caban-complex burial contained two tripod plates typical of Early Postclassic ceramics of the Petén Lakes region in shape and type (P. M. Rice 1979b).

SPECIAL BURIAL STUDIES

Several studies of burial ceramics show that considerable information remains to be derived from investigating still unexplored facets of the mortuary patterns of ceramics. It would be even more revealing, of course, to do full burial analyses that include the context of burials and all the material within them.

Vessel Locations in Early Classic Elite Burials

In an important study, Kerry Sagebiel (2000) has analyzed the location of vessels in the major Early Classic elite Bus. 10, 22, and 48

TABLE 2.3

Numbers of Vessels in Ik and Imix Complex Burials at Tikal

Number of Vessels	Ik Number	Ik Percent	Imix Number	Imix Percent
1	3	18%	15	23%
2	3	18%	6	9%
3	1	6%	32	49%
4	7	41%	8	12%
5			1	2%
6	2	12%	2	3%
6+	1	6%	2	3%
Total	17		66	

from Tikal and comparable Early Classic elite Bus. A22, A29, and A31 from Uaxactun. Her results show that vessel location was very strongly patterned. A category of special ritual vessels including cache vessels, *candeleros*, effigies, and *incensarios* occurred between 74 and 82 percent of the time toward the head and left side of the principal body and to the east. Cylindrical tripods showed the same locational preference in frequencies between 74 and 86 percent. Jars (although only eight examples were located in the burials) showed an equally strong tendency in the opposite direction, with 88 percent at the feet, 75 percent to the west, but still 63 percent to the left of the principal body. Serving vessels (plates, small bowls and dishes, but excluding cylindrical tripods) distributed about equally between alternatives. These data, which as far as I know have never been examined before, open endless possibilities for expansion into other materials, times, and sites.

Numbers of Vessels in Late Classic Burials

An analysis of the number of vessels in Late Classic burials at Tikal also demonstrated that mortuary customs were by no means random (see table 2.3).

The data from the Imix complex are the most striking because of the size of the burial sample. Even a brief inspection of the data makes it obvious that choices about the number of vessels to include as burial offerings were strongly patterned in Imix. There was a strong

TABLE 2.4

Number of Vessels in Imix Burials by Tikal Report Number

Number of Vessels	TR 19	TR20	TR21	TR22
1	4	2	8	
2	2	1	2	1
3	6	7	16	1
4		1	6	1
5				1
6			1	
Total	12	11	33	4

preference for three vessels, and there was an obvious avoidance of offering two.

The sample of Imix burials was large enough to compare figures from several excavation sets reported in different Tikal Reports. Tikal Report 19 (Haviland 1985) covers excavations in Small Structure Groups 4F-1 and 4F-2; Tikal Report 20 (Haviland n.d.a.) includes investigations of other Small Structure Groups without shrines; Tikal Report 21 (Becker 1999) is the study of structure groups with shrines on the east; Tikal Report 22 (Haviland n.d.b) consists of research in the medium-size Group 7F-1. Raw numbers of burials from these four sets are included in table 2.4.

The data in table 2.4 show that the general pattern of number of vessels included in Imix burials is sitewide. Only Group 7F-1 proves an exception, but the small number of burials encountered in the group makes it uncertain whether Imix mortuary customs there actually represent an anomaly.

Although the sample of burials from the Ik complex (table 2.3 above) is considerably smaller than that for Imix, it is clear that the patterns were quite different. In Ik, four vessels were preferred and three vessels strongly avoided. What occasioned these differences in mortuary choices is unknown, as is the question of whether they were accompanied by differences in other parts of the mortuary ritual.

At Uaxactun (R. E. Smith 1955), the number of vessels in burials in Tepeu 1 and Tepeu 2 does not fit the Tikal pattern. In Tepeu 1, the number of vessels in the nine burials was about equally divided between one, two, three, and four (three burials had three vessels, while one, two, and four vessels were present in two burials each). In Tepeu 2, five of the nine burials had two vessels, the number avoided in Imix at Tikal. Although the sample size is small at Uaxactun, there is a strong suggestion that the Tikal patterns were not shared with its neighbor site.

CONCLUSION

The ceramic collections from Tikal are superb. Given the significance of the site, the length of time during which the University of Pennsylvania and the various projects of the Instituto de Antropología e Historia de Guatemala have worked at the site, the scale of research, and the care exercised in archaeological recording and analysis, it is hardly surprising that the collections have few counterparts in Maya archaeology. The analyses that have been done with Tikal ceramics have produced a ceramic sequence that has already replaced the Uaxactun sequence as the standard point of comparison for the central Petén. It is already obvious that the combination of ceramic data from the University of Pennsylvania project and that of the Proyecto Nacional Tikal provide a sequence of exquisite sensitivity and detail. When the final effort necessary to integrate the work of the various analysts has been done and published, the results will be a landmark and the standard reference for generations to come.

What do ceramics tell us about the economic, social, and ritual structure of the ancient Maya? It is clear that ceramics bear most directly upon the economic system. Yet it is obvious that understanding the production and distribution systems of ceramics at Tikal and other Maya sites has been a particularly intractable problem. Although Fry and I are agreed that ceramics were produced by specialists, we have located only one specific center of production and have identified the products of a few other centers that remain unlocated. In addition, although we agree that ceramics were mostly distributed through a market system, we have no real information about the operation of this system. There is a potential for more information to be gained by both technical and stylistic analysis, but the task would be very large and would lack a guarantee that the results would be successful.

Analyses indicate that the separation between social classes in the use of ceramics was quantitative: essentially, architectural groups whose size indicates higher status used more of the decorated serving vessels. Refuse-disposal patterns and the constant movement of materials in the process of construction make the assignment of collections to specific structures impossible. For small groups or clusters of groups that are isolated from others, one can presume with some security that material found within the group represents activities that took place locally. For material associated with large groups, the situation is even is more difficult. Refuse found near the central groups of major structures at Tikal could have originated anywhere within an area of many hectares that included structures of many kinds and a variety of activities.

There are two points in the Tikal sequence at which the ceramic assemblage of Tikal changed profoundly: the boundary between Preclassic and Early Classic and that between Early and Late Classic. At these points the change involved the domestic monochrome types and shapes, as well as decorated serving vessels. The evidence indicates that the changes were gradual, with the introduction of some new types and shapes, at times, well before the transitions were complete. These changes, of course, occurred not only at Tikal but also throughout the southern Maya Lowlands. The first period correlated to some degree with the still little-understood changes at the end of the Late Preclassic, marked by the fall of El Mirador and transformations at other sites, while the second correlated roughly with the political events associated with the start of the monument hiatus at Tikal and some other sites. I would be very loath, however, to associate the ceramic change with these political events because I doubt that such events would have had impact on domestic ceramics.

Changes in decorated ceramics, especially those associated with the upper-level elite, may be more susceptible to interpretation as political indicators. The first instance of such changes is the ceramic transformation between Manik 2 and 3. At this point domestic ceramics remained unaffected, but elite burials, especially those of the North Acropolis, show the deemphasis of polychromes and the rise of black and gouged-incised elite decorated ceramics and cylindrical tripods. As has been suggested (Coggins 1975; Krejci and Culbert 1995), these changes were closely tied to the complex and fascinating dynastic affairs that in some way involved Teotihuacan (Laporte and Fialko 1990; Culbert 1994).

The beginning of the Ik complex correlates with the defeat of Tikal by Caracol and the beginning of the long monument hiatus. As Coggins (1975) has pointed out, some influences from the general direction of Caracol, such as the Ahau plates in Bu. 23 and the melon-style vessels and monkey depictions in PD 34 (looted Bu. 200), occur in elite Ik ceramics. In addition, the lesser quality of ceramics in Ik chamber burials and the wider spread of inscriptions and elegant vessels in other burials probably do suggest something about a changed social-class structure, as Moholy-Nagy (this volume) suggests on other grounds.

The beginning of the Imix complex correlates with the inauguration of Ruler A (Jasaw Chan K'awiil), the end of the monument hiatus, and the resurgence of Tikal's political power. Again, there was a striking change in decorated ceramics, with the increase in figural polychromes in the most elite burials and changes in polychrome types and vessel shapes that affected all social classes.

Finally, the appearance of the Terminal Classic Eznab complex occurs after the cessation of major aspects of elite leadership. By that time the major decline in population had already occurred, and range structures were occupied by the nonelite. The ceramics of Eznab were still well made—almost surely produced by specialists—and most types and shapes continued with little change. The near disappearance of polychromes, however, was a major change in tradition. It seems likely that the extra cost involved in polychrome decoration was simply beyond the budgets of Terminal Classic inhabitants of the site.

Those of us who have worked with Tikal ceramics have come a long way since the Pennsylvania project opened in 1956. But recent research on special patterns in Classic burials such as the nonrandom location of vessels in elite Early Classic burials and nonrandom choices in the number of vessels placed in Late Classic burials offers hints of many more possibilities for studies that have not yet been done.

3

Beyond the Catalog

The Chronology and Contexts of Tikal Artifacts

Hattula Moholy-Nagy

A large sample of artifacts was collected by the Tikal Project of the University of Pennsylvania Museum during its fourteen years of survey and excavation of the site. Even though it was acquired before the salutary influence of the New Archaeology, the collection is outstanding in its size, variety, and excellent documentation. What we have are the durable remnants of an assemblage of portable material culture that figured into virtually all the activities of those who once lived at Tikal. When these remnants and their recovery contexts are arranged chronologically, they contribute to our present understanding of Tikal culture history, supporting or contradicting hypotheses derived from other archaeological or epigraphic data.

The emphasis in this chapter will be on those durable materials conventionally defined as "artifacts," which became my field of research. Detailed and fully illustrated descriptions of the body of material reviewed here will be published as Tikal Report 27, Part A (in preparation) and Part B (in press). The publication of this volume, intended as an interim reference work to Tikal, also presents an opportunity to mention figurines and censers of pottery, two classes of portable material culture about which little has been published to date. The information on pottery figurines was contributed by Virginia Greene (pers. comm. March 2000). The information on censers comes from Lisa Ferree's doctoral dissertation (Ferree 1972).

Throughout this chapter I have made extensive use of the Tikal Reports series, especially T. Patrick Culbert on ceramics from special deposits (Culbert 1993), William R. Coe on Gp. 5D-2 (W. R. Coe 1990), Christopher Jones and Linton Satterthwaite on carved monuments (C. Jones and Satterthwaite 1982), and Dennis Puleston and William A. Haviland on the Tikal Sustaining Area (D. E. Puleston 1983). I can only touch upon the important body of data from the excavations of the Proyecto Nacional de Tikal of Guatemala (Laporte 1989; Laporte, this volume).

The dates of materials from burials, problematical deposits, and general excavations (secondary contexts) are almost entirely derived from the associated ceramics. With one exception, the end of the Late Late Classic period Imix ceramic complex, they follow the dates published by Culbert (1993:table 1). Artifacts from the construction fill of monumental architecture and many Classic period caches could be dated by Maya inscriptions on associated stone monuments and wooden lintels. In some structure groups, notably Gp. 5D-2, which was the civic-ceremonial heart of the city during much of its existence, such dates could often be spatially extended by architectural stratigraphy.

Artifacts are grouped by assumed function, as derived from typology, recovery context, and ethnographic analogy, and are presented by chronological period. A summary follows of the contributions their study makes toward a fuller comprehension of specific aspects of Tikal's past.

EARLY MIDDLE PRECLASSIC PERIOD, C. 800–600 B.C., THE EB CERAMIC COMPLEX

This was the period of initial, permanent settlement. The associated pottery is characterized by vessels of simple form and high technical competence.

Recovery contexts: The two largest samples of materials come from redeposited lots. One of these is from general excavations just above bedrock under the North Acropolis in Gp. 5D-2. The other had been deposited into a chultun 2 km. to the northeast during Early Classic times. This latter group of materials is the earliest example of what I have elsewhere referred to as *burial-like problematical deposits* (BPDs) (Moholy-Nagy 1999). BPDs are characterized by secondarily interred human remains, materials that are not found in traditional burials, such as household trash, and artifacts of social and ceremonial function that ordinarily do not occur in middens.

Utilitarian: Utilitarian artifacts of materials obtained through long-distance exchange are already present in the form of a few prismatic blades of obsidian, probably from the Highlands of Guatemala. Another imported substance is a light-colored quartzite, probably from Belize, which predominated among Tikal manos and metates throughout its entire occupation.

Hammerstones, waste flakes, and cores indicate knapping of local chert, at least on an expedient level. The chert sample also includes used flakes, prismatic blades, and scrapers. Small, nicely shaped limestone hemispheres with a central depression in the flat face may have also had a utilitarian function.

There was a heavy reliance on locally available freshwater snails *(Pomacea flagellata)* for food. These large snails are common in Preclassic and Terminal Classic general excavations but are rare during the Classic period, suggesting that their availability was strongly affected by the size of the human population.

Social: Occurring now and continuing throughout Tikal's permanent occupation are pottery artifacts that probably had nonutilitarian functions. The collection includes flat and cylindrical stamps of modeled pottery and potsherds with shaped edges in the form of ovals, oblongs, disks with and without a central perforation, and eccentrically perforated worked sherds that may have been worn as pendants.

Ritual/Unidentified: Modeled pottery figurines are present throughout the Middle and Early Late Preclassic periods. Solid human figurines predominate during the Preclassic, although the sample does include a few zoomorphic whistles.

The function and use of pottery figurines is uncertain. It can be noted, however, that at all times they are closely associated with residential structures and they were never placed in traditional caches or burials.

LATE MIDDLE PRECLASSIC PERIOD, C. 600–350 B.C., THE TZEC CERAMIC COMPLEX

The somewhat more plentiful and varied remains of this period are attributed to an increase in population and more diversified activities.

Recovery contexts: Most of the sample recovered from general excavations came from construction fill or was otherwise redeposited. There were, however, several special deposits, including burials and problematical deposits resembling burials and caches, some of which are probably related to ritual activities. The North Acropolis of Gp. 5D-2 had become a locus of ritual significance by this time.

Utilitarian: William Haviland (1981:103) defined a basic assemblage of artifact types found in all Classic period households. This assemblage includes pottery figurines, chert flake cores, used flakes, unmodified flakes, scrapers, ovate bifaces and elongate bifaces, prismatic blades of chert and obsidian, and manos and metates of pecked and ground stone. We now know that all of these artifact types were in use by the Late Middle Preclassic period, and all but the chert bifaces have been attested for the time of initial settlement.

Haviland also identified another six artifact types that were common at Tikal: pottery censers, centrally perforated worked sherds, chert drills, chert and obsidian thin bifaces (projectile points and knives), hammerstones, and rubbing stones. Stemmed chert projectile points appear during the Early Late Preclassic period, but only become common during Classic times. An important aspect of Tikal's basic and common utilitarian assemblages, from at least the Late Middle Preclassic to the end of permanent occupation, is the prominence of imported stone and specialist-produced artifacts.

Definitely present by the Late Middle Preclassic are the first bifaces (ovate, elongate, and large stemmed types), prismatic blades, and polyhedral blade cores of local chert. The chert blade cores and bifaces suggest the inception of specialized lithic production at Tikal itself. There is an increase in obsidian prismatic blades. A single obsidian prismatic blade core, but no other obsidian debitage, was recovered, so it is not certain that blades were locally produced at this time. Concentrations of used chert flakes indicate the processing of softer materials, such as shell, bone, wood, and fiber. There are also scrapers and perforators retouched from chert flakes. Rubbing stones made of fist-size limestone pebbles are thought to have been used to finish plaster walls and floors. They are characterized by one or more facets that are flat along both axes. Narrow spatulate artifacts of uncertain use were made from mammal long bones.

Social: Ranked social organization may have been present by this time, suggested by the appearance in two special deposits of artifacts that were associated with the elite in later times. In this chapter, *elite* loosely refers to the social group that possessed a complex of archaeologically visible and socially restricted artifacts and features considered to be markers of elevated rank. Jade, *Spondylus* shell, pearls, cinnabar pigment, stingray spines, stone monuments, buildings with corbeled vaults, cached offerings, and chamber burials are some examples of elite markers at Tikal. *Nonelite* refers to the rest of Tikal society, which did not possess the material complex identified as elite.

A necklace composed of three jade beads and three *Spondylus*-shell beads was buried with an adolescent, and a stingray spine occurred in a problematical deposit that included an adult male. Both deposits were found in the North Acropolis of Gp. 5D-2.

Cut and polished beads and tubes of long bone appear in general excavations at this time. These types are associated with nonelite in later times.

THE EARLY LATE PRECLASSIC PERIOD, C. 350–1 B.C., THE CHUEN CERAMIC COMPLEX

Elite display pottery vessels are brightly decorated in black on red in resist technique.

Recovery contexts: The earliest public and domestic structures found by the Tikal Project date to this time. The construction fill of the North Acropolis was very rich in broken and worn-out, but otherwise well-preserved, potsherds (Culbert, this volume) and artifacts, so the available sample of domestic goods is much larger than that for the Middle Preclassic period. Several special deposits are known from the North Acropolis and from the outlying Minor Center of Uolantun.

Utilitarian: Several new types of specialist-produced domestic artifacts appear during the course of the Early Late Preclassic period. These types include chert chopping tools; tanged chert macroblades very likely brought from Belize as finished artifacts; rare thin bifaces (stemmed projectile points) of local and imported chert; jadeite celts; bone perforators, including awls, pins, and needles; centrally perforated bone disks; and sherds with edges reworked into scrapers. The proportion of imported to local materials increases. Impressions of plain weave cloth were found on plaster adhering to the base of a pottery vessel from a North Acropolis burial, although no formed spindle whorls of pottery and stone are reported until the Classic period. This early occurrence of woven cloth suggests that spindle whorls were ordinarily of perishable material, such as wood (for example, Coggins 1992:figs.8.100, 8.101; Taschek 1994:fig.44b).

A few fragmentary prismatic blades of green obsidian date to this period or to the previous one, evidence that goods from as far away as the Central Mexican Highlands somehow reached Tikal.

There is a strong emphasis on *Pomacea* snails, turtles, and dogs as protein sources in the Late Preclassic. All of these are locally available and easily obtained.

Social: The offerings in one of the four burials of this time from Gp. 5D-2 included elite status markers: three jade beads, 27 uncut *Oliva* shell tinklers, and a stingray spine coated with cinnabar pigment.

Nonelite ornaments of bone and modeled pottery, including beads, pendants, and earspools, date to this period or to the end of the previous one.

Ritual/Unidentified: Two modest North Acropolis structure caches are the earliest known examples of a long-lived elite tradition that attained great importance during the Classic. Each offering consisted of an obsidian blade fragment placed in a pottery vessel. An additional six caches had been placed into the construction fill of Str. SE-486, the main building at Uolantun. They contained smoothed lumps and fragments of jade that look very much like materials a jeweler could rework into smaller ornaments. These may indicate that production of jade ornaments was being carried out in the area during the Preclassic.

The first censers appear. The material, belonging to the Zinic complex (Ferree 1972), is sparse and fragmentary and comes from general excavations. Basic forms consist of dishes, plates, and covers and are similar to domestic pottery vessels. Different types are embellished with exterior spikes, interior prongs, and pedestal supports.

LATE LATE PRECLASSIC PERIOD,
C. A.D. 1–150, THE CAUAC CERAMIC COMPLEX

Elite display pottery is an exuberant adaptation of the Usulutan pottery style originating beyond the Maya Lowlands. Pottery vessel shapes become more complex and include animal effigies.

Recovery contexts: The construction fill of the North Acropolis continues to provide the best preserved and largest collections of material, but there are also some large midden and debitage deposits in small structures and chultuns in outlying areas.

Some specialist lithic production took place in the peripheries, indicated by hundreds of pounds of chert debitage recovered from a chultun (Fry 1969:144). This chultun was first used as a dump for ordinary household trash. The subsequent inclusion of quantities of chert debitage in the upper part of the deposit suggests, among other things, that by Late Late Preclassic times there was not enough free space available to create large surface dumps (Shafer and Hester 1983; Black and Suhler 1986). From this time onwards, quantities of chert and obsidian production debris too large to be accommodated by the household midden went underground.

The inclusion of both household and production refuse in the same dump may indicate that specialist knappers worked in or near their residences. This mode of production of craft specialists working at home becomes the principal one for Tikal during the remainder of its permanent occupation.

Thirteen special deposits are assigned to this period. Eight are from Gp. 5D-2, testifying to its ongoing ceremonial function.

Utilitarian: All of the important utilitarian artifact types present during the Early Late Preclassic carry over to the latter part.

Two fragmentary ground stone bark mallets and fragments of material that appear to be bark cloth date to this time. Bark cloth is well attested by impressions on plaster from several North Acropolis structure caches of the Late Classic period, and its production and use probably continued into Terminal Classic times. The Late Late Preclassic bark mallets may, of course, also attest to the local production of paper.

The earliest identifiable maize *(Zea mays)* in the form of charred cob fragments comes from North Acropolis construction fill. Maize kernels, cob fragments, and husk impressions continue to occur sporadically in general excavations, chamber burials, BPDs, and structure caches into the Terminal Classic period.

Social: By this time Tikal was a socially stratified society with a ruler, or king (Martin, this volume). Three North Acropolis chamber burials are the earliest examples of a mortuary program accorded rulers throughout the Classic period. One of them may include a sacrificed retainer.

Jade, *Spondylus* shell, and red pigment sprinkled over the corpses and offerings occur in all of these burials. Other types of artifacts appearing for the first time are a mask of green serpentine with inlaid eyes and teeth of *Spondylus* shell, a small anthropomorphic greenstone sculpture, a pearl pendant, bracelets composed of several strings of hundreds of small *Spondylus* shell beads attached to spacer beads of polished bone, a scraped and perforated valve of the large and distinctive Pacific coast species, *Spondylus calcifer,* dishes and bowls of wood and gourd coated with gesso painted red and green, and modeled cylinders tentatively identified as copal that were furnished with twig wicks.

Ritual/Unidentified: A fibrous material that we nicknamed "seaweed" was included among the offerings in one of the chamber burials. This is the earliest known occurrence of a material that continued to be offered in caches, and occasionally in burials, until the end of the Classic period. Our samples of seaweed went astray in the Smithsonian Institution before they could be identified, but it is likely that this material is lime-producing marine algae.

Pottery figurines decline dramatically and may have gone entirely out of use.

Censers of this period compose the Holom complex (Ferree 1972). The sample is larger than that known for the Zinic complex, and the shapes are more diverse. Effigy masks appear at this time. Censers were found in a burned deposit on the steps of Str. 5D-sub.1-1st on the North Acropolis, the earliest example of an association of censers with temples that lasted throughout the permanent occupation of Tikal. Although censers were used in several kinds of ceremonies throughout the subsequent Classic period, their most explicit association is with termination rituals that marked the end of the use life of sanctified structures, monuments, and portable artifacts (Walker 1995:73–77). Censers are rare in structure caches and have not, to date, appeared as offerings in Tikal burials or monument caches.

TERMINAL PRECLASSIC PERIOD,
C. A.D. 150–250, THE CIMI CERAMIC COMPLEX

The last century or so of the Preclassic era, formerly referred to as the Protoclassic period, is characterized by changes in pottery style, but in other respects it is poorly demarcated in the inventory of material culture.

Relatively unmixed Terminal Preclassic deposits occurred in the central part of Tikal and at Uolantun. The North Acropolis remains an important ceremonial locus. The earliest-known chamber burial with an exterior deposit of chert and obsidian debitage is attributed to this period. Other special deposits include a chamber burial in Uolantun and two deposits of obsidian blade production waste dumped into a chultun in the peripheries (D. E. Puleston 1983:fig. 21 shows the epi-central, central, and peripheral areas of Tikal).

This may have been the last period in which chultuns were used as lithic dumps. Throughout the subsequent Classic period, small concentrations of chert and obsidian debitage of less than 1,000 pieces continue to appear in construction fill and in some kinds of structure and monument caches. But by far the largest deposits are found exterior to the chamber burials of rulers and the most powerful elite. In all such deposits, the chert component consists overwhelmingly of biface thinning flakes and production failures. It is usually accompanied by a lesser amount of obsidian prismatic blade production debris, mostly small pressure blades, core fragments, exhausted cores, error-correction and core rejuvenation flakes, and occasional macroblade fragments.

The deposition of lithic production debris exterior to chamber burials and in structure and monument caches may indicate episodes of patronized production of craft specialists who usually worked independently. Besides increased inputs of labor, construction of the chamber burials and associated temples would have required increased numbers of tools of all kinds. Although this hypothesis was not tested by refitting, the debitage in caches may pertain to the flaked chert and obsidian eccentrics included in the same offerings.

EARLY CLASSIC PERIOD,
C. A.D. 250–550, THE MANIK CERAMIC COMPLEX

Hieroglyphic texts mark the beginning of this period, which ends in apparent political disorder marked by a hiatus in the sequence of known inscribed monuments and a pause in construction, offertory, and mortuary activities in Gp. 5D-2. During the Early Classic, Tikal grew rapidly into the most populous settlement of the core area, becoming its economic, administrative, and ceremonial capital. As at other Classic Maya sites, the variability of structure groups, features, and artifacts indicates a socioeconomically heterogeneous society.

The new style of display pottery is characterized by polychrome decoration and other kinds of labor-intensive surface finishes, as well as elaborate forms made possible by the use of volcanic ash temper. From the time of the Manik 3A complex (c. A.D. 378–476) to the end of the Classic period, some of the motifs and inscriptions on the display pottery are identical to motifs and inscriptions on monuments (C. Jones and Satterthwaite 1982; Culbert 1993; Iglesias and Sanz 1999).

During the time of the Manik 3A ceramic complex, the Teotihuacan horizon style (Willey 1991) was adopted for elite-associated monuments, architecture, and some types of portable objects, including pottery vessels, censers, pottery figurines, and milling stones that were also used by the nonelite (Iglesias 1987; Moholy-Nagy 1999).

Recovery contexts: Most materials from general excavations still come from construction fill. There is a great emphasis on cached offerings in the elite tradition. The placing of caches with temples continues from Preclassic times, and they are now occasionally associated with elite range structures and burials. Caches also accompany stone monuments, invariably placed with stelae. No difference has yet been noticed between the offerings placed with plain and carved stelae. Four chamber burials and many problematical deposits also date to this period.

Utilitarian: There is a sudden, large increase in thin bifaces made of fine, dark, nonlocal chert and in metates of siliceous and igneous stone. This was the time of maximum importation and use of Mexican obsidian, preponderantly as prismatic blades and stemmed thin bifaces.

A number of important changes can be seen in the basic domestic assemblage used by all social groups.

Polyhedral blade cores of chert disappear and are replaced by large, thick flake cores from which small chert bladelets could be removed (Arnold 1985). Large, carefully shaped scrapers made on macroflakes of local chert up to 15 cm long are probably specialized masons' tools. Limestone bark beaters mounted in wooden handles replace the monolithic bark mallets of the Late Late Preclassic. The troughed boulder metates of the Preclassic period are gradually replaced by troughed turtleback metates with rounded undersurfaces shaped by pecking. Granite, thought to be from Belize, appears in the form of turtleback metates and accompanying manos and becomes increasingly common during the course of the Classic period. Flat slab and large tripod metates and manos appear now but are always relatively rare. The earliest tripod examples are of vesicular basalt, possibly from Highland Guatemala.

Pottery cord holders fitted with tie rods of wood or human long bone are sometimes set into the interior walls on either side of the doorways of masonry structures. They are specially formed or reworked from jar necks. Limestone hemispheres with central depressions and large stemmed chert bifaces are no longer made.

Some pottery artifacts and ornaments are now made wholly or partly in molds, which may represent a technology borrowed from Central Mexico. Molds in this period were used to form the handles on the lids of cylindrical tripod vessels and the decorations applied to their bases, the *adornos* added to censers of Teotihuacan style, some types of figurines and whistles, and formed pottery spindle whorls. The spatial and temporal distributions of objects made in the same mold have great potential in determining patterns of distribution and consumption.

Edible fauna, consumed by everyone, was imported to Tikal. Exotic animals include iguanas from the savanna and blanca turtles (*Dermatemys mawei*) and large Pomacea snails and freshwater mussels from permanent rivers and lakes. Rare plant remains other than maize come mainly from protected contexts such as structure caches, chamber burials, and BPDs and include beans (*Phaseolus spp.*) and three species of cucurbits (*Cucurbita moschata, C.pepo,* and the wild squash, *C. lundelliana*).

Social: Elite chamber and crypt burials are richly furnished with jade and *Spondylus* ornaments, although *Spondylus* declines in favor of jade during the course of the Classic. There are many new types of labor-intensive sumptuary goods, such as elaborately carved jade beads and pendants, finger rings, large earflares, life-size mosaic masks of greeenstone and shell, slate-backed pyrite mosaic mirrors, carved alabaster bowls, large marine bivalves such as *Spondylus* and scallops that were modified for use as ornaments, and small anthropomorphic sculptures of bone. Some of these artifacts incorporate elements of the Teotihuacan horizon style. Most no longer occur after the Early Classic period, and the chamber burials of Late Classic rulers are lavishly furnished with other kinds of valuables. Among unworked materials, red mineral pigment and stingray spines are frequent offerings. The use of mollusks from the Pacific Ocean peaks at this time, although—like artifacts of Central Mexican obsidian—they also occur in earlier and later times.

Earspools of polished black pottery, usually decorated with gouged-incised geometric designs, are associated with nonelite.

Ritual/Unidentified: Cached offerings receive great emphasis during the Early Classic period, and new kinds of pottery vessels, artifacts, and raw materials are now especially created or assembled for them. Chert and obsidian eccentrics, statuettes of deities of gessoed wood embellished with stone and shell mosaic work, and imitation stingray spines of terrestrial bone make their first appearance. Small anthropomorphic cutout figurines ("Charlie Chaplins") are concentrated in this period. They are predominantly of *Spondylus* shell, but rare examples are also made of nacreous and white marine shell, jade, and bone. Debitage of jade, specular hematite, *Spondylus,* and nacreous shell is offered in this period and the next.

Much value is placed on materials of marine origin. There are quantities of unworked shells, unworked and elaborated stingray spines, and nonmolluscan invertebrates, including various kinds of corals, bryozoans, lime-producing algae, sea whips, sea urchins, sponges, and worm shell colonies. Even waterworn pebbles with holes made by boring shells were offered.

Other unworked fauna in caches and burials, deposited more or less whole, include snakes, turtles, crocodiles, large *Pomacea* snails from Lake Petén Itzá, and several species of birds. White-tailed deer are represented by phalanges.

Early Classic cached offerings are an interesting mix of parsimony and lavishness. Parsimony is suggested by offering goods that could not be used for other purposes. The obsidian eccentrics are made on exhausted blade cores, and the chert eccentrics are often of poor-quality local chert not ordinarily used for artifacts. The small elements of jade, *Spondylus,* and other marine shell encrusting the deity statuettes appear to be bits of production waste and reworked broken ornaments. Most of the marine shells are small, thin walled, or of odd shapes not suitable for ornaments. The occasional inclusion of complete ornaments of socially valued jade and *Spondylus* shell appears extravagant by contrast.

There is a reintroduction of pottery figurines on an almost imperceptible scale. They occur almost exclusively in BPDs but are so fragmented that we overlooked them for years. Some show affinities with figurines types from Teotihuacan (for example, Iglesias 1987:fig.110a, c). Some appear to be partially mold-made.

Censers belong to the Kataan complex (Ferree 1972), whose Early facet is coeval with the Manik 1 and 2 ceramic complexes and whose Late facet is contemporary with Manik 3A. Some Holom complex forms carry over into the Early facet. Overall, the Kataan complex is characterized by specialized forms used only for censers, paralleling the increasing specialization seen in other kinds of ritual artifacts. An important technological innovation is the gradual substitution late in the period of volcanic ash temper for carbonate temper, permitting thinner walls and more elaborate forms. The elaborations apparent among Late Kataan censers form the basis for the complex forms of the Late Classic period.

The Teotihuacan horizon style is seen in such censer shapes as the Early and Late Kataan bowl form with three loop handles used as either a container or a cover and in the Late Kataan hourglass form used with a composite or conical cover. Besides these types, which do not last beyond this period, small one- and two-chambered *candeleros* appearing at this time continue into the Terminal Classic period.

Other forms are pronged dishes on pedestal supports, ladle censers, and flanged cylinders, a uniquely Lowland Maya form. Often, censers are embellished with modeled or mold-made masks and other *adornos.*

Censers continue to be most frequently recovered from contexts that can be interpreted as termination rituals carried out in the decommissioning of temples and monuments. But they are also included in

Early Classic period BPDs and occasionally in general excavations in residential groups. Although not mentioned by Ferree, I think it possible that some fragments classified as censers on the basis of paste and surface finish might be from utilitarian braziers.

EARLY LATE CLASSIC PERIOD, C. A.D. 550–700, THE IK CERAMIC COMPLEX

The Early part of the Late Classic period is equivalent to the Intermediate Classic period of the Gp. 5D-2 construction and offertory sequences (W. R. Coe 1990). The gap in inscriptions appearing towards the end of the Early Classic extends through this period. Around A.D. 600, however, there is a resumption of elite activity in Gp. 5D-2 and the beginning of a century-long period of widespread material prosperity.

Among the most intriguing of the elite construction projects are the two or three Twin Pyramid Groups built to commemorate K'atun endings in the Maya calendar (C. Jones 1969). These groups include stone monuments accompanied by caches in the elite tradition, but all of the known monuments are plain.

The Early Late Classic period, like the Early Classic, marks a break in the stylistic sequences of several classes of material culture, followed by innovations in architecture; stone monuments; display pottery; elite offertory assemblages; artifacts of utilitarian, social, and ritual function; pottery figurines; and censers.

Ik complex display ceramics have simple shapes decorated with elegant, masterfully executed designs in polychrome slip, carving, incising, and painted stucco (gesso). Hieroglyphic inscriptions are greatly emphasized, a development that appears especially significant in the absence of inscribed monuments.

Recovery contexts: A larger proportion of material is now derived from domestic middens. The many special deposits of this period produced an abundant sample of artifacts.

Utilitarian: The domestic inventories from nonelite residential groups indicate a broader access to specialist-produced commodities and imported materials than at any other time. Two new artifact forms are small tripod metates of sandstone and both carved and plain spindle whorls of limestone and marble.

Social: New types of goods come from the chamber burials of this era. Composite ear ornaments consisting of a small jade flare mounted upon a pipe-shaped backing of white marine shell replace the large greenstone earflares worn during the Early Classic. Persons of high rank, including rulers, sometimes inlaid their front teeth with disks of jade and pyrite. Bright green jade begins to replace the grayish green stone favored during the Early Classic. Minor stone sculptures of animals now occur. The serendipitous preservation and meticulous excavation of the contents of a chamber burial on the North Acropolis produced evidence of several kinds of wooden artifacts covered with a coat of painted gesso, such as a set of four sculptures of the rain deity, Chac; a throne; and floorboards decorated with inscriptions. There were traces of a feather headdress and the cast of a small wickerwork basket that had held beans. By this time sacrificed retainers were no longer included in burials.

Nonelite persons wore plain and carved beads, pendants, and ear ornaments of white marine shell, freshwater mussel shell, bone, and pottery.

Ritual/Unidentified: Large and diverse structure caches are characteristic of this time. Developments in the production of ceremonial lithic artifacts contrast with earlier practices of reserving some kinds of nonlocal materials for utilitarian use. Some eccentrics are now made of the fine dark, imported chert usually used for thin bifaces. A new innovation is the incised obsidian. Incised obsidians are macroflakes, macroblades, and core tablets struck directly from the large polyhedral cores brought to Tikal for local prismatic blade production. They are engraved on the ventral surface with deities and symbols (W. R. Coe 1967:103). The eccentric obsidians of this time are also occasionally made on macroblades and macroflakes from large polyhedral cores and are the largest and finest known. The use of fine chert and obsidian for ceremonial lithics demonstrates a ready access to trade goods during this hiatus period.

Marine shells continue to be frequent inclusions in structure caches, as they were in the previous period. Additionally, there is an increased emphasis upon nonmolluscan marine invertebrates, such as corals, gorgonians, and sponges, and on prickly fishes, such as stingrays and porcupine fish *(Diodon spp.)*.

Small heads of deities modeled of unfired clay appear in some

Early Late Classic structure caches, apparently replacing the small-element mosaic statuettes of the preceding period. Jade and *Spondylus* ornaments are no longer offered.

At the beginning of this period pottery figurines are only somewhat more plentiful than during the Early Classic, but there is a definite surge in number and diversity by its end. Most are now partially made in molds, although it is possible that the more compact mold-made figurines have preserved better than modeled ones. Flutes and panpipes appear. In contrast to Preclassic figurines, whistles are more common than solid figurines, and their relative numbers continue to increase into the Terminal Classic period. Figurines mounted on four pottery wheels appear to date to this time. Almost all of these types continue into the Terminal Classic. As noted by Haviland (1981:103), figurines are used by everyone, constituting part of the basic domestic inventory. During the Late Classic period, however, they are relatively more frequent in lower-ranked Small Structure Groups than anywhere else.

The Tulix complex (Ferree 1972) has an Early facet and a Late facet that are contemporaneous with the Early and Late divisions of the Late Classic period. Generally, Early Tulix types are characterized by a proliferation of new forms, which become standardized in the Late Tulix facet.

Effigy Group censers predominate in both facets. In Early Tulix there is an abrupt transition from masks to full figures, invariably male. Effigy censers do not show evidence of burning, and by this time they may have been transformed into deity images, themselves becoming objects of veneration. Spiked censers, ladle censers, and *candeleros* are the only types that actually show signs of use. Flanged censers increase in importance until they predominate in Late Tulix.

Much of the information we have about the construction of woven cloth and matting comes from impressions on the backs of censer flanges and other flat censer elements.

THE LATE LATE CLASSIC PERIOD, A.D. 700–870, THE IMIX CERAMIC COMPLEX

The last part of the Late Classic period is marked by the reappearance of inscribed monuments and a vast amount of public construction. During the next two centuries Tikal is governed by strong—even autocratic—rulers, who are able to maintain order. A favored motif on the splendid polychrome display pottery of the Imix ceramic complex of this era is the unsubtle depiction of a king enthroned in his palace receiving homage and gifts from men of lesser rank.

Innovative style and technical excellence characterize the portable material culture that marked high social or political rank. Otherwise, increasing simplification and standardization of form and decoration are evident in artifacts of utilitarian and ritual function.

Recovery contexts: Much of the large artifact sample comes from midden deposits. The number of special deposits, especially nonelite burials, is also greater than in previous periods.

Utilitarian: Quantities of imported materials of predominantly utilitarian function continued to reach Tikal, including obsidian from Highland Guatemala and Mexico; fine, dark chert; granite; and other igneous and metamorphic rock.

Small side-notched points retouched from thin flakes and thought to be arrowheads are present during this time. A specially formed pottery spindle whorl shaped like a small perforated cupcake resembles examples from northern Yucatan (Kidder 1943).

There is an increased reliance upon white-tailed deer and larger wild birds as meat sources during the Late Late and Terminal Classic periods.

Social: Two undisturbed royal chamber burials from Gp. 5D-2 are the richest known from Tikal. Their exterior chert and obsidian debitage deposits are huge and can be regarded as an indirect measure of the increased amount of construction during this time. Both graves included quantities of superb, labor-intensive goods. Many types appear for the first time, such as diadems of small jade flares; composite ear ornaments of jade flares and beads of jade or pearl; cufflike bracelets and anklets made of long jade beads arranged side by side; assemblages of dozens of pearl pendants made of true pearls and composites pieced together from blister pearl or nacreous marine shell; composite pendants of cut nacreous shell; vessels of pottery, banded calcite *(tecalli),* and wood coated with gesso and elaborately painted; wooden cylindrical lidded jars covered with a veneer of rectangular jade plaques; jade sculptures of humans and animals; and tweezers carved of bone with shell overlays. One burial possessed a spectacular set of bone artifacts, many carved and incised with hieroglyphic texts and pictures (Trik 1963). Two carved bones occurred with the other burial. In addition to the actual mortuary offerings, there are many depictions of rulers and nobles on stone monuments, wooden lintels, pottery vessels, and figurines, which show the mode of use of jade, shell, and pearl jewelry; feathered headdresses; jaguar mittens and boots; and richly decorated capes, loincloths, and *huipils* of woven cloth. The men shown on the pottery vessels and figurines usually wear only loincloths, headdresses, and ornaments, while those depicted on the stone monuments and wooden lintels are virtually obscured by their highly ornate costumes. Nonelite burials have even fewer durable offerings, usually only one or two pottery vessels, if any. Ornaments are very rare.

Ritual/Unidentified: The emphasis on caches diminishes noticeably after c. A.D. 730. Chert eccentrics and incised obsidians become smaller, and obsidian eccentrics are no longer offered. On the other hand, sawfish snout barbs may occur only during this period.

There is a considerable increase in pottery figurines, continuing the trend seen at the end of the previous period. A unique deposit of 26 mold-made and modeled figurines sprinkled with specular hematite was found in a chultun in the central area. Some of the figurines had been deliberately abraded before deposition, and none of them were whole. This deposit is either Early Late or Late Late Classic in date.

Censer molds are introduced in Late Tulix as part of the trend towards standardization. They are used for spikes, some masks on cylinders, the faces of seated effigies, and some effigy headdresses. Painted designs on effigy censers replace earlier decoration done in appliqué. Censers are carefully and skillfully made, which suggests workshops devoted exclusively to their production.

The winged *candelero,* resembling a candleholder with a curved base (Ferree 1972:fig.31), appears during Late Tulix or at the end of the Early facet. Winged *candeleros* invariably show burning.

The largest known censer deposit is associated with Str. SE-486 at Uolantun. Early and Late Tulix censer fragments in sealed pits in the floor of the temple may be the residues of ceremonies. Hundreds of other fragments and some whole censers found on the substructure surface suggest temple furniture stored in the superstructure that was scattered when its walls collapsed.

THE TERMINAL CLASSIC PERIOD,
C. A.D. 870–950, THE EZNAB CERAMIC COMPLEX

The Late Classic ended around 10.2.0.0.0, or A.D. 869, the date inscribed upon Stela 11 in Gp. 5D-2, the last dated monument known from Tikal itself. Some time afterwards, Tikal's rulers vanish. The succeeding Terminal Classic period is a time of dwindling population and the end of permanent occupation.

Decorated pottery vessels continue to be produced as part of the Eznab ceramic complex, but in much smaller proportions than during the Late Classic. Modeled-Carved Fine Orange pottery is present, as well as a local imitation of this trade ware.

Recovery contexts: The large sample dated to this period comes mainly from protected middens in the rooms of range structures of Gp. 5D-11, so preservation is better than usual. There are a number of special deposits, some also quite rich in artifacts.

Utilitarian: All of the major utilitarian artifact types of the Classic period are still present in the abundant sample of domestic material culture. Unique objects were recovered from Gp. 5D-11, such as the large proximal fragment of a wooden atlatl with carved bone finger grips and a chert thin biface that still carries traces of the adhesive used to attach it to its now vanished wooden handle. A large sample of charred seeds from the Central Acropolis gives the impression of an increased use of gathered wild plants. This impression is reinforced by an increase in *Pomacea* snail shells in middens, suggesting a recovery of some local, wild food resources.

Regional and long-distance exchange continue, but the proportion of exotic goods and materials to local ones declines.

There is evidence from Gp. 5D-11, in the form of debitage and failed artifacts, for the continued production by local specialists of chert bifaces of various kinds, obsidian prismatic blades, utilitarian bone artifacts, and possibly some shell ornaments of white marine shell and freshwater mussel, although the latter might also be food remains.

An increase in bone debitage at Tikal, as well as at other sites in the

Petén, indicates an emphasis on utilitarian bone artifact production, which some researchers (for example, Emery 1997:573) regard as an adaptive response to the unsettled times. This may well be the case. However, bone preservation in the Maya Lowlands is uneven and generally miserable, and much debitage from earlier times may have simply disappeared.

Craft specialists presumably also produced the plentiful pottery figurines, censers, and vessels of this period.

Social: A number of burials and problematical deposits can be attributed to this time. Some elite may have still lived at Tikal. Two crypt burials of women of high rank were made in Gp. 5D-2. One of them, in Temple I (Adams and Trik 1961), was covered by a layer of over 660 pieces of chert debitage, showing that the tradition of including lithic waste with special deposits was still practiced. Some obsidian blade cores and flakes were included in a large problematical deposit on the Central Acropolis. Three burials had offerings of a few jade and *Spondylus* beads, and a few bits of jade and *Spondylus* debitage were recovered from general excavations. A nonelite burial from the central area had been well furnished with attractive rosettes and pegs carved of white marine shell and thought to be ear ornaments, as well as a set of finely made, short bone pins.

Ritual/Unidentified: The specialized artifacts and materials of the elite offertory tradition disappear from the record. On the other hand, there are various kinds of problematical deposits, especially of large quantities of smashed censers in epicentral Groups 5D-2, 5D-10, and 5D-11 and around Stela 1 at Uolantun. Presumably, these censer deposits are the remains of termination rituals.

There was considerable disturbance of Gp. 5D-2 monuments and special deposits at this time, which involved the resetting of monument fragments and the looting and rearrangement of Classic period caches and chamber burials.

The pottery figurine industry flourished, showing only a slight decline from the previous period. An interesting development in figurines is that they tend to be larger than previously.

Censers continue to be locally produced, but the quality of craftsmanship indicates that they are no longer made by specialists. The repertory of shapes is greatly reduced and consists of ladle censers, spiked cones, and several types of effigy censers. Of these, only the ladle forms show signs of use as censers.

THE EARLY POSTCLASSIC PERIOD,
C. A.D. 950–1200, THE CABAN CERAMIC COMPLEX

Tikal is thought to have had no permanent residents by this time; nevertheless, scattered finds of pottery and artifacts, usually mixed with material from earlier times, show that people still visited the city. Perhaps the main purpose of such visits was to perform rituals in Gp. 5D-2. Traces, in the form of abundant copal deposits and heavily burned floors, remained in the rooms and at the base of Temple I (Adams and Trik 1961). A cache, or possible storage locus, of four modeled balls of copal, painted blue, had been intruded into an inside step in Temple I. The apple-sized balls had been furnished with twig wicks.

Two censers and several censer fragments from another deposit in Temple I were assigned to the Xnuc complex (Ferree 1972). This complex is intrusive and has affiliations with northern Yucatan.

SUMMARY

Developments in selected aspects of Tikal's culture history, abstracted from a study of its portable material culture and considered in conjunction with other research, are summarized below as the following topics: social structure, the nature of political power, warfare and factional conflict, site settlement pattern, and aspects of the economy. These should be regarded as a sample of many that can be enhanced by studying the associated artifacts.

Social Structure

Burials often provide useful information about past social structure. The earliest indicators of ranked social structure appear in Late Middle Preclassic interments in Gp. 5D-2. From then on until the city's abandonment, different mortuary programs were accorded Tikal's elite and nonelite residents. The appearance of richly furnished chamber burials in the Late Late Preclassic period lends support to the establishment of hereditary kingship during the first century A.D., proposed on epigraphic evidence (Martin, this volume). During the Classic period caches also distinguished elite residential groups.

By the beginning of the Classic period, the social rank and political power of elite women apparently declined further at Tikal than in other Lowland polities. Elite women were no longer buried in the royal necropolis of Gp. 5D-2, and they are notably underrepresented in burials in most other areas of the site. Women are seldom depicted on monuments or pottery vessels and are only shown in significant numbers on Late Classic pottery figurines.

Burial offerings, again, are the material evidence that some form of ranked social structure may have persisted into the Terminal Classic period after Tikal's rulers had vanished. It is of interest that women were once again buried in Gp. 5D-2.

The Nature of Political Power

The establishment of hereditary kingship during the Late Late Preclassic period around the first century A.D. is lent support by the range structures and chamber burials that make their first appearance at that time, because they imply the presence of a ruler who had the power to command resources and labor for personal projects (for example, Flannery 1998:21). By the Early Classic and Early Late Classic, both caches and chamber burials were well stocked with large quantities of durable goods, suggesting strong rulers who also had important ceremonial roles. From relatively modest beginnings in the Early Late Preclassic, caches in the elite tradition grow larger and more elaborate and appear in new contexts.

There is a short period towards the end of the Early Classic period when public construction, inscribed monuments, and chamber burials disappear from the archaeological record (W. R. Coe 1990:838–40, chart 1). This appears to have been a time of considerable unrest when no ruler was able to maintain political control.

The political situation changed with the beginning of the Early Late Classic period, when the material culture inventory and its spatial distribution demonstrate a high level of general prosperity. On the one hand, the rulers of this period initiated a number of construction projects, including Twin Pyramid Groups and the first of the Great Temples, Temple V (Gomez 1999). Four of these hiatus-period kings were given well-furnished chamber burials in Gp. 5D-2. Their graves are associated with the construction of new temples or major renovations of existing ones. Large quantities of chert and obsidian debitage were associated with three of the four burials. On the other hand, no inscribed monuments can be associated with the rulers of this time.

The nature of political power changed conspicuously during the course of the Late Late Classic period. The reappearance of inscribed monuments, a great increase in public construction, a trend towards deemphasizing temple and stela caches, and two exceptionally rich chamber burials all demonstrate that this was a time of increasingly autocratic rule, with attention focused more upon the person of the ruler than upon his role as a leader. A remodeling of the range structures of the Central Acropolis to make them less accessible (Harrison 1999:186) is also observed at Tikal's closest large neighbor, Uaxactun (A. L. Smith 1950).

The abrupt end of dynastic rule occurred during the succeeding Terminal Classic period. No new monuments, caches, and chamber burials were made in Gp. 5D-2, and there was a widespread disturbance of earlier ones. The Terminal Classic period in Gp. 5D-2 is also characterized by the placing of numerous nontraditional and therefore problematical deposits.

Warfare and Factional Conflict

There is no unambiguous evidence of interpolity warfare in the portable material remains. On the contrary, during the middle of the Classic period, when written records report considerable warfare ({A. F. Chase and D. Z. Chase 1998; Martin, this volume), the artifact inventory indicates the highest level of general prosperity.

But artifacts and their recovery contexts do support the inscriptions in the matter of factional conflict, particularly during the Early Classic period. In Manik 1 and 2 times, chamber burials were not made in the North Acropolis of Gp. 5D-2 but rather in Gp. 5C-11, the Mundo Perdido (Laporte and Fialko 1990). Such burials are again present on the North Acropolis during Manik 3A times, but the only Manik 3B chamber burial known at present is in an outlying structure group in the central area (Haviland 1981). Another important development during Manik 3A times is the adoption of certain elements of the Teotihuacan horizon style by some nonelite segments of Tikal society, most striking in goods included in the BPDs, and the adoption of other elements by the elite, most clearly seen in stone monuments and burial furnishings. The Early Classic period ends during a lull in construction and ritual activities in Gp. 5D-2 and a gap in inscriptions, caused at least in part by the energetic destruction and relocation of many inscribed monuments.

Site-Settlement Pattern

From the initial, dispersed settlement of the Early Middle Preclassic to the end of major construction at the close of the Late Classic, there is a trend towards nucleation. Over the course of one and a half millennia, Tikal expanded and filled in to become a city concentrically structured around a monumental, civic-ceremonial architectural core.

The social correlates of some residential groups changed over the course of the Late Preclassic and Classic periods as Tikal's settlement pattern evolved. This is suggested by the presence of Late Preclassic elite burials in Small Structure Groups that became the residences of nonelite during the Late Classic period.

During the Classic period, if not earlier, the city's most important civic-ceremonial, ritual, and economic functions were performed by four structure groups at its core. Gp. 5D-2 was the civic-ceremonial heart of the Tikal polity. The rulers lived in Gp. 5D-11, the Central Acropolis, on the southern border of the Great Plaza of Gp. 5D-2, and lesser but powerful elite families lived in Gp. 5D-10, bordering the western edge of the North Acropolis. The principal marketplace was in Gp. 5D-3 (C. Jones 1996), directly to the east of Gp. 5D-2. The epicentral area also included important temples and groups of ceremonial structures, such as Tikal's Great Temples, Twin Pyramid Groups, and Gp. 5C-11. Raised causeways linked some of these groups to Gp. 5D-2.

In contrast to the Late Preclassic period, nonelite craft specialists, with the probable exception of potters, were concentrated in Small Structure Groups in the central area during the Classic. Their social rank and economic activities are attested by the juxtaposition of simple architecture and modest special deposits with copious domestic middens that also include quantities of production waste. Small Structure Groups are the most common type of residential group in outlying areas, their material culture inventories becoming smaller and simpler with distance from the core.

Intermediate Structure Groups are found interspersed among Small Structure Groups in the central and peripheral areas. The sporadic occurrence of stone monuments, caches, richly furnished burials, and a Manik 3B chamber burial demonstrates that at least some of these groups housed elite families, but the inadequate excavated samples do not permit us to say that all of them did.

During the course of the Classic period, Tikal is nearly surrounded by a ring of satellite Minor Centers. With a couple of exceptions, Minor Centers occur beyond a distance of 4 km. from the core. They are found to the east, south, and west of Tikal but not to the north, where there is an earthwork approximately 9 km. long at a distance of 4.5 km. from Gp. 5D-2 (D. E. Puleston 1983:fig.20; Haviland, this volume). Traces of a similar earthwork were identified approximately 5 km. to the southeast of the core (D. E. Puleston 1983:fig.20). These constructions are generally considered to have been defensive in nature, and they may also have been related to long distance and regional exchange, as suggested by Culbert. By the Late Classic period, some of the Minor Centers possess public architecture and stone monuments, yet their artifact inventories are poor in specialist-produced goods compared with those of structure groups in the epicenter and center. However, more work needs to be done in these Minor Centers to determine their function and social correlates.

In the Terminal Classic period, much of the remnant population remained in or moved into the larger, formerly elite residential groups located in the epicenter of Tikal. Occupation also continued in a few structure groups in the central and peripheral areas, suggesting a reversion to the dispersed settlement pattern of the Preclassic.

Economy

The basic domestic artifact assemblage was already in use at least as early as the Late Middle Preclassic period. Production by craft specialists of goods used by everyone and their exchange through some kind of market system are well established by the Early Late Preclassic period. Specialization is indicated by standardization of form, a high degree of technical competence, large quantities of production debitage, and special site-maintenance practices for coping with the waste. By these criteria, specialist production in chert, obsidian, bone, and pottery continued without interruption into the Terminal Classic. Expedient industries in chert, bone, and worked sherds—all abundant local resources—also existed at all times.

The long-delayed identification of the production waste associated with elite burials and caches has led to an underestimation of the importance of Tikal and other large cities as production centers of both domestic and status artifacts (Moholy-Nagy 1997). Regular cleanup of work areas and the absence of permanent facilities make it very difficult to identify the actual loci of craft production. Debitage and failed artifacts, unfortunately both highly portable, are the best evidence we have at present, since only special deposits were screened. It appears that the production of pottery vessels may have been carried on in the peripheries at all times (Fry, this volume). The production of chert bifaces and obsidian prismatic blades and the processing of now perished material with lithic artifacts are attested for the peripheries during the Late Preclassic. During the Classic, however, most craft specialists of all kinds were concentrated in the Small Structure Groups of the central area. Craft specialists probably worked independently at their residences, producing for the market and their own needs. Nevertheless, the presence of chert, obsidian, jade, and *Spondylus* debitage in elite contexts may be evidence that the same artisans occasionally worked in the attached mode upon elite demand.

The permanent facilities constructed for the Gp. 5D-3 central marketplace are the architectural evidence for a market system. These facilities took the form of long, narrow buildings with many doorways, which probably served as vendors' stalls. More significantly, the market exchange of domestic goods is indicated by the broad spatial distribution of artifacts produced by craft specialists from locally available and imported raw material (Hirth 1998).

During the Early Classic period, Tikal became the most important administrative, economic, and ritual settlement of the northeastern Petén. It was the apical central place in a regional settlement hierarchy that probably conformed to Christaller's k=7 or administrative pattern and the center of a marketing system resembling Carol Smith's solar system type (C. A. Smith 1976:317). In addition to regional and local commodities, this system drew in large quantities of domestic and status goods from well beyond its area. Tikal was the gateway site for these exotics. They have been recovered there in greater quantities and higher proportions than from any other settlement in the region.

The consumption of specialist-produced durable artifacts during the Classic period was higher in the residential structure groups of the city's epicenter and center than on the peripheries. Beyond a radius of approximately 2 km. from Gp. 5D-2, such artifacts show a steep drop in density, approximated by count per defined excavation lot, although expedient artifacts do not show such a drop. Several likely reasons for this disparity come to mind, such as more limited excavation in the peripheries, shorter spans of occupation, or poorer preservation of shell and bone. However, this kind of distribution may also indicate that the residents of outlying areas did not have the means to acquire much in the way of specialist-produced goods distributed through the market.

Imported artifacts and raw materials of regional and extraregional origin figured prominently in Tikal's economic, sociopolitical, and ritual activities throughout its existence. Long-distance exchange is evident from the time of initial settlement. The circumstance that several of the significant utilitarian imports are present well before the rise of ranked society suggests that early long-distance exchange was in the hands of a suprahousehold organization, perhaps the lineage (Freidel 1981a).

By the Late Late Classic, several of the peripheral Minor Centers possess distinctive plans characterized by public architecture, grand plazas, and long causeways with one or more structures at their outermost end (for example, D. E. Puleston 1983:figs.9, 14). Their layouts resemble the Late Classic causeway termini groups at Caracol (A. F. Chase and D. Z. Chase 1996), and I suggest that they, too, may have been entrepôts for imported goods. Markets could well have been held in their ample plazas.

A decrease in overall prosperity, measured by decline in the spatial distributions and proportions of specialist-produced goods to expedient ones and of imported materials to those available locally, is observable during the Late Late Classic. Local craft production of basic domestic goods, however, persisted into the Terminal Classic, and some long-distance imports continued to reach Tikal until the city was abandoned.

CONCLUSION

In the past, just as in our own time, artifacts facilitated almost every aspect of human behavior and, accordingly, have the potential to inform us about virtually all other aspects of past culture. The study of portable material culture of past complex societies is especially rewarding because large quantities of different kinds of objects have often survived.

There are, to be sure, significant problems in placing artifacts into their past cultural contexts, but these problems can be greatly reduced as we make better use of the theory and field and laboratory methods now available to us and as we continue to develop more efficient methods and more inclusive theory.

Note

This paper has greatly benefited from the discussions we held at the advanced seminar on Tikal at the School of American Research in Santa Fe in September 1999. I also thank Jerry Sabloff for specific comments and suggestions. I am especially appreciative for nearly four decades of information exchange with my fellow tikalistas in our attempts to understand the archaeology of Tikal. Bill Haviland inspired me to look beyond the catalog, and my special thanks go to Ginny Greene for contributing the results of her research on Tikal figurines.

4

Settlement, Society, and Demography at Tikal

William A. Haviland

When the University of Pennsylvania began the original Tikal Project in the late 1950s, little was known about ancient Maya settlement, let alone the related subjects of demography and social organization. Sites were generally not mapped in their entirety, and attention to archaeological features beyond major architecture and public monuments was sporadic at best (Haviland 1966a). Moreover, investigations were usually geared toward supporting existing notions about the Maya rather than toward seriously testing alternative ideas. But with rising interest among American archaeologists in settlement studies and what these might tell us about the nature of ancient societies, the time was ripe for a concerted effort to investigate the full range of Maya ruins, and efforts in this direction were made (Bullard 1960; Willey, Bullard, Glass, and Gifford 1965). Still, not until the work of the Tikal Project was a Maya site of the Classic period mapped in such detail, over so extensive an area (Carr and Hazard 1961; D. E. Puleston 1983), nor were so many "house mounds" as thoroughly investigated (Becker with Jones 1999; Haviland et al. 1985) (fig. 4.1). Although full publication of the excavations did not immediately follow (and is still not completed),

FIGURE 4.1

Str. 4F-2 is typical of many house ruins at Tikal. Even after a thorough clearing of vegetation, it was scarcely visible before excavation.

interim publications (Haviland 1965, 1970) made preliminary conclusions available and caused a revolution in our thinking about Maya society. Clear evidence that ancient populations were far larger than previously thought prompted a search for subsistence alternatives to simple "slash-and-burn" farming (D. E. Puleston 1968; Siemans and Puleston 1972). At the same time, the richness of the data permitted new reconstructions of the ways in which Classic Maya society was organized (Haviland 1966b, 1972; Haviland and Moholy-Nagy 1992).

Unfortunate though the lag in publication of final field reports has been, it has also had unexpected benefits. Subsequent investigations throughout the southern Maya Lowlands have provided a wealth of comparative data that have informed, enriched, and sometimes altered our interpretations in important ways (compare Becker 1973a, b; Becker with Jones 1999; Haviland 1985, 1992a, 1997). Given this, it is worth revisiting the topics of settlement, demography, and social

TABLE 4.1

Excavated and Tested Residential Groups

| Quadrangle | Excavated Residential Groups | | Tested Residential Groups | |
	Major Excavations	*Minor Excavations*	*Major Test*	*Minor Test*
Bejucal		2B-1 3C-1		2C-1 3C-3 2C-2 3C-4 3C-2
North Zone	3D-3	3D-9		3D-4 3D-8 3D-5 3E-1 3D-6 Ch. 2E-2 3D-7
Encanto	2F-1 3F-1 2G-1 3F-2 2G-2 3F-3 Str. 2G-61	Ch. 2F-5 3G-1 3G-2		2G-3 Str. 2G-48 Vacant Terrain
Temple IV	5B-2 5C-3 Str. 5C-56	Ch. 5C-6	Str. 4C-34	4C-1 4C-6 4C-2 5B-3 4C-3 5C-4 4C-4 5C-5 4C-5 5C-6
Great Plaza	4E-1 4E-2 5D-1			4D-3 5E-2 4D-4 5E-3 5E-1 5E-4
Camp	4F-1 4F-2 4F-3 4G-1 5G-1 5G-2	5F-1	4F-5 4F-7	4F-4 5F-3 4F-6 5F-4 4G-2 5F-5 4G-3 5G-3 Ch. 4G-2 5G-4
Perdido	6C-1 6C-5 Str. 6C-60 7C-1 Str. 7C-62	6B-1 6C-2 6C-4 7C-2	6B-3	6C-6 7B-1 6C-7 7C-3 6C-8 7C-4 6C-9 7C-5 6C-10
Corriental	6E-1		7E-3	6D-1 6E-9 6D-2 6E-10 6D-3 6E-11 6D-4 6E-12 6D-5 6E-13 6D-6 6E-14 6E-3 7E-1 6E-4 7E-2 6E-5 7E-4 6E-6 7E-5 6E-7 7E-6 6E-8 Vacant Terrain
Inscriptions	7F-1	Str. 6F-62 7F-2 7G-1		7F-3
Peripheral	4H-1 4H-4	3H-1 4H-5		1D-1 1D-6 1D-2 1D-7 1D-3 1D-8 1D-4 1E-1 1D-5

organization at Tikal as they are currently understood. The basic data came from 29 extensively excavated groups of residential structures, 17 groups less extensively excavated, and 89 groups explored solely by test pits (table 4.1). These include almost all residential structures investigated within the central 16 square km. of Tikal, the major exception being the elite "palace" compounds at the city's epicenter. They also include a number of "invisible" groups of which no traces could be detected prior to excavation (cf. Strs. 5F-42–47, Puleston 1983:10, and compare his fig. 2a with the same locus as mapped by Carr and Hazard 1961: Camp Quadrangle). Obviously, the presence of houses not detectable by surface survey raises serious issues for interpretation of the site map, and awareness of the problem led to systematic exploration of seemingly vacant terrain over several seasons, beginning in 1961 (W. R. Coe and Haviland 1982:29–31). Such work was virtually unheard of at Maya sites previously.

At Tikal, the search for invisible structures revealed that wherever chultuns were found in the absence of visible ruins, excavations invariably revealed the one-time presence of associated architecture (cf. Haviland 1963:119–42). Moreover, in seemingly vacant areas devoid even of chultuns, tests revealed structural remains (the aforementioned Strs. 5F-42–47 are a case in point). Clearly, there were a great many more structures in the central 16 sq. km. of Tikal than those shown on the site map. On the other hand, it is now certain that the "invisible" structures were all abandoned by the time Imix (or at least late Imix) pottery came into production, so they do not affect interpretation of Tikal settlement in its latter years before the collapse. Such structures do greatly complicate our interpretation of earlier Tikal settlement, as I shall subsequently discuss.

I have drawn the data that follow from two final field reports (Becker with Jones 1999; Haviland et al. 1985) and from the complete drafts of Tikal Reports 20, 22, and 27 (W. R. Coe and Haviland 1982:57–59), in my possession.

CHRONOLOGY

As even a quick glance at the Tikal map (Carr and Hazard 1961) (fig. 4.2) shows, residential buildings rarely occur as single isolated features. Rather, they are usually found in groups of two or more,

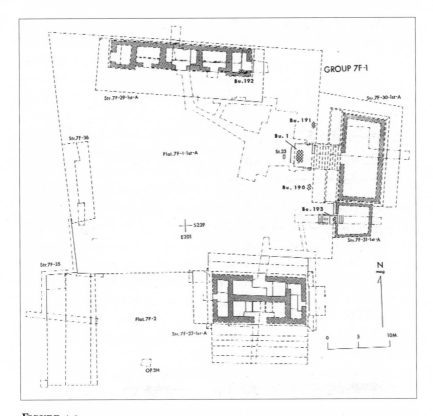

FIGURE 4.2

Gp. 7F-1, an elite residential compound, exemplifies the Maya practice of grouping houses together around open plazas.

arranged around the edges of common plazas. When one consults the time spans defined for the 23 best-known groups, it is apparent that for the most part the structures within each functioned as a unit rather than sequentially, one replacing another. Some, of course, were constructed earlier than others, and some old structures might be replaced by new ones. In the latter case, the abandoned structures were normally at least partially razed and buried beneath new construction. As the use of a given group continued through time, the number of structures in most—but not all—cases increased.

The chronological data from all residential structure groups excavated or tested are summarized in table 4.1. For a number of reasons, these data are heavily dependent upon the ceramic chronology established for Tikal. Chief among these reasons are the sheer abundance of potsherds and the marked changes ceramics exhibit over fairly limited periods of time. While other classes of artifacts, as well as architecture, provide some chronological control, these data tend not to be as readily accessible and/or as precise in providing information on blocks of time as ceramics are. The dates given in figure 4.3 are those for the beginnings and ends of the various Tikal ceramic complexes as provided by Culbert (this volume). Of course, these dates provide only outside limits within which the construction, use, and abandonment of particular structures or groups took place. For example, Manik sherds within the fill of a particular piece of construction do not mean that the construction was built in A.D. 250 but merely that construction was no earlier and perhaps later. Although it appears in figure 4.3 as though there were sudden bursts of building activity at a few particular moments in time, around 600 and 350 B.C. or A.D. 1, 250, 550, and 700, this was probably not so. It is more likely that building was going on more or less constantly. Similarly, the presence of Imix, but not Eznab, ceramics in late occupation debris does not indicate that a group was abandoned precisely in A.D. 850.

A number of other problems involved in ceramic dating need to be mentioned. One of these is the occasional presence in early fills of a few sherds that predate the bulk of those present. For example, a fill with a large number of Manik sherds may include a few from Preclassic vessels as well. While the lower limit date for such construction would not be in doubt (A.D. 250 in this case), the Preclassic sherds raise the possibility that the group's occupation began earlier. Or perhaps the earlier sherds represent a basket load of trash brought in from some nearby group. This sort of problem arises most often in the case of tested, rather than more extensively excavated, residential groups. In my interpretations I assume that one or two sherds from an earlier ceramic complex are probably strays, unless the total sample is small and/or there is no likely nearby source for such strays. The more abundant such sherds are, the more likely it is that they represent occupation of the group where they were found.

A related problem is that much of the fill used for construction in one group could have been brought in from another group. An early construction full of Manik sherds, for example, could have been built

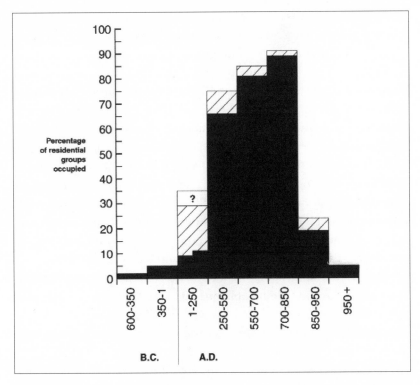

FIGURE 4.3

Percentage of residential groups occupied, by major blocks of time. Certain occupations are indicated in solid black; possible occupations are indicated by crosshatching (see text for further explanation).

after A.D. 550, with no earlier occupation of the group of which it was a part. Again, this is a particular problem where tested, rather than more fully excavated, groups are concerned. I have assumed that fill material was readily procured nearby for small-scale architecure, whereas larger construction would more likely require that fill be hauled in from some distance (see Haviland et al. 1985:161–62). Hence, unless there is a specific reason to think otherwise, I assume that the earliest sherds from test pits (except for strays) pertain to the initial occupation of the group in question. Such sherds may be redeposited (for example, Manik sherds in the excavated Str. 2G-59) or not (for example, midden beneath Str. 6C-45-8th-C).

Still another problem is that sherd collections cannot always be precisely identified as to complex. In the case of a number of tested residential groups, later sherd collections are identified only as "Late Classic" (Ik and/or Imix). Of all groups known to be in use when Ik ceramics were in vogue, only two definitely (but four possibly) were abandoned by the time of Imix production. Furthermore, only nine, or at most ten, groups that were occupied when Imix ceramics were in vogue had no earlier Ik-related occupation. Consequently, I assumed that collections identified as Ik and/or Imix indicate that a group was likely in use ca. A.D. 700, with the strong possibility of occupation as early as A.D. 550 and as late as 850. If Manik sherds are also present, an Ik occupation is virtually certain; if Eznab sherds are present, a late Imix occupation is probable. This assumes continuous rather than periodic occupation of small-structure groups, as excavation has shown was usually the case (at least by Intermediate and Late Classic times).

Just as some collections are identifiable only as Ik and/or Imix, so other collections are identifiable only as "Late Preclassic," a period of time spanning the use of Chuen, Cauac, and Cimi (though Cimi is now considered "Terminal Preclassic") ceramics. But were all groups with such pottery occupied continuously from as early as 350 B.C.? The answer is, probably not. Three unequivocal Tzec, 7 definite Chuen, and 11 certain Cauac (two of them Cimi facet, but no earlier) occupations are known, so most collections diagnosed as "Late Preclassic" are probably later rather than earlier.

Another problem with the tested groups within the central 9 sq. km. of the site map is that concentration on architecture for test pits did not always produce late occupation samples. Fry, in Square 1D, used a different approach (D. E. Puleston 1973:135–36), so this is less of a problem there. Lack of late occupation samples, if not allowed for, could make a group appear to have been abandoned before it actually was.

Keeping all these considerations in mind, a number of conclusions about residential structures are possible. First, the dates of the structures of the excavated sample for which there is evidence of modification and which were in use during the era of Imix pottery production (table 4.2) suggest that modifications were carried out on the average of about every 60 years or so. However, there are three reasons why this figure is too high. The first has already been alluded to: The structures used for this calculation were not all built precisely when ceramics of

TABLE 4.2

Structures Built by A.D. *700 or Later That Were Subsequently Modified before* A.D. *850*

2G-14-2nd	4E-51-2nd	5D-6-3rd
2G-15-2nd	4E-53-2nd B	5D-7-4th
2G-56-B	4F-2-2nd	5D-8-C
2G-58-2nd	4F-3-2nd A	5G-4-3rd
2G-59-2nd	4F-4-B	5G-5-2nd
2G-60-2nd	4F-5-B	5G-8-3rd
3C-15-3rd	4F-6-B	5G-9-2nd
3F-12-1st C	4F-7-C	5G-10-2nd
3F-24-3rd	4F-16-1st C	5G-11-3rd
3F-25-2nd	4F-21-2nd	5G-12-2nd
3F-26-3rd	4F-47-2nd	5G-49-B
3F-29-2nd	4G-10-B	5G-51-2nd
3G-1-3rd	4H-4-2nd B	5G-52-2nd
3G-20-4th	4H-15-B	5G-53-2nd
3H-2-B	4H-16-2nd	5G-54-2nd
3E-16-2nd	4H-18-2nd	6C-41-1st B
4E-31-D	5B-6-2nd	6E-26-3rd
4E-50-B	5B-7-2nd	7C-7-2nd

the Ik-Imix transition appeared, nor were they all abandoned simultaneously in A.D. 850. For example, Str. 4E-16-2nd was not built until after late Imix ceramics had appeared, probably after A.D. 770. Conversely, for all we know, Str. 2G-59-1st could have been abandoned by then, even though other structures in the group (2G-1) of which it was a part were not yet abandoned.

Second, this calculation is too high. If these structures consisted in part of pole-and-thatch buildings, as evidence indicates, the buildings were undoubtedly rebuilt when their platforms were altered, as a conformity in shape between the two could be expected (fig. 4.4). This is the case for twentieth-century Maya houses (C. F. Wauchope 1938:14), and it was true of some—and perhaps all—houses in the past (Haviland 1963:274 and Haviland et al. 1985:118). On the other hand, if only the building was renovated, its platform might not be affected,

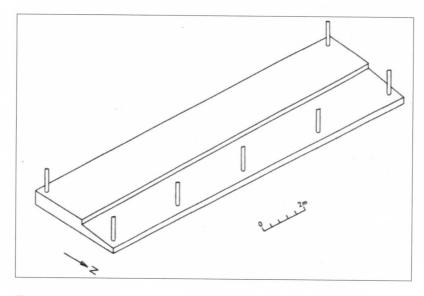

FIGURE 4.4

This isometric drawing of Str. 3F-25 shows how the main posts of houses (revealed by post-holes) were positioned relative to the walls of supporting platforms.

and there would be no archaeological trace of such an alteration.

Third, even in Intermediate and Late Classic structures (about which more is generally known than is known of earlier ones), the state of preservation differs considerably. One may compare, for example, Strs. 2G-15 and 6E-26. For the former, a poorly preserved structure, there is evidence of only two Late Classic architectural developments. For the latter, better-preserved structure, six architectural modifications are known for the 150 years or so during which Imix (and transitional Ik-Imix) ceramics were in vogue. This last case suggests alteration about every 25 years. There are other structures that suggest a similar time interval for alterations: Str. 5G-11, about every 25 years while Imix ceramics were in use; Str. 6C-45, about every 11 years during the time that late Manik ceramics were in vogue; Str. 2G-59, every 50 years during the interval when Ik ceramics were in vogue; Str. 4E-16, about once every 20 years, while late Imix ceramics were in vogue. In Groups 4F-1 and 4F-2, (Haviland et al. 1985), over the 150 years that Ik ceramics were in use, there were three modifications at the loci of Str. 4F-10 and of Strs. 4F-15 and -43 (once every 50 years). In the same interval, Str. 4F-14 was altered four times (once every 38 years). Similar intervals are indicated for Strs. 3G-20, 4E-31, 4H-4, 5D-7, and 5G-9 during the era of Imix production. Thirty-year intervals are indicated for Strs. 5G-4, 5G-8, 5G-12, and 5G-54 over the same period. I am of the opinion that these various examples are closer to the truth than the figure of 60 years mentioned above.

The possibility was once raised that houses were used, abandoned for a significant length of time, and then rebuilt (see Sanders and Price 1968:165). Probably few people would accept this possibility today, for it is not consistent with several lines of evidence. First, an apparent 25- to 35-year interval between alterations is inconsistent, especially given the fact that by age 55, 68 percent of the men and 80 percent of the women at Tikal had died (Haviland, in prep.b). For men, who were most likely the heads of households, mortality was highest in the 40s. This would suggest modification of a house upon death of its inhabitant. Second, when a house was altered, portions of older floors and walls commonly remained in use. Had the structure stood exposed to the elements for very long in the northeast Petén climate, the component floors and walls would have deteriorated rapidly and would not have been in any condition for re-use. Third, there are middens such as those associated with Strs. 4F-3 (Haviland et al. 1985), 6C-45, 6E-26, and 5F-Sub. 1 that show continuous deposition. Had the associated architecture stood abandoned for any length of time, at least some soil would have accumulated over the middens prior to further deposition of trash. This would have left stratigraphic evidence in the form of layers in the middens, which in fact they lack. One rare exception is the midden behind Str. 6C-45-5th, but its building was clearly in use before and after the break; there is presently no evidence of its abandonment and subsequent modification. Fourth, household burials suggest continuity of occupation in two ways. One is the rarity of disturbed burials in building platforms, which implies remembrance of their location over several generations. This is particularly evident in the case of Str. 2G-59, with its 11 undisturbed burials but only one secondary burial. It is also evident in the case of Str. 6E-Sub. 1 (buried beneath the platform on which Strs. 6E-25 and 26 were built), in or near which at least nine inhumations took place over a period of some 700 years. The only disturbance of a burial was apparently due to its position relative to planned large-scale architectural alterations. It appears to have been disturbed by design rather than by accident. Such remembrance would not be expected in the absence of continuous occupation. Nor, it may be added, would one expect the locus of Str. 6E-Sub. 1 to continue as a favored spot for burial after it was abandoned and covered over by fill of Plat. 6E-1 (as it was), unless an old tradition relative to burial location was continuing. This is the second argument in favor of continuity of occupation from the burial evidence.

These four points were touched upon in an earlier article of mine (Haviland 1970:191), and D. E. Puleston (1973) added two other supportive arguments to them. One is that if the cultivation of fruit trees around houses was an important element of Classic Maya subsistence, then householders would not be expected to shift their residence periodically. If they did so, they would be abandoning productive trees important to their livelihood. Puleston's second argument is that the construction of sometimes substantial building and group platforms seems more consistent with a degree of residential permanence than it does with shifting residence.

A final observation pertaining to architectural modification is that several structures, along with their common plaza, were often altered at the same time rather than individually. Evidence for this is especially clear in the case of Groups 4F-1 and 4F-2 (Haviland et al. 1985) and Groups 2G-1 (Haviland 1988), 3F-2, 6C-1, and 6E-1. While the evidence is not so clear in other groups, at least it is not inconsistent. I shall return to the implications of this later in the chapter.

As is clear from figure 4.3 (above) and the data just discussed, there was a substantial increase through time in the number of residential groups in use at any given time. In Preclassic through Terminal Classic times, 40 to 48 household groups (30 to 36 percent of the total sample) are known to have been in use. In the period during which Manik ceramics were in use, the figure is 89 to 101 (66 to 75 percent). When Ik ceramics were in vogue, 110 groups almost surely (115 possibly) were in use (81 to 85 percent). Finally, 120 groups were almost surely in use, another three possibly so, between A.D. 700 and 850, when Imix ceramics were in vogue (89 to 91 percent). This, of course, is a rather gross breakdown of figures. Although greater precision is difficult, some can be achieved. Working backward in time, we can be

TABLE 4.3

Residential Groups or Loci Surely or Almost Surely Occupied When Late Imix Ceramics Were in Vogue

1D-1	3G-2	5G-2
1D-8	3H-1	6B-1
2C-1	4C-5	6C-4
2G-1	Str. 4C-34	6C-8
2G-2	4E-1	6D-1
3C-1	4E-2	6E-1
3C-4	4F-1	6E-6
3D-6	4G-1	6E-12
3F-1	4H-1	7C-3
3F-2	4H-4	7E-3
3F-3	4H-5	7E-5
3G-1	5F-1	7F-1
	5G-1	

reasonably certain that 37 household groups in use between A.D. 700 and 850 were still in use in the era of late Imix pottery production, probably after A.D. 770 (table 4.3). A 38th is highly probable. On the other hand, only two loci with Imix ceramics are known to have been abandoned by the time late Imix ceramics appeared; conversely, only two groups or loci are known to have had their first occupation after the appearance of late Imix pottery (though a third possibility exists). Overall, it looks as though the number of residential groups in use while Imix ceramics were in vogue was fairly constant, with abandonments matched by new occupations. Furthermore, residence appears to have been quite stable, with a minimum of shifting about.

To pursue this further, it appears that with only one certain exception (and one possible but very doubtful one), all the groups of both the excavated and the tested samples depicted on the site map (Carr and Hazard 1961) were in use between A.D. 700 and 850, even though the antecedents of some reach further back into antiquity than others. A complicating factor, though, is the existence of other structures that were probably occupied between A.D. 700 and 850 but do not appear on the map. This brings us back to the previously raised issue of "invisible" structures. Seven of these at four different loci on the 9-sq.-km. site map are not truly "invisible," as they are marked by prominent ruin mounds

TABLE 4.4

Visible Small-Structure Ruins to Be Added to the Central 9-Sq.-Km. Site Map

Structure	Location
3D-126	S 150 E 222
4E-54	S 248 E 352
4E-55	S 271 E 347
4G-11	S 288 E 53
4G-12	S 296 E 64
5B-21	S 25 E 400
5B-22	S 15 E 410

that were missed by the mappers. These seven (table 4.4) may simply be added to the total for the central 9-sq.-km. mapped portion of Tikal and treated as mapped structures. I believe that the sample is sufficient to state with confidence that 99 percent of all groups of small structures that appear on the 9-sq.-km. site map were in use in this last part of the Late Classic time period.

The situation for the peripheral squares of the 16-sq.-km. site map is more complex. Unlike the squares of the central 9 sq. km., these were originally mapped by reconnaissance methods rather than by plane table survey. Later investigation of six peripheral squares (table 4.5) suggests that numbers of visible ruins should be increased by 50 percent. Thus, 272 structures should be added to the 543 actually shown on the 28 peripheral squares of the map, for a total of 815. Of these structures, those groups that have been tested suggest all but one to have been occupied between 700 and 850. The exception is Group 4H-5 (Becker with Jones, 1999:50), which was not founded until ca. A.D. 775. On this basis, I am inclined to extend the preceding conclusion to state that 99 percent of all groups of small structures that appear on the 16-sq.-km. map were in use in Late Classic times.

Of the Ik-related small structure groups, 79 surely or almost surely were occupied by A.D. 550 (table 4.6). The number may have been considerably higher, for none of the groups are known to have been first occupied in Intermediate Classic times. Only one structure, "invisible" 6C-60, was surely abandoned by then, while two groups were probably abandoned by A.D. 700. A third may have been abandoned as well, but

TABLE 4.5

Numbers of Structures to Be Added to the Outer Squares of the 16-Sq.-Km. Site Map

Square	No. of Structures Originally Mapped	No. of New Structures Discovered	% Increase
1D	28	28	100
3H		8	
4H	17	1	6
5A	13	0	0
5H	23	11	48
8D	26	5	19
Total	107	53	50

TABLE 4.6

Residential Groups or Loci Surely or Almost Surely Occupied When Early Ik Ceramics Were in Vogue

1D-1	2G-2	4C-2	4H-1	5G-1	6D-1	6E-14
1D-2	3C-2	4C-6	5B-3	5G-4	6D-2	7C-1
1D-3	3C-4	4D-3	5C-4	6B-1	6D-3	7C-2
1D-4	3D-4	4D-4	5C-5	6C-1	6D-4	7E-3
1D-5	3D-5	4F-1	5C-6	6C-2	6D-5	7E-4
1D-6	3D-7	4F-2	Ch. 5C-6	6C-5	6D-6	7E-5
1D-7	3D-8	4F-3	Str. 5C-56	6C-6	6E-1	7E-6
1D-8	3F-2	4F-4	5D-1	6C-7	6E-6	7F-1
1E-1	3F-3	4G-1	5E-3	6C-8	6E-1	7F-2
2B-1	3G-1	4G-2	5F-1	6C-9	6E-12	7F-3
2C-2	3H-1	4G-3	5F-5	Str. 6C-60	6E-13	7G-1
2G-1	4C-1					

this is doubtful. Again, residential stability rather than shifting residence is suggested.

Of the 89 Manik-related groups, one surely was abandoned by late Manik times, and others may have been. One (Group 7F-1) was abandoned around A.D. 525 but was immediately reoccupied by another family (Haviland 1981:93). Of the remaining groups, ten (seven of them "invisible") are known to have been abandoned by A.D. 550 at the latest, although two of these do have later occupations. Seven groups surely did not exist until middle to late Manik times. What these figures suggest is that residential stability may not have been as great prior to

A.D. 550 as it was later on. I shall return to this point shortly.

A breakdown of Preclassic through Terminal Preclassic occupations, as far as they are now known, has already been given. There are three definite occupations associated with Tzec pottery. Two others are not certain; ceramics from these groups were identified only as "Preclassic." We can be certain of only seven Chuen occupations, but other possibilities may exist. Similarly, definite Cauac occupations are known for 16 groups; two or three of these do not predate the Cimi facet, but some or all of the others do. One group was abandoned by the time Cauac ceramics appeared, never to be reoccupied. Four other groups were abandoned by A.D. 250 in Preclassic times but were reoccupied when late Manik or later ceramics were in vogue. One group was abandoned earlier (by 350 B.C.) and not reoccupied until ca. A.D. 550. Finally, Group 5G-1's earliest occupation ended by 600 B.C. (Becker with Jones 1999:77–78). Following a lengthy hiatus, the locus was reoccupied, then abandoned by A.D. 250, but again reoccupied when late Manik pottery was in vogue. Once again, some shifting of residence is suggested, as it was for Early Classic times. Some confirmatory evidence comes from an examination of 12 groups or loci occupied prior to A.D. 550, for which sufficient information exists to indicate whether individual structures were built and continuously occupied with occasional modification or built, occupied, and replaced by new structures. The former was the case in eight groups; the latter was the case in two and possibly four others. In addition, the "invisible" Str. 7C-62 seems to have been very briefly occupied, while in the group comprising the previously mentioned Strs. 5F-42 through 47 (Group 5F-2), there were essentially only two rebuildings. Obviously, there seems to have been considerable residential stability, but I think that this was somewhat less than after A.D. 550.

It is clear from figure 4.3 (above) that there was a dramatic abandonment of residential groups by ca. A.D. 850. This observation, of course, is not new (see Culbert 1973:67–70). Twenty-five groups (possibly 32) show traces of Eznab-related occupations (19 to 24 percent of the sample). Twenty-two of these may represent continued occupation of the groups in question for a time after A.D. 850, before final abandonment. Group 7F-1 is a particularly clear case in point (Haviland 1981). Three others seem to represent late reoccupations. Obviously, a dramatic drop in population is indicated. While these Eznab-related occupations are widely distributed, there may have been some tendency to congregate near sources of water. Six occupations known for the camp and five to seven for the Corriental Quadrangles suggest a focus of interest on the Tikal and Corriental Reservoirs.

Caban-related occupations are rarer still (fig 4.3 above). Seven are known, of which four are located in the Camp Quadrangle at no great distance from the Tikal Reservoir. A fifth and sixth are near the Inscriptions Reservoir. The concentration near the Tikal Reservoir is of interest; two of the three known Tzec-related occupations occur here as well. This apparent focus on reservoirs on the part of Tikal's last prehistoric inhabitants was a return to one of the earliest localities chosen for settlement.

Having looked at the number of residential groups shown on the site map that were in use between A.D. 700 and 850, we can now look at the number of individual structures that were so occupied. In the excavated sample of household groups, 103 mapped ruins were actually investigated. Of these, Str. 3F-13 probably and Strs. 3F-28, 4F-8, 4F-11, 4F-12, and 7F-34 surely turned out not to be structures at all, while five unmapped ("invisible") structures (3D-127, 4F-48, 4F-49, 6E-162, and 6E-163) were discovered. The numbers to be eliminated and added, therefore, come close to balancing out. Of all Imix-related structures, 2B-7, 4F-14, 4F-42, and possibly Strs. 4F-15 and 4F-43 were abandoned by ca. A.D. 770. Structures 3C-14 and -15, 3F-27, 4C-34, 4E-14, -15, -16, -50, 4G-10, -11, 4H-13, -18, 5G-5, -6, -7, -10, -49, -50, -51, -52, -53, -55, and 6B-9, however, all appear to postdate these structures. There is no evidence that any other excavated mapped structures were abandoned by A.D. 770, although some, such as Strs. 2G-59 or 7C-4, may have been abandoned not long afterward.

The structures just noted do not exhaust the number in use between A.D. 700 and 850. "Invisible" Str. 5C-56 is not a part of any mapped group. Structures were almost certainly built close by Ch. 5C-6, as Str. 5C-56 was near Ch. 5C-5. Finally, the possibility exists that Ch. 2E-2 and Ch. 4G-2 might indicate the nearby presence of unmapped Intermediate or Late Classic structures. It seems obvious that there are more such structures to be found, but there is no way to estimate how many. Although these known "invisible" structures, along with those of unmapped Gp. 3H-1, were in use in Intermediate/Late Classic times, there is no evidence regarding whether or not most were still in use by A.D. 770. Group 3H-1 surely was in use, but quite possibly the rest were not; Str. 5C-56-1st with Plat. 5C-1-1st, for example, was built while Ik ceramics were in vogue, and there is no evidence of further modification. The Imix ceramics around the structure cannot be identified as early or late, but a logical interpretation is that the structure and plaza remained in use for a time after the appearance of Imix ceramics yet were abandoned soon thereafter, surely by A.D. 770. The early abandonment of this locus is probably the reason for the absence of a visible ruin, as opposed to those structures that were abandoned in the last days of Tikal.

Consequently, I am inclined to the opinion that most such "hidden" structures and groups were abandoned by ca. A.D. 770 and need not be considered in calculations of the number of residential structures in use at that time. To reinforce this opinion, in addition to the cases noted above, 13 other tests of "vacant terrain" produced as many indications of "invisible" structures, but all were abandoned by A.D. 700. On the other hand, it is important to know whether or not A.D. 770 represents the high point for Tikal in terms of residential-structure density. Certainly, structures were many times more numerous then than in Preclassic times, as is evident from the previous discussion, which demonstrated that structure density surely increased in Early Classic times; just how much is uncertain. And certainly, there are many Early Classic "invisible" structures that remain to be discovered at Tikal, though it is impossible to estimate just how many. On the other hand, this is offset by the fact that not all Early Classic structures were in use contemporaneously. However, almost as many groups of small structures were in use between A.D. 550 and 700 as by A.D. 770. This, coupled with the undoubted existence of more "hidden" structures in use between A.D. 550 and 700, suggests that structure density was at least approaching a peak by A.D. 550.

DEMOGRAPHIC AND SOCIAL IMPLICATIONS

The demographic implications of the preceding information are obvious; from small beginnings, Tikal's population grew dramatically to a peak reached by A.D. 700. I shall refrain from estimating actual numbers of people, as data are not yet sufficient for a final, definitive figure. For present purposes, overall trends through time are sufficient. As for existing estimates, my feeling is that earlier tendencies to underestimate have been replaced by a tendency to overestimate. As yet, I have seen no compelling reason to adjust my own earlier estimate of ca. 45,000 up or down (Haviland 1970:193).

Perhaps there was a particular surge of growth at the end of the Preclassic, though the potentially deranging factors of "invisible" houses and possibly shifting settlement are particularly difficult to control. Some shifting of residence in Early Classic times, too, may inflate estimates of population for this era, but perhaps the "invisible house" factor offsets this. For the Intermediate and Late Classic, the picture is clearer; although numbers of structures within groups increased somewhat after A.D. 700, numbers of groups themselves remained more or less constant. Then, around A.D. 850, a population crash was underway. All available evidence indicates that this was not a long, drawn-out process but took place relatively rapidly.

The earlier observations that houses and associated outbuildings (such as household shrines, kitchens, and storage facilities) were usually grouped together around the edges of common plazas, that the number of structures in these groups often increased through time (table 4.7), and that they appear to have undergone reconstruction on average once per generation suggest occupancy by extended families. The common association of burials with reconstruction is consistent with this suggested cycle. With few exceptions, interments in favored locations—either a shrine on the east (Plaza Plan 2; see Becker, this volume) or the oldest and most prominent house (Haviland 1988)—are those of males who are thought to have been senior heads of their households (fig. 4.5). Overall, the pattern suggests that residence was commonly patrilocal, although more flexible ambilocality may have characterized Preclassic and Terminal Classic practices (Haviland 1997). Given what we now know about the importance of warfare to the Maya of the Classic period, patrilocality makes sense because warfare is the strongest predictor of this practice cross-culturally (Ember and Ember 1996).

In some instances at Tikal, extended family households appear to have been parts of larger social groupings that are usually interpreted

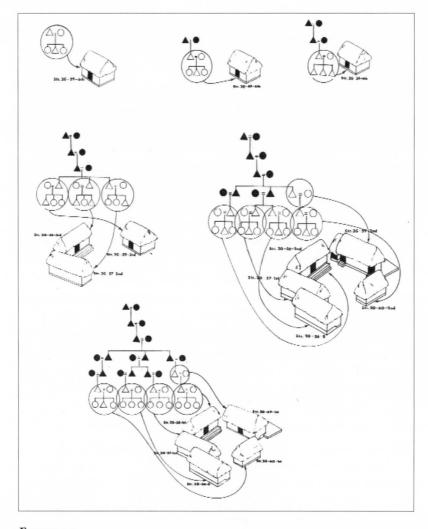

FIGURE 4.5

This drawing of Gp. 2G-1 shows how the group developed over its history and who may have lived in the various structures. The genealogies are reconstructed from burials associated with periodic rebuildings of the houses.

as lineages, that is, corporate groups, membership in which is based on descent (ambilineal, matrilineal, or patrilineal) that can be traced genealogically to a known ancestor (Haviland 2000:610). Because the core members of lineages (those through whom descent is reckoned) commonly live in proximity to one another, the distribution of house-

TABLE 4.7

Numbers of Houses in Best-Known Residential Groups When First Built and When Abandoned

Group or Locus	Number of Original Houses	Total Number of Houses Added	Number of Houses in Use Just Prior to Abandonment
2G-1	1	5	4
Str. 2G-61	1	1	1
3C-1*	1?	1?	2
3D-3	2	3	3
3F-1	1	1	2
3F-2	1	2	3
4E-2	2	2	4
4F-1a*	1 or 2	0 or 1	2
4F-1b	1	1	2
4F-1c	1 or 2	2 or 3	4
4F-2	1	5	4 or 5
4F-3	2	0	2
4G-1	1	3	4
4H-1	?	2	2
4H-4	3	0	3
4H-5*	1?	1?	2?
5B-2	2	0	2
5F-1*	1?	3?	2
5F-2	2	1	3
5G-1	?	5	5
5G-2	2	5	7
6C-1*	1 or 2	2 or 3	4
6C-5	1?	1?	2?
Str. 6C-60	1	2	1
6E-1	1?	4?	2
7C-1	2	0	2
Str. 7C-62	1	0	1

holds might be expected to reflect the existence of lineages. Two likely cases of this at Tikal consist of several groups in proximity to Str. 5G-8 (Becker with Jones 1999) and Groups 4F-1 and 4F-2 (Haviland 1992a:938–39; Haviland et al. 1985:184–85). In both instances, the special nature of founding burials suggests the sort of ancestor veneration characteristic of lineages, numbers of people resident in constituent households are within the expectable range for lineage membership,

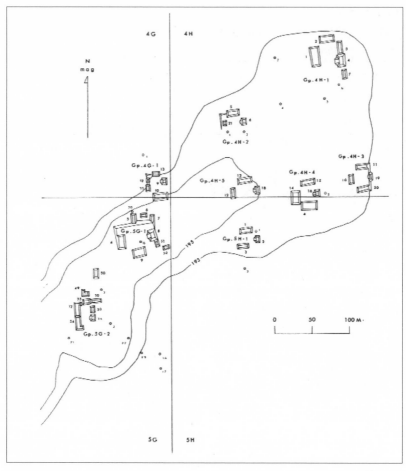

FIGURE 4.6

This relatively discrete grouping of residential compounds may have been occupied by core members of a lineage with their spouses.

and special-purpose buildings (5G-4, 5G-8, and 5G-9 in one instance, 4E-31 in the other) seem appropriate for affairs relating to the several households together (fig. 4.6). While comparable clusters of households exist elsewhere at Tikal—Strs. 3F-11 through 3F-15 and nearby groups, for example—few other such situations are detectable. For this reason, I have argued that lineage organization was not a universal feature of Tikal society in the Classic period (Haviland 1972:5).

Cross-culturally, lineages are typically found in agrarian societies, where they function as landholding corporations, allocating plots as necessary for their members to farm. At Tikal, farmland must have been increasingly scarce by Early Classic times, and by A.D. 550, osteological data suggest that provision of sufficient food for the city's large population had become a problem (Haviland 1967 and in prep.b). Under the circumstances, it seems likely that land management would be taken over by an elite ruling class, which we know was emerging in the first century A.D. (Haviland 1997:9–10; Haviland and Moholy-Nagy 1992:57–58). With this usurpation of lineage functions, exacerbated by the ability to attract or coerce commoners away from their kin to become "live-in" servants in noble households (Haviland 1992a:939), one would expect lineage organization to decline. The exceptions would be in cases where special circumstances favored their continued existence. Among the ruling elite, this ongoing existence might be expected to protect monopolies of power, privilege, and wealth, but what about people of lower social rank?

In Groups 4F-1 and 4F-2, evidence indicates that the occupants were engaged in the specialized production of figurines and objects of shell and obsidian (Haviland et al. 1985:177–78, 184). In those groups focused on Str. 5G-8, occupants appear to have specialized in the production of polychrome ceramics (Becker 1973a). The implication is that those commoner lineages that survived in the Classic period did so because they found functions for themselves other than landholding. In these two cases, they appear to have been transformed into organizations for the production of special goods.

As implied by the above references to elites and commoners, Tikal society was organized by social class, as well as by residence and kinship. Indicators of differential class standing include differential access to favored residential localities, differences in scale of domestic architecture, differential treatment of the dead, differential access to particular kinds of objects and raw material, apparent dietary differences, and differences in "life chances" (see Haviland and Moholy-Nagy 1992:51–57 for discussion). Clearly, the higher a family's social class, the more space its members could command for themselves (in death and in life), the more access they had to other peoples' labor (live-in servants, for example; see Haviland 1992a), the more access they had to wealth goods, and the better their diet and general health.

Unlike the situation at some Classic Maya centers (Copan, for example), class structure at Tikal did not crosscut such lineage membership as existed (Haviland 1992a). Indeed, the origins of social classes at the city may lie in differential ranking of lineages (Haviland and Moholy-Nagy 1992:57–59). Nor was stratification a simple matter of elites versus commoners. For example, the families living in Groups 4F-1 and 4F-2 and the groups focused on Str. 5G-8 stand in fairly sharp contrast to those who lived in major "palaces," such as those of the Central Acropolis. Their status as "commoners" seems clear. Nevertheless, there are clear differences between them, especially in architecture, burials, and life chances. Although there is overlap, the buildings of Groups 4F-1 and 4F-2 are less impressive overall, burials are less reflective of wealth, and differences in physical stature suggest a less favorable diet and overall health status. In all respects, the individuals who used Str. 5G-8 and lived nearby are intermediate between those living in the large, epicentral "palaces" on the one hand and those at the bottom of Tikal's social scale at the other. One hesitates to call them a "middle class," given the meaning of that term in modern industrial societies; the safer course might be to label them an "upper class of commoners."

ELITE CLASS POWER AND THE BOUNDARIES OF TIKAL

The issue of elite class power inevitably draws our attention to the two sets of earthworks, associated with a significant drop-off in settlement density, that mark the northern and southern boundaries of Tikal (fig. 4.7). Each set consists of a deep trench with a parallel raised embankment on the inside. Located 4.6 km. north and ca. 6.5 km. south of the Great Plaza (Puleston 1983:19 and 24), only those on the north have been mapped fully. Running a minimum of 9.5 km. from end to end, excavation reveals the trench to be 4 m. wide and 3 m. deep, with nearly vertical bedrock walls (D. E. Puleston and Callender 1967:42 and fig. 2). The associated embankment, composed of earth and limestone rubble from construction of the trench, survives to a height of 1.75 m. but must originally have stood higher. Faced on either side with limestone rubble, its width is about 5.5 m. (fig. 4.8). Obviously intending to impede the movement of people, the Maya constructed

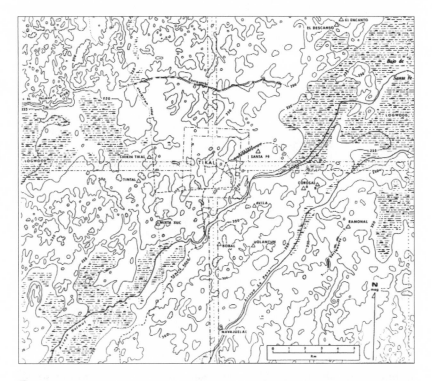

FIGURE 4.7

This drawing shows the northern earthworks and the mapped portion of the southern earthworks of Tikal.

four or five narrow causeways to allow movement across. Clearly, it would provide a strong position for forces defending Tikal against invasion, and I see no reason not to accept Puleston and Callender's (1967:43) suggestion that it was constructed for purposes of defense. While this does not preclude its use as a means of regulating commerce to and from Tikal as well, it is difficult to imagine its construction for that purpose alone.

Though only a small segment of the southern earthworks has been mapped (Puleston 1983:fig.1), it is clear that they closely resemble those on the north and must have been constructed in the same way, for the same purpose. If, like those on the north, they terminated in the bajos east and west of Tikal, then they were at least twice, if not three times, as long.

These earthworks represent major projects undertaken for the

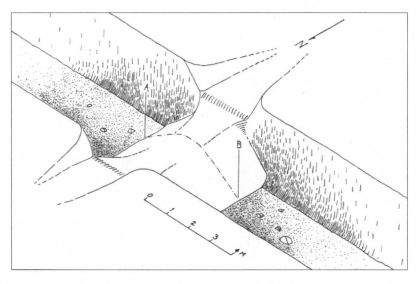

FIGURE 4.8

This drawing is a reconstruction of the north earthworks where a causeway crosses the trench.

public good. The northern trench *alone* required excavation of something like 114,000 m.^{3} of material, which had to be piled up and augmented to form the embankment. Nor was the work over when construction was finished, as constant maintenance was required. As Puleston and Callender (1967:47) note, where the earthworks cross low, swampy areas, each rain causes black muck to flow into the trench. On higher, dryer ground, the problem is not so severe; still, periodic cleaning would have been required lest the effectiveness of the barrier be negated by infilling. With an even more extensive defensive barrier to construct and maintain on the south, the project's magnitude becomes even more impressive. Clearly, the ruler responsible (or rulers, since we do not know that they were constructed at the same time) had considerable power to successfully plan and mobilize the labor force necessary to carry out such large-scale construction and maintenance. It is also clear that Tikal's rulers had reason to fear attack, or there would be little motivation to undertake such a formidable task.

The question is, what Tikal king or kings were responsible for this undertaking? At what time in Tikal's history were the earthworks built, and how might this relate to the growth of Tikal's population? The dating of the earthworks was originally considered by Puleston and Callender (1967:43–45) and later reconsidered by Fry (n.d.). Three excavations carried out by Puleston and Callender (1967:fig.1) provide some data. The westernmost excavation, through a low, swampy area, provided few data of chronological significance. The small quantity of sherds, all from the trench, contained nothing identifiable as other than Preclassic, mostly late, including Terminal Preclassic Cimi. Given the already mentioned tendency for soils to flow into the trench after every rain, it is clear that these sherds were carried in as part of this process. Ceramic testing has documented the presence of Preclassic settlement nearby, and this is the most likely source of the sherds. They could have washed in several centuries after the trench's construction.

The easternmost excavation, too, produced few sherds: two rims and a "handful" of body sherds according to Fry (n.d.), four sherds altogether according to Puleston and Callender (1967). Fry says that all were from the trench, but Puleston and Callender report the presence of one Manik sherd in the original topsoil beneath the embankment. Since they were the excavators, I see no reason not to accept their report. It suggests construction of the earthworks/trench complex after Manik ceramics had been in vogue for enough time for such pottery to have been used, broken, and discarded. However, construction could easily have been two or more centuries after the appearance of Manik pottery.

The third excavation was through one of the causeways that gave access to Tikal from the north. Here, Fry, Puleston, and Callender agree that a Manik sherd (from a basal flange bowl) was found beneath the embankment in ancient topsoil, confirming the discovery in the easternmost excavation. Clearly, the earthworks were constructed sometime after A.D. 250, but how much later is the question. In the trench itself, close to .75 m. of silt had accumulated prior to construction of the causeway. Few sherds, none identifiable as to complex, were present in this silt, nor were many present in the causeway's fill. They, too, were not identifiable; although their paste suggests Manik, this is far from certain. Sherds were, however, abundant on either side of the causeway, above the underlying silt. Of these, 80 percent pertain to the Ik Complex and have identical paste. Only three major shape classes are present: barrel-shaped vases, lateral ridge plates, and pottery drums. While fine pottery was not altogether absent in households some distance away from more elite settings closer to Tikal's center, its sheer quantity, uniformity of paste, and restricted shape inventory here strongly suggest that one or more persons carrying sacks of fine pots to or from Tikal dropped them off the edges of the rather narrow causeway. Another possibility is that the sherds were in material used for a later widening of the causeway, but I consider this less likely. So much fine pottery would probably not be present nearby in trash likely to be drawn on for construction fill. A third possibility, suggested by Fry (n.d.), is that this part of the trench was used opportunistically for the firing of fine pottery. If so, one would expect substantial deposits of ash and charcoal, yet none are mentioned by the excavators. Nor is the situation at all similar to that of the groups in which Becker (1973a) argues that the production of polychrome ceramics took place.

Scattered among these Ik sherds in low frequency were some from Manik and Cauac pottery that likely washed in from surfaces nearby. A scatter of Imix sherds found near the surface is associated with a widening (to 10 m.) of the original causeway. Fry (n.d.) thinks that they may have been scattered by users after the widening, whereas Puleston and Callender (1967) regard them as part of the fill.

What this evidence seems to add up to is this: Use of the original causeway dates to a time when Ik ceramics were in use (between A.D. 550 and 700). The causeway is unlikely to have been constructed before the appearance of such ceramics, or a few Manik pieces might be expected on top of the silt but beneath the Ik deposits. By how much it predates the end of Ik ceramic production we do not know, but it could not have been at the very end. The widening of the causeway appears to be associated with Imix ceramic production.

In his attempt to date the earthworks, Fry (n.d.) considers their resemblance to fortifications at Becan. As he notes, the resemblance is not precise, as the Becan trench is deeper and wider and protects only the central portion of that site. Yet their general resemblance to Tikal's fortifications might support a similar Early Classic time of construction for the latter. He also notes that, like the one causeway investigated at Tikal's northern earthworks, four of seven such causeways were eventually widened at Becan sometime between A.D. 600 and 750. While all of this is consistent with what has already been said of the dating of the Tikal feature, it does not help to pin down the time of construction with any more precision.

A third, indirect way of approaching the problem, explored by Fry (n.d.), has to do with shifts in settlement in areas adjacent to the earthworks. To follow his lead, I have gone back to Puleston's (1973, esp. figs. 12 and 13) original presentation of data from Fry's test pits on the 12 km. north and south survey strips (Puleston 1983:fig.1). Inside the north earthworks, 24 of 71 probable residential groups north of the 16 km.[2] site map were tested, of which 21 certainly and one possibly produced Manik sherds. While a few of these could be identified as early Manik, none could be identified as definitely late. However, most Manik sherds occurred in small numbers at the base of deposits that represent accumulations of material, the bulk of which consists of Late Classic sherds. Only three groups may not have had Late Classic occupations (and even this is uncertain). My interpretation of this is that not all of the Early Classic occupations are contemporary; some groups with early Manik pottery were probably abandoned before most of the other groups were established, likely after the appearance of late Manik pottery.

Thirteen of the tested groups certainly and another six possibly produced Ik pottery; 14 definitely and seven possibly produced Imix pottery. Two that produced Ik produced no Imix, while four with Imix had no earlier Ik. Although it may look as though there was a decline in settlement between the periods when Manik and Imix ceramics were in vogue, I think this was not so. As just noted, not all groups with Manik pottery were necessarily contemporary. It looks to me as though several residential groups were established in the period of late Manik ceramic production, with continued population growth through Ik into Imix times. Assuming that construction of the earthworks provided a sense of security for those living inside this barrier, the founding of several groups toward the end of the Early Classic period might support Puleston's (1973:313) contention that this was the time of the earthworks' construction.

In the intersite area between the earthworks and the outskirts of Jimbal, test pits were sunk in 14 randomly selected residential groups. Thirteen groups produced Manik sherds, seven surely and six possibly Ik sherds, six surely and four possibly Imix sherds. Only one group produced Manik without Ik sherds (but Imix were present). Puleston (1973:313) appears correct in his statement that Early Classic settlement is nearly as dense outside as inside the earthworks. It appears to hold constant during the era of Ik pottery production but then drops off in Imix (Puleston 1973:148, 208, 314). This seems counterintuitive, in view of evidence that movement across the trench was most restricted when Ik pottery was in vogue but less so with the advent of Imix ceramics. Why would settlement be heavier outside the earthworks when Tikal felt the greatest external threat, but less heavy as the city felt less threatened? One possibility is that houses north of the earthworks were abandoned for a period, but one too short for our dating to pick up. Elsewhere at Tikal, evidence suggests that political upsets between A.D. 562 and 682 had little effect on most people. This being so, it may be that those living to the north of the city moved back to their houses as soon as possible after Tikal's defeat. Left unexplained, of course, is the reason why a similar reoccupation to the south did not take place.

Inside the south earthworks, test pits in 29 randomly selected probable residential groups reveal Manik pottery definitely present in 21, possibly present in seven. All but one of these produced Ik sherds, but Imix sherds were present in the latter. Five test pits with Ik produced no Imix, but two without Ik had Imix. It looks as if settlement did not increase or decrease particularly after A.D. 550, until a slight decrease did take place about the time that Imix ceramics appeared.

In the 3.5 km. just south of the earthworks, ten groups were randomly selected for testing, while eight groups were more extensively excavated. Puleston (1973:228) states that Manik sherds were present in eight of ten tests, though his table 13 shows nine probable and one possible. All eight extensively excavated structures produced Manik pottery (Puleston 1973:106). None revealed significant evidence of Late Classic occupation, nor did six of the test pits. Of the other four, Ik (but not Imix) was present in one, two had "very slight" evidence of possible Intermediate or Late Classic pottery, and one had possible Imix (Puleston 1973:228). A sharp decline in settlement in this region of well-drained upland soils is, as Puleston (1973:314, 319) noted, well established. This strongly suggests abandonment of an area beyond newly constructed fortifications.

Although uncertainties remain, it looks to me as though construction of the earthworks took place at the time of, or just before, the inauguration of Wak Chan K'awiil ("Double Bird") as king of Tikal. His accession date (C. Jones and Satterthwaite 1982:table 6), 9.5.3.9.15 (A.D. 537), is shortly before the appearance of Ik ceramics, an event that took place around A.D. 550 in Wak Chan K'awiil's reign. It was in his reign, too, that Tikal suffered a major military defeat at the hands of Caracol or Calakmul (Martin, this volume). Perhaps it was concern over a possible threat from Caracol that led to construction of the southern defenses and near abandonment of settlements outside their protection. Similarly, glyphic evidence indicates that by A.D. 546 Calakmul, located north of Tikal, was becoming a force to be reckoned with (S. Martin and Grube 1995:45), perhaps triggering construction of the northern defenses. Prior to his later military misfortunes, Wak Chan K'awiil appears to have begun his career as king with sufficient strength to see to his city's fortification. As Martin notes (this volume), his accession represented a dynastic refounding, and he enjoyed wide power beyond Tikal.

Wak Chan K'awiil was the first ruler to be buried (in Bu. 200) with Ik ceramics (Haviland 1994:267). The last was the one buried in Bu. 24 (W. R. Coe 1990:543; once considered the tomb of an associate of Nuun Ujol Chaak ("Shield Skull"), Tikal's 25th numbered king and thought to be the subject of Bu. 23, it now appears that the latter may be the tomb of the 23rd ruler, with Bu. 24 that of his successor; see Martin, this volume). Throughout this time, access to and from Tikal across the earthworks remained restricted. When Nuun Ujol Chaak died, his son, Jasaw Chan K'awiil, became king, in 9.12.9.17.16 (A.D. 682; C. Jones and Satterthwaite 1982:table 6). Associated with his rise to power was replacement of Ik by Imix ceramics, following which the access causeways were widened. This act suggests an increased confidence on the part of Tikaleños, no doubt related to Jasaw's military successes (S. Martin and Grube 1995:45). Even so, there was no rush to resettle previously abandoned land to the south. To the contrary, some previously occupied residential groups to the north were abandoned. Since Calakmul was no longer much of a threat, there must be some other explanation for this. It might be the case that the new king brought more people into the city for work other than food production. But, as alluded to earlier in this chapter, osteological evidence indicates that by ca. A.D. 550 undernutrition had become widespread at Tikal. Could it be that, in the face of food shortfalls induced (or at least exacerbated) by previous decades of conflict, Jasaw Chan K'awiil used his power to promote farming rather than settlement in these rural areas? Perhaps we shall never know, but Jasaw clearly was a powerful king, and by preventing resettlement to the south and encouraging removal from the north, he would have maximized the land available for production of food to feed the hungry people of the city.

FINAL REFLECTIONS

Writing exactly 40 years after settlement studies began at Tikal, I can say that we have a reasonable understanding of the nature of settlement, demography, and social organization at the site. Though Tikal shares many elements in common with other Classic centers, in some ways it is unique (see Haviland 1992a). No doubt its distinctive features relate to historic contingency, as well as its unusually large size. In any event, just as we should be cautious about generalizing from other Maya sites—especially smaller ones—so should we be cautious about generalizing from Tikal. Variation surely existed within the Classic Maya world, but we need to have a better understanding of it.

The fact that we have a reasonable understanding of the topics addressed here does not mean that there is not more to learn. This is most evident in connection with the earthworks scenario described above. Nothing is more important than further work on the earthworks, which define the ultimate extent of Tikal. While those on the north have been adequately mapped, those on the south have not. They need to be, but to do so will undoubtedly require excavation to confirm their presence where surface traces cannot now be seen. Excavations beneath the embankment are needed for purposes of dating. The same is true for causeways, assuming that such exist. The northern earthworks, too, are deserving of further attention. Additional excavation of the earthen parapet has the potential of providing better sherd samples for dating. Excavation of one or more of those causeways that have not yet been investigated could also provide tighter chronological control. Here is an opportunity for important, problem-oriented research; let us hope someone rises to the challenge.

5

The Peripheries of Tikal

Robert E. Fry

The investigation of the peripheries of Tikal began as an attempt to find the boundaries of the numerous groups of structures surrounding the epicenter of the site. Early settlement surveys in the Maya Lowlands, such as the Ricketsons' cruciform survey at Uaxactun (Ricketson and Ricketson 1937), the first systematic survey beyond the edges of a site core, had merely sought out the range of structure types around a center. Bullard's trailside surveys of the late 1950s (Bullard 1960) indicated that settlement density in remote areas of the Petén were surprisingly higher than were thought possible, given the supposed dispersed nature of slash-and-burn agricultural systems. The mapping of the 16 sq. km. map around central Tikal also had shown no natural boundaries within the areas mapped (Carr and Hazard 1961). The Tikal Sustaining Area Project was created in order to ascertain the limits to a major ancient Maya center (D. E. Puleston 1983). Systematic mapping and excavation eventually led to the definition of its epicentral and central zones based on density and size of groups of structures. Areas of less dense population were defined as peripheral Tikal, while the formal boundaries of the Tikal earthworks were used to define the boundary of Tikal with intersite areas (see D. E. Puleston 1983 for definitions). The focus of this chapter is the relationships among peripheral Tikal, central Tikal, and intersite areas north and south of Tikal (fig. 5.1) in light of the changing views on the nature of Maya sites over the past 30 years. I will be concerned with the nature of the boundaries of Tikal as an entity and with the nature of economic interaction and social variation within peripheral areas of the site and larger regional contexts. I will refer primarily to the ceramics from peripheral Tikal, but other data will be used to supplement this primary ceramic focus.

Another major research objective involved the relationship of Tikal with its hinterland. What were the agricultural necessities required by the population of Tikal, and what were its relationships with the surrounding rural communities? The concept of a sustaining area reflected the assumption that each site would have a proximate rural-settlement zone that would provide the basic foodstuffs necessary for the elite and other population resident at the center. Each center would have a sphere of support and influence proportional to its resident population. Of course, there were alternative views of the nature of Maya sites. Robert Rands in his important 1967 article discussed two polar models: an inward-looking model that saw Maya sites as being semiautonomous and relatively self-sufficient units with a high degree of focused economic activity, and an outward-looking model suggesting that individual households or groups of households had less obligatory ties to nearby centers and a more voluntaristic association with a number of centers (Rands 1967). In the latter model, economic ties were thus less affected by mere proximity. I tested these alternative models using ceramic data from peripheral Tikal. My studies of distributional patterns of locally produced ceramics strongly supported the inward-looking model for Tikal (Fry 1969, 1979; Fry and Cox, 1974).

BOUNDARIES OF TIKAL

The question of whether there had been formal boundaries to Tikal was answered positively with the discovery of the northern Tikal earthworks in 1966 during the mapping of the north survey strip (D. E. Puleston and Callender 1967). Survey in 1967 encountered a similar earthworks and moat system located southeast of the site center, though the full extent of the system could not be determined. Its rela-

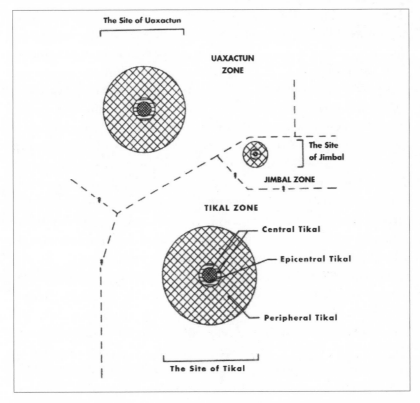

FIGURE 5.1

Schematic presentation of the terms used to describe the main subdivisions of Tikal and Jimbal. From Tikal Report No. 13 (Puleston 1983).

tionships to the northern earthworks are still unknown because traces of such systems are not readily apparent from the surface in intervening *bajo* areas. Dating of the northern earthworks proved a challenge. Since there were few households or other structures with abundant occupation debris near the earthworks, few sherds were found in the construction fill of features. Excavation within one of the ramparts showed at least that portion of the earthworks had not been constructed before Manik ceramics were in use. The earthworks do not show signs of active use, as seen at sites such as Becan, where causeways were chopped out (Webster 1976). Thus, we had to date termination by use of the ditch in ways that would have impaired its functioning for defensive purposes. We found abundant pottery (very scarce in other excavations) in a thick deposit adjacent to one of the causeways. This deposit would have compromised the effectiveness of the very narrow causeway. These ceramics are uniformly from the Ik ceramic complex. This implies that use of this portion of the earthworks was at least impaired by Ik-complex times. I have argued that this deposit was the byproduct of deliberate use of the ditch as a firing channel by potters (Fry 1979). Over 90 percent of the pottery recovered from the ditch was of a locally distinctive Saxche paste variant, with only three shapes represented: barrel-shaped vases, flaring-side dishes, and pottery drums. This argues for an Early Classic date of construction for the northern earthworks and a cessation of major use during Ik-complex times. (Compare this argument with the discussion in Haviland, this volume.) In addition, testing of large-structure groups north of (outside) the earthworks indicated the initiation of construction at the end of the Early Classic. Thus, it is possible that the abandonment may have been even earlier, in the later Early Classic.

If the period of use of the earthworks was significantly long and the challenge to the site core serious enough (Martin, this volume; Haviland, this volume), some impact should be seen in the distribution of settlement. Although the excavation strategy of the peripheral-area test-pitting program resulted in the highest reliability for the latest periods of occupation, it is clear that there was a major pullback of population from habitable areas in peripheral Tikal and intersite areas near Tikal during the earlier portion of the Early Classic period (Fry 1969; D. E. Puleston 1973). Sampling of structures to the north of the earthworks shows that many of them—including the largest complexes of mounds, bordering in size on that of Minor Centers—show initial construction during the later portion of the Early Classic. These continued to be occupied throughout most of the Late Classic. This pattern would also support an inference of a middle Early Classic date for construction and major use of the northern earthworks.

Boundaries for earlier and later periods are more difficult to reconstruct. The southeastern earthworks was not traced over an extensive area and was never tested. The southeastern earthworks is similar to the northern earthworks in scale and in distance from the center. Although it is also highly likely to be an Early Classic construction, this remains an untested hypothesis. Extensive areas of *bajo* with low or no occupation serve as natural breaks in the distribution of settlement. The Tikal-Yaxha transect survey by Ford (1981a, 1986, 1991) did not generate data adequate to demonstrate whether there are settlement-density dropoffs in the Early Classic. The more recent research of the Proyecto Triangular–Intersitios (Fialko 1995; Fialko and Culbert 1999) will make such definition much more clear-cut. Preliminary reports indicate that in the Early Classic Minor Centers to the southeast of Tikal, Uolantun and Corozal "had been incorporated as part of the sub-urban system of Tikal" (Fialko and Culbert 1999:8). They also state that "by Tepeu 2, Chalpate, the main political center in the Bajo de Santa Fe, had probably been incorporated within the expanding suburban zone of Tikal" (Fialko and Culbert 1999:9).

CERAMIC DISTRIBUTION AS EVIDENCE FOR SITE BOUNDARIES AND REGIONAL INTERACTION

Another method for discerning community boundaries uses the distribution of commonly used artifacts, especially if there is a formal marketing system present. Sharp boundaries in the mix of locally produced items can give clues about the presence and location of economic boundaries. It has even been suggested that the Tikal earthworks may have functioned more effectively as a commercial barrier than as a defensive one. Ceramics are one of the best indicators, being very common and being produced in large quantities at a number of specialized centers during the Classic. Because of the emphasis on testing for occupation debris (Fry 1972), we encountered few burials and no caches in the test-pitting program and none earlier than the Late Classic. The more extensive excavations at Uolantun and Navahuelal (Green 1970) produced caches and several additional burials with accompanying ceramic vessels. The bulk of the collections derive from occupation debris contexts.

Middle Preclassic occupation was difficult to find, given the emphasis on house mounds dating primarily to the Classic period and the sampling strategy used (Fry 1972). The bulk of ceramics from the Eb and Tzec phases came from the tunneling in the main temple at Uolantun (Structure SE[S]-486). Only scattered occupation was found elsewhere, mainly on ridge tops. The fill ceramics recovered from Uolantun are very close to the norms of Middle Preclassic ceramics from central Tikal. The only widely traded exotic ceramics are of the Savanna Orange Group from Uolantun and a small possible temple located at the edge of peripheral Tikal (Structure NE[N]-60). Occupation dating to the Late Preclassic (Chuen, Cauac complexes) was much more widespread in peripheral Tikal, with construction at a series of public buildings at sites such as Uolantun and Structure NE-N-60. The ceramic uniformity of the Late Preclassic does not allow us to create boundaries based on the distribution of types or varieties. The only collection with a significant number of exotic types, comparable to those of central Tikal, came from in front of Structure NE(N)-65. This collection mainly derived from the filling of a chultun (NE[N]-35) in the plaza in front of the structure. It contained several imported examples of Flor Cream and Chic Red-on-orange-trickle decorated dishes reminiscent of pseudo-Usulutan. The bulk of the deposit consisted of Sierra Red bowls, vases, and medial-ridge bowls. Uolantun does not seem to have had as many exotics as the materials from the north-survey-strip chultun.

Early Classic Manik-complex ceramics are much more frequently encountered than Preclassic in the peripheral zone collections. Minor Centers, including Navahuelal and Santa Fe, were constructed. Early in the Early Classic a stela was erected at Uolantun (S. Martin 1998c, this volume), and there was also more investment in construction. Norms of pottery production are almost as uniform at the regional level in the Early Classic as in the Late Preclassic. Cache vessels fit closely with central Tikal shapes and slips (figs. 5.2, 5.3). Peripheral-area collections differ from Central Tikal collections in the paucity of polychromes like Dos Arroyos Orange polychromes. This may in part be a result of our concentration on house-structure sampling and construction fills rather than burials. One unique settlement just south of the Laguna Verde *aguada* on the south survey strip was more extensively tested. The settlement dated to very early in the period of use of Manik ceramics— Manik I. It was apparently a rural community with relatively small household groups centered on a 9-m.-high public building. Excavations produced limited quantities of occupation debris, perhaps reflecting a relatively short-term occupation. This settlement was unique in showing no evidence of construction in the later Early Classic or Late Classic, thus revealing a more intact Early Classic community.

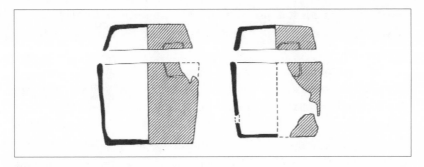

FIGURE 5.2

Early Classic cylindrical cache vessels from Cache 215, Navahuelal.

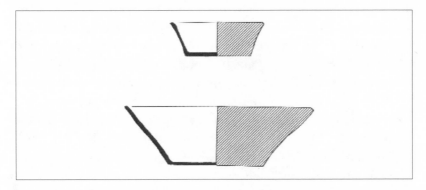

FIGURE 5.3

Early Classic dish-shaped cache vessels: large vessel from Cache 215 at Navahuelal; small vessel from Cache 219 at Uolantun.

The reasons for the abandonment of the community are not obvious. It was located in excellent agricultural lands. The increasing centralization at Tikal later in the Early Classic may have recruited this population or coerced it into close proximity. It is also possible that clashes with competing polities may have forced the community from its economically favorable location. Later in the Early Classic, some of the previously more autonomous communities were abandoned or at least ceased construction at public buildings, including communities such as Uolantun. It is worth speculating that these changes were largely directed by the political changes taking place during the Early Classic. Unfortunately, the lack of more tightly definable ceramic complexes and the lack of diagnostics in the peripheral-area collections leaves the settlement changes still too imprecise in time to be tied directly to the vicissitudes and triumphs of Tikal's Early Classic political elite (Martin, this volume).

We have more clear-cut examples of economic boundedness in the Late Classic. Most of the structures, with the few exceptions given above, were occupied during the time periods when both Ik and Imix complexes were in use. My earlier studies have demonstrated a high degree of specialization in ceramics within the peripheries of Tikal (Fry and Cox 1974, Fry 1979). The most parsimonious explanation for the observed distribution is a complex marketing system, with more localized consumption of less portable wares such as large coarse-ware jars and a larger radius of circulation for utilitarian wares such as Tinaja Red bowls and jars. The vessels with the widest circulation would have been serving wares, especially the beautiful vases, bowls, and dishes and plates of the Saxche and Palmar Groups. Paste similarities between some vessels in the Saxche and Palmar Groups and some of the monochrome utilitarian wares (probably Tinaja Red) indicate to me that some workshops made almost the total range of slipped ceramics. It is likely that others produced only unslipped utilitarian wares. The distribution patterns of coarse wares are less synchronous with those of slipped wares, and it is likely that separate production centers were involved (Fry and Cox 1974). Except for the possible firing area for Saxche vases and drums, we found no direct evidence for specialized pottery production. We still do not know if there were large sections of whole communities involved primarily in pottery production or widely scattered households with a low proportion in any one neighborhood or community—a topic for further research.

I used a standard geography formula based on population size for determining the potential break point for the Late Classic boundary between Tikal and the nearby center of Jimbal. I originally assumed populations of 50,000 for Tikal and 10,000 for Jimbal, given the relative density of population and the size of the centers. Recent estimates for Tikal are substantially higher (Culbert et al. 1990), but the relationship is probably not that different because the Late and Terminal Classic settlement of Jimbal and intersite areas near Jimbal is substantial. The formula predicted a boundary between 8 and 9 km. north of the site center. To test whether such a boundary could be delimited, I examined the patterns of resemblance of collections of single-shape classes from the sampled settlement areas north and south of Tikal in peripheral and intersite areas, plus selected contexts from central and epicentral Tikal. My earlier research indicated that the circulation patterns of serving wares and slipped utilitarian large bowls would be the best measures to discern a boundary of interaction. Narrow-mouth jars were more likely to be circulated over large geographic areas, due to their scarceness and the high desirability of certain high-quality workshop products (R. H. Thompson 1958). Heavy and bulky wide-mouth jars would have been more likely to demonstrate supply-zone behavior (Renfrew 1977), with distribution limited to areas of easiest access. In the Tikal region, unlike other areas in the Maya Lowlands, there would have been fewer large streams or watercourses to facilitate canoe-based hauling of bulkier items.

Since collections were not very large for most of the sampled groups, collections were aggregated by sampling stratum (Fry and Cox 1974). Measures of similarity for aggregated collections using stylistic characteristics of the pottery were utilized to examine whether stylistic boundaries were present in the collections. The basic assumption is that although the pooled collections of each shape class would contain examples from a variety of sources, proximate assemblages would resemble each other if they shared a large number of vessels from the same source. If there was a strong economic boundary, fewer vessels would have been traded across the boundary, and this collection would be sharply distinguished from collections inside the boundary. Technological characteristics were rejected for this analysis because clay and paste similarity might be related to localized clay sources, which—given the relative uniformity of the geological substrate at Tikal—might not show any discrete source patterning.

Figure 5.4 shows the location of the grouped assemblages used in the analysis. The pattern of similarity picked out by the multidimensional scaling programs can be seen in figures 5.5–5.8. The solutions for Ik-complex serving wares (figs. 5.5, 5.6) tend to treat ceramics from Jimbal and the area north of the proposed boundary as quite distinct, the Jimbal area being placed at some distance from the other samples. This breaks down in the analysis of Imix-complex serving forms (figs. 5.7, 5.8). Here the Jimbal area collections are not placed at such a

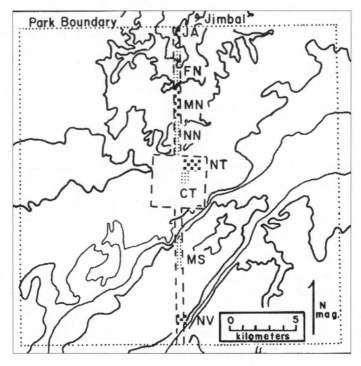

FIGURE 5.4

Map of the Tikal zone showing the location of grouped collections in peripheral and central Tikal used in the analysis.

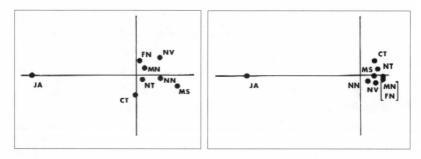

FIGURE 5.5

Two-dimensional multidimensional scaling solution for Ik-complex vases. Stress is .012.

FIGURE 5.6

Two-dimensional multidimensional scaling solution for Ik-complex plates. Stress is .012.

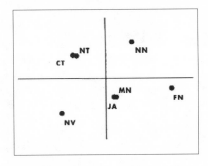 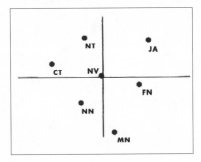

FIGURE 5.7

Two-dimensional multidimensional scaling solution for Imix-complex vases. Stress is .042.

FIGURE 5.8

Two-dimensional multidimensional scaling solution for Imix-complex plates. Stress is .091.

distance, and in the case of cylindrical vases are not distinct at all. This tends to confirm that as far as utilitarian ceramics are concerned, Tikal was a bounded economic unit in the earlier Late Classic. The boundary may have broken down during the time of use of Imix ceramics. I have modified the map from TR 13 to demonstrate where I think the boundaries of Early Late Classic Tikal may have been (fig. 5.9).

New pottery-paste traditions and even more distant sources of pottery were encountered in the Terminal Classic, during the period of use of Eznab ceramics. More imported pottery is found, even in serving wares. New shape classes such as tripod *molcajete* bowls appear (fig. 5.10). Sites such as Navahuelal, which previously had norms that were close to central Tikal and received pottery that may have been distributed throughout the central Tikal market, began to show resemblance to more distant sites. The Terminal Classic cache from in front of the main temple of the central groups at Navahuelal has a cache vessel closely resembling Eznab-phase cache vessels (fig. 5.11), but the plate and dish from the same cache more closely resemble vessels from near the Petén-Belize border to the east (figs. 5.12, 5.13). New wares include Altar Orange and Pabellon Modelled carved from sources in the Pasión–Upper Usamacinta region (Bishop 1994). This further opening up of the system of production and consumption does not betoken an even greater commercialization. The Terminal Classic at Tikal is a period of steep decline in local population. It is likely that many potters

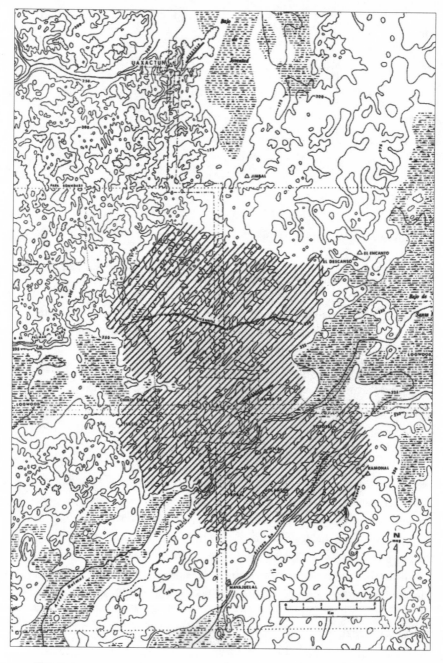

FIGURE 5.9

Boundaries of early Late Classic Tikal, based on settlement density and economic interaction (modified from a figure appearing in TR 13 [Puleston 1983]).

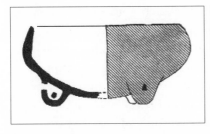

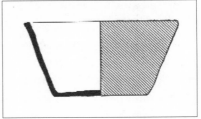

FIGURE 5.10

Eznab-complex tripod redware vessel from Uolantun.

FIGURE 5.11

Eznab-complex cache vessel from Burial 206, Navahuelal.

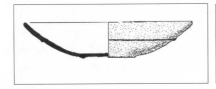

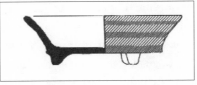

FIGURE 5.12

Eznab-complex polychrome plate from Burial 206, Navahuelal.

FIGURE 5.13

Eznab-complex polychrome dish from Burial 206, Navahuelal.

had to restrict production or even give up manufacture and/or emigrate. The diversity we see may reflect the shambles of a collapsing system. New centers that arose would have also attracted interest in consumption of their own distinctive pottery types.

SOCIAL DIFFERENTIATION IN PERIPHERAL TIKAL

The social position of residents in peripheral Tikal compared to central and epicentral Tikal can be assessed by a number of means, including volumetric assessment of households, or the number of courtyards in multiple-courtyard grouping. This, however, may be unduly influenced by the length of occupational history. Incremental additions in generation upon generation of remodeling and expansion can create an impressive mass of architecture. Another means of assessment is the nature of the architecture itself, with a continuum of construction choices from ground-level or near ground-level construction with a platform edging and pole-and-thatch construction through masonry, including corbel-vaulted roofs and impressive high platforms. This elaboration is still not completely coterminous with simple volumetrics. Associated artifacts have also been used to infer social position, despite negative evidence from ethnoarchaeological studies (Hayden and Cannon 1984). Certain items may be indices of relatively high social status, from decorative items such as stelae and carved thrones to portable personal items such as fans (shell-fan handles), sandals, and so forth. Often, as in the case of peripheral Tikal, these are not numerous enough to reach the level of statistical significance. In order to search for patterning in the more common attributes, I undertook a factor analysis using data from the midden debris from peripheral Tikal, with enough artifacts to provide reasonable statistical grounding for the analysis. As variables, I included frequencies of vessel shapes, counts of vessels present, counts of artifacts, and counts of chert and obsidian debitage. A total of 84 assemblages were used in the analysis from both the north and south survey strips. All of the excavations were test pits chosen using the stratified random-sampling research design of the peripheral Tikal test-pitting program (Fry 1969). The major factors that were discriminated confirmed my classifications based on assessment of raw-artifact category frequencies: workshops, with high frequencies of obsidian cores; a small house mound, with polished axes and some fine Saxche bowls; a place of primary chert reduction.

The first three factors seem to be the most significant and useful, with a falloff in eiegnvalues below the first three. These three factors explain in total about 44 percent of the variance in the data. Factor 1, which I call the occupational midden factor, has an eigenvalue of 8.38, which explains 24 percent of the variance. Simply an occupational deposit dominated by pottery, it includes all but two of the pottery-shape classes. It also includes the total number of vessels that actually had the highest loading. These are the large midden deposits, which tend to be dominated by pottery, with only a few categories of other artifacts that are not consistently associated. Factor 2, the lithic workshop, has an eigenvalue of 4.31 and explains 12.4 percent of the variance. This is an obvious lithic workshop factor, dominated by broken and unbroken chert nodules and obsidian chips. Loading at a lower level on this factor is one shape variety of large redware bowls. This may be a chronological marker or simply an artifact of the program. Factor 3 had an eigenvalue of 3.91 and explains 11.2 percent of the variance. This unique factor included jadeite celts (very rare in peripheral collections), round-side vases, pointed flakes, and used and unused flakes. It is likely that this is a woodworking shop for making fine finished items. There is only one locus, on the Bobal ridge on the south survey strip. This group was also distinctive because of the discovery of several fine Saxche Orange polychrome bowl fragments, which are associated with this small, unprepossessing group. The other three factors have much lower loadings and explain between 6 and 7 percent of the variance each. Two have higher frequencies of obsidian, one with used and retouched chert flakes, the other with biface tools and metate fragments. These may well be workshops that used obsidian as part of the production process, perhaps for working organic material or possibly for woodworking or even textile making or featherwork. The other factor includes cores and biface ovates. Loading lower are pottery panpipes, biface elongates, and unused flakes, which may also be due to a temporal factor.

It is my impression that basic agricultural tools such as biface ovates are proportionately more frequent in Eznab times than earlier in the peripheries. Given the evidence in support of dispersed production of craft items and/or elite ritual paraphernalia in peripheral Tikal, is it possible that many of the residents of Classic-period peripheral Tikal and intersite areas within the Tikal zone were not involved in any major agricultural production? Did the collapse of the Maya realm at Tikal at the beginning of Eznab times doom the remaining local population to a reversion to subsistence agriculture? The relative frequencies of differing classes of tools or debitage and ratios of obsidian to chert did not provide any consistent pattern in the data. This is not unexpected, as a wide range of activities went on at household groupings, including production of craft items and of items used to legitimize social, religious, or political rank. Vagaries of refuse disposal and sampling anomalies might also obscure any clear-cut indicative signals in the assemblages.

SHAPE COUNTS, WEALTH, AND SOCIAL RANK

In the first stage of my research on social variation in peripheral

TABLE 5.1

Percentage of Shape Classes—Early Classic

Shape Class	Navahuelal Fill Sample SE(S) – 430	SE(S) – 382 SW(S) – 157
Serving forms	66%	28%
Monochrome bowls	28%	25%
Slipped jars	2%	19%
Unslipped jars	4%	28%

Tikal, I did cross-tabulations of shape classes to see whether there were any social factors reflected in the relative frequencies of differing shape classes of pottery. It is generally assumed that greater wealth should be reflected in both higher-quality pottery and/or a higher frequency of functionally redundant serving forms—vases, small bowls, and dishes. Social rank was inferred from a typology using numbers of plaza groups and average structure height. Minor Centers (D. E. Puleston 1983) were groupings with one or more large, temple-type constructions and large plazas, as exemplified by sites such as Navahuelal and Bobal. Large structures had two or more plazas in most cases and had an unexcavated mound height of 3 m. or more. Medium-size structures had a mound elevation ranging from 1.5 to 3 m., while small structures had elevations of under 1.5 m. There were only scattered examples of occupational debris from the Preclassic periods, so no assessment could be made of variability in ceramic assemblages from the earliest time periods.

There were very few collections with enough vessels to be reliable for the Early Classic Manik complex. I compared the two largest assemblages from Structures SE(S)-382 and SW(S)-157 and the fill of the main temple in the central group at Navahuelal SE(S)-430 (table 5.1). The latter was a redeposited fill context, but it did have many midden-like characteristics, including a pure later Manik deposit with large sherds having relatively fresh breaks. The comparison shows a very high frequency of serving forms for the Navahuelal sample. The small house-mound sample had few serving forms and a high frequency of slipped jars, higher than Manik averages.

There were more abundant data for the Late Classic, with many more occupation middens and relatively pure deposits (table 5.2). As expected, the largest residential structures had proportionately higher

TABLE 5.2

Percentage of Shape Classes for Differing Size House-Mound Groups—Late Classic

Shape Class	Minor Centers No.	Minor Centers %	Large Mound No.	Large Mound %	Medium Mound No.	Medium Mound %	Small Mound No.	Small Mound %	Peripheral Tikal %	Central Tikal %
Serving vessels	101	34%	110	51%	163	41%	104	41%	42%	42%
Large slipped bowls	106	35%	39	18%	103	24%	60	24%	27%	20%
Narrow-mouth jars	45	15%	19	9%	36	12%	31	12%	12%	14%
Unslipped wide-mouth jars	49	16%	46	22%	93	23%	58	23%	19%	24%
Total vessels	301		214		395		253			

frequencies of serving forms than were found in medium-size or smaller structure groups, which tended to be quite similar. One of the most significant ceramic associations of larger groupings, however, is the simplest measure—the number of vessels represented. Such activities as feasting by higher-rank individuals could have led to a much higher consumption of all classes of pottery vessels. Overall proportions of shape classes tended to be very close to the proportion recovered from central and epicentral Tikal contexts. The major differences are a somewhat higher proportion of slipped large bowls and a lower frequency of unslipped wide-mouth jars. This may relate to a higher proportion of cooking in the residential zones of peripheral Tikal and a somewhat lower need for storage. A surprising finding was the low frequency of serving vessels at small centers and the higher proportion of both slipped large bowls and narrow-mouth jars. I would have predicted a profile closer to that of large households. It may be that public feasting rituals, involving larger groups and without a need for serving vessels, may have been an activity at the small centers. Another confounding factor may be the high frequency of Eznab-period occupation at the centers in comparison to occupation in central and epicentral Tikal. However, the Eznab complex, although witnessing a sharp decline in the use of serving vessels, also sees a sharp increase in the use of wide-mouth jars, which is the opposite of the pattern in peripheral Tikal.

SOCIAL RANK AND THE CONSUMPTION
OF CERAMICS IN PERIPHERAL TIKAL

Over the years, I have investigated several means of assessing social-group differences. One approach, which uses the production-step method, has been used with success elsewhere in highland Mesoamerica (Feinman 1982) and in the Maya Lowlands (LeCount 1996; Heredia 1998; Heredia and Fry n.d.). One major drawback preventing the use of this technique in peripheral Tikal was the lack of well-preserved surfaces. In the case of the better-preserved Early Classic collections, it is clear that the serving wares from peripheral areas of the site were much less likely to be painted or elaborately decorated than those from epicentral and central Tikal.

In order to extract information on status differences from both central and peripheral Tikal, I used multidimensional scaling analysis of attributes of differing shape classes of pottery. All larger collections recovered by the random sampling test pits along the north and south survey strips were included. In addition, I included collections from the nonrandom excavations in the small, nucleated groups of Bobal and Navahuelal, oversampled large groups from the north survey strip, and ceramics from small-scale excavations at Jimbal. For central Tikal, I used ceramics from excavations off the East Plaza, which probably came from the marketplace located there (C. Jones 1996), and ceramics from adjacent portions of the Central Acropolis. In addition, I used ceramics from excavations by William Haviland in the northeast quadrant of central Tikal (Haviland 1963). Only specimens representing separate vessels were used in the analysis. Ceramics were coded using a standardized format for 19 technological, functional, and stylistic attributes. These were also categorized using the Tikal shape-classification system. No surface-finish attributes were coded, since only a few of the vessel fragments had sufficient slip preservation.

Although I intended to utilize ceramics from individual household clusters as the minimal unit of analysis, the small sample size precluded any meaningful comparison and would have severely limited the number of cases. Instead, I combined all the vessel samples from within each sampled universe and Minor Center in peripheral Tikal within the fourfold group typology. The same fourfold classification of groups and the same criteria that I used in the earlier research were used again. I also included a separate ceremonial category for the public architecture of Minor Centers such as Bobal and Navahuelal. Thus, a data point in the solution for far north Tikal would reflect the pooled characteristics of middle-size mound groups in that area. The solutions present the scaling of resemblances of these pooled provenience contexts. Nine technological variables that could be considered to represent vessel quality were selected for this analysis, including paste texture, temper frequency, and firing characteristics. It was assumed that higher-quality pastes would tend to have less temper and smaller temper size and would show better control of firing. Separate analyses were run for six major shape classes of pottery, two for vases of differing time periods and one each for serving plates, large bowls and basins, narrow-mouth jars, and wide-mouth jars. Separate analyses for each shape class meant that differences in frequencies of these classes, with their differing paste characteristics, would not skew the results.

In an exploratory analysis, one should be able to predict the outcomes—where the various groupings of shape classes should fit in multidimensional space. If quality was being properly assessed by the variables used, one would predict that large groups would have the highest-quality pottery and smaller groups would have lower-quality pottery. There would be an axis in the graph reflecting consumption of high-quality pottery. Another axis might reflect proximity to a major source. In an earlier article, I emphasized that the central market at Tikal was marked by extremely high-quality, well-fired pottery (Fry 1979). Proximity and access to the market should affect the position of even lower-rank households in the central portion of the site, making them similar to higher-ranking ones.

I will start with the analysis of serving vessels. Such vessels are found in most household debris, making up 51 percent of vessels from large mound groups down to 41 percent at medium and small mound groups (see table 5.2). The multidimensional scaling solution for the Ik-complex barrel-shaped vases is presented in figure 5.14.

Stress, the measure of quality of fit, was quite acceptable at .086.

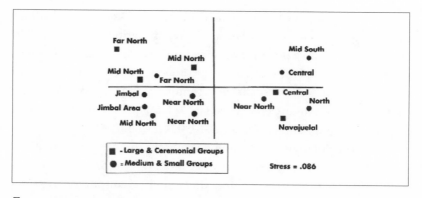

FIGURE 5.14

Social variation in peripheral Tikal. Two-dimensional multidimensional scaling solution for Ik-complex vases. Stress is .086.

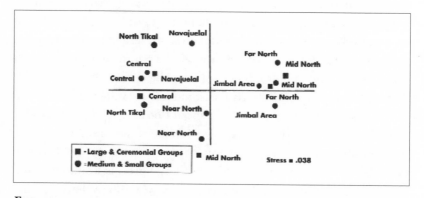

FIGURE 5.15

Social variation in peripheral Tikal. Two-dimensional multidimensional scaling solution for Imix-complex vases. Stress is .038.

The solution does demonstrate some emphases on rank differences. There is less obvious clustering by geographic area. The three cases in the upper-right quadrant are medium and small groups from central and southern parts of the site, but the group in the lower-right quadrant is an assortment of all ranks from the central and southern portions of the site. The sites to the left of the axis are all from the north survey strip, with the lower quadrant largely from medium and small groups and the upper quadrant mainly from large and ceremonial ones. The multidimensional scaling solution for Imix-complex cylindrical

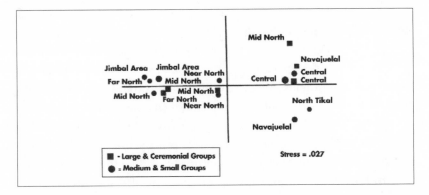

FIGURE 5.16

Social variation in peripheral Tikal. Two-dimensional multidimensional scaling solution for Imix-complex plates. Stress is .027.

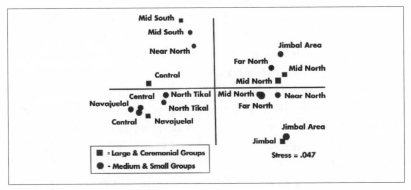

FIGURE 5.17

Social variation in peripheral Tikal. Two-dimensional multidimensional scaling solution for Late Classic large slipped bowls. Stress is .047.

vases is seen in figure 5.15, where stress was .038 for the two-dimensional solution. There are two broad groupings, based more on geography than rank. For the Imix vases, geography trumps social factors.

There were not enough cases to make the analysis of Ik-complex plates and dishes feasible. The solution for Imix-complex plates and shallow dishes (fig. 5.16) has an excellent stress of .027. At the left can be seen one tight cluster near the axis, all from the northern portion of the north survey strip and the Jimbal area. A smaller cluster near the intersection of the axes is mainly from the near and mid-north survey strips. Another tight cluster near the axis on the right side is from central Tikal, near the marketplace, and from ceremonial associations at Navahuelal, while the cluster on the lower right represents the small structure from northeast central Tikal and medium-size structures from near Navahuelal. Geography again tends to be more important than rank, with the unique case of Navahuelal once again.

In the solutions for more utilitarian pottery, we would not expect a factor for quality, especially for the large coarse-ware jars. These seem to have been produced by different workshops than the slipped vessels and to have had a more supply-zone pattern of distribution, being highly localized. On the other hand, water-carrying jars were often a class of ceramic with potentially greater prestige value, being widely traded in colonial Yucatan and often the most highly decorated of utilitarian vessels (R. H. Thompson 1958).

The solution for large slipped bowls and basins is presented in figure 5.17, with a stress of .047. Here there is a tight cluster of items from central Tikal and from Navahuelal. Another cluster on the upper-left quadrant is from the mid-south and near-north survey areas, again with mixed rank. Yet another large, loose cluster on the center of the right side is from the north survey strip, again at all ranks, while a smaller cluster in the lower portion of the same side is from Jimbal and its vicinity. Again, social rank does not emerge as very powerful, except in the case of Navahuelal.

Stress was low, at .033, for slipped narrow-mouth jars (fig. 5.18). There are three distinct clusters, again mostly geographical: one cluster predominantly from the far-north survey areas and Jimbal on the upper left; another cluster, including central and northeast Tikal, Navahuelal, and the small, nucleated site of Bobal on the right; and a small cluster made up of middle and small structures from the edges of peripheral Tikal to the north and south at the bottom. Finally, geography tends to override rank for the wide-mouth coarseware storage jars (fig. 5.19), with a stress of .063. There are fewer signs of clear-cut clustering or axes, with collections primarily from south of Tikal and the near north on the upper-left quadrant, the epicentral and the northeast quadrant of Tikal on the lower left, the nearer-north survey strip on the upper right, and the far north on the lower right.

Overall, it is clear that consumption of locally produced ceramics

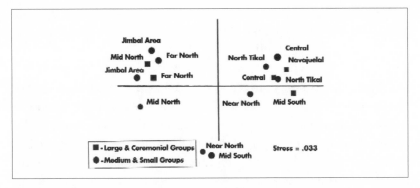

FIGURE 5.18

*Social variation in peripheral Tikal. Two-dimensional multidimensional scaling solution
for slipped narrow-mouth jars. Stress is .033.*

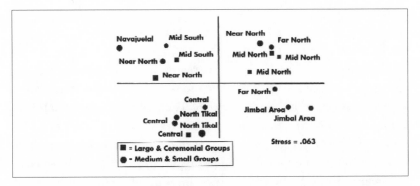

FIGURE 5.19

*Social variation in peripheral Tikal. Two-dimensional multidimensional scaling solution
for Late Classic unslipped wide-mouth jars. Stress is .063.*

tended to overshadow social-rank factors. People consumed local products for most of their needs, not seeking exotic higher-quality items on
a regular basis. Serving forms, especially vases, are the only category
that is somewhat of an exception. The only people who seem to have
been concerned enough to choose high-quality, presumably imported,
serving vessels in some number were the residents of Minor Centers
such as Navahuelal. The few whole vessels we recovered at Navahuelal
included a number of examples identical to types common in central
Tikal. Although the sample size was too small to admit to the analysis,

high-quality Ik plates were also found at Bobal. The fact that the consumption patterns of people living at Minor Centers mirror those of central and epicentral elites shows that these centers were the residence of the highest-ranking or wealthiest people in the peripheries.

The period of maximum social distinction in ceramics is that of the Ik ceramic complex, a time when Tikal was under great political stress. A potential explanation for this distinction is to be found in the increasing political marginalization of Tikal and the consequent reduction in access to wealth and elaborate status markers implied by this marginality. During this time period it is possible that fancier, locally produced ceramics served as substitutes for the now restricted supply of prestige goods. The presence of such ceramics in Minor Centers may reflect a deliberate strategy of providing those items in order to recruit and reward potentially wary followers and retainers.

OCCUPATIONAL SPECIALIZATION
IN PERIPHERAL TIKAL

At the onset of the peripheral-area excavations, we were unsure about the possible presence of craft and other occupational specialists in any numbers in the peripheries of Tikal. Traditional models had tended to emphasize the concentric nature of sites in terms of social rank, but little emphasis had been placed on the location of specialists. The sampling strategy of the test-pitting program in peripheral Tikal was geared towards the small-scale sampling of a larger number of structure groups for dating purposes. Occupation debris was usually assumed to reflect casual debris from household occupation, and we were not specifically searching for or expecting to find materials reflecting occupational specialization. Although my previous publications on peripheral Tikal ceramics have emphasized production and distribution systems for ceramics, in only one case did we produce locational evidence for a ceramic production locus. Even that one case— the possible firing area for Saxche paste vases, plates, and drums—is equivocal.

Ceramic production areas were inferred from the distribution of distinctive paste classes of pottery around the supposed locus of production. Our study indicated that there were at least five or six workshop traditions, producing large slipped bowls that were routed at least in part through the central Tikal market (Fry 1980). Determining whether these were specialized communities heavily involved in production or simply individual households will require additional research. Given the scale of production and the likely use of open and pit firing rather than formal kilns, it may be difficult to locate these centers. Traditional clues used to identify pottery-production locations in the Mexican-highland surveys may not be appropriate for the Lowland Maya. Forming tools were probably made of hardwood rather than stone. Old metates could have been used for grinding the calcite temper, and no washing of clays was done. All the raw materials were abundant locally, except for the volcanic ash sometimes used for temper in the Late Classic. The differing patterns of clustering of assemblages indicate that coarse wide-mouth jars were made in separate production centers from those that produced serving forms and slipped wares.

We also found evidence for specialized areas involving lithics, though none seem to be highly concentrated. This may reflect the concentration of production in central Tikal during the Late Classic (Moholy-Nagy, this volume). In some of the areas, lithic tools were used to produce other items, rather than being an indication of lithic workshops. These areas include the probable woodworking location 4.5 km. north of the site center studied by Olga Puleston (O. S. Puleston 1969), with its high frequency of drills. Still other areas produced large numbers of exhausted obsidian cores and utilized flake blades. These locations are near the borders of Tikal, as defined on the basis of the earthworks and settlement density. Several locations on top of the ridge in the middle of the south survey strip showed large quantities of unmodified nodules and primary debitage. The surface pattern of disposal contrasts with the disposal of lithic debris in pits and chultuns in central Tikal (Moholy-Nagy, this volume). There is also abundant evidence of small-scale surface quarrying in this upland zone. The small scale of this activity reflects the production of informal or expedient tools for localized consumption. The evidence for workshops involving large-scale production and/or consumption of lithic tools may be underrepresented if the disposal pattern of lithic refuse in below-surface pits or dumps was also used in peripheral Tikal. Evidence that this disposal pattern was followed in peripheral Tikal as early as the Cauac complex of the Late Preclassic comes from the filled-in chultun excavated in the plaza in front of Structure Ne(N)-65. This was a serendipitous discovery because we were looking for rubbish deposits adjacent to the staircase of this structure. The test pit encountered a debris-packed Cauac-complex refilled chultun. Large quantities of nodules, unworked and used cores, and debitage had been used to make a tight packing of the mouth of the chultun. I suspect that the high frequency of lithics and the higher quality of the Cauac ceramic assemblage reflect the debris associated with a Minor Center. This chultun was very close to the woodworking area documented by Olga Puleston.

CONCLUSION

In looking backward over the past thirty years since the conclusion of our fieldwork in the peripheries of Tikal, we can see how the research we carried out was part of the broad movement of change sweeping through American archaeology. Archaeology had begun to change from a site-oriented focus to a regional focus; perhaps more slowly, but inevitably, this change took place in the Maya area. A concern for the lives of the nonelite Maya also reflected a growing interest in bottom-up theories of social change rather than an elite-dominated narrative. The interests in demography and ancient economies resonated with the materialistic trends in cultural anthropology and archaeology. Concerns about ecology and economy, which were coming to the forefront of research agendas, were an important part of our project (D. E. Puleston 1968, 1983; Olson and Puleston 1972). The project's research design and methods were innovative in both method and technique. Transect sampling was, in part, derived from natural-science approaches; random sampling (see Tourtellot 1988 for a contemporary example) and the use of multivariate statistics for data analysis and hypothesis testing were just coming into vogue. The Tikal Sustaining Area Project was one of the earliest to use these techniques in the Maya Lowlands.

In the 1960s and 1970s, ecological factors were more strongly emphasized in explaining settlement dynamics. We investigated carrying capacity and sought evidence for land shortages and exhaustion, which were seen as major factors in changes in the location and density of settlements. We now realize that these early studies were often too limited in scope for polities of the Classic and even the Late Preclassic. The programs of regional analysis begun in the 1960s have extended our understanding of the scale of the political and economic systems. The results of these studies (Sanders et al. 1979; Blanton et al. 1982) should caution us against using portions of regional landscape that are too small to allow generalizations about the causes of settlement shifts. The successful translation of the hieroglyphs involving political events has allowed us to re-create the dynamics of the political forces that shaped major centers (Culbert 1991a; S. Martin and Grube 2000). The political elites are back with a vengeance. We cannot hope to understand the settlement dynamics of a major political and economic center such as Tikal without considering a much wider economic and political arena (Haviland, this volume). The boundedness of Tikal is now a political and an economic issue. Distribution of both the volume and quality of artifacts was influenced by the political fortunes of the rulers of Tikal, though not always in the predicted way (Moholy-Nagy, this volume). Also, social stratification in the Tikal zone involved the peripheries as well as the center, Minor Centers being an important component. Hierarchies were dynamic, with wealth and status markers changing as political fortunes changed.

The advantages of studying in the peripheries of a major site such as Tikal lie in the boundedness of the settlement and economic systems as they fluctuated through time. Patterning is often easier to see in the peripheries, for in many cases there is less intense use of the land and structures. There is also less smearing of the archaeological record by large-scale programs of construction, which destroy whole settlement segments and suck up occupation debris for fills. In addition, one can sometimes find earlier settlements that have been preserved fairly intact, providing a clearer picture of activity patterns. Studies can thus be used as guides to unraveling the more complex histories of occupation nearer the vortex of a center's activities.

Although the concepts that helped shape the research of the Tikal peripheral-studies program have been shown to be overly simple, they were a good starting point for the path that has led to our current viewpoints. When the program began, the urban nature of Maya centers was still a hot topic of debate, the roles of conflict and warfare were highly controversial, and nobody had discovered systems of intensive agriculture. It was plausible to see a small, shifting population of agriculturalists being seduced into visiting and supporting the ceremonial center of their choice, however distant. The new complexity of information is both intimidating and refreshing. It is both surprising and gratifying that the data we collected and sweated over are still productive and useful in answering contemporary questions.

Note

Ceramic data from peripheral Tikal were collected and studied while the author was ceramicist for the Tikal Sustaining Area Project, William A. Haviland, Director. The project was supported by National Science Foundation Grant GS-1409 and the University Museum of the University of Pennsylvania. Funding for the data analysis was provided through a grant from the Penrose Fund of the American Philosophical Society. I was assisted in the analysis by Scott C. Cox and Steve Durand, with statistical consultation by the late Dr. Andy B. Anderson. I have benefited from discussion over discussion on Tikal ceramics and settlement with the late Dennis E. Puleston, as well as T. Patrick Culbert and William A. Haviland. Christine Fry critiqued the manuscript and prepared the originals of the vessel illustrations.

6

The Central Acropolis of Tikal

Peter D. Harrison

IN THE BEGINNING

When I first saw the city of Tikal in 1959, the Central Acropolis was completely tree-covered, not perceivable as an entity, and distinguished only by the presence of a handful of buildings with standing architecture (fig. 6.1). These buildings were already known through their publication by Maler (1911), who described them as having multiple stories, a few preserved wooden lintels and one carved lintel, and a maze of rooms in standing structures.

Excavation began under my supervision in 1962 and continued for seasons of varying length until 1967, for a total of 40 months of excavation, which peaked in intensity and numbers of workmen employed in 1966. Of the 43 numbered structures that were tabulated, 25 were wholly excavated. The complex was revealed as a definable entity in which the large majority of structures were "palaces" arranged around six courtyards, all at different absolute levels. Some structures appeared at the time of original mapping (Carr and Hazard 1961) to be mounds of earth overgrown by large trees. When cleared, these "mounds" yielded complex structures with multiple rooms (figs. 6.2, 6.3). The

FIGURE 6.1

Painting by Santa Fe artist Carlos Vierra, completed in 1915, based upon plans by Maler and photographs by Maudslay. Despite his never visiting the site, Vierra's vision of post-abandonment Tikal is remarkably accurate (photo courtesy of the Museum of Man, Balboa Park, San Diego).

difference from their counterparts with standing architecture was simply degree of preservation (fig. 6.4). Despite all the labor expended, the Central Acropolis is still not fully excavated, and many questions remain unanswered. A policy was established favoring broad surface excavation rather than depth, contrasting with the policy in the North Acropolis. This policy of breadth over depth was compensated by one deep pit in Courtyard 3 connecting to two tunnels that penetrated beneath structures 5D-50 and 5D-52 (fig. 6.5). Other pits extending to bedrock were excavated in Courtyard 1; Courtyard 6, where the bedrock was very close to the final surface; and Courtyard 2, but only to the level of a lower platform. Excavations made in the ravine to the south investigated not only the Palace Reservoir but also parts of the base of the great wall that forms the southern defining boundary of the Acropolis.

In 1970 I presented an analysis on the structural forms during the Late Classic period as my doctoral dissertation. At the time, the word *palace* seemed too culturally loaded and too simple a distinction to separate this architectural sample from the temples of the Great Plaza and

FIGURE 6.2

During initial excavation in 1964, Structure 5D-46 was primarily an earthen mound.

FIGURE 6.3

After excavation and partial restoration of Structure 5D-46, in 1969, the earthen mound yielded a fine and ancient palace.

FIGURE 6.4

The second story of 5D-52-1st exemplifies the appearance of standing architecture surrounded by foliage in 1959, prior to excavation.

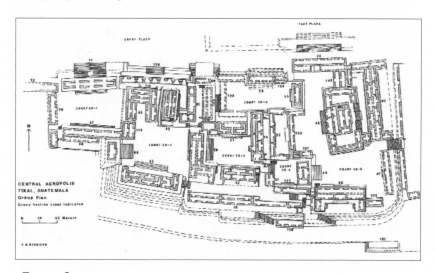

FIGURE 6.5

General map of the Central Acropolis of Tikal prior to final rectification.

North Acropolis, which they adjoin (fig. 6.6). Further, the European term did not seem to accommodate the large variety of form and complexity exhibited in the Central Acropolis structures. The clumsy term

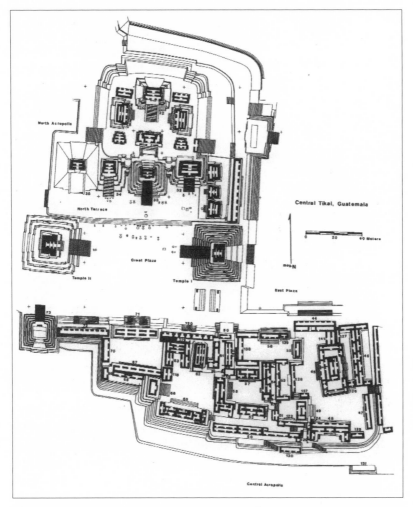

FIGURE 6.6

Map of the power core of Tikal, showing the relationship of the Central Acropolis, North Acropolis, and Great Plaza (map prepared by Amalia Kenward).

range-type buildings was substituted for *palace* in an effort to achieve a more objectively descriptive phrase. As a starting analytic base, I utilized the variations in floor plan according to the ranged quality of the rooms, using the terms *tandem* and *transverse* (fig. 6.7). This device worked well to segregate the structures according to their complexity. A single-roomed structure was by definition *non-tandem* and *non-transverse.*

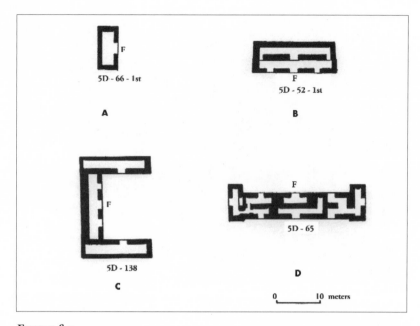

FIGURE 6.7

Examples of the four levels of complexity in palace ground plan, (a) *non-tandem/non-transverse,* (b) *tandem/non-transverse,* (c) *non-tandem/transverse, and* (d) *tandem/transverse.*

Intermediate levels of complexity included *tandem with non-transverse* and *transverse with non-tandem.* The most complex possible combination was *tandem and transverse.* The architecturally established assumption was made that complexity of function would be reflected in complexity of form. There were plenty of further variables to be tested for their presence or absence and their clustering within certain structures. These included the addition of architectural elements, such as whole rooms or stories; modification of floor plan through time by closure or opening of access routes; and presence/absence of windows, niches, burials, caches, Special Deposits, and benches. The latter variable was complex enough to require its own analysis due to the variety of shapes and sizes of masonry benches throughout the Acropolis.

Perhaps predictably, clustering attributes were distributed in accordance with the complexity of floor plan. The most complex plans exhibited the greatest history of change and addition and the presence of feature variables, with the exception of burials and caches. Burials were very rare in the Central Acropolis, and four of these clustered in a single building, 5D-46. One burial was placed as an apparent dedicatory cache beneath an external stair and was devoid of grave goods (Bu. 180). Burial 177, which included a small chamber cyst in the fill of Courtyard 1 and was arguably a very important personage from the Manik ceramic period, was located precisely on the sacred axial line of the North Acropolis. This line also serves as the axis of Structure 5D-71. A small number of other burials were interred in the base of a structure (in one case) and into middens (in two other cases) and were of post-collapse (Eznab) date. Among burials included in the fill of structures, only 5D-46 had received this honor. I will discuss this structure in some detail below.

Turning to the question of function, I examined the ethnographic literature and the Mesoamerican analogies for structure functions observed in the Colonial period. This exercise indicated that complexity of form did indeed indicate residence as a function, while ritual uses fell into the somewhat less complex configurations of attributes. The simplest structures with one or two rooms and few additional attributes left me puzzled, and at the time I suggested storage of ritual paraphernalia as a legitimate building function in this centralized locale.

Residence remained a problem because there were numerous complex tandem-transverse buildings but none with contained burials other than 5D-46. Archaeology elsewhere, both at Tikal and other large Lowland sites, had demonstrated that burial of the dead within the house was a common practice. The solution lay in a distinction between *residence* and *residents,* which is the difference between permanent and temporary residence. Only permanent residence represented family living. Because of the central location and the opulence and complexity of the structures, such residence would presumably be of the royal family. My conclusion was that only one structure fulfilled all the criteria for royal residence, and this was 5D-46. These criteria were the presence of burials and caches and a high incidence of all the other variables that were examined and found in normally lesser degree in other structures. Other complex and equally opulent structures, but devoid of burials and axial caches, represented functions of some form of temporary residence. The nature of these temporary residences was likely quite varied, but my two favored interpretations in 1970 suggested that they were schools and/or priests' housing and ritual retreat houses, both of which had strong analogues in the Colonial record.

A great many changes and advances have occurred since the 1970s, some as the result of further archaeological excavation, analysis, and thinking and some as the result of interpretive reading of hieroglyphic texts. It is important to note that both these types of reference material (archaeological and epigraphic) require interpretation. I now add one other structure to the list of family residences—5D-57—which was only excavated on the exterior, revealing two images of a ruler and a short text. Translation of the text identified the protagonist as Jasaw Chan K'awiil I,1 the 26th ruler of Tikal. The floor plan of this structure qualifies it for residence, but the absence of excavation leaves us without data about the other attributes found in 5D-46. The signature of the builder convinces me that this building is an excellent candidate for family residence. The carved scene commemorates a capture of a high personage from near the city of Calakmul, Tikal's traditional enemy and nemesis for centuries (S. Martin and Grube 1995:42–46). The event dates the structure to soon after A.D. 695. Two other structures are dated with confidence—5D-52-1st (1st Story) and 5D-46. The first story of 5D-52 contains a carved lintel in the preserved central doorway identifying the date of installation as 26 June A.D. 741, placing it as contemporary with lintel dates on Temple IV and authored by Yik'in Chan K'awiil, son of Jasaw. The placement of this edifice on the south side of Court 3—seemingly blocking the view from his father's "house"—seems strange, but only from the Western point of view. The ritually decorated building replaced the scenic view with the eye of K'inich Ajaw, the sun god, not likely an insult.

Structure 5D-46 is dated by a combination of C14 results and an inscription carved on a cache vessel that was dedicatory to the primary west stair (fig. 6.8). It is now known that this inscription identifies the building as the *na* or house of Great Jaguar Paw or Chak Tok Ich'aak. The date is approximately A.D. 350. The remarkable feature of 5D-46 is that this early building (see fig. 6.3) was never ravaged during conquest nor covered over in peacetime by the people of Tikal. Many additions and changes were made, but the original structure, interpreted as a clan house of the Jaguar Paw clan, was never touched. Other palace

FIGURE 6.8

The black incised cache vessel that displayed an inscription identifying the na *house of Jaguar Claw the Great, shown in situ in 1965.*

structures of this period are known to be buried beneath the present courtyards, in the common Maya practice of rebuilding new architecture over the walls of the old.

NEW VIEWS AND VIEWPOINTS

The opening of the Central Acropolis through clearing of vegetation, along with excavation and some restoration of many of the buildings, has revealed an architectural group with a semblance of how it appeared in ancient times (fig. 6.9). Of course, much is lacking—the plaster finishes, the color, most of the sculptured decoration—but nonetheless, a whole new perception is now possible. Visiting the group today, one sees the Central Acropolis to be a gallery of enclosed, boxlike spaces—a three-dimensional maze—with as much emphasis on vertical variation as on horizontal spread (fig. 6.10). Moving from courtyard to courtyard, one sees a constant series of surprises, with external spaces that range from intimate to publically grand. The outdoor spaces of the final configuration are livable and stimulating to the

FIGURE 6.9

View from Courtyard 6, with Courtyard 4 on the left and the multiple structures of 5D-52 rising in the background, showing the interplay of plans and levels that characterizes the Central Acropolis (1967).

FIGURE 6.10

Artist's conception of the reconstruction of the north face of the Central Acropolis, with the plaza ball court in the foreground. The crested structure on the right is 5D-63; the adjacent 5D-62 has a viewing chamber on the axis of the ball court in its second story.

FIGURE 6.11

The interior of Structure 5D-65 shows the plain, plastered, undecorated walls of a normal palace interior. Graffiti scratched into the walls are a feature that helps to identify function. The absence of furniture and wall hangings belies the probable opulence during ancient occupation.

senses, in contrast to the present apparent starkness of the interior spaces (fig. 6.11). These outdoor spaces are four-sided but not square. They are surrounded by architectonic decoration, a series of textured sculptures made up of symbolic and historic faces, mythic creatures, and carved texts. Each courtyard is an open-air gallery that encloses the viewer. When these courtyards were intact, the effect must have been overwhelming even to the jaded resident.

To the modern eye, the final product appears to be the master-work of a brilliant sculptor who has produced an enormous cubist entity showing his great sense of humor and love of the interplay between dizzying heights and flowing stairways. The multistoried buildings themselves resemble giant steps (see fig. 6.9), reflecting the high, stacked terraces of the Great Temples nearby.

The pleasing, three-dimensional interplay of stairs, stepped stories, and multilevel courtyards is the final product of more than half a millennium of construction, not a program planned with the end result in view. However, planning was present, and the three-dimensional quality of the Acropolis has existed from the earliest times. The time span does not detract from the aesthetic and does not mean that the builders were unaware of what they were creating. Certain rules were clearly observed throughout the long period of occupation and growth. These included the use of ever-different levels of courtyards. While the absolute levels and range of inter-courtyard accessability did indeed change through time, the basic principle of multiple levels among courtyards appears to have been intentionally maintained.

Another rule had to do with the nature of the enclosed courtyard, which served as a decorated gallery—often a setting for ritual—as well as a lush, tactile, and serene setting for daily life. Throughout time the configuration flowed and changed, but in all its manifestations it invites us to rethink our conceptions of interior versus exterior spaces.

Another visually exciting feature is the use of stairs, which form connecting lines that flow from one courtyard level to another and among building stories, from level to level. The use of stairs as architectural connectors borders on the obsessive and possibly has a mythological metaphor, such as representing connected levels of the heavens. At one location, between Courtyards 3 and 4, there are three adjacent stairs (fig. 6.12)—as if one were not enough—connecting different destinations from a single starting level. These are differentiated both physically and visually by separate sloped planes. The effect on light and shadow is stunning, changing with the movement of the sun through the day. A planned playfulness with interacting planes is indicated that borders on indulgence. That these differing stairs served mildly discrete functions does not diminish the visual effect of the juxtaposition.

Visual Deception in Architectural Planning

External disguise and visual deception are features in the presentation of many facades, especially where high elevations above the

FIGURE 6.12

The multiple stairs leading from Courtyard 4 to a variety of rooms and levels above provide an interplay of light and shadow, as well as restricting access.

surrounding terrain are involved. For example, the conglomerate of constructions that is labeled 5D-60 (see fig. 6.5) is little known by excavation, with only small portions of the exterior surfaces preserved and revealed. However, enough has been seen to allow us to understand that the appearance of a very high, terraced temple facade is turned toward the side of Great Temple I (see fig. 6.10). This is, in fact, a false facade. The details of what lies beneath are not known, but the small structure at the summit was accessible only from the summit and does not have the characteristics of a temple room. The terracing visible at the bottom is merely a facade affixed to much earlier, now buried construction.

Another, even better example of this type of visual disguise is found on the west end of Structure 5D-65 (Maler's Palace). The west supporting wall of the Acropolis was faced with terraces at the time the large palace above was built, partly to cover the fill of new construction and partly to bury earlier courtyard levels. While this terracing might be considered normal acropolis facing, it is the treatment of the west-end room of the palace above that reveals the intended visual deception. The interior of the room contains a huge false doorway, complete with a lintel. This false doorway leads nowhere except to its own shadowed recesses. Viewed from below, the illusion of a temple interior is complete, with the inner doorway dimly visible, but it is not a doorway, just an illusion.

There are many examples in the Lowlands of the Maya, using this facade device to disguise changes of level, whether of natural or artificial origin, and then facing the level change with either a stair or a series of terraces to give the appearance of a massive new work. Examples can be found at Yaxchilan, where the steep terrain was used in this manner, and at Kabah, where even a low rise in the natural terrain was converted into a contrived facade.

GROWTH THROUGH TIME

Pending the final analysis, it is safe to characterize the span of occupation of the Central Acropolis from Chuen ceramic times (350 B.C.–A.D. 1) to the end of the Eznab ceramic phase (A.D. 950). According to known evidence, it was always a place of palace-type structures.

Chuen Period

The earliest constructions are masonry platforms with large postholes, indicating a totally perishable structure above its masonry platform. None of these structures were wholly exposed, and they are known mainly from a cross-section "peek" that is provided in a tunnel excavation. Examples were found beneath Structure 5D-71, facing the Great Plaza, and at several deeply buried points below structures 5D-50 and 5D-65. Most prominently, immediately south of 5D-46, an early structure was more fully exposed due to its proximity to the present surface (fig. 6.13). Although spotty, these locations suggest that the entire present span of the Acropolis has great antiquity.

The early building beneath 5D-71 was encountered on the sacred axis of the North Acropolis, but since neither of its dimensions is known, it is impossible to say whether this early perishable structure formed a southern boundary for the Plaza or even whether it was centered on the axis. It can be said that the axis of the North Acropolis, referred to as an *axis mundi*, did cross a Chuen-date building on the south side of the Great Plaza.

The buried remains of structures of this date on the southern

FIGURE 6.13

The plastered surface of Irma Structure (1966), with large primary and smaller secondary postholes, exemplifies a Chuen-period platform that supported a perishable building. The unexcavated portion is the level of the final courtyard floor, dated some 500 years later.

boundary of the present Acropolis occurred at a much lower absolute level, likely marking the surface of the ridge bedrock at the start of occupation. Their existence, however, does suggest that the configuration of the Acropolis in its horizontal boundaries was established by Chuen times. Subsequent development was vertical.

The best-known structure from this period, dubbed Irma Structure (fig. 6.13 above) during excavation and located immediately south of the South patio of 5D-46, was the most impressive platform found for the time period. This patio was constructed quite late in the history of the Acropolis as an addition to the original fourth-century building. By the date of the addition (ninth century), the Chuen building had already been covered by subsequent flooring. Its buried remains were partially overbuilt by the larger palace's south patio wall. Since a tunnel beneath 5D-46 did not reveal any earlier architecture beneath its precise axial location, it seems reasonable to assume that Irma Structure was the Chuen-period prototype for a royal residence at the east end of the Acropolis. It had been constructed immediately over leveled bedrock. In form, it is quite reminiscent of the very early platforms excavated by N. Hammond at the Belizean site of El Cuello (Hammond 1991), although "Irma" is not as early as Hammond's buildings, which date to either Swazey or Bladen ceramic phases.

Manik Period

This period is better known but is still limited to those surface buildings that survive to the present and a few glimpses into the lower depths of the Acropolis, mainly beneath 5D-50 and 5D-52. From A.D. 250 to 550, masonry construction was introduced. The palaces of this period on the surface include 5D-46 (as mentioned earlier), 5D-71 (fig. 6.14), 5D-58, and 5D-120. Remains of a buried palace found directly below 5D-52-1st shared the axial point of the structure above, but the buried palace was oriented north instead of south. This structure, known as The Palace of the Red Dado, had been razed to a level below the vault spring, but the remaining interior walls were very well preserved, exhibiting the tandem/transverse room arrangement of the residential complex. Interestingly, the building was devoid of any masonry benches, suggesting that in the Central Acropolis at least, such benches, with all their important forms and functions, were a later feature, introduced after A.D. 550. The "red dado" was a band of decorative paint around the base of the interior walls, in the fashion of a painted low wainscoting. As yet undated, it cannot be said whether this structure is older than 5D-46 or not, despite the former's being buried and the latter's still being on the surface.

Structure 5D-46, constructed around A.D. 350 by Great Jaguar Paw, may well be the earliest Manik building in the Acropolis, built as it was almost directly over leveled bedrock. The original building displayed a deviation from the standard tandem/transverse pattern in that there were three tandem rooms instead of the more common two. It was constructed as a single-story building, raised by a walled platform surrounding it on all four sides. There were dual staircases, providing approach from the west and the east. It was beneath the western stair that the now-famous cache vessel was interred as a primary deposit (fig. 6.8 above), identifying the building as the house of Great Jaguar Paw. This western stair suffered little addition over the next five centuries. The

FIGURE 6.14

The stubs of the walls of Manik Structure 5D-71 show white against the uncut foliage of Courtyard 1. The stair facing the Great Plaza is unexcavated (1966).

eastern stair, on the other hand, was altered with each shift in ceramic phase, and each stair renewal was dedicated by a human burial with grave goods. The original Manik-phase stair and burial were almost completely destroyed during the first renewal by the construction of another stair with burial in the Ik phase. This burial, of an elderly woman, included two painted bowls and her bone-encased sewing kit, suggesting an old family retainer—a nanny or long-term servant of the royal household. The final, Imix-phase stair also contained a burial, but it was less elaborately endowed with grave goods. There was, in fact, a very final addition to this eastern stair, which demonstrates the exceptional continuity of occupation of this building. This was a single, broad Eznab-period (A.D. 850–950) step added to the base of the stair, with Eznab sherds contained in the fill. While the repeated rebuilding of the eastern stair may have been prompted by successive family occupations of the palace, the placement of a dedicatory burial beneath each reconstruction suggests to me a reflection of the residential nature of the building. The inclusion of burials beneath the architecture of residential structures has been established for lower levels of Maya society at Tikal

FIGURE 6.15

The unique interior stair in the north ground-floor chamber of 5D-46 is secondary and well preserved (1966).

(Haviland 1985). The ultimate placement of burials on the east side of the structure further suggests a residential marker.

Meanwhile, the western side of the building became increasingly enclosed and shut off from access even from the rest of the structure. The three western doorways were constricted by masonry buttresses, and the western platform or porch was enclosed by a thin masonry wall, further shutting the western view from the external world. When the late-period patios were added sometime in the eighth century, they were oriented with access routes only from the east, and these were guarded by highly restricted entryways. Another feature of this building is unique at Tikal. Still during the Manik phase but presumably much later, a second story was added in such a feat of clever engineering that its secondary status was very hard to detect. Access was achieved through a spiral stair constructed in the north gallery (fig. 6.15), essentially sacrificing that room to access function. The giveaway that revealed this as a secondary addition was the sealing of a door access from the west gallery into the north gallery, which was necessary for the stair construction. Very little of the second story remains—just enough to establish its ancient existence. The remains suggest that this upper story was a single gallery in width with an open platform facing the east—in the direction of the rising sun.

Evidence of other structures of this period was glimpsed immediately beneath the wall bases of Structures 5D-57 and 5D-54, suggesting that an earlier Manik-period courtyard was now buried below the present configuration, nearly identical to it but at a lower level. These buildings would have formed the north and east sides of a patio with the buried Palace of the Red Dado, indicating that Courtyard 3 had an entire Manik phase, which is partially reflected by the palaces on the present surface. The western side of this group was formed by Structure 5D-58, also of late Manik phase and built in the unusual form of an L. It is not known whether the two wings of this building are contemporary. The north face of the south wing exhibited a rare and unique mask with a "duck-billed" creature surmounting a human head (fig. 6.16). This mask was first published by Maler (1911:pl.7 [1]).

Within present knowledge of both ruler dates and the often exotic forms of iconographic rendition, it is quite possible and even likely that this creature is a crocodile and that the structure was a palace of the 15th ruler, Yax Nuun Ayiin, formerly known as Curl Snout. Whoever raised this palace, it towered high over courtyards both to the east and west at the time.

Structures 5D-71 and 5D-120 are also related to this ceramic phase and were constructed in that sequence, with 5D-120 being quite later than 5D-71 (fig. 6.5 above). This latter structure has several features of interest. Originally built with a stair from the plaza level on the north and another stair on the east, the structure was accessed by "pass-through" (one of numerous structures with this function at Tikal), but not to the level of Courtyard 1 as now seen (fig. 6.14 above). There was a much earlier courtyard reached by a taller stair. The axis of 5D-71 lies

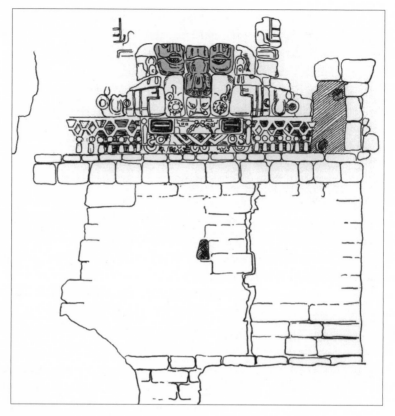

FIGURE 6.16

1965 drawing by Merle Greene Robertson of mask decorating the north wall of the east wing of 5D-58 in Courtyard 3. The mask, which may represent a crocodile, is shaded.

on the sacred axis of the North Acropolis, and this structure may well date to the 16th ruler, Siyaj Chan K'awiil II (Stormy Sky).

For its part, Structure 5D-120 was built very late in the Manik period and yet served a uniquely important function. With its nine doorways, it completes the Great Plaza as a cosmic analogy for the Twin Pyramid Groups of Tikal. Since 5D-120 was constructed long before either Temples I or II, and because 5D-120 is nowhere near the axis of the North Acropolis, explanation of this phenomenon invites thought.

Ik and Imix Periods

The period from A.D. 550 onwards was one of explosive development, particularly triggered by the 26th ruler, Jasaw Chan K'awiil I, with the construction of 5D-57 around A.D. 695. Tikal's period of great prosperity and architectural expansion occupied the next 105 years, involving major construction across the city, such as Temples I, II, IV, and VI and several Twin Pyramid Groups, among many other projects. This prosperity of architectural expansion is well reflected in the Central Acropolis. The concentration of centralized power around the precincts of the Great Plaza was not continuous, as shown by Laporte's excavations in the Lost World Group (Laporte and Fialko 1990). Nevertheless, the functions of the Central Acropolis were never abandoned at this location either.

All the rest of the architecture of the Central Acropolis dates to the Ik and Imix periods (A.D. 550–850), although the majority are confined to the contributions of the 26th through 29th rulers.

Some of the major architecture can be sequenced, and this sequence does reflect a crescendo of centralized power followed by a denouement. Other than 5D-57, the works of Jasaw Chan K'awiil I are difficult to attribute because of a lack of accurate dating materials, texts, and stratigraphy. It is likely that 5D-54-1st was built slightly later than his postulated "house," 5D-57.

In turn, the next known additions were the first story of 5D-52-1st (A.D. 741) by the 27th ruler (Yik'in Chan K'awiil) and, very likely, 5D-141, two structures connected by the iconography of a court dwarf, at a time that was too late for Jasaw's authorship. Second and third stories are hard to attribute, but we do know that the second story of 5D-52 was built later than 5D-51. We also know that a single massive project was surveyed in Courtyards 4 and 6 and included the whole of the platform of Courtyard 4 (fig. 6.17), Structures 5D-49, 5D-53, and 5D-55. This project was unified by a continuous walled platform that defined a new western boundary for Courtyard 6. It was surveyed from the primary axial points of 5D-54 and 5D-46 jointly in a sophisticated series of alignments, right angles, and quadrangles, serving to unify the complex. I will discuss the methods of surveying and manner of planning the Central Acropolis below.

Many of the later structures can only be attributed in sequence rather than to ruler. These include 5D-50, a two-story complex that was added to the face of the south wall of the Acropolis at a date later than

FIGURE 6.17

View of Courtyard 4 and part of Courtyard 6 in 1966 during excavation and consolidation. Structure 5D-49 is on the left, 5D-53 on the middle right.

the first story of 5D-52. As Bill Coe always advised those of us who served as students under his stewardship: "A stratigraphic time gap does not tell the difference between ten minutes and ten years." This very true dictum of reading stratigraphy at Tikal comes into play more frequently during the late period of high development than ever before.

The massive construction program that resulted in the rise of the most carefully surveyed building in the Central Acropolis was 5D-65 (Maler's Palace, fig. 6.18). The physical labor and amount of fill moved rivaled that of Temple VI, for example, simply because an earlier and much lower platform (courtyard) had to be filled for the creation of Courtyard 2, as well as owing to the structure of the great palace itself. The specific methodology used to survey this building—the most complex, yet most clearly demonstrable, of all surveying examples found in the Acropolis—has been published several times elsewhere (Harrison 1989, 1999). The floor stratigraphy directly connecting 5D-52 and 5D-65 clearly indicates that the latter was built later. The development in masonry style and art in the upper zone suggest that this was at least

FIGURE 6.18

The most carefully planned structure in the Central Acropolis is 5D-65 on the left, with the later "oratorio," 5D-66, on the right (1966).

a moderately significant time difference, enough to account for the succession of the next ruler, Yax Nuun Ayiin II, formerly known as Ruler C, the 29th ruler of Tikal. The extraordinary alignments and structural affiliations that link 5D-65 to Temple V suggest that the two were a joint construction project, facing each other across the Palace Reservoir. Dating of Temple V by recent joint Guatemalan/Spanish excavations has been inconclusive, showing a great deal of fill from the Manik and Chuen periods but no datable tomb.

We are left with a great deal of the Acropolis unaccounted for by date. There is much left to be excavated and dated in future investigations. Just as Tikal exploded into phenomenal architectural prominence as a city between A.D. 695 and 810, so did the Central Acropolis. During this period the city expanded its cosmic greatness out to Temple IV in the west and to Temple VI in the east, while the Central Acropolis simply expanded upwards, in the process creating an architectural enclave that may be unique in the Maya Lowlands in its power and beauty.

THE CONCEPT OF THE ROYAL COURT

Perhaps the greatest change and advancement in interpretation has been the recent focus on the properties and functions of the Maya Royal Court and the application of these concepts to the Central Acropolis. Stephen Houston and Takeshi Inomata focused our attention on these concepts beginning in 1996, when—based upon their own work in the Petexbatun region—an examination of this feature of Maya political organization was initiated. A series of symposia organized by a number of scholars ensued, culminating in a symposium at Yale in 1998. Besides both new and old archaeological data, there were new sources of data brought to bear on the subject that have altered and enriched the topic. These sources included inscriptions revealing the complexity and extensiveness of conflict in the Maya Lowlands and the concomitant machinations of diplomacy, intermarriage, and political alliance. All of these matters required a place where they could occur, and it is generally conceded that they were played out in the structures traditionally called "palaces." Although still considered inadequate, the old term is easier to deal with than my cumbersome "range-type structures."

The other new source is derived from the subject content of the multitude of painted vessels, many without provenience but a significant number of which have been archaeologically recovered. Justin Kerr's corpus, *The Maya Vase Book* (Kerr 1989–97), with five volumes published to date, contains an enormous range of informative iconography. Many of the scenes are clearly set in an architectural framework, complete with details that match known archaeological data, such as benches, as well as other information about the perishable panoply that accompanied scenes in the royal palaces (fig. 6.19).

In my original view of the Central Acropolis, I used the Vatican as a model, albeit this is a rough analogy. The concepts of government, education, residence, and religion embodied in a single architectonic enclave fell just a little short of the concept of the Royal Court. A list of expected functions was largely deduced in the earlier period of interpretation, but this list can now be supported by the additional data sources described above. Functions of the Royal Court included limited royal residence; militaristic affairs; diplomatic affairs, including the receipt of allies and feasting; domestic social events, such as marriage

FIGURE 6.19

*Roll-out photograph by Justin Kerr of painted vessel excavated by Laporte in the Lost World
Group, showing a reception throne scene with a tribute presentation of a baby jaguar skin.
The elaborate headdresses demonstrate the importance of "livery" as royal identification
(Kerr File No. 2697).*

arrangements; the judiciary; ritual and divinatory events; and very
likely torture and execution of prisoners, an important subset of military affairs. In the Central Acropolis of Tikal, I would also insist upon
including special forms of ritual housing of the retreat-house and
guest-house variety, especially those related to teams of visitors partici-
pating in the ritual ball game. As I have published elsewhere, I believe
this latter to be the specialized function of 5D-63, due to the cumulative
factors of the proximity to the plaza ball court, the large number of
bed-benches, the U-shape of the floor plan, and the large number of
decorative roof crests.

From the new data sources, we can draw a few conclusions about
palace structures. They were multifunctional, one function being residence of both a permanent and a temporary nature. Permanent residence is relatively rare in a large complex the size of the Central
Acropolis. There is reason to believe that the seat of the Royal Court at
Tikal moved on more than one occasion but that, despite these demographic shifts within the city's boundaries, the Central Acropolis never
ceased to serve some of these functions. Presumably, in the face of an
ever-growing population and an ever-expanding royal family, there was
no lack of candidates to occupy a palace formerly the residence of
an ancestor. If a current, late-period ruler chose to move his physical

residence, including his immediate family and his immediate affairs, to another locale in Tikal, there was surely an heir apparent or a cousin who would happily take over 5D-46 in the Central Acropolis. Even extended families tend to extend further, and growth of the architectural entity would follow suit, as long as prosperity permitted. Speculation on the locales of other sites of the royal residence goes beyond the subject matter of this chapter, but interested readers can consult my other publications on the subject (compare Harrison 1999).

Throne Buildings

One of the original interpretations in my 1970 report has changed quite radically—that regarding the function of the simplest floor plan (nontandem/nontransverse), which is essentially a one-room structure. The current interpretation results from new ideas regarding the functions of the Royal Court and new data available from painted vessels. One-room buildings occur in the Central Acropolis both as free-standing structures and as additions to existing buildings. These have now been interpreted as Throne or "Reception" Buildings, reflecting the most commonly depicted activity on the painted vessels. The presence of a masonry bench in the form of a throne with sidearms and often a backrest as well identifies this function. The example illustrated in figure 6.20 is a reconstruction of 5D-123, a freestanding structure of late date located close to the southeast corner of 5D-52.

Despite the late appearance of separate Throne Buildings, throne benches were found in all of the excavated structures that exhibit the most complex floor plans. It must be assumed that, at least during the middle phases of the city's development (Manik to Ik), throne rooms were normal even in permanent structures. For example, 5D-46 has a throne bench prominently centered on the axis of the east side of the house, which was added in Ik or later times.

ALIGNMENTS, TRIANGLES, AND PLANNING IN GENERAL

The introduction to "Pythagoreanism" in the *Encyclopedia Britannica* says in part: "The character of the original Pythagoreanism is controversial, and the conglomeration of disparate features that it displayed is intrinsically confusing." I wish to state most emphatically that

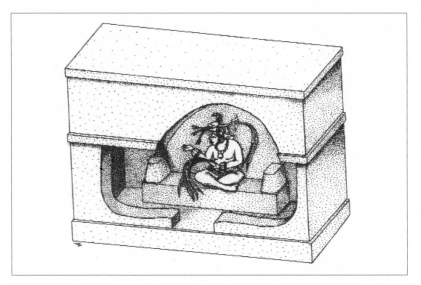

FIGURE 6.20

Reconstruction by Amalia Kenward of Structure 5D-123, showing the proportions and size of the freestanding Throne Building, with sidearm bench.

in no way am I invoking the mystical and confusing attributes of Pythagoreanism when I make specific observations concerning the layout of the architecture of Tikal. The fact that alignments, right angles, and integral right triangles, which figured in Pythagoreanism, also occur in Maya architecture is an observation, not a subscription to a particular philosophy. I will observe that highly respected scholars in the field of Egyptology do not find the use of such geometry in any way unusual or questionable (for example, see Mark Lehner's description of the Gizah Plain in *The Complete Pyramids* [1997:106–107]). A. F. Aveni (1982) and H. Hartung (1982, 1984) have been writing about this subject for years, but so far they seem not to have been heard.

In the progression of the mathematics of integral right triangles, the literature refers to a "natural" progression that begins with a 3-4-5 right-angle triangle, followed by a 5-12-13 right-angle triangle. These are the only two progressions that I will refer to here, and the ancient Maya of Tikal seem to have used both with equal frequency. But the triangular relationship of buildings was only one aspect by which important Maya structures were related to each other. The most important and undeniable facts are that all Maya monumental buildings were

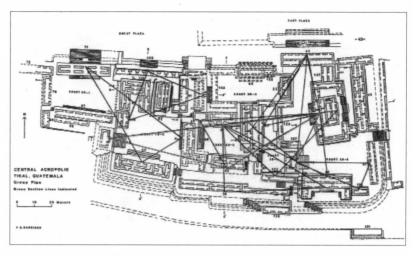

FIGURE 6.21

Twelve integral right triangles connecting the PAPs of palaces in the Central Acropolis. The highlighted pair anchor the east-west and south of the Acropolis.

constructed in a *place* that was predetermined by the locations of two earlier structures and that the progression of architectural growth occurred as a result of this referencing based upon ancestral reverence. Moreover, the progression was carefully planned in advance, often by decades. The two basic principles of Maya planning are alignment and right angles. The two together often coincide with triangles, which are distinct from the concept of the *triad,* but, I suspect, not unrelated to it.

My observations of the layout of Tikal over the past two decades suggest that there is a tendency for the 3-4-5 triangle to cover large spatial areas, while the 5-12-13 triangle is utilized more frequently (but not exclusively) for smaller spatial intervals.

In the Central Acropolis, I have previously pointed out (Harrison 1989) the presence of 12 significant triangular relationships that span the Manik through the Imix periods (A.D. 200–850) (fig. 6.21) and nine alignments of significance (fig. 6.22). Of course, the earlier end of the spectrum is harder to trace because so many buildings in that portion of the site history have been buried.

Alignments

The use of alignment between certain important architectural fea-

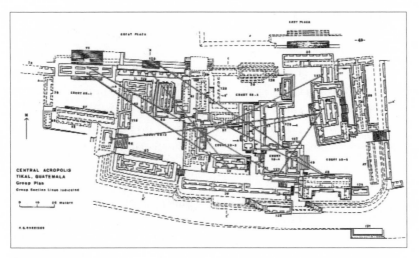

FIGURE 6.22

Nine alignments of PAPs and other significant structural points connect late buildings to early buildings.

tures is so common at Tikal that it was clearly a basis for planned structural interrelationship. In a prior publication on the subject, I defined an alignment as the deliberate same-line occurrence of no fewer than three significant points. Most commonly, these points are the Primary Axial Point [PAP] (Harrison 1989, 1999) but can also be the midpoint of noncentral doorways, corners of structures, and other architecturally delineated features on a building's exterior. In figure 6.22 above, nine such alignments in the Central Acropolis alone are illustrated. The alignments coincide frequently with right-triangular arrangements, as it is logical that they would do. The basic premise is that no building was constructed in a random place or position, but rather that each was planned in terms of its relationship to other, earlier buildings in a complex system of mathematical obeisance to ancestors. Of the nine such alignments defined thus far—and the study is by no means exhaustive—the most prominent one extends from 5D-46 in Courtyard 6 through 5D-57 in Courtyard 3 and continues to 5D-66 in Courtyard 2. The dating is in the same order, from east to west. There are at least two possible explanations for this use of alignment. In the simplest explanation, it may be a progression through time of ancestral veneration and nothing more, but one leading to a geometric network

199

that results from the combination of alignment and triangulation. The alternative explanation, expounded convincingly by Schele and Mathews (1998), is that the alignment has an astronomical significance, contemporary with the setting of the location of the second or third structure that creates such an alignment. I have not yet tested this explanation in my studies. The strength of the sequencing for ancestral continuity, where it is known, is such that I do not feel astronomical bases need to be invoked as an explanation for alignment.

Triangles

The example of Structure 5D-65, Maler's Palace, has been cited so often in the past (Harrison 1989, 1997, 1999) that I am reluctant to reiterate the discussion here. This structure was without doubt one of the most carefully placed buildings at Tikal and certainly in the Central Acropolis. Attention was paid to the location of the primary axial point first to locate it in such a way that two Manik buildings were the points of reference: 5D-58, possibly built by Yax Nuun Ayiin I, and 5D-71, possibly built by Siyaj Chan K'awiil II (Stormy Sky). These would certainly be important ancestors upon which the location of a new, equally important building should be based. The point from which the new building was surveyed has been identified and the method explained (ibid.). The final and most interesting feature is that the single primary window in this structure was located in the one asymmetrical room in such a manner that a direct line from the PAP of Temple I crosses through this window to connect to the PAP of Temple V, which supports the interpretation that 5D-65 and Temple V had to be constructed in tandem in order to achieve the alignment.

That said, I will describe two other sets of relationships in the Central Acropolis that also demonstrate referential surveying from earlier buildings to new projects. The simplest example connects 5D-52-1st, 1st Story, to the alignment described above, which extends across most of the east-west axis of the Acropolis, from 5D-46 to 5D-66. At the midpoint, which occurs at the PAP of 5D-57 (built by Jasaw Chan K'awiil I), a right angle turns south to the PAP of 5D-52-1st, 1st Story (see fig. 6.21). If one connects the dots, there are two nearly identical 5-12-13 right-angle triangles that together unify most of the Central Acropolis. There is good evidence for the identity of the authors of all but one of these buildings. Str. 5D-46 was built by Great Jaguar Paw, the earliest ancestor in the series; 5D-57 was built by Jasaw Chan K'awiil I; 5D-52-1st, 1st Story, was built by Yik'in Chan K'awiil, son of the latter; the author of 5D-66 alone is not known, though it is known that it was constructed later than 5D-65 and is therefore one of the latest structures in the Central Acropolis. Its placement was dictated by the long east-west alignment, and its stratigraphic position is later than 5D-65; hence, it should postdate the reign of Yik'in Chan K'awiil.

One of the by-products of the method of surveying a new building by using earlier buildings to place its corners is the production of a space that is rhomboidal in shape, as are all of the excavated courtyards in the Acropolis. This quick visual test can be applied to any part of Tikal, and in fact to any major Lowland city, to detect the presence of this system of city planning. One should look for rhomboidal courtyards, and the rest will follow.

The second example I will describe involves a large construction project that included at least three structures, defined the western boundary of Courtyard 6, and was built sometime between A.D. 700 and 800. It was a more complex survey job because it involved sightings from two base points rather than one (figs. 6.23, 6.24). From the PAPs of Structures 5D-46 *and* 5D-54, a series of right-angled surveys of the space between served to set up, in a single operation, all of the following: the layout of Courtyard 4, the facade of 5D-128, and 5D-55. All were unified by a single wall with one major inset—a survey project that defined the entire west side of Courtyard 6. At a later date other structures and stairs were added in front of the unifying wall, hiding its presence. This was a single construction project with a *terminus post quem* of A.D. 700, but it could easily be as late as A.D. 750. Given subsequent construction history and the short time left for the high period of Tikal's florescence, I would favor the later date, but not a date later than that.

The century between A.D. 700 and 800 was a period of nearly frantic growth at Tikal, and this growth is as evident in the Central Acropolis as at any other part of the site.

Figure 6.22 above shows the strict use of right angles to lay out the development of the west side of Court 6. Two of the new buildings, 5D-53 and 5D-49, each have their new PAPs related to earlier structures: 5D-122 and 5D-51, respectively. Where the baseline between

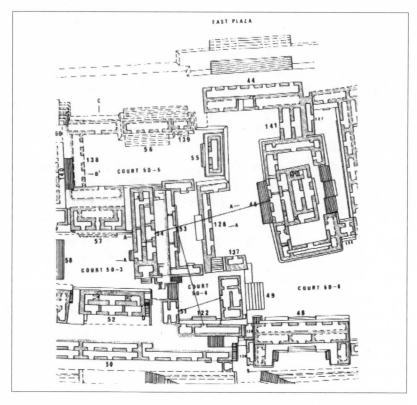

FIGURE 6.23

The baselines for surveying of a large construction project in Courtyards 4 and 6 form rigid right angles when the PAPs of the old and new buildings are connected.

5D-54 and 5D-46 crosses the proposed PAP for 5D-53, a right angle connects to the older 5D-122. In Courtyard 4 the intersection of these planning lines crosses with four squared right angles in negative space (that is, in open space of the Courtyard, not touching any of its surrounding architectural entities)—not in the center of Courtyard 4, because of the displacement between the older 5D-51 and the new 5D-49, but nevertheless out in negative space. The courtyard shape is rhomboidal as a result, and this geometric shape of the space enclosed by buildings is a clear indicator of the surveying technique that produces the shape.

Figure 6.23 above shows the resultant survey lines from both 5D-54 and 5D-46, which pinpoint the critical locations of corners of the new buildings 5D-49, 5D-53, and 5D-55. The older 5D-51 was also utilized as

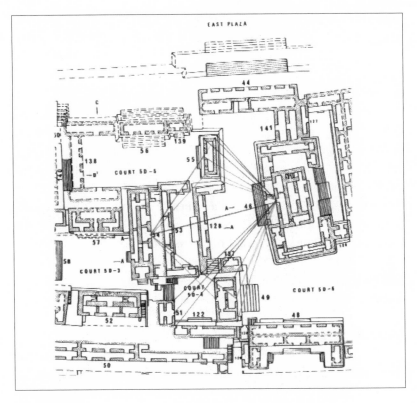

FIGURE 6.24

The actual right angles turned from sighting points in 5D-54 and 5D-46 show how the new project was laid out.

a reference for turning right angles in the laying out of this major planning project. The adjacent structures 5D-137 and 5D-128 were even later additions, so they did not figure in the results of the particular survey project I have described here.

Previously published examples for the survey of Structures 5D-63 and 5D-65 in Courtyard 2 were achieved by the use of a single survey vantage point. This example in Courtyard 6 is more complex because it involved two earlier survey vantage points.

Thus far, I have confined my observations within the boundaries of the Central Acropolis, which is clearly a false constriction since planning could not be contained by a single architectonic entity alone. Of necessity, such a system, which relates new structures to older ones, had to be extended beyond the boundaries of a single group if ancestral veneration was the primary motivation of planning. The ancestors might have lived in this group (the Central Acropolis) and built part of its components, but they were neither buried here nor confined in their residence to this complex.

Two examples, also previously published, are (1) the placement of Temple III by triangular reference to the sacred axis of the North Acropolis as it connected with Structure 5D-71 in the Central Acropolis (Harrison 1999:176, fig.111) and (2) a 3-4-5 triangle that connects the PAPs of 5D-52-1st, 1st Story, in the Central Acropolis to Temple III and hence to 5D-104, the central temple structure atop the South Acropolis, about which nothing is known by excavation. In this case, we know the relative dates of the two ends of the hypotenuse: A.D. 741 for 5D-52-1st and A.D. 810 for Temple III. My prediction is that the last named structure in the South Acropolis (5D-104) is the latest of the three connected points, a "last hurrah" at Tikal before the final decline.

CONCLUSION

Even before the final analysis is completed, a number of major steps have been achieved in understanding the Central Acropolis architectural complex. Through reconstructions on paper, we can begin to appreciate both the complexity and the beauty of the Maya achievement in the realm of elite residence and palace structures (fig. 6.25).

Despite attempts at other forms of definition, the old term *palace* remains the most useful. Although we still know that it does not correlate perfectly with the European model, there are enough areas of coincidence that analogies to European palaces no longer seem ridiculous. The Maya palaces were as complexly functional bases of both religion and government as their counterparts in Europe.

Royal residences are somewhat rarer than rulers; continuity of use is demonstrated by the example of 5D-46, which continued to be used into Eznab times (A.D. 850–950), during the very collapse of the city. However, not all the royal residences of Tikal have yet been identified. One royal residence, 5D-57, has been added to the list of those in the Central Acropolis—a strongly based speculation. Other functions of the architectural complex are proposed on the basis of a multitude of painted vessel scenes depicting military, judicial, social administrative,

FIGURE 6.25

This reconstruction of 5D-65 by T. W. Rutledge imagines a royal court reception scene taking place outdoors on the porch of the palace. While the iconography of the upper zone incorporates known imagery, much is imaginary. The stone screens flanking the top of the stair were found partially intact.

and diplomatic activities and the oversight of domestic affairs, including food production and ritual feasting. In short, a complex such as the Central Acropolis is a physical demonstration of centralized power. It happens to be an excellent example because of its location at the visual center of a large city, adjacent to a central place—the Great Plaza—and opposite the royal necropolis, which served this purpose for centuries—the North Acropolis (fig. 6.6 above).

Throne buildings have been added to the list of specific building functions. A distinction between permanent and temporary residence has particular importance to population estimates because the temporary residents should not be counted in such an estimate. Many of the most complex structures of the Central Acropolis fall into this category, such as 5D-65.

Finally, the Maya of Tikal built not only for function but also with an acute awareness of the aesthetic of their product. Perhaps this aesthetic had a dual function, having an intrinsically pleasing quality as a workplace for the insiders while at the same time serving to intimidate those who entered into its precincts as outsiders, either friendly or otherwise.

IN THE FUTURE

The Central Acropolis has not yet yielded its full story. We still know little of the earliest phases of occupation, and we have only a few glimpses into the configuration of its courtyards during the Early Classic period (A.D. 200–550). Three courtyards are in desperate need of further excavation. The first is Courtyard 3 and its two adjacent buildings, 5D-57 and 5D-58, each with enormous potential for the history of Tikal. Both may have been the houses of rulers, and the specific sequence between them and what lies beneath both are of particularly great interest.

The second, Courtyard 5, has been virtually untouched and thus is a blank slate. Structures 5D-56, 5D-138, and 5D-139 are unknown by date or author. Also, they border an important interconnective with the East Plaza and the Great Plaza, overlooking the official entrance to the Great Plaza.

The third, Courtyard 1, provides a link between the Early and Late periods in Tikal's rulership. It is a possible area of transition between influences from Teotihuacan and their abandonment for purely Maya modes of art and architecture. This courtyard is strangely isolated from the rest of the Acropolis, and the reasons for the separation would be useful to know.

In an extension outside the Central Acropolis, I see the three most important investigations as centered on 5E-38, which may indeed house the tomb of a ruler who lived in the adjacent Acropolis. Marshall Becker has noted the appearance of a Barringer Group in the relationship between this small temple and 5D-46 (Becker, pers. comm.). We need to know more about it. In addition, the contents and construction histories of Temple VI and the South Acropolis demand attention. Only a small part of Tikal's history is yet known.

Notes

1. The names, spelling, and numeration of the Tikal Rulers are standardized throughout this volume. These are readings that are neither permanent nor necessarily accepted by the author of this chapter.

7

The Tikal Renaissance and the East Plaza Ball Court

Christopher Jones

The University of Pennsylvania Museum of Archaeology and Anthropology excavated the East Plaza at Tikal in 1964 and 1965. I directed strategy and recording the first season and was joined in 1965 by Nicholas Hellmouth and Miguel Orrego. Brief preliminary reports appeared soon after (W. R. Coe 1964, 1965a, 1965b, 1967). Tikal Report 16 (C. Jones 1996:83–84) concluded that the East Plaza Ball Court and Shrine (Structures 5D-42, 5E-31, and 5D-43) may have commemorated the A.D. 695 victory of the Tikal ruler Jasaw Chan K'awiil I over Jaguar Paw of Calakmul, which had been recorded on Lintel 3 of Temple I (C. Jones 1977, 1985, 1991; Freidel, Schele, and Parker 1993:310–17; S. Martin and Grube 1994; S. Martin 1994, 1995; Schele and Matthews 1998:70–75; Harrison 1999:130–33).

Late Classic Tikal prosperity and creativity began around the time of this event and continued in full force for more than a century. Construction projects during this time included most of the "Great Temples" and palaces, the causeways, and the Twin Pyramid Groups. This chapter reviews evidence that the ball court and shrine were built shortly after Jasaw I's victory in A.D. 695 and suggests that they aided in

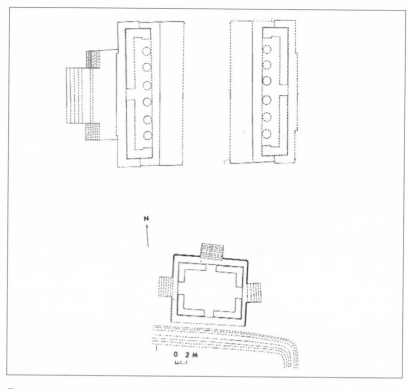

FIGURE 7.1

Plan of the East Plaza Ball Court and Shrine, Structures 5D-43, 5D-42, and 5E-31 (from C. Jones 1996:figs.8a,19a).

the success of the Tikal renaissance by linking the triumph to the mythological victory of the hero twins Hunapu and Xbalanque over the Lords of Death, as told in the Popol Vuh.

THE BALL COURT AND SHRINE

The East Plaza Ball Court is composed of Structures 5D-42 and 5E-31 (figs. 7.1, 7.2), which define a playing alley with vertical bench fronts and sloping plaster surfaces rising gently up to vertical back walls. The structures have paneled upper and lower zones that imitate vaulted buildings. Overlooking the playing alley are true vaulted buildings with cylindrical columns. Stairways to these upper buildings have not been found.

Beyond the southern end of the playing alley stands Structure

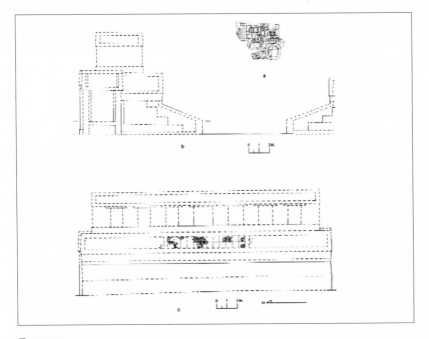

FIGURE 7.2

*Elevations of the East Plaza Ball Court, Structures 5D-42, 5E-31, (a) central fragment of
inscription on Str. 5E-31, (b) north ends of Str. 5E-31 and 5D-42, and (c) west side of
Structure 5E-31 (from C. Jones 1996:figs.151,8b,8d).*

5D-43 (figs. 7.1, 7.3). In its original form it was a square four-doorway
room on a three-stairway platform (C. Jones 1996:figs.19a, 19b, 22a).
Roofing of the large single room, before the addition of a secondary
medial wall, was supplied by half-vaults on all four walls, spanned by
wooden beams.

The platform carries distinctive profiles made up of a sloping
lower member or tablero decorated by Venus-star designs (Carlson
1991), a vertical middle panel or *talud* with the eye-guards of the
Mesoamerican deity Tlaloc, and an outward-sloping upper member or
reverse *talud* with the Venus designs. The upper zone is decorated by
shallow-relief front-view representations of deity faces with full lips;
molars; large bifurcated tongues; humanlike incisors; long, curving
side fangs; sky glyphs; and pendent human hearts. The roof was topped
by pyramidal merlons, one of which was found in the debris (C. Jones
1996:fig.74a).

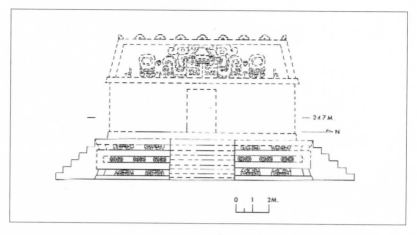

FIGURE 7.3

Elevations of the East Plaza Shrine, Structure 5D-43, (a) *north side,* (b) *details of east side, and* (c) *detail of south side (from C. Jones 1996:figs.20,21,22a).*

The radial four-stairway design, three-member moldings, Venus and Tlaloc decorations, and merlons link the structure to those depicted on ceramic vessels and clay models from sites in Western Mesoamerica (Gendorp 1985:figs.2, 4b, 5, 8a,b) and mark it as a sacrificial chamber as identified by Carlson in the iconography of Teotihuacan, Cacaxtla, and other Western Mesoamerican sites (Carlson 1991). A Tikal antecedent may lie in the Early Classic structure that held a Venus-Tlaloc effigy war banner commemorating an earlier Tikal victory (Laporte 1989; Harrison 1999:80; figs.41–43). The battle standard is like one represented in the famous Tlamimilolpa mural of Teotihuacan as a marker in a game of ball.

There are vivid examples of the association of the ball game with sacrifice. Stairway panels of Structure 33 of Yaxchilan show a bound prisoner on a large rubber ball bounced against a stairway by the Yaxchilan ruler Bird Jaguar, who is wearing ball-game gear (Freidel, Schele, and Parker 1993:356–62, 372–74). Also, a ball court at Tonina displays statues of bound prisoners as side markers. Structure A-13 at Seibal, a four-stairway platform on the long axis of ball-court Structure A-19, contained the disarticulated and fragmentary bones of 11 or 12 individuals, mostly young males, buried in the center of its summit surface (Tourtellot 1990:90–91).

Four-stairway platforms at the ends of ball-court alleys are also found in Late and Terminal Classic sites of Quiche and Huehuetenango, Guatemala, and Chiapas, Mexico (Taladoire 1981:190–95, 242–44, pls. 41–44,58), providing a link between the Classic Period Lowland Maya and Highland Maya cultures that produced the Popol Vuh.

DATING THE EAST PLAZA BALL COURT BY STRATIGRAPHY

Precise dating of Maya architecture is becoming possible because of ongoing decipherment of hieroglyphic inscriptions on stone stelae, altars, lintels, wall panels, and burial artifacts. A date or a ruler's name can place a structure in time or link it to a dated reign. Buildings without directly asssociated dates can also be placed in time by stratigraphic connectives.

Initial paving of the East Plaza (Platform 5D-2) with Floor 4 created a broad expanse of plaster surface that stretched from one end of the plaza to the other (C. Jones 1996:fig.9). The western edge of the floor turned up to a Great Plaza stair or terrace (Platform 5D-1: Unit 17) in almost certain contemporaneity (W. R. Coe 1990:fig.254). Unit 17 was assessed to have been built in conjunction with a Floor 4B paving of the Great Plaza around A.D. 0 (W. R. Coe 1990:chart 1).

In time the East Plaza received two thick new pavements (Floors 3 and 2). The second one turned up to a second Great Plaza stair or terrace (Unit 18), and the underlying mortar layer almost assures contemporaneity. A set of twin four-stairway pyramids, Structures 5D-Sub.16 and 5E-Sub.1, were erected with Floor 2 (C. Jones 1996:figs.4,5). East and west of each other, five terraces high with four stairways, the pyramids are identical to later Twin Pyramids from 9.13.0.0.0 to 9.18.0.0.0 (A.D. 692–790). The Twin Pyramid Groups at Tikal probably housed the ceremonies of the new year, presided over by the ruler, who scattered seeds on the ground in prognostication of the year's fortunes (C. Jones 1969).

East Plaza Floor 2 is connected by contemporaneous joinings of floors and walls to Floor 2A of the Great Plaza, floor Unit 26 of the North Terrace, and Floor 3 of the North Acropolis (W. R. Coe 1990:838–40), all of which seem to have been built as a single project later than Structure 5D-33-2nd and its painted Burial 48 chamber date of 9.1.1.10.10 (A.D. 457). W. R. Coe estimated a date of A.D. 475, which places the Twin Pyramids into the reign of Kan Boar or his son Jaguar Paw Skull.

The East Plaza Ball Court was erected over the Twin Pyramids, burying them completely within its fills. The ball-court shrine and it were abutted by Floor 1 (C. Jones 1996:figs.9, 12a,b,c, 13, 19d, 22c). In all cases, the walls and floors are on mortar layers, so Floor 1 is probably contemporary as a finishing pavement.

Floor 1 on the western side of the plaza lies under Temple I and the Unit 15 stairway behind it (W. R. Coe 1990:fig.254a; C. Jones 1996:figs.2c, 9). Because Temple I, which covers the burial of Jasaw, could not have been built after 9.15.3.6.8 (A.D. 731), when Jasaw's son Ruler B took the throne (C. Jones 1977), the ball court must precede that date.

Coe concluded that Floor 1 of the East Plaza and Floor 1 of the Great Plaza were contemporaries, coinciding with Unit 8 under Temple I and a two-stage Unit 71 facade to the north (W. R. Coe 1990:842). Floor 1 of the Great Plaza contemporaneously abuts a rebuilding of the North Terrace stairway (Unit 209A) and a terrace summit floor (Unit 25) that abuts Str. 5D-32-1st (W. R. Coe 1990:141–42, 840–42, chart 1). Unit 25 on the North Terrace was not laid at the time of Str. 5D-32-1st, however, as had previously been concluded (C. Jones 1996:83–84). That discussion of the stratigraphy overlooked the fact that Unit 25 possessed three or four sequent plaster surfaces near Structure 5D-32-1st and not elsewhere on the North Terrace (W. R. Coe 1990:figs.196, 205a) (fig. 7.4). The lower surfaces turning up to 32-1st disappear as they spread out from it. Only the upper one, which must be far later than Structure 5D-32-1st, extends across the terrace toward the south and east and was laid with the Unit 209A terrace steps, Floor 1 of the Great Plaza, Floor 1 of the East Plaza, and the ball court and shrine. Coe suggests (1990:141) that the floor was put in around 75 years after 5D 32-1st, just before the burning activity that occurred between Burials 24 and 23 (see below). This revision of the stratigraphy means that Structure 5D-33-1st, not Structure 5D-32-1st as had been thought, is associated with these major plaza refurbishings. The change is of major importance in that these important construction activities can no longer be assigned to the years prior to

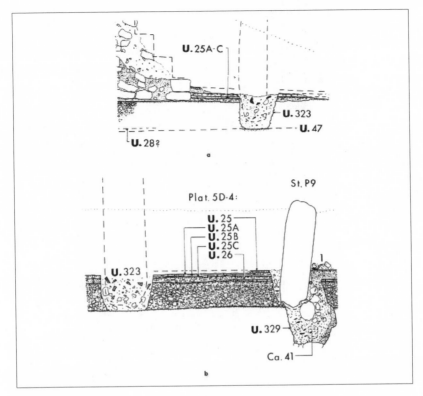

FIGURE 7.4

*North Terrace floors (Platform 5D-4), (a) Units 25A–C, under unmarked Unit 25, abut-
ting Stela 6 and the stair of Str. 5D-32-1st (from Coe 1990:fig.196), and (b) the same
floors between Stela 6 and Stela P9 in an E–W section (from Coe 1990:fig.205A).*

Jasaw. The burial of Animal Skull in 5D-32-1st was not accompanied by
large-scale constructions as had been suggested.

Other important constructions coincided with the building of the
East Plaza Ball Court. Floor 1 extended onto the northern Maler
Causeway and eastern Mendez Causeway, becoming the first of their two
pavements. These new causeways greatly transformed the appearance of
Tikal at the time of the ball-court project. Also, the first gallery of the
East Plaza marketplace (Structure 5E-95-2nd) was erected at the far east-
ern edge of the open space, blocking the only access stair up to the East
Acropolis (C. Jones 1996). Behind Structure 5D-43 rose a massive new
terrace of the Central Acropolis (C. Jones 1996:fig.19d). This rebuilding

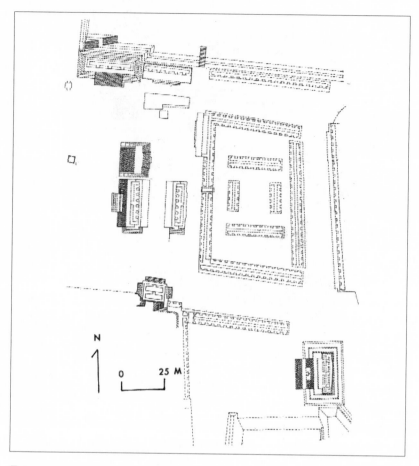

FIGURE 7.5

The East Plaza Marketplace (from C. Jones 1996:fig.1).

of the eastern end of the Central Acropolis was labeled Platform 5D-27-B, C, and D, respectively, under Structures 5D-47, 45, and 44 (Harrison 1970:figs.10, 11, 12, 13). Where the terrace met the Great Plaza platform at the southwest corner of the East Plaza, it is also clear that it was built with East Plaza Floor 1 (C. Jones 1996:figs.2c, 66a).

After construction, neither the ball court nor the shrine was ever dismantled or buried. A tall, pyramidal structure to the north, though very close, faced west and apparently did not hinder the ball-court function. The southern ends of the court were buttressed, and the western stairway was expanded to cover the entire west facade. The shrine room was divided in two by an internal transverse wall, with a central doorway eliminating the rear and side doorways. The Venus and Tlaloc designs on the structural platform were covered by wider stairways, but the corners of the three-member profile remained visible. Successive constructions of long multi-doorwayed galleries eventually completed a large complex east of the ball court composed of an enclosing rectangle, protected inner galleries, gallery-lined streets, possible guardrooms, and judges' stands for what was probably a marketplace (C. Jones 1996:fig.1) (fig. 7.5). The market was begun by Jasaw, but its final form was built with pavements later than Temple I and must be credited to Jasaw's son Ruler B or his grandson Ruler C.

DATING THE EAST PLAZA BALL COURT BY MASONRY

Structures can also be dated by comparisons of style and technique. Technical changes that are hidden in the final product—for example, wall blocks covered by plaster—are especially reliable for chronology.

The masonry of the ball court and shrine (Structures 5D-42, 5E-31, and 5D-43) is uniform in dimensions and installations (C. Jones 1996:figs.13a,b, 14d,e, 20, 22c) (figs. 7.3 above, 7.6, table 7.1). The soft marl wall blocks generally measure 0.45 to 0.55 meters in length, 0.25 to 0.30 in height, and 0.20 to 0.25 in thickness; that is, they stand up on their sides in the walls. Tops of courses are often undulating, and thin flat stones are used to even out the undulations for a horizontal line. Headers are placed between every one or two stretchers. Decorative elements are carved in low relief, as on the hieroglyph panels of the ball court (fig. 7.2 above) and the designs of the shrine (fig. 7.3 above).

When compared to masonry elsewhere in Tikal (table 7.1), these characteristics best match Structure 5D-33-1st (compare fig. 7.6a, b, c). They are also seen in Structures 5D-2-1st and 5D-1-1st (Temples II and I) and Twin Pyramid Structures (3D-99, 5C-14, and 4D-32), which date to A.D. 692, 711, and 731. Stratigraphically earlier Structures 5D-32-1st and 5D-22-1st (fig. 7.6d) were built with stones of similar dimensions laid on their largest surfaces rather than on their sides. This masonry is also seen in Twin Pyramid Structures 5E-Sub.1 and 5D-Sub.16 beneath the ball court (table 7.1). Later structures, such as those of

TABLE 7.1

Measurements of Three Consecutive Masonry Types at Tikal (from Coe 1990; Jones 1969, 1996)

Structure	Length	Height	Depth	Date A.D.: Time Span (m.) and Range	
Early Masonry					
5D-22-1st	0.35	0.1	0.25	Gr.5D-2:TS.6	475–630
5D-32-1st	0.22–.6	0.11–.18	0.2–.4	Gr.5D-2:TS.5B	630–670
5E-Sub.1	0.35–.5	0.15–.2	0.2–.3	Gr.5D-3:TS.6	475–630
Early Late Masonry					
5D-33-1st	0.65	0.3	0.25	Gr.5D-2:TS.5A	670–730
5D-2-1st	0.6	0.3	0.2	Gr.5D-2:TS.4B	700–730
5D-1-1st				Gr.5D-2:TS.4A	730–800
5D-42	0.4–.7	0.25	0.2	Gr.5D-3:TS.5	630–730
5E-31	0.55	0.3	0.2	Gr.5D-3:TS.5	630–730
5D-43	0.5	0.3	0.25	Gr.5D-3:TS.5	630–730
3D-99	0.51	0.26	0.15	9.13.0.0.0	692
5C-14	0.49	0.24	0.19	9.14.0.0.0	711
4D-32	0.54	0.28	0.17	9.15.0.0.0	731
Late Masonry					
5E-32-1st	0.55–.63	0.32–.4	0.17	Gr.5D-3:TS.4	730–770
5E-34	0.5	0.35	0.2	Gp.5D-3:TS.3	770–810
5D-40	0.5	0.35	0.18	Gp.5D-3:TS.3	770–810
5D-37-A	0.50–.60	0.35	0.18	Gp.5D-3:TS.3	770–810
5E-41-2nd	0.56	0.36	0.19–.24	Gp.5D-3:TS.4	730–770
5E-95-1st	0.55	0.35	0.25	Gp.5D-3:TS.3	770–810
3D-44, 45	0.58	0.3	0.21	9.16.0.0.0	751
4E-36	0.57	0.31	0.22	9.17.0.0.0	771
4E-40, 41	0.51	0.34	0.17	9.18.0.0.0	790
Later Masonry					
5E-22	0.45–.60	0.35–.44	0.2	Gp.5D-3:TS.3	770–810
5D-134	0.55–.60	0.3	0.15	Gp.5D-3:TS.2	810–900

the marketplace adjacent to the ball court, have larger blocks averaging 0.55 to 0.60 m. in length and 0.30 to 0.35 m. in height, as do the later Twin Pyramid Structures (3D-44, 3D-45, 4E-36, 4E-40, and 4E-41 of table 7.1 above) at A.D. 751, 771, and 790.

In sum, three sequent masonry types can be observed in the Tikal Late Classic (table 7.1):

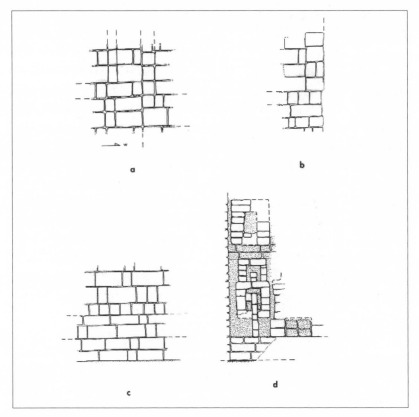

FIGURE 7.6

Masonry examples from structures at Tikal, (a) Ball Court Structure 5E-31, (b) Ball Court Structure 5D-42, (c) Structure 5D-33-1st, and (d) Structure 5D-32-1st (from C. Jones 1996:figs.14d,e; Coe 1990:figs.190e,201a).

- Flat-laid blocks (Structures 5D-Sub.16, 5E-Sub.1, 5D-22-1st, and 5D-32-1st)

- On-edge blocks (Structures 5D-42, 5E-31, 5D-43, 5D-33-1st, 5D-2-1st, 5D-1-1st, and Twin Pyramid Groups before A.D. 731)

- Slightly larger on-edge blocks (Structures 5D-74, 5E-32-1st, 5E-34, 5D-40, 5D-37-A, 5D-41-2nd, 5E-95-1st, 5E-22, and Twin Pyramid Groups after A.D. 751)

The East Plaza Ball Court and Shrine belong to the middle group from A.D. 692 to 731, and their closest match is Structure 5D-33-1st.

DATING THE EAST PLAZA BALL COURT
BY EPIGRAPHY

Several hieroglyphically inscribed stones were recovered from text panels overlooking the ball-court alley on Structures 5D-42 and 5E-31 (C. Jones 1996:27, fig.8d, 15) (fig. 7.2a, c above). Only two fragments were recovered from what was probably the first half of the text on the western side, and the remainder is yet to be recovered. The eastern side (Structure 5E-31), on the other hand, was completely excavated. Several blocks from the central area were fitted together (fig. 7.2a above) and carry the distance number 1 katun, 15 tuns (35 years), with possible additional months and days, a count-forward glyph reading iwal-ut, and a glyph-block with coefficient 1 and the day-sign Ahau. Although a period ending sign was not found, the Tikal Emblem Glyph that ends the inscription is suitably placed for a Period Ending dedication. 1 Ahau tun endings at 0, 3, 5, 10, 13, or 15 tun within the typological and stratigraphic range of the architecture are as follows:

9.10.0.0.0	1 Ahau 8 Kayab	(A.D. 633)
9.10.13.0.0	1 Ahau 3 Kankin	(A.D. 646)
9.13.5.0.0	1 Ahau 3 Pop	(A.D. 697)
9.16.10.0.0	1 Ahau 3 Zip	(A.D. 761)
9.17.3.0.0	1 Ahau 3 Cumku	(A.D. 771)

The first two dates are early for Structure 5D-33-1st, and the last two are later than Temple I. The middle date, 9.13.5.0.0, is just a year and a half after Jasaw's 9.13.3.7.18 (A.D. 695) victory over Jaguar Paw of Calakmul. Five-tun dedications are not common at Tikal, but one does occur forty years later on Stela 21.

High above the south side of the East Plaza stood Structure 5D-57 (Schele and Grube 1994b:142; Harrison 1999:131, fig.76). The upper zone of the building depicts a figure dressed in a Venus-Owl headdress holding a rope attached to a seated, bound prisoner. A calendar round date falls just 13 days after the battle and states the name and Calakmul origin of the captive. The raked angle of the upper zone, the low flat relief of the carving, and the masonry dimensions match those features in Structures 5D-43, 5D-42, and 5E-31. The structure was built on Platform 5D-18, which raises the courtyard between earlier Structures 5D-58 and 54 and, with them, forms a secluded courtyard facing out over the southern ravine (Harrison 1970:figs.5, 6). The rear doorway of the building opens onto a terrace that commands a view down over the East Plaza and the newly built causeway to the North Zone (Harrison 1970:figs.13, 15). Without the crowding of later Structures 5D-140 and 59 beside it, this building would have stood prominently at the central and highest point of the palace complex.

SHIELD SKULL AND STRUCTURE 5D-33-1ST

In the hieroglyphic text on Lintel 3 of Temple I, Jasaw extolled his victory over Jaguar Paw of Calakmul. In addition, he stated that his mother was Lady Jaguar Throne and his father was Shield Skull, ruler of Tikal. The same parentage statement is repeated on hairpinlike bone objects found with his body in Burial 116 under Temple I. No inscriptions from Shield Skull's reign have survived at Tikal, but recently much has been learned about Shield Skull and his career from inscriptions outside Tikal (Houston 1993:100; S. Martin and Grube 1994:11–13; S. Martin 1994; Schele and Grube 1994b:122–33; Harrison 1999:125–26). Pertinent dates are

- A.D. 657 (9.11.5.4.14), a "star wars" defeat of Tikal and exile of Shield Skull by Calakmul (Dos Pilas Hieroglyphic Stair 2)

- A.D. 659 (9.11.6.16.17), an "arrival" by Shield Skull at Palenque after participation in a successful war by Palenque against Yaxchilan and Pomona (Palenque Temple of the Inscriptions)

- A.D. 672 (9.12.0.8.3), a "star wars" victory by Shield Skull over Dos Pilas (Dos Pilas Hieroglyphic Stair 4)

- A.D. 679 (9.12.6.16.17), a "he tore down the flints and shields" defeat of Shield Skull by Ruler 1 of Dos Pilas (Dos Pilas Hieroglyphic Stair 4)

- A.D. 682 (9.12.9.17.16), accession of Jasaw, son of Shield Skull, presumably after the latter's death (Temple I, Lintel 3)

- A.D. 695 (9.13.3.7.18), a "he tore down the flints and shields" defeat of Jaguar Paw of Calakmul by Jasaw

- A.D. 697 (9.13.5.0.0), dedication of the East Plaza Ball Court

Maya texts often cite a prior defeat of the home polity in order to glorify a victory as a vindication, as in the Dos Pilas Hieroglyphic Stair 4 text above (Houston 1993:108; S. Martin 1995:2). The 35-year distance number on the ball court that counts forward to 1 Ahau probably does so from missing dates around A.D. 662 (9.11.10.0.0), five years after Shield Skull's first defeat and five years before his victory over the ruler of Dos Pilas. Jasaw's use of the phrase "he tore down the flints and shields" on the Temple I lintel text, duplicating that used previously by Dos Pilas against Shield Skull, suggests that Jasaw linked his triumph with the hard times inflicted on his father.

Recent discovery of what may be Jaguar Paw's tomb at Calakmul verifies that "he tore down his flint and shields," when used by Jasaw to describe the victory over Jaguar Paw, did not necessarily mean that Jaguar Paw was captured and sacrificed (Carrasco et al. 1999). By the same token, we do not know whether Shield Skull was captured or sacrificed in his A.D. 679 defeat.

Burial 23, beneath Structure 5D-33-1st, is the possible but by no means certain resting place of Shield Skull. The Ik ceramic complex vessels in the grave are chronologically appropriate for that ruler, and a C-14 sample in the fill material of the burial shaft gives a date spread from A.D. 620 to 740, with the 680 midpoint close to the A.D. 682 accession of Jasaw (W. R. Coe 1990:807–9, appendix F). Placement of the previously shattered Stela 31 remnants within the rooms of Structure 5D-33-2nd before construction of 33-1st would have been a logical reverential act on the part of Jasaw.

There are not one but two important burials in Structure 5D-33-1st. The chamber and shaft of Burial 23 were sealed and filled, and the cut stairway of the old Structure 33-2nd was restored for use. Burning charred this repaired stair and summit and the old terrace floor in front. The Unit-25 floor mentioned above as being contemporary to the ball courts covered this burned flooring prior to the new temple (W. R. Coe 1990:141). A second shaft was dug through the repaired stair, and another body was placed to rest in a new chamber, Burial 24, above—and almost as large as—the earlier one. The body lay on an identical rectangular area of rotted organic material that was probably a bier or litter. *Spondylus* shells were arranged similarly around both bodies and were worn on the heads as a sort of cap. Both skeletons had jade inlays in their upper-front incisor teeth and stingray spines near their right shoulders. Both were adults, male in Burial 23 and undetermined in Burial 24. Ceramic inventories were complementary in a way; Burial 23 had nine drinking cups and three Ahau-decorated plates, whereas Burial 23 contained four rounded bowls and two plates, one with a drawing of a catfish.

Although Coe called the occupant of Burial 24 a hunchback (1990:844), the 120-cm. height estimate from skeletal positions (Burial 23 was 150 cm.) was not necessarily the correct height of the individual in life. The chest and upper backbones were not preserved, and the skull could well have been displaced toward the hips after death by battlefield mutilation, transportation, or roof collapse. The limb bones themselves are only slightly shorter than those of Burial 23. Axial setting, chamber size, and furnishings suggest that the personage in Burial 24 was a full member of the royal family, perhaps a wife, brother, son, or nephew. For that matter, either burial could be Shield Skull. In fact, because Burial 24 initiated Structure 5D-33-1st, it may be the better candidate.

THE POPOL VUH AND THE PLACE
OF BALL GAME SACRIFICE

The Popol Vuh is a Maya mytho-historical epic poem written in Highland Guatemala in the middle of the 16th century, probably by members of the ruling Quiche Maya lineage, in their language and in roman script (Tedlock 1985:28). One chapter tells the story of the triumph of the twin dieties Hunapu and Xbalanque over the Lords of Death. As I have mentioned, the plans of some Postclassic ball courts in the Highlands have their precedents in Classic-period Tikal and Seibal. Furthermore, scenes from the ball-game story and the names of the hero twins appear in Classic Maya art (Freidel, Schele, and Parker 1973:340–72). There can be no doubt that the tale was centuries old when it was written down.

Before the twins are born, their father and uncle, One Hunapu and Seven Hunapu, go to Xibalba to play ball with the lords but are tricked and killed before they can play a game. Their bodies are buried at the *puzbal chaak,* the "Place of Ball Game Sacrifice," but the head of One Hunapu is hung on a tree and impregnates a maiden, who gives birth to Hunapu and Xbalanque. The boys go back to avenge the deaths of their father and uncle by playing ball with the lords. They triumph over every trick the lords try on them, allow themselves to be burned to death, then return to life and trick the lords into being cut to pieces. The boys ascend to rule the sun and the moon after the father and uncle are put back together and left at the Place of Ball Game Sacrifice:

> And the first to die, a long time before, had been their fathers, One Hunapu and Seven Hunapu. And they saw the face of their father again, there in Xibalba. Their father spoke to them again when they had defeated Xibalba.
>
> And here their father is put back together by them. They put Seven Hunapu back together; they went to the Place of Ball Game Sacrifice to put him together. He had wanted his face to become just as it was, but when he was asked to name everything, and once he had found the name of the mouth, the nose, the eyes of his face, there was little else to be said. Although his mouth could not name the names of each of his former parts, he had at least spoken again. And so it remained that they were respectful of their father's heart, even though they had left him at the Place of Ball Game Sacrifice: "You will be prayed to here," his sons told him, and his heart was comforted. "You will be the first resort, and you will be the first to have your day kept by those who will be born in the light, begotten in the light. Your name will not be lost. So be it," they told their father when they comforted his heart. We merely cleared the road of your death, your loss, the pain, the suffering that were inflicted upon you.
> (Popol Vuh, Tedlock 1985:159)

Contrary to Dennis Tedlock, if I play with the punctuation, this passage may refer almost entirely to the father, One Hunapu, with the reference to Seven Hunapu being an aside stating that he, too, is put back together (Tedlock 1985:40–46, 233–35, 295–97). The father, One Hunapu, is the one who lost his head and clearly is "the first resort....the first to have your day kept by those who will be born in the light." His name is the day One Ahau and the name of Venus as morning star, the "first resort," which precedes the sun in the morning sky.

This name for Venus derives from the selection of the day One Ahau as the first heliacal rising of Venus in a 104-year cycle (J. E. S. Thompson 1950:217–29). Seven Hunapu, the uncle, may be Venus as the evening star, which is seen in the sky only eight or so days before its morning appearance. Tedlock points out that Seven Ahau is the previous appearance of Ahau in the 260-day calendar before One Ahau. Therefore, One Ahau and Seven Ahau are an "Alpha and Omega" expression representing the entire cycle of Ahau in the Sacred Calendar.

This probably ancient story of revenge and victory would have been appropriate for Jasaw of Tikal if he wished to stress the importance of his recent victory. By using it, he could set the triumph into the context of national Maya mythology and convince his supporters that Tikal's reborn strength was just part of the natural order. No better way to make the connection would exist than to build a grand ball court and Venus-Tlaloc platform in which the defeated lords and armies could be offered in sacrifice. The fact that the current five-year period ended on the Venus day 1 Ahau would not have escaped his notice, and the centering of this hieroglyphic date on the eastern side of the ball court does honor to the name of Venus as morning star in the eastern sky. Even his father's name, Shield Skull, may have recalled to him or to his advisors the bone-white skull of One Hunapu, which had hung on a tree in the story. Perhaps it is significant that Ahau signs on the plates in Burial 23 carry coefficients of six, seven, and eight and may therefore refer to Seven Hunapu, or Seven Ahau, the brother of One Ahau (fig. 7.7a). The catfish painted on one of the plates in Burial 24 recalls the catfish forms taken by Hunapu and Xbalanque as they returned to life after leaping into the fire (fig. 7.7b).

If the stratigraphic connectives between the ball court and Structure 5D-33-1st are followed in their most reasonable interpretation, they conform to the narrative. Jasaw came to the throne in 682, while Tikal's power was still low. He erected his first Twin Pyramid Group ten years later at 9.13.0.0.0, erecting the first carved monument (Stela 30) at Tikal in nearly 150 years. Three years later he achieved his great triumph and erected the Place of Ball Game Sacrifice over the old Twin Pyramids. In a long-overdue reconstruction effort, he rebuilt the East Plaza; the eastern end of the Central Acropolis; the sides, stairs, and floors of the Great Plaza; and the North Terrace. As a result of the

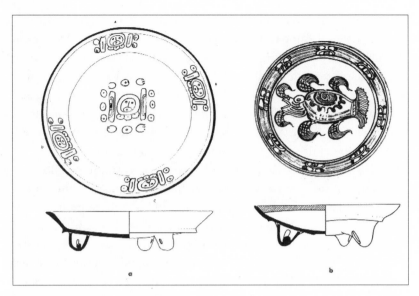

FIGURE 7.7

Ceramic plates from Burials 23 and 24, (a) Ahau plate from Burial 23 and (b) Fish plate from Burial 24 (from Culbert 1993:figs.40a,42a).

victory, as in the Popol Vuh story, he was perhaps able to recover the bodies of his father and uncle from the lands of the defeated enemy, one slightly later and more deteriorated than the other, and cap their twinned burials by Structure 5D-33-1st.

In this chapter I have attempted to show that the ball court and the Venus-Tlaloc shrine in the East Plaza date to the time of Structure 5D-33-1st and Burials 23 and 24, sometime in the late seventh century A.D. in the 15th year of the great Tikal king Jasaw I. The 1 Ahau date on the court fits the Period End 9.13.5.0.0 (A.D. 697), just after Jasaw's victory over Calakmul. The iconography of the court and shrine are associated with the sacrifice of war captives. The choice of a ball-court complex is appropriate to this particular victory, which avenges prior defeats, because it recalls the similar story of the revenge of the hero twins for the death of their father and uncle. Burials 23 and 24 may contain the bones of Jasaw's father and uncle—Shield Skull and an unknown brother.

These conclusions carry interesting implications. Construction projects that covered contiguous areas of central Tikal can be demonstrated through careful examination of juncture points of floors and walls. Furthermore, masonry typology can be inserted in the chronological placement of otherwise undated constructions. Finally, hieroglyphs can help to date architecture, and architecture, in turn, can enrich the facts obtained from those inscriptions.

At times, architectural history has been written as the personal history of a great leader. The existence of the East Plaza of Tikal, in its enormous outlay of material, manpower, creative energy, and transformative thought, may be in some sense due to the will of an individual. At the same time, it must be acknowledged that Jasaw did not achieve the victory or the building program by himself. History must reach beyond the individual to look at cultural contexts such as geography, trade, architecture, art, religion, common culture, and settlement. Because of careful data gathering during the years of excavations at Tikal, we are in a position to see more of that context than usual.

8

The North Acropolis

Monumentality, Function, and Architectural Development

H. Stanley Loten

High, pyramidal temples like Great Temple I at Tikal are the popular icons of ancient Maya civilization. Their familiarity implies that we know them very well, but the truth is quite different. They stubbornly guard their secrets. Their precise functions, the fundamental reasons why they were built, and the ends they were meant to accomplish remain uncertain. Bassie-Sweet (1996:118), for example, has suggested that temples may have been conceived as places where the gods came to receive offerings. There have been few suggestions more specific than this. We assume that elaborate rituals were staged on and around temples. We know that caches and interments were placed within their fabrics and that fires were burned on their floors. We can imagine the clouds of incense billowing out of their doorways. But we can only speculate about the fundamental cultural pressures that produced them and required that they should be monumental in form.

This chapter presents an exploratory model based on the proposition that temples would not have been built on the scale and in the abundance that we find, or with such impressive monumentality, in the absence of very compelling reasons for such investment. Further, I propose that the fundamental motivations for temple building might have been practical in nature rather than symbolic, a presumption based mainly on the large number of temples built by all Mesoamerican cultures. I have developed the model under the assumption that temples would not have been built in the forms and numbers that we see unless some kind of readily understandable material benefit could be expected to flow from them.

If pragmatic, material considerations prompted temple building in the first place, epiphenomenal by-products such as support for rulership, social status, and elite authority may have emerged later. Temples initially may have evolved out of the settings established very early for shamanic activities. Places similar to the contemporary shrines described by Dennis Tedlock (1985) and Evon Vogt (1969) might have become increasingly elaborated in ways intended to enhance the shamanic function. Elaboration might have developed into architectural treatments intended to reinforce shamanic objectives of managing animistic or metanatural forces for practical, material benefit. Temples might have begun in this way and later come to be employed for ideological purposes, to validate elite status and dynastic legitimacy—objectives that might have been absent or much weaker initially.

In considering how temples might have been understood initially as tools or instruments able to serve shamanism, I have employed the North Acropolis at Tikal as a case study and have emphasized the architectural feature of monumentality. If a model based on the North Acropolis can account for monumentality in terms of its practical utility rather than its symbolism, the same argument should be applicable to some degree in Maya temple architecture generally.

Tikal epitomizes monumentality in Maya architecture (compare Webster 1998:14). The Great Plaza, the North Acropolis, and the Late Classic Great Temples stand as prime examples of monumentality at a level hardly surpassed by other world traditions. Tikal, therefore, is an appropriate context in which to raise the general question of monumentality as it relates to cultural development. Traditionally, monumental architecture has tended to be regarded as an epi-phenomenon of political power, wealth, and social status—an expression of the desire for self-aggrandizement and memorialization. This view has been most clearly articulated by Bruce Trigger (1990) but is implicit in many accounts of Maya architecture. I propose not to discredit factors such as conspicuous consumption, display, and symbolism, which undoubtedly did apply, but to suggest that monumental architecture might have initially emerged in response to very different concerns—pragmatic, practical matters addressed within an animistic worldview, in which shamanic techniques were expected to produce material results. Such concerns may have provided the fundamental motivation for temple building even after political powers had to some extent co-opted the ritual dimension of ancient Maya civilization.

After proposing a speculative model that suggests how monumentality might have contributed to a primary function for temples, I review the architectural sequence documented for the North Acropolis at Tikal. A prolonged developmental experiment in monumentality can be seen at Tikal that may extend from primary temple functions into a more complex secondary role associated as much with political ambition as with management of metanatural forces.

Most studies of monumental architecture emphasize symbolism, commemoration, and reference to cosmic templates as aspects of meaning (Ashmore 1991, 1992; Dunning 1992; Schele and Mathews 1998; Webster 1998; Grove 1999; Lewis and Stout 1998). Although they have greatly advanced our understanding and their findings are not in question, these studies do not propose interpretations more fundamental than symbol and metaphor. The model I advance here assumes that enterprises such as centering the world and replicating cosmic or underworld orders, though of some importance, would not have been the fundamental reasons for building temples. I suggest that simpler, more directly profitable motivations are called for in view of the magnitude of the investment that temples represent and the universality of the practice of temple building. Artifacts of such prominence in Mesoamerican cultures surely must have been made for very tangible reasons.

Monumentality in architecture is not merely a matter of size. Peter Murray and Linda Murray (1959:216) define the term as "grand, noble, elevated in idea, simple in conception and execution, without any excess of virtuosity, and having something of the enduring, stable and timeless nature of great architecture....not a synonym for 'large' [parenthesis in original]." Lewis Mumford (1961:65) suggests that "what we now call 'monumental architecture' [parentheses in original] is first of all the expression of power,...the purpose [of which]...was to produce respectful terror," a definition that seems very appropriate to the Mesoamerican context. However, there is another dimension to monumentality that may have been even more directly effective.

Monumentality produces a sensory effect that can be used for symbolic purposes and can be interpreted as physical, metanatural power. A tangible sense of such power is generated directly by the strength and character of architectural form. Very few visitors to the Great Plaza at Tikal—even those unaware of the symbolism it contains—fail to notice this effect. This palpable emanation is something that ancient people might have interpreted as metanatural, animistic force. In the context of the Classic period at sites such as Tikal, this immediate apprehension of physical power, still perceptible today, would have been far stronger when institutions operating in the monumental centers were staging their dramatic, sanguinary rituals.

Within the ancient Maya worldview, the sensory effect of architectural power might have been understood as the action or presence of metanatural power and not simply as an effect produced by the architecture or mere symbolic referencing. Physical power would be expected to produce material, pragmatic results such as good crops, good health, and victory in battle. Temples thought to be infused with metanatural power might be expected to function as instruments facilitating management of that power for the benefit of society. The way in which this might work is most succinctly suggested by Frankfort et al. (1946:15) in his depiction of the Nile, which, if it does not rise, "has refused to rise [parenthesis in original]." To remedy this, the animistic power controlling the Nile must be somehow persuaded to act more favorably. Egyptian temple architecture and sacrificial ceremony provided the instruments needed to accomplish this kind of metaforce management. Mesoamerican monumental temples may be a parallel development.

In recent decades researchers have identified a number of Maya terms that seem to refer to basic vitalizing forces that animate the cosmos—terms such as *ch'ul* or *K'ul* (Schele and Freidel 1990), *ch'ulel* (Ringle 1999), and *its* (Freidel, Schele, and Parker 1993). These refer to animistic forces of nature, elsewhere labeled as "meta-cosmological" or "meta-meteorological forces" (Tate 1999) and identified here as metanatural forces. Joyce Marcus, Kent Flannery, and Ronald Spores (1983:37) and Marcus (1989:150–51) describe a force called *pee* for the Oaxaca region, which could "occupy animate beings as well as some inanimate objects." Richard Townsend (1979) discusses *teotl*, a similar force recognized by the Aztecs.

For simplicity's sake, and because Bernal Diaz del Castillo (1963) referred to temples by the term *cu*, I will use *k'u* as an umbrella term for these forces. The word adopted by Castillo probably reflects a term employed by the Maya at the time. Whether or not it is correct to characterize the referents of *c'u* as gods or as more abstract forces has been a subject of much discussion (compare Taube [1992a:7–9]; Townsend [1979]; Tate [1999]; Marcus [1989]). Our desire to make this kind of distinction may be a reflection of our own outlook, alien to the ancient Maya worldview, in which it might have been quite possible for both concepts to be active at the same time (compare Gillespie and Joyce 1998).

K'u, which seems to refer to forces that cause things to move, to grow, and to live, might potentially affect any and all human affairs. *K'u* forces were apparently seen by the ancient Maya nearly everywhere. They were manifest in wind, lightning, rain, blood (Stuart 1988), nectar of flowers, birth, death, breath, utterances such as song and incantation, dance, fire, smoke, reflections in mirrors, and perhaps the fleeting glimpses of strange marine creatures dimly visible beneath surfaces of water. The ancient Maya may have understood the sensation of extreme pain as the presence of *k'u* (compare "vision quest," Schele and Freidel 1990).

The ancient Maya saw *k'u* forces in certain plants, animals, and celestial objects such as the sun, moon, and planets and, perhaps, in calendric time periods. Certain places or natural landscape features may have been seen as places of *k'u* power. Mountains (Sugiyama 1993), distinctive landforms (Ortiz and Rodriguez 1999; Grove 1999), and some caves (Bassie-Sweet 1991) may have been understood as locations where these forces were most proximally present and resided or visited. The term *witz* (Stuart cited in Schele and Freidel 1990) refers to this aspect of temples as mountains, specifically as man-made mountains, often elaborated with *witz* masks.

If the ancient Maya considered that *k'u* forces caused or influenced both natural phenomena and human affairs and temples were seen as places of *k'u* power, then the aura generated by monumentality might have been taken as the presence of physical *k'u* power, not merely as symbolic references to power. This might have provided the basic motive for both monumentality and scale, since size certainly amplifies the impact of monumentality.

Mountains, caves, and other natural places may have provided appropriate settings for ritual because *k'u* forces were thought to be present in those locales. At some point the Maya might have realized that they could build equivalent places—a realization that would have profoundly affected their intellectual, political, and social development. Man-made temples, since they are cultural artifacts, might have seemed more effective than natural places for human intercession with metanatural forces. The sensory effect generated by monumental temples might also have substantiated belief in the presence of *k'u* forces. Man-made temples possessed by established political powers may have been able to serve a broader range of social agendas than the natural places frequented by shamans. With their design controlled by humans, they could be tied to social groups such as dynastic lines in ways that natural places could not.

From primordial times the ancient Maya may have understood certain natural features to be places of *k'u* power, believing that *k'u* forces not only affected natural phenomena but also potentially could determine the outcome of any human enterprise or personal destiny. Natural places of ritual might have become progressively more elaborated, as can be seen in the Zinacantan shrines illustrated by Vogt (1969). Eventually, the natural surface of these places might have become layered over with artifacts intended to enhance the effectiveness of ritual. The possibility that places of ritual could be entirely man-made thus may have evolved gradually. Monumentality, then, might have developed as a way to validate temples by making the presence of *k'u* forces more directly obvious. The sensory effect of monumentality, expressing power, would be the key property for this validation. Temples able to generate such an effect may have seemed more likely to be effective as instruments for managing the *k'u* power that was apparently present. Other aspects of monumentality, both ritualistic and political symbolism, would then flow from this fundamental belief.

The architectural sequence in the North Acropolis at Tikal provides a case study of this process. The architecture of the North Acropolis has been mapped and designated as a series of distinct entities identified by individual structure numbers (Carr and Hazard 1961). From the ancient Maya point of view, though, the acropolis might have been one among the series of temples at the site center. Formal complexity of the North Acropolis, suggesting a multitemple makeup, may reflect multiplicity and complexity of the metanatural forces that Maya-ritual specialists attempted to confront at this locus.

THE NORTH ACROPOLIS ARCHITECTURAL DEVELOPMENT

Tikal Report 14 (W. R. Coe 1990) presents the architecture of the North Acropolis in a clear evolutionary sequence, a spate of construction, occupation, modification, demolition, and reconstruction that was continuously active over many centuries. I will concentrate here on features directly related to monumentality, skipping over many other features.

The earliest material encountered, dating to about 800 B.C. (W. R. Coe 1990, vol. 3:chart 1), suggests that deep cuts into the bedrock and trashlike deposits of debris resulted from both residential and ceremonial activities that likely antedated any substantial architecture. William Coe suggests (1990, vol. 3:815) that the site may have been a "natural prominence...[favoring]...ideology" and for that reason might have been chosen for ritual activities—in other words, a natural place of *k'u* power.

Another example of this kind of place may be Cerro Manati (Ortiz and Rodriguez 1999) in southern Veracruz, where metanatural forces were understood to be present and ritual activities were focused on a distinctive landform feature with a pyramidal form. Constructional elaboration of the North Acropolis might have been intended either to make certain that it was understood in the same way or perhaps to increase the likelihood that *k'u* would be present at appropriate moments when ritual performances were set in motion.

The feature illustrated here as NA 12 (fig. 8.1), which falls within Coe's Time Span 13 (1990, vol. 3:816–17), dating to the second century

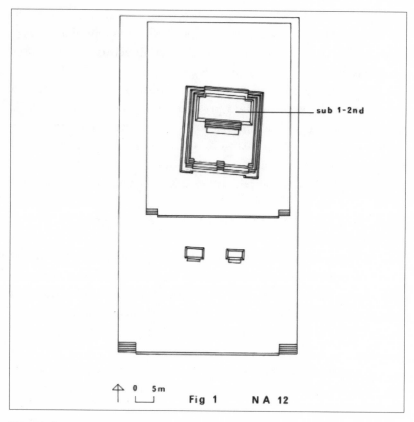

FIGURE 8.1

After Coe 1990, figure 6a.

B.C., is the earliest recorded example of acropolis architecture. An uncertain number of earlier structures preceded it but had suffered extensive demolition. Coe suggests that destruction went beyond what would have been necessary for new building, as though some kind of cleansing had set the stage for a new program. This program might have been based on the realization that man-made architecture could equal or even surpass the power of natural places for ritual. With earlier evidence so fragmented, it is impossible to know whether the physical evidence would support this assumption.

NA 12 possessed a clear formality that seems intentionally aimed at a monumental effect, though quite modest in scale. A major format of NA 1 (fig. 8.12 below), built six centuries later, is already present here.

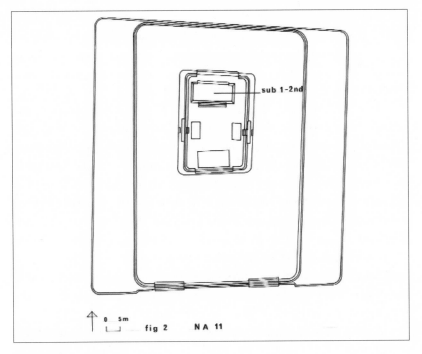

FIGURE 8.2

After Coe 1990, figure 6b.

The three NA 12 focal elements formed by two small frontal platforms and the north axial dominant feature (Sub.1-2nd) prefigure the triadic arrangement of the three summit temples (5D 23, 24, and 22) in NA 1.

Figure 8.1 (above) hypothetically shows completed lower platforms excavated across their front faces. Their northern extent and complete forms are uncertain, but their effect appears to be that of very low basal terraces not strongly integrated with the upper body, except for the paired lateral stairs that repeat at each level. The effect is that of two distinct parts: an upper body of three terraces, a building platform, and a building and two lower terraces with two small shrine structures out in front. The broad surfaces of the lower platforms might have been designed to accommodate specific activities. Although a progression of elements rising toward the north might have been appropriate ideologically, the lower elements are only weakly integrated into this movement, a condition that would diminish the sense of power that the structure could project.

This defect was retained in the next rebuilding of the acropolis, NA 11 (fig. 8.2). This rebuilding, which is more fully known than NA 12, appears more integrated as a single entity. Coe places this acropolis in Time Span 12, which covers the whole first century B.C. NA 11 might relate to roughly the first half of this period.

Two architectonic features in NA 11 are most obvious: the rounded corners and the quadrangular arrangement of anciently demolished summit buildings, now seen only as building-platform footprints. Rounding of corners tends to bring diverse elements together as one complex body composed of distinct parts, and this would tend to augment monumental impact. The quadrangle of summit buildings presumably reflects both functional and conceptual, or iconographic, programs. It may be that the functions and meanings associated with the two frontal shrines of the preceding acropolis were now incorporated into the upper quadrangle. It is worth noting that a south, central building of some kind recurred throughout later developments, except for a briefly entertained alternative immediately following NA 11.

A most surprising aspect of this acropolis is the absence of "front" at its upper level, although this might have been partially supplied by upper elements of the south, central (anciently demolished) building. Access appears to be possible only from the east and west flanks. The north-south axis is marked by outsets, a larger one to the north and a smaller one to the south. Directional implications of outsets can be assessed more confidently for centuries later than that of NA 2 (fig. 8.11 below). There is no front or central stair—a most odd departure from prevailing norms.

The quadrangular plan accepts buildings that face in different directions. Whereas all NA 12 features face south, NA 11 features face north, south, east, and west. Since directionality was a constituent aspect of metanatural forces in all Mesoamerican systems (compare J. E. S. Thompson 1934), acropolis form may have been revised to embody changes in this factor. Directionality in the architecture could refer metaphorically to a mythological order but might also be seen as a way to increase the possibility that directionally identified forces or beings would choose to be present at the site. Beyond this, one can imagine that the summit buildings of this acropolis housed ritual objects with directionally specific associations. Thus, this particular rebuilding might be seen as an effort to improve the functionality of the acropolis for ritual (shamanic) purposes.

The quadrangular organization also tends to suggest residential architecture, although most Maya residential complexes are somewhat less rigorously ordered. If the central objective was to encourage the presence of metanatural or *k'u* forces, residential architecture could satisfy this by establishing a *k'u* "home" place. Of course, as Christopher Jones has suggested (pers. comm.), residential architecture might simply mean residential function—that the acropolis was the rulers' residence. This is very attractive as a parsimonious interpretation, but there are several arguments against it. First, most versions of the acropolis are much less residential in form, though some elements of residential form are very common in structures that seem clearly nonresidential in function—Great Temple I, for example. Second, Diego de Landa (1978) described rulers' residences as being close to central monumental complexes but not actually in them, as the North Acropolis very clearly is.

NA 10 (fig. 8.3), probably built in the latter half of the first century B.C. (Coe places it together with NA 12 in TS 11), presents a decisive revision of acropolis architecture. For this new version, the upper body was broadened to accommodate two identical summit features with elaborate substructures and partly vaulted buildings (Sub. 1 and Sub. 9). Monumentality would have been greatly enhanced by the central, front stair on the upper platform body and further reinforced by the two (demolished) buildings flanking it at the summit.

In most architectural traditions, axial compositions are established by the use of flanking elements to define the axial line and confirm its importance. For this reason it is surprising that this arrangement did not persist in the North Acropolis once it had been put in place, even if this arrangement persisted briefly. It is tempting to think that there must have been some strong conceptual or functional reason for placing subdominant features directly on the axial line. The low basal terrace in NA 10 and 11 had flanking elements formed by two lateral frontal projections first introduced in NA 11.

The upper dominants (Sub. 1 and Sub. 9) work against overall monumentality by projecting equally in two different directions, each of which likely possessed its own significance. The absence of a single,

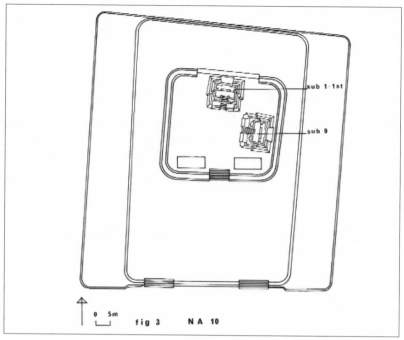

FIGURE 8.3

After Coe 1990, figure 6c.

clear dominant would definitely reduce the overall strength of the cumulative monumental effect. It may be that a complex program of competing or divergent concerns governed the institution that the acropolis served and that the development of monumentality had to contend with this factor. The same weak integration of upper and lower elements that had impaired the two preceding versions continued to have the same effect.

The time span for the construction of NA 10 (TS 11) includes initial paving of the Great Plaza as a large horizontal, plastered surface in front of the North Acropolis—a development that must have greatly increased the impressiveness of the Central Zone. In this context, a relative feebleness of acropolis architecture would have been glaringly evident. This elaboration of the Great Plaza may reflect a ruler named Yax Ehb' Xook or Yax Moch Xok (compare Martin, this volume) and known as the "founder" of the subsequent dynastic line. The radical change in architectural form and increased richness of Burial 85,

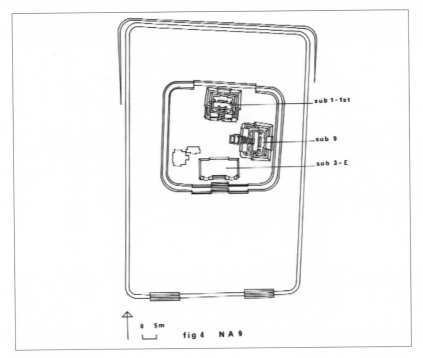

FIGURE 8.4

After Coe 1990, figure 6d.

which may (or may not) contain the remains of this individual, might embody a more ambitious claim for both dynastic legitimacy and shamanic capability than had been made earlier. This, in fact, might be the real significance of the term "founder" and might pinpoint a moment in which politics began to compete with or supplant shamanism in the social significance of the North Acropolis.

NA 9 (fig. 8.4) seems calculated to address these issues and to upgrade the acropolis to the new level demanded by the now formalized Great Plaza and an expanded dynastic role. Structure 5D Sub. 3E was now placed squarely at the head of a new axial stair flanked by mask panels. These moves amplified the frontality that was tentatively developed in NA 10 by reverting to an earlier strategy that seems peculiarly tied to the North Acropolis and rarely is seen elsewhere—that of marking the axis by a subdominant feature placed upon it. Commonly, axial compositions reserve such positions for the dominant feature, which is usually at the end of the axis, the position occupied by Sub. 1 but not

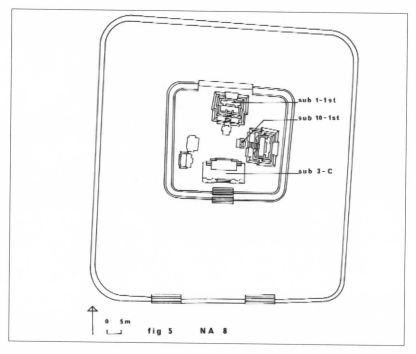

Figure 8.5

After Coe 1990, figure 6e.

Sub. 3. Nevertheless, with Sub. 3 as a south-facing, frontal, axial feature, the unbalanced effect caused by Sub. 9 would have been somewhat reduced, at least from the Great Plaza area.

NA 8 (fig. 8.5), still within Time Span 11, saw a subtle but very significant enhancement of architectural form. The lower acropolis terrace was now made much broader, whereas previously the width had been less than the front-to-rear depth. All elements, top to bottom, were now at least similarly proportioned, though at the cost of an even larger gap between the lower platform and the upper body. Still, this certainly suggests that the designers of the acropolis were intent on pulling all the elements together to be perceived as one entity, a strategy essential to the maximal monumental effect. At the same time Sub-3 developed as a portal building, channeling entry to the acropolis through its rear wall. This development may reflect the (unknowable) reason why the building was placed initially on the central axis as an extension of the central stair.

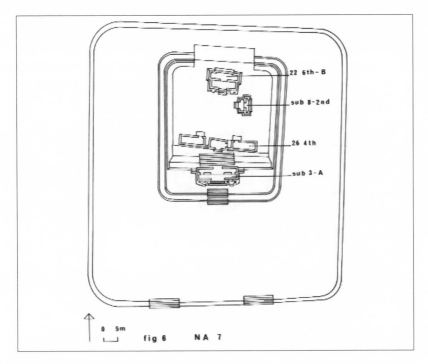

FIGURE 8.6

After Coe 1990, figure 6f.

It is noteworthy that Structure 5D-Sub.10-1st and the tomb under it in this Time Span sport murals depicting anthropomorphic figures in scrolls descending from something very like a sky-band. These may be ancestor images and may constitute further evidence of dynastic appropriation on the acropolis, perhaps achieved by the "founder" in NA 10.

The next acropolis, NA 7 (fig. 8.6), in Time Span 10, from A.D. 75 to 170, presents a most decisive revision, clearly aimed at greater monumental effect that for some reason was only partially realized. In what may be a further response to earlier enhancement of the Great Plaza, five meters of height were now added just behind the frontal structure (Sub. 3) that had stood for some time at the head of the upper stair. Three new structures were located on the new, higher summit, reemphasizing the venerable secondary orientation to the west. The axial stair was made wider and higher. A new north-axial structure (5D-22-6th) introduced the format that developed into the final completion of the

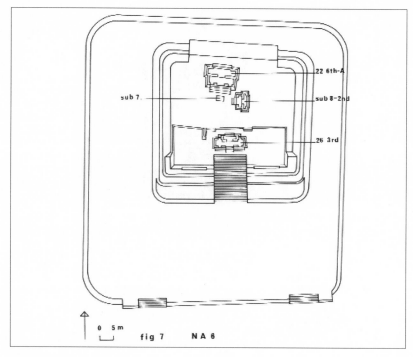

FIGURE 8.7

After Coe 1990, figure 6g.

Acropolis. The lower platform, however, still reflected a separate central axis slightly off to the west.

Although the intent seems clearly linked to the scale of the Great Plaza, the unresolved, fragmentary nature of the upper south front must have undercut this aim. The form seems temporary, as though Sub. 3 was to be completely buried but something prevented this from happening. Again, we may be seeing a conflict between different elements within the group operating the acropolis.

Acropolis 6 (fig. 8.7), in short Time Span 9 (A.D. 170–190), retains this unresolved formal treatment of the south front while installing a large axial stair scaled to the new, higher acropolis. Frontal elements flank the axial line in the basal terrace, but they are small and formally weak in relation to the whole structure.

Time Span 8, A.D. 190–325, the second longest in the North Acropolis sequence, contains two reconstructions, NA 5 and NA 4 (figs.

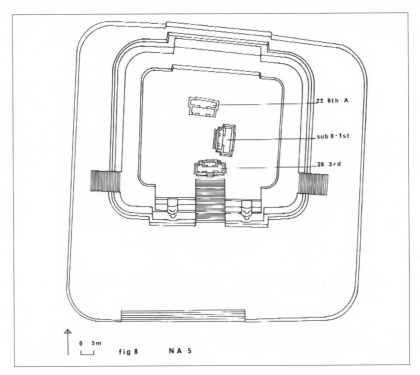

22 6th·A

sub 8-1st

26 3rd

0 5m
fig 8   N A 5

FIGURE 8.8

After Coe 1990, figure 6h.

8.8, 8.9). The initial substage (NA 5, fig. 8.8) sets out the format for final resolution of earlier formal problems through an amplification of the upper body and a stronger integration with the lower terrace, although its single stair, conspicuously off the upper axis, impairs this effect. At this time frontality and monumental treatment were greatly enhanced by the installation of large mask panels flanking the upper stair. Working against this, the three upper features were most tentative in nature, crowded into the center and too small to complete the effect initiated by the stair and its mask panels. It seems as though there were two different teams at work with different notions about architecture. Those working on the middle-body terracing and stair understood the scale, but those responsible for the upper features did not. Once again, the conflicting emphases of both south-facing and west-facing features persisted at summit level.

An interesting aspect of this acropolis is the appearance of substantially scaled lateral stairs, allowing retention of the old dual-stair

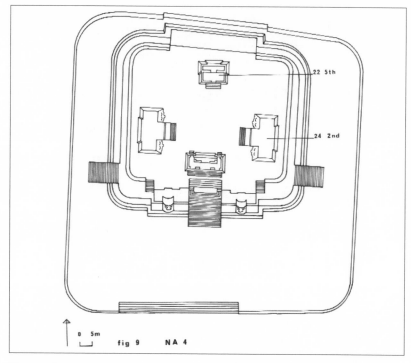

FIGURE 8.9

After Coe 1990, figure 6i.

system but in a new form. This might reflect functional demands of ritual processions moving on the central axis, off axis, and back on again, quite possibly as a part of ritual performance harking back to the very earliest surviving fragments.

Acropolis 4 (fig. 8.9 above), emerging later in Time Span 8, may again reflect the resolution of a recurrent programmatic conflict in establishing equal east and west orientations at the summit, with the north-south line clearly dominant. The spacing of the group seems to anticipate subsequent growth by allowing room for enlargement of the north-dominant element (5D 22), still too diminutive at this time to exert a commanding presence effectively.

Acropolis 3 (fig. 8.10), in Coe's (1990) longest Time Span, T.S. 7 (A.D. 325–475), represents a culmination of the long search for the most effective monumental form for the North Acropolis at a scale appropriate to the Great Plaza. Only one relatively minor touch

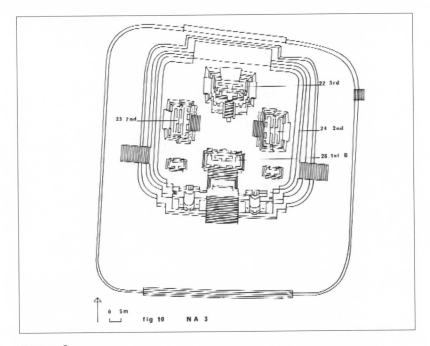

FIGURE 8.10

After Coe 1990, figure 6j.

remained to be added (see NA 2). This assessment reflects my fundamental assumption that the intent driving architectural development and elaboration at this locus was in part concerned with the *k'u* forces assumed to be literally present, or at least potentially present, during ritual performance. Presumably, the designers of this and preceding versions of the acropolis wanted to make the architectural form such that the presence of those forces could be more confidently secured, and they appear to have succeeded more fully here than in earlier attempts. Merely comparing plan diagrams of the acropolis sequence suggests that none of the earlier versions possessed the formal power equal to that of NA 3. This more powerful form might have been understood as encouragement for *k'u* forces to choose to be present and take up residence, at least for the duration of ritual performances. The perceptible effect of the form might have been felt as proof that this desired end had been achieved.

It may be no coincidence that this particularly coherent version of

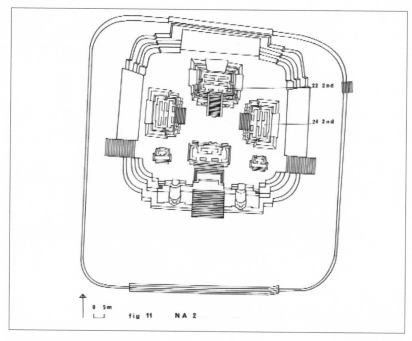

FIGURE 8.11

After Coe 1990, figure 6j and k.

the North Acropolis appeared at precisely this time. Time Span 7 includes a most profound political development. It was the time of the A.D. 378 war event involving Uaxactun and the installation of a new ruler, Curl Nose, who may have been from outside the traditional Tikal dynastic lineage (C. Jones 1991; Culbert 1991b). This new rulership, perhaps with some kind of link to Teotihuacan, may have elevated Tikal to a new level as a regional power. If the monumentality of the North Acropolis and Great Plaza had initially reflected metanatural power, it now almost certainly expressed political power, probably layered on to the older priestly institutions. The sacerdotal aspect of the acropolis may not have been diminished by this development. Greater architectural power might have reinforced the conviction that priestly ritual really could manage *k'u* forces through the efficacy of the temple. At the same time, such ritual would provide an aspect of the support and credibility desired by a more ambitious dynastic establishment. If NA 3 was uniquely linked to the new dynasty, this may explain why it was never subsequently obliterated completely, despite pressures that caused its front face to rapidly disappear behind abutted new structures.

The next acropolis, NA 2 (fig. 8.11), in Time Span 6 (A.D. 475–600), is a very special case, but a hypothetical one in that the acropolis may never have existed. Three new outsets at the east, west, and north sides of the middle body were added in the same stratigraphic level as the structures facing onto the Great Plaza (see fig. 8.12 below). The sequence between outsets and frontal additions is simply not demonstrable. Isolating NA 2 arbitrarily as one possible form that the acropolis could have reached in Time Span 6 if the outsets were added prior to the frontal structures reveals it as the most coherent and most monumentally powerful form realized within the North Acropolis.

As seen in conjectural figure 8.11, the considerable formal complexity of the North Acropolis now became thoroughly integrated as one unified architectural vision. It can be compared in this regard with Temple I. Both appear as single entities composed of numerous, very strongly integrated formal parts. If this version of the acropolis ever did exist, it raises the question of how the acropolis was conceptualized. If it was thought of and designed as a single structure at this particular time, perhaps the same was true from the beginning. NA 2 may have been the version in which design ideals that were present from the outset were finally most fully embodied. The whole architectural development might have been a process of modifying what was always thought of as a single entity, despite the number of different features contained within it.

If a TS 6 acropolis did exist, as illustrated in figure 8.11 (above), then subsequent radical departures from previous practices (fig. 8.12) might be understandable as reactions to it. Presumably, the cultural pressures responsible for the continual enlargement and redesign of the acropolis did not suddenly cease. Yet a new attitude now appeared. New additions were no longer thought of as reshaping the whole but as attachments to it—separate features posed frontally. This attitude allowed new construction to preserve the NA 2 Acropolis form. That the acropolis became somewhat cut off from the Great Plaza may have been acceptable because it possessed sufficient power of its own to allow its continued functioning. In turn, this suggests another possibility—that the formal properties of the acropolis may not have been

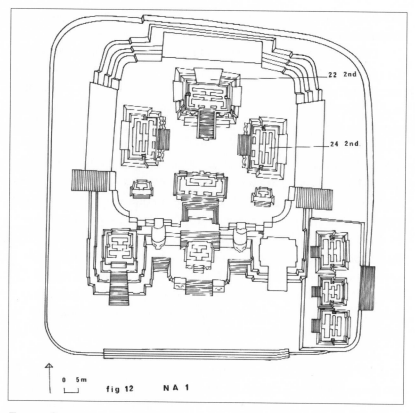

FIGURE 8.12

After Coe 1990, figure 6k.

entirely a matter of the way in which they projected into the plaza, but rather of the way in which they communicated with metanatural entities existing in an "otherworld" domain of *k'u* forces. If this was the case, blocking off the front of the acropolis from the Great Plaza would not greatly impair its primary function.

In any case, whether or not the figure 8.11 (above) acropolis did exist in that particular form, it certainly did not do so for very long. Frontal structures arrived within the same time span (NA 1, fig. 8.12 above). If ever an acropolis in the form of figure 8.11 did see the light of day, it most likely would have emerged during the reign of Curl Nose. The initial motivation for locating new structures on the south front may well have been his tomb, housed in 5D-34, as well as, perhaps, that of his son Stormy Sky (see Jones, this volume), which was placed so as to minimize obstruction of the acropolis as it matured during his tenure.

NA 1 (fig. 8.12 above) illustrates the final result of the process perhaps initiated by the construction of 5D-34. At first glance, this acropolis seems to embody a rejection of earlier approaches, but as I suggested above, it may indicate a high regard for the preceding sequence and a sense that this development had reached an unsurpassable fruition. If the forgoing is true, this version of the acropolis closed off a sequence of development begun roughly eight centuries earlier and finally evolved to such a point of architectural finality, clarity, and monumental strength (NA 2) that further change may have seemed regressive.

Semifictional NA 2 (fig. 8.11 above), if it never did exist, raises an issue central to the question of how monumentality might have served a practical function. The side and rear outsets that distinguish this structure from its predecessor were added as separate elements, suggesting that these features possessed some particular significance of their own. They do not add surface area that might have accommodated ritual performances, and they solve no obvious structural problem. They may, however, reflect the fundamental function of temples as instruments designed for management of metanatural forces. The outsets seem essentially related to directionality and might have been seen as connecting with *k'u* forces, which the Maya thought of as having directionality (J. E. S. Thompson 1934). In the shamanistic process of engaging with these forces, directionality would have been one of the factors taken into account. The outsets, then, may have been seen as features added to embody directionality in the architecture. Formal expression of directionality might, in a shamanistic view, allow or encourage the presence of the forces addressed by the ritual. In this regard, it is worth noting Vogt's observation (1969:375) that the crosses erected on shamanistic shrines in the hills around Zincantan are not Christian cross symbols, as they initially appear, but are "a means of communication with either the ancestral gods who live in the mountain or the earth god who lives beneath the surface of the earth." The NA 2 outsets exactly parallel these crosses as expressions of directionality like crossroads (compare Bassie-Sweet 1996:22). This is the most explicit indication that monumental architectural form in the North Acropolis was designed to enhance shamanic function—that is, to achieve practical results, not merely to symbolize mythology. By extension, the quadrangular formats of NA 14 and NA 11 can be interpreted in the same way, although these more complex structures would also house additional functions and invoke the very extensive mythology of four-sidedness (compare Bassie-Sweet 1996:28–31).

Bassie-Sweet (1996:118) suggests that temples may have been places where "the deities and ancestors came to receive their offerings." Earlier in the same work (1996:21–24) she reviews ideas of directionality, citing crossroads as a general form of place at which supernaturals were likely to be encountered. These observations further support the interpretation I have suggested above.

By Time Span 6, it seems virtually certain that the North Acropolis reflected a dynastic tradition as well as a shamanic one. Earlier, in Time Span 13, this might have been less the case. Because the earlier levels are so much smaller, dynastic presence seems weaker in them. It may be that early versions of the acropolis were formed around shamanic specialization and that dynastic exploitation took over later. The final form of the acropolis might embody both dynastic and sacerdotal functions. If this highly speculative interpretation is accurate, the symbolic aspects of meaning, such as memorialization, display of wealth and power, and metaphoric embodiment of cosmic orders, might have been layered onto forms initially expected to work on a more practical level by connecting with animistic forces. The basic architectural language of terrace profiles, plan shapes, and architectural character may have evolved out of a materialistic, functional application of shamanic knowledge and practice, which we can see clearly in relation to the crosslike forms, but which remains obscure in other details. Monumentality would have possessed a definite, positive value in this context, and, once developed, could have been very conveniently arrogated for the self-interest of the dynastic elite.

The North Acropolis exemplifies a constituent feature of Mesoamerican monumental architecture: the habit of building, rebuilding, ripping out, demolishing, and renewing in a constant process of construction, at the same locus, as though the same structure had to be built over and over again. Shook and Coe (1961) proposed the term "architectural development" for this phenomenon. We have numerous examples of it, but as yet there has been no systematic study specifically of architecture developments. The Copan acropolis sequence (Sharer et al. 1999), which begins later than the North Acropolis, follows a similar course from modest beginnings toward something very large and complex that looks like a group of structures rather than one individual work.

Future projects will no doubt provide more data, but it is probably not too soon to look at patterns of superimposition that we can already see in monumental construction at various centers. Studies looking at patterns of change within architectural developments over a range of examples will no doubt yield different results. The North Acropolis sequence reviewed here shows a progressive trend toward increasing monumentality and greater formal coherence, followed by stasis in the face of continued development, as though some kind of search had been underway, seeking and eventually finding the most powerful architectural expression appropriate to that particular place. Other sequences may show quite different patterns, suggesting different intentions. The hypothesis I have presented for the North Acropolis here obviously needs to be tested by comparison with other architectural developments.

If the more fundamental inference explored here—that temple architecture was expected to produce practical results beyond the symbolic and metaphoric content that it surely conveyed—is valid for Tikal, it surely must have some application not only to Maya monumental temple architecture but perhaps also to ancient-world traditions generally.

Notes

Although this chapter was not presented at the seminar and therefore was not formally discussed, the participants encouraged me to write it. I was uncertain about proceeding, because the subject is so speculative and I could see no objective way to develop it. I am very grateful to my colleagues for their encouragement. The faults are entirely my own.

1. William Coe's group plans (1990:fig.6) were redrawn to graphically convey architectural form as distinct from the strict record of archaeological evidence actually seen. For example, figure 8.1 is Coe's figure 6a. Where he left the lower platforms incomplete because of limitations of excavation, they have been completed, but, of course, this has been done on a purely hypothetical basis.

Uncertainties due to preservation or accessibility (broken lines) have been suppressed in the figures in favor of a clear morphology. For the sake of simplicity in discussion, sequential units are labeled as NA 12 (earliest), through NA 1 (latest). Other units did precede NA 12. Figures 8.1–8.12 all derive from Coe's figure 6.

9

Plaza Plans at Tikal

A Research Strategy for Inferring Social Organization and Processes of Culture Change at Lowland Maya Sites

Marshall Joseph Becker

The identification of architectural patterning among groups of structures at Tikal provides insights into the ways that the Classic Period Maya organized their residences and ritual complexes. Each group pattern, or "plaza plan," reveals an architectural grammar that can be used to understand urban and rural settlement patterns throughout the Maya realm. Recognition of these patterns, achieved through the use of the Tikal survey maps alone, provides a basis for developing effective research strategies for all Maya sites.

Plaza Plan data taken from maps and confirmed by archaeological testing enable us to reconstruct synchronic sociocultural interactions among the several "classes" within these proto-complex societies and to reveal the dynamics of activities within and among Maya "cities" during a single period of time. These architectural patterns also aid us in understanding the diachronic processes leading to the emergence of a complex society at the beginning of the Classic Period and the reverse processes leading to the devolution of these systems. Documenting these relationships enables the reconstruction of processes of culture change through time and space in this part of the Maya realm, serving to verify aspects of the extensive textual evidence that is now available.

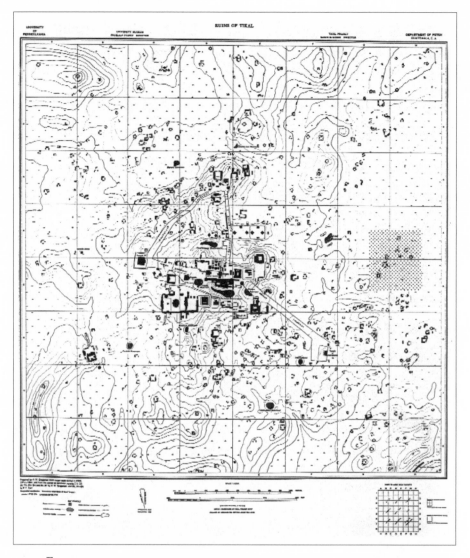

FIGURE 9.1

The Carr and Hazard (1961) map of the ruins of Tikal, Guatemala. The principal area at Tikal where groups conforming to Plaza Plan 2 can be found is in the shaded area at center right (see fig. 9.2).

PLAZA PLAN FORM REVEALS MEANING

Settlement research at Tikal in the early 1960s verified the accuracy of a major mapping project (Carr and Hazard 1961, fig. 9.1) and demonstrated that careful survey is an important element of basic research in the Maya region. It was subsequently discovered that the form of an architectural group at this enormous Lowland Maya site can be more significant than its physical size (Becker 1971, 1999:197–205).

At other Maya sites, groups of structures continue to be evaluated using the absolute size of the buildings within the cluster and the technology employed in construction (for example, superstructures of pole and thatch versus masonry). Ranking groups by size may elicit information on status variables, or "ranking and stratification" (Becker 1988; Hendon 1991) among the families occupying or using these groups, but such descriptive archaeology provides only a limited reflection of cultural differences or processes of change through time.

Reviewing the literature two decades ago, Don Rice and Dennis Puleston (1981:138–39) noted that the study of "structure aggregates," as suggested by William A. Haviland (1963:466), would be the preferred way to examine Maya settlement patterns. This approach remained very much in the background as most research continued to focus on group size (see Willey 1982). Recently, the interpretation of social relationships among the residents of the extended families occupying these household groups has reemerged as an important subject of study (see Haviland 1988; Manzanilla and Barba 1990; Mcanany 1993) for two reasons. First, the study of residential groups aids in making more accurate estimates of populations; Maya ethnographic data indicate an average of about 25 people per extended family household (Becker 1971). Thus, the population of the 690 groups in the mapped portion of Tikal can be estimated at 17,250 people, if all of these groups were residential. The greater Tikal area may have had a population of around 25,000 people (compare Culbert et al. 1990). Second, as the functions of Maya houses become better understood, we see patterning among both residential and nonresidential groups.

The architectural patterns recognized in 1962 led me to propose that a group's form, whether residential or ritual, is more predictive than its physical size (compare Becker 1982, 1999). When applied to the architectural groups at Tikal, this approach amplifies the information gathered there during four decades of excavations. In addition, the examination of similarities and variations in form among household groups within Tikal, as well as among sites, provides a mechanism for formulating hypotheses regarding culture change in time and space.

MAYA COGNITIVE MODELS: THE DISCOVERY
OF PLAZA PLANS

Each "Plaza Plan" (hereafter *PP*) recognized at Tikal conforms to an architectural grammar (cognitive model or mental map) employed by the Maya builders and users of these building clusters. PPs reflect those aspects of the architectural grammars that relate to the structures within a group rather than those that reveal individual-room function (see Hendon 1991; Harrison, this volume). Each grammar reflects cultural choices in the specific order in which the various components of a group were assembled and the form that they took. Each PP incorporates rules followed by the builders that can now be interpreted from excavated groups. At many sites the fundamental rules of these grammars can be identified from surface observation alone (Becker 1999, fig. 9.2). At other sites the grammatical rules may be less evident from the surface, such as at Piedras Negras, where rolling terrain masks details of structural form and orientation (compare Escobedo and Houston 1997).

Surface observation of the group's arrangement and the form of the structures provides the first level of identification for a PP. Statistical analysis of building measurements, gained through excavations, is the second level. Analysis of other unique traits, such as burial or cache placement and contents, is the third level of analysis. For PP2 and PP3 (see below), the extensive work at Tikal has permitted us to refine our ability to distinguish between two very similar architectural patterns and to infer residential functions for both of them (compare Laporte and Iglesias 1999). These three levels of identification should lead to the consideration of a fourth level—why changes occur through time (P. S. Martin 1971:3–4). It remains our ultimate goal to determine what factors led a Maya family to follow one template in the construction of their residence rather than any of the others. The appearance and proliferation, as well as the disappearance, of various plaza plans through time also serve as useful indicators of cultural change within ancient Maya society.

On the basis of the first three of these levels of identification and analysis, we can conclude that those groups at Tikal that are oriented around a single plaza, with a relatively square and tall structure on the east and relatively low, rectangular structures in other positions, conform to a distinct arrangement now designated as PP2. Consideration

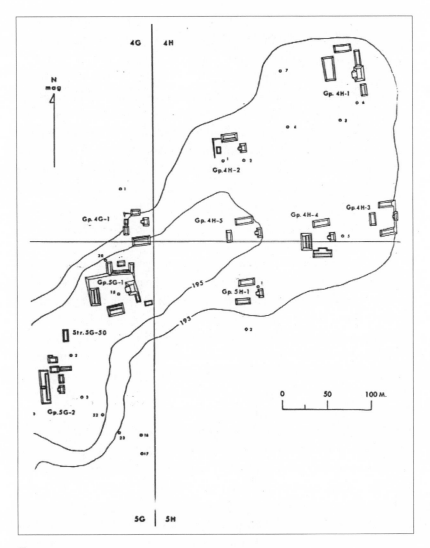

FIGURE 9.2

The peninsula on the eastern side of the city of Tikal, on which nine groups conforming to Plaza Plan 2 were identified. This plan was redrawn by Becker (1971, 1999) after excavations in 1962.

of other traits that distinguish the structures on the east from those in other positions indicates a ritual function for the former as a shrine (family temple or oratorio) within the context of a residential group. The nonsquare, noneast buildings are inferred to have served other domestic purposes, such as "bedroom," dormitory, men's house, kitchen, or storage area. Details of these relationships and extensive PP2 data from other sites are presently being gathered (Becker in prep.).

At all sites excavation is essential to confirm observations made during the course of mapping. Excavation also reveals elements of the grammar not evident from the surface, such as associated mortuary complexes. The definitions provided below for ten PPs at Tikal need to be scrupulously followed when making evaluations of PPs at other sites. The statistical data related to PP2 (Becker 1999) and other plans are as essential to their specific identifications as are the details of patterning noted by C. Jones (1969) for twin-pyramid groups.

Plaza Plan 1

Following the verification, by excavation, of the "temple-on-the-east" pattern central to PP2 (Becker 1971), I searched for other architectural patterns (PPs) at Tikal (Becker 1982). Among those found was an architectural pattern already described by Shook (1957:48) as a "twin-pyramid" group (also W. R. Coe 1962:479; C. Jones 1969:128–29, 141). The "grammar" defining "twin-pyramid groups," including architecture, building positions, and stela pattern, led to my suggestion (Becker 1982) that this plan should be considered as PP1 because it was the first predictable group pattern identified at Tikal.

The regularities of the PP1 architectural grammar, with its associated monuments, enabled C. Jones (1969; compare Becker 1982:117) to identify a seventh example of a PP1 near Tikal's East Plaza and to suggest the presence of two other examples near Temple IV. C. Jones (1996:1, 91) concluded that PP1 groups served as Katun markers. Since PP1 groups have no association with residential buildings, they must have had only ritual and calendric functions. PP1 groups can be compared with parallel examples at Uolantun, a small site near Tikal, as well as at Chalpate, on the eastern periphery of Tikal, and at Yaxha (Laporte, this volume), where some PP1 elements vary from those at Tikal. Other examples of PP1, as well as variant forms of PP2 such as PP2B, continue to be recognized at other Lowland sites (see Becker in prep.).

Plaza Plan 2

The frequency and distribution of PP2 within a site and among sites provides a means by which many Maya cities can be compared. PP2 can be initially identified by the presence on the center of the eastern side of the compound of a relatively square, relatively tall, and often relatively small structure (Becker 1999). These structures are now commonly called "shrines" (see below). Of the 690 architectural groups delineated at Tikal, a total of 96 (14 percent) were predicted to conform to PP2 solely on the basis of their mapped configurations (Becker 1982). Dennis Puleston's (1983) study of the South Brecha at Tikal, extending 12 km. out from the site center, identified a total of 128 architectural groups, of which 19 (15 percent) conform to PP2. The remarkable similarity in these percentages and their random appearance throughout the test area suggest that PP2 has a consistent distribution throughout the greater Tikal region.

Nine of the PP2 groups located in central Tikal are on a peninsula jutting into the Bajo Santa Fe (Carr and Hazard 1961, fig. 9.3). In 1962, six of these groups were excavated, and the other three were resurveyed. These nine groups provided the type-plan for PP2. Subsequently, six of the other 87 groups at Tikal that had been predicted to conform to PP2 were randomly selected for testing to validate the hypothesis that PP2 configurations could be recognized by surface survey and evaluation of architectural pattern. The 1963 excavations, focused on the east-lying structure in each group, demonstrated the predictive power of this architectural grammar. Each of these east-lying shrines includes high-status burial, in each case made prior to the construction of the first structure at each locus. Usually, each subsequent rebuilding was preceded by the intrusion of another high-status burial (Becker 1971, 1999). This associated mortuary pattern, plus ceremonial activity in the form of on-floor burnings, helps to indicate the function of these buildings, now identified as shrines. Only the largest examples of PP2 shrines were vaulted, with the smaller examples supporting only thatched structures.

A primary question that was asked regarding the definition of the PP2 architectural grammar concerns the validity of characterizing an entire group on the basis of the configuration and position of only one of its structures: east location plus high width to length ratio (>.70). Platforms of buildings in noneast positions in these groups have a low ratio of width to length (consistently <.70; Becker 1971, 1999).

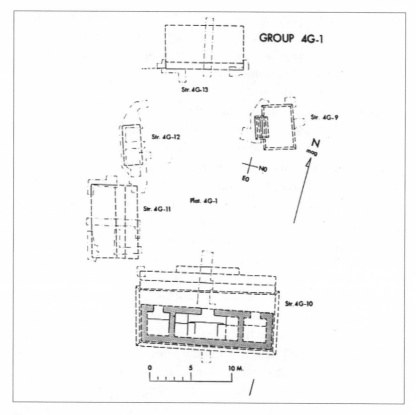

FIGURE 9.3

Tikal Group 4G–I. Detailed plan of one example of Plaza Plan 2 on the peninsula depicted in figure 9.2. The small shrine on the eastern side of the plaza is Structure 4G-9.

Excavations of PP2 groups provided specific architectural details characteristic of each east-located shrine (Becker 1999) plus precise measurements that demonstrate, when subjected to statistical analysis, that structures on the east of PP2 groups are significantly distinct in plan from all other structures in the same group. Squareness of structure plan remains the critical variable in identifying these "temples on the east" from surface survey alone.

Of particular interest at Tikal is the recent discovery by the Proyecto Nacional Tikal (PNT) of a second area with a clustering of PP2 groups. These are in the area of the Bajo Pital. That both clusters of PP2 groups at Tikal are in areas surrounded by bajo may not be a matter of chance within this large and complex site. The relationship between the forms of residential groups and the bajos, a juxtaposition explored by Fletcher et al. (1987:23–26) at Calakmul, may also be a consideration in the location and interpretation of variant examples of PP2 (see Kunen et al. ms. A). The construction of residential groups using the PP2 grammar in areas near bajos may reflect a social phenomenon that remains to be elucidated.

Directionality, Origins, and Evolution of PP2

The location of the diagnostic structure or shrine on the east of PP2 groups calls to mind Clemency Coggins's (1980:729) suggestion that, among the Maya, "east" is invariably the position of honor. Maya maps that date from the Colonial era place east at the top. Ashmore (1991:200, 1998) addresses questions of directionality in Classic Maya site planning, providing valuable insights and interesting interpretations of the cultural processes underlying the organization of space among the ancient Maya. The earliest known examples of PP2 at Tikal date from the Early Classic period (Becker in prep.), suggesting an evolution from an earlier pattern in which the structure on the east is also significant. I believe that PP2 evolved from E-groups (PP10) and that the transition may be part of the process of social and cultural transformation leading into the Classic period throughout the Maya area.

Soon after the recognition of PP2 at Tikal in 1962, looters applied this predictive model at Tikal, Caracol, and most other Lowland sites with great success. Their functional application of these data to maximize the return on their efforts (see Pendergast 1991; Lynott 1995; Lynott and Wylie 1995) demonstrated the utility of this archaeological model. The application of this research strategy by scholars searching for tombs began with the proposal that Str. 16 was the burial locus of the kings of Copan (Becker 1980). Other archaeologists dealing with large sites have found these grammars useful in the organization of survey data and in making intersite comparisons. For example, Arlen Chase and Diane Chase (1994:54) believe that 60 percent or more of all groups at Caracol are "eastern shrine groups," as compared wiith only ca. 15 percent at Tikal (see Becker in prep.).

Studies of culture change as reflected in architectural change (Fletcher 1978, 1983; Freidel 1981b:311–14) offer a means by which the transition to the Postclassic period can be understood. This change may be seen at Postclassic-period Lowland Maya sites, perhaps reflecting the devolution from organized, Classic-period PPs (see D. S. Rice 1988) that parallels a devolution in social organization (Becker 1988).

RECOGNIZING A GRAMMAR OF PPS AT TIKAL: EIGHT NEW EXAMPLES

The recognition of a PP2 at Tikal, with a residential function distinct from the public function inferred to be associated with PP1, led to the examination of the Tikal map to search for other PPs. Eight additional PPs were soon identified at Tikal, based on examination of the map alone (see fig. 9.4). Excavation enables us to verify these patterns and to infer functions for these groups. Each of the PPs must reflect some aspect of cultural dynamics essential to our understanding of the history and social organization of Tikal. A description of these eight plans follows.

Plaza Plan 3: The "Normal" Tikal Residential Plan

Approximately 70 percent of the 690 architectural groups at Tikal are residential clusters with a simple rectangular arrangement, generally with low rectangular platforms evident on two or more sides (for example, Gr. 7C-XVII, see Becker 1982). This PP developed during the Preclassic and remained common at Tikal, the size of the structures becoming larger during the Classic period. PP3 is also the most common group arrangement at Calakmul, with PP5 probably the second most frequent (Fletcher et al. 1987:94–96).

Some PP3 groups include one or more vaulted buildings that range greatly in size, reflecting family resources. These regular ("white bread") groups have no shrine on the east and no distinct mortuary complex. As is the case in PP2, some PP3 groups are small (Gr. 3B-XI, Haviland in prep.b), while others are extremely large (for example, Gr. 6D-V, Iglesias 1987). Refining the identification of PP3 is one of the major contributions of a recent report by Juan Pedro Laporte and Josefa Iglesias (1999; see also Haviland in prep.b).

Plaza Plan 4: Central Altar Plan

The diagnostic architectural feature of these PP3-like residential groups, formed by only rectilinear structures, is a small platform (low

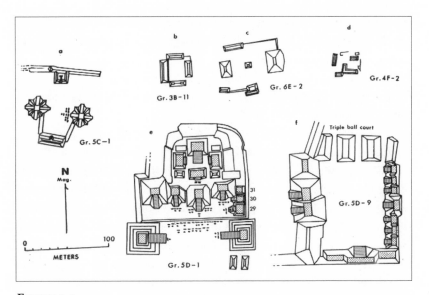

FIGURE 9.4

Examples of other Plaza Plans identified at Tikal, (a) Plaza Plan 1, Twin Pyramid Groups (Gr. 5C–I), (b) Plaza Plan 3, example of a typical Tikal residential-group plan (Gr. 3B-11), (c) Plaza Plan 4, central-altar plan (Gr. 6E-2), (d) Plaza Plan 5, informal residential grouping (Gr. 4F-2), believed to be low-status residences, (e) Plaza Plan 6, the "Temple Triad" plan, as represented by the three northernmost structures on Tikal's North Acropolis (Gr. 5D-1), with an example of a ball court (Plaza Plan 8) at lower right, and (f) Plaza Plans 7 and 8, "Seven Sisters" plan and ball courts. Seven temples along the eastern margin are incorporated or linked to Gr. 5D-9, and the northern structures form a triple ball court.

altar?) in the center of its plaza (fig. 9.4c). Since this diagnostic feature is often extremely small, these groups are detected only by careful mapping. One should note that the PP4s now known are usually in relatively large groups, probably because the diagnostic pattern in such groups is proportionally large and therefore easily visible during mapping. Thus, an example of PP4 composed only of small structures might have a relatively small platform or "altar" in the center of the plaza—a structure that could be invisible except through careful excavation. Excavations in several of these central, altarlike platforms found caches of diagnostic artifacts in the form of human "trophy heads" (for example, Tikal Groups 6E-3, 6F-1, 7F-15, 5C-3, 6D-1, and 10). The use of skulls as trophies and in caches is often noted in the Maya area but remains a subject meriting further study (compare Becker 1996; see also D. Chase 1988; A. Chase 1994; Becker 1992; D. Chase and Chase 1998). The platform west of Str. 7F-30 (W. R. Coe and Broman 1958:figs. 2 and 3, feature 1) may reflect the presence of a PP4. This feature was covered ca. 10.1.0.0.0, perhaps with the entire group function being altered.

A possible example of an altar in the center of a group's plaza is the early-period structure that Laporte (1989:42) calls "banqueta" (Str. Sub-27 of Gr. 6C-XVI-Sub), located in front of Strs. Sub-23 and Sub-26 of this group. This location suggests that the 0.30 m.–tall structure may be a prototype of a PP4 platform. Haviland (pers. comm.) notes that some of the much later examples of these central "altars" at Tikal have *tablud-tablero* architecture. C. Jones (pers. comm.) suggests that some of these altars may relate to the Venus-Tlaloc deity complex that is also associated with ball courts. PP4 altars thus may be ancestral to the Venus platform at Chichen Itza, with its skull associations. Many other sites also have such structures (compare Becker in prep.), and PP4-like features appear as far away as Puebla, Mexico (Op. 11 and 12 of Plunket and Uruñuela 1998).

Plaza Plan 5: Informal Groupings

Structures in these groups are always small, never vaulted, and arranged in an irregular or "messy" pattern without an evident central plaza (for example, Tikal Groups 4F-II [fig. 9d], 4F-I, and 6F-IX; compare Ashmore 1981:49; Webster and Gonlin 1981). Although one might predict that the size and irregularity of such groups relates them to the lowest social class, it is significant that the smallest architectural groups at Tikal do not conform to PP5 but generally conform to PP2 or PP3.

Plaza Plan 6: "Temple Triad"

Temple triads (see also "Triadic Temples" in Folan et al. 2001) are best exemplified by Tikal's North Acropolis plan. These ritual groups include a series of major temples placed on the east, north, and west of a relatively large plaza (see fig. 9.4e). A PP6 arrangement developed on the North Acropolis at Tikal (Group 5D-II) during the Early Classic period and was rebuilt several times in this form throughout the Late Classic period (W. R. Coe 1964:411, 1967:42).

An important question in the evaluation of PP6 is the location of the most important structure in the group as defined by size or mass. My assumption is that the principal structure of such groups is always located on the north, as in the Tikal North Acropolis. This variable may shift through time at other sites (see Becker in prep.). Smaller variants of PP6 groups remain to be recognized. Coe (1990:943) refers to this pattern as a "trinal arrangement."

Plaza Plan 7: "Seven Sisters Plan"

In this plan, seven "temples" or ritual structures are situated along the eastern side of a rectangular plaza (for example, Group 5D-9 with Strs. 5D-92/99, see fig. 9f) of an elite residential complex. PP7 may be a variation or elaboration of Tikal PP2B (see above), but one found only in large and probably high-status residential groups (Maler 1911:52–55; Becker in prep.).

Plaza Plan 8: Ball Courts

Constructions identified as ball courts have long been recognized as a distinct type of Maya building group (Blom 1932:499; Strömsvik 1952; Scarborough and Wilcox 1991; C. Jones this volume). C. Jones (1996:86–87) also suggests an association between ball courts (PP8) and markets (PP9), a relationship that might be helpful in identifying both categories. A great deal is known about ball courts in Mesoamerica and elsewhere. Such knowledge of spatial distribution provides opportunities to use PP8 for comparative research on this complex (Whalen and Minnis 1996; Becker in prep.).

Plaza Plan 9: Markets

A common feature in a complex society is the presence of centralized and regulated markets. The late E. Shook suggested that markets must have existed within Classic-period Maya cities, and specialists such as R. Rands (1967:147, 149) note that markets must have been part of any system that produced complex and specialized goods. Hattula Moholy-Nagy (this volume) elaborates on this theme, noting that the artifactual evidence alone suggests that several markets existed within Tikal (compare Fry 1979, 1980). Markets may be identifiable by architecture designed to meet the needs of business activities (C. Jones, this volume) and by the artifacts recovered from associated dumps. Identification of markets depends on finding large, open squares within a quadrangle formed by long, narrow structures that presumably held market stalls similar to those known from the *stoa* in Athens.

C. Jones (1996) offers convincing architectural data from the East Plaza at Tikal to suggest that the eastern portion had been used as a market area over a considerable period of time (but see Potter and King 1995:23–24). C. Jones (1996) notes that "stalls" in the Tikal market are only ca. 1.5 m. wide, suggesting that a form-function relationship is important. Public markets have been "recognized" at several other large Maya sites, such as Calakmul (in square M29, see May Hau 1990; Folan et al. 2001), Sayil (Tourtellot and Sabloff 1994:88, 90), Yaxha (C. Jones 1996:86–87), and Copan, where one is situated just west of the Acropolis area.

Plaza Plan 10: "E-Groups" and Astronomical Rituals

One of the earliest observations of regularities in Maya structure groupings was the recognition of a pattern reflecting astronomical activities ("E Groups"; see A. Chase and Chase 1995a). Near Tikal, ca. 1997, V. Fialko found an example of a large PP10 south of Navahuelal, associated with a huge pyramid and dated to the Middle Preclassic period (Laporte and Fialko 1990:47; see also Green 1970). Laporte (pers. comm.) notes that E-groups are central to ca. A.D. 200 sites in the Tikal region and that many appear to date from the Classic period. I now believe that "E-Groups" were antecedents of PP2, with all surviving examples having early origins. At small, peripheral sites one might expect PP10s to continue in use into the Classic period.

The first clear delineation of an "E-Group" from the surface appears on C. L. Lundell's (1933) map of the Calakmul site core. Folan et al. (1995:315, fig.4) identify this group as Str. VI on the west, with the buildings of Str. IV on the east (compare Fletcher et al. 1987:fac.p.30). J. Bolles (in Ruppert and Denison 1943) provides details of the Calakmul E-group (Strs. 4 and 6 in Sq. M29; see May Hau et al. 1990; Folan et al. 2001; compare Carrasco et al. 1999:50, fig.2) and also notes that similar groups could be found at Hakun and Uaxactun.

"Excavations" at Uaxactun (Ricketson and Ricketson 1937:105–8; A. L. Smith 1950) revealed a group of structures with associated monuments erected in a pattern reflecting astronomical and calendric functions. Oliver Ricketson (1937:105–8) describes the pattern as including a series of three "temples" along the eastern margin of a plaza, with another "temple" (Str. E VII) on the west serving an "astronomical" function. Laporte (in prep.) continued this research at Uaxactun during the 1974 and 1984 seasons. Karl Ruppert (1940) listed 19 architectural groups similar to the E-Group at Uaxactun within 100 km. of that site, and other examples have been reported from elsewhere in the Maya realm (Blom 1924; Laporte 1993; see also Becker in prep.).

Although A. Chase associates PP10 with the beginning of the stela cult and Coggins (1980:731) suggests that PP10s are ancestral to twin-pyramid groups (PP1; see also Schele and Mathews 1998:180), I believe that PP10 groups are precursors of PP2. I suggest that Tikal Gr. 5D-XI is an analog to the Uaxactun "E-Group" complex, with Str. 5C-54 (Tikal's principal "Lost World" pyramid) on the west and Strs. 5D-84, 86, and 88 as the eastern trio (see Laporte 1989:figs 135, 138). Laporte and Fialko (1990) identify Burial PNT-022 as the earliest associated with a Tikal E-group, noting that it is set in front of the central platform. I believe that this easily tested thesis relates to the later PP2 mortuary complex, and I offer two predictions. First, I believe that a mortuary complex will be found associated with the central structure on the east of E-groups. Second, I think that traces or remnants of solstice markers will be found flanking the central structures of the first Early Classic examples of PP2.

THE TEN PLAZA PLANS NOW IDENTIFIED

Overlaps in the elements that are diagnostic of each of these architectural grammars are strikingly rare. Data derived from excavations in noneastern structures within PP2 groups at Tikal and in various buildings from groups conforming to PPs 3, 4, and 5 all seem to reflect the use of these groups as household units (residences for an extended family). Differences in various details of arrangement among the groups may reflect social-class differences—a matter to be considered in future research. Excavations at Tikal in 1963 were focused on PP2 and PP3 groups in order to demonstrate the accuracy of the map and indicate differences that could be seen only through archaeological recovery (Becker 1999; Haviland in prep.b). The success of this program led to a more intensive program by the Proyecto Nacional Tikal

(PNT) to explore group variations in one part of Tikal and to compare PP2 groups (for example, Gr. 6C-IX and XV) and PP3 groups (6C-I, XVI) with the much larger structure assemblages that are less easily classified (for example, Gr. 6D-VI, XVII: see Iglesias 1987; see also Laporte and Iglesias 1999). New data from these excavations allow us to infer functions from the PPs, providing a separate line of research (compare Becker in prep.).

ARCHITECTURAL GRAMMARS VERSUS GRADATIONS BY SIZE

Among archaeologists interested in settlement studies, fascination with structure size has detracted from research on architectural grammars. Very small structures, usually unseen by even the most diligent mappers, were sought at Tikal in a special project directed by Bennett Bronson. Research targeting very small structures continues in the Maya area (compare King and Potter 1994:65; Webster and Gonlin 1981). Considerable success has been achieved recently in the Northern Lowlands, where surface visibility is good. These studies may provide us with important clues to the organization and social structure at Maya sites. More problematical in Maya studies is not the attention directed toward large architectural groups but the belief that relative size is the only variable that matters.

The Three Bears and Other Fairy Tales

The viability of predictions based on the arrangements that can be identified in architectural groups is a primary concern of this chapter. We have established that group form alone has extremely high predictive value as relates to the behaviors of the group's occupants or builders. These predictions hold true *regardless of the absolute size* of the group. While economic variations may be reflected by differences in the size of architectural groups, other speculations based on the size of structures within a group are of little use in explaining how the Maya lived. Attempts to infer site organization and meaning from the relative size of specific residential groups (Webster 1998:17) risk creating circular arguments. The evaluation of any large group as the residence of the "elite" requires confirmation through sets of architectural and artifactual evidence that remain to be determined (see Webster 1998:24).

Thus, "Goldilocks and the Three Bears" provides us with an important cautionary tale for interpreting studies that seek meaning in the relative size of architectural groups.

The "Three Bears" approach to Maya architecture involves the use of "group size," variously calculated, to evaluate the social class of the users of specific groups of structures (architectural complexes). These size-related studies yield descriptions of architectural groups that always sound like stories about the three bears. One may ask, "What is the gender of the baby bear?" One does not know because it is irrelevant to a story in which size is emphasized. Now that gender has an important place in archaeological interpretation, the story of the three bears—like size-based analyses of groups—may not be relevant (see Becker 1999). Although commonly employed, the "three bears" approach has not produced any useful predictive models, despite the fact that groups of large size yield useful data in the form of objects and texts. These findings reflect riches and very possibly elite status, but "going for the gold" lacks methodological order and explanatory value.

In Maya archaeology, as in modern American society, the distinction between elite and rich is rarely addressed and remains unclear to most scholars (see D. Chase and Chase 1992; Moholy-Nagy, this volume). Patterning among architectural groups at Tikal, rather than size, produces data that are useful in understanding factors other than wealth (see Hendon 1991). At Tikal the range of variations in the absolute size of the individual groups conforming to a specific pattern is vast. Wealth, as reflected by group size, is not correlated with any particular PP. Since any specific PP (for example, PP2) at Tikal was built in all sizes (Becker 1982, 1986, 1999), use of architectural grammars may provide an important research strategy for understanding what these groups mean both at Tikal and at other Maya sites (compare Ashmore 1987).

Tikal PP2 groups range in size from extremely small to extraordinarily large, with the largest PP2 groups within greater Tikal exceeding the size of many small Maya sites. This indicates that something else is involved in the configuration of these groups—something embedded within the culture that transcends status or wealth. Inasmuch as the form of a specific PP is more predictive than the evaulation of the size of the architectural cluster, this suggests that a nonranked view (heterarchy) of these groups might be useful.

HETERARCHY

Classic-period Maya houses sharing the same PP vary in size from quite simple (see Pyburn 1989) to very elaborate. While the most elaborate houses might represent high-status or elite residences, Gair Tourtellot (1988:362) notes a lack of correlation between dwelling size and wealth or status. Ranking "houses" or "courtyard groups" by size in areas where discrete architectural groups are common is an extension of the regional rank-size analysis of Maya sites pioneered by Adams and Jones (1981; see also Adams 1982). But many enormous residential groups within Tikal are located far from the elite residences on the Central Acropolis. We may be seeing the earliest "suburbs" in the New World, with the traditional "center city" people at Tikal living near the Great Plaza and their "commuting cousins" living in impressive residences such as Gr. 7F-I or Gr. 6B-II (the "Barringer Group"), both of which conform to PP2.

Heterarchy, as an alternative to hierarchy (Ehrenreich et al. 1995) among the Maya, is a research focus of E. King (2000), who examines Maya settlement patterns using a "multiscalar, dialectical" approach. Carole Crumley (1987) addresses the problem of trying to order data using contemporary notions of social stratification and class. She suggests that hierarchichal arrangements based on size of structures, for example, may not reflect the cognitive systems of the people who created the evidence that is recovered by archaeology: "Heterarchy may be defined as the relation of elements to one another when they are unranked or when they possess the potential for being ranked in a number of different ways. For example, power can be counterpoised rather than ranked" (Crumley 1995:3, 1987:158). This approach provides a means by which we can understand some of the issues regarding size variations in residential groups that share the same PP. King (2000) also provides inferences regarding heterogenous, or nonhierarchichal, social forms based on findings of regional rank-size analysis.

Crumley (1987) notes that confusing the hierarchichal nature of Maya settlements by ranking them by size, with implied complexity, obscures our ability to elicit patterns from the archaeological evidence (see also King and Potter 1994:67). Social classes may be blurred in the archaeological record by the conversion of wealth into architecturally elaborate groups. While Classic Maya society clearly had a hierarchichal sociopolitical structure (Feinman 1995; Marcus 1995:13–16, 19–20, 27–29), the considerable variation in the size of PP2 groups and other types of groups demonstrates the need to consider how the concept of heterarchy might be useful. The many size-ranking models proposed for the Maya have generated no predictive means by which we can understand variability within Maya society, except for differences in wealth (see Marcus 1995:25–27). A shift of emphasis in Maya settlement studies toward the form of clusters of buildings (PPs) representing households or other units, along with the correlary realization that the individual parts need to be evaluated independently, provides momentum to this line of research.

The term *nonhierarchichal*, applied to PPs, suggests that there is no way of ranking these groups rather than that there are various ways of ranking them, as by size. Crumley (1995:4) also notes the important point that "governmental heterarchies (e.g., peer polities; Renfrew and Cherry 1986) can move over time to become hierarchies and vice versa" (Crumley 1987:164–65). These changes may occur without the need to invoke what can be termed the "rhetoric of collapse." David Potter and Eleanor King (1995:21) note that there is no evidence of elite or hierarchichal regulation of many aspects of the Classic Maya economy, such as corvée labor, nor any evidence for an elite controlling local economies. Perhaps, as King (2000) suggests, Maya society during the Classic Period had achieved the complexity that is apparent from variation in architecture (wealth) without a hierarchichal social structure (compare King and Potter 1994; Potter and King 1995; Palka 1997b). A hierarchichal economic structure is evident from wide variations seen in the size of various groups sharing the same PP, but differential access to wealth does not correlate with sociopolitical power. Therefore, shifting resources (wealth) may have been a factor in the changing power structure at Maya sites and may reflect "dynastic" changes that are documented in the ancient texts.

PLAZA PLANS AND CULTURE CHANGE THROUGHOUT THE MAYA AREA

The ten distinct PPs at Tikal provide a typology that may subsume most groups within any Maya city under a relatively smaller number of headings. Thus, the grammars defined above can be used to order the archaeological data more effectively (Becker 1971, 1982), allowing us to study processes of cultural change through time and space (de Montmollin 1988). All this, of course, depends on the evaluator's having good site maps and skill at pattern recognition.

Variations in Classic-period Maya sociopolitical organization are increasingly evident both within and between sites (Hendon 1992), but there are many elements shared among these ancient city-states. PP2, as defined at Tikal, is a group arangement commonly distributed throughout the southern Maya Lowlands (Becker 1971:16–18) and easily identified far beyond this region. Recognition of elements of a PP2 configuration at Quirigua (Becker 1972) enabled me to predict the origins and functions of Structure 6, first cleared some 100 years ago. This was an early demonstration that the architectural grammars defined at Tikal could be identified at other sites. The same theory regarding PP2 was also used to predict that Copan Str. 16 (Becker 1980:20–21) held the tombs of the kings of Copan.

Alterations in the PP of a group reveal cultural changes in ways not duplicated through the study of the forms of individual structures alone. The continuities or discontinuities among these group patterns reveal a great deal about cultural continuity. Documenting the first appearance and the subsequent "evolution" of residential groups conforming to PP2 at Maya sites is but one way in which change may be characterized (see Hendon 1999; Ringle 1993).

At Tikal the building that had originally covered Bu. 35 suggests that PP2 had Late Preclassic origins (Haviland et al. 1985). PP2 matured during the Early Classic period, became common during the Late Classic, and ultimately was used for 14 percent of all known architectural groups at Tikal (Becker 1982). The meaning of these changes and the possible evaluation of ideological and cosmological implications are based on data derived from site mapping alone (see Shaw, King, and Moses 1999).

The shrine in a PP2 residential group may focus or legitimize the power of a lineage head belonging to a specific kin group, or moiety. If so, then the shrine would define lineage association or membership. Association between the location of a household shrine and the residence of that lineage head may be noted from a cross-cultural perspective (Sanders et al. 1979; but see Hageman 1999). In the Maya

Lowlands the high degree of shared community interaction of the Preclassic period, with a ritual focus at the center of the village, was followed by urbanizing expansion during the Early Classic (see Feinman and Marcus 1998). This led to the formation of an "urban" royal elite, a specific class that lived in the Central Acropolis at Tikal (Harrison 1970), near the focus of the rapidly specializing, complex ceremonialism on the North Acropolis. Many but not all lower-status residents lived at some distance from this ritual center. Distance from the site center appears unrelated to wealth but may reflect differential access to power or to powerful people.

If the ritual focus of a PP2 household at Tikal was its own shrine and not the large temples built by the elite, this might reflect centripetal forces acting on rituals and might be associated with urbanization. We still do not know why some families wished to have their own shrines and others did not, but no concentric zonation is seen at Tikal or at any other Maya site. At Tikal the apparent clustering of residential groups with shrines (PP2) near *bajos* suggests an alternative theory (see Laporte and Iglesias 1999), possibly that PP2 groups represent immigrant families or specialists in some trade such as pottery production.

Plaza Plans and Temporal Change

The distribution of examples of PP2 throughout a site may provide important clues to cultural change and "urban" organization in Maya cities. Similarly, the decision of a group to change its PP tells us something about cultural processes. At present we remain unable to interpret this information. Examination of temporal change relating to PP2 reveals three variations in the construction of the diagnostic temple in the east reflecting cultural process. First, we can describe what appears to be the original category, in which the initial construction on the eastern margin of the residential plaza is a characteristic small shrine covering a new burial chamber that must be cut into the bedrock. Through time, accretions to this structure reflect the fortunes of the occupants of this residential group, but each subsequent stage of construction conforms to the size and shape rules, or grammar, for PP2.

A second category of PP2, "changed to," began its existence in conformity with a PP3 or other residential-group plan, but at some point this plan was deliberately altered to conform with the rules associated with PP2. In these cases, the initial burial shaft had to be cut through the entire existing nonsquare structure on the east and down into the bedrock, as exemplified by Tikal Bu. 116, beneath Temple 1. The Temple I tomb represents the introduction of the PP2 concept into the very center of the Tikal ceremonial area, if the temporal origins of nearby Str. 5E-38 and the impressive burials within it are not earlier.

The process of "change" involved in the construction of Temple 1 as a "shrine" on the east required that the ritual burial "consecrating" the ground beneath it be made in a tomb that cut completely through (not just into) the existing structure at that site. Since that structure was not a shrine, the PP2 tomb had to penetrate the existing structure and go down into the bedrock. The ritual building, then "sealing," of that tomb performs a "cognitive" covering function, wholly or at least in part encapsulating the existing structure at that eastern location. Thus, Tikal Bu. 116 is not centered below Temple I, as is the case with an "original" PP2 shrine, but had been intruded through the southern part of the existing platform (nonshrine) already at this locus. The center of this platform lies north of the Temple I axis, but the tomb cut was required to go through the earlier structure as part of the grammar of PP2 construction.

This burial pattern beneath a structure on the east side of a plaza differs from the Tikal tradition of making interments of "kings" below the temples arrayed over the North Acropolis. In 1962 I predicted that no burial would be found beneath Tikal Temple II, III, or IV but that a major tomb would be found beneath Temple VI, which faces west from the east side of its plaza (see Becker 1982:119). Most of the first 22 rulers of Tikal may be buried within the North Acropolis (but see Laporte, this volume). The shift to a PP2 mortuary pattern at Tikal's epicenter that is indicated by the burial of Jasaw Chan K'awiil II (after S. Martin and Grube 2000, formerly Hasaw or Ruler A) beneath Temple I leads Haviland (1994) to suggest that Jasaw had his origins at Caracol, where PP2 is common. Jasaw may also have been the victor in a "war" with Tikal. In an alternative scenario, Jasaw's wife or consort comes from Caracol. The presence of Jasaw in a PP2 "shrine" at Tikal may reflect the introduction of PP2 to the Tikal elite from Caracol, where residential groups commonly conform to this plan (see above). Regardless of the origins of Jasaw Chan K'awiil II, this shift in mortuary ritual at Tikal appears to signal an important alteration in the political history of the site. The burial beneath Temple I suggests that the rituals of people using PP2 had become the primary religious rite used at the site.

A third category of PP2 groups began by using the normal PP2 plan, but at some point the occupants chose to abandon this tradition and convert the shrine to a nonritual function. This important third category, "changed from," reflects a process that is the reverse of "changed to." The remodeling of the east building to serve a new purpose (see Webster 1998:16) is generally not evident from the surface (Becker 1971). This process can be seen in Bu. 35, located below Str. 4F-8 at Tikal and dated to the Manik ceramic period (see Culbert 1993:figs. 27 and 28). The same process applies to Quirigua Str. 6, which changed its function at some point (see Becker 1972).

The spatial and temporal distribution of architectural groups throughout the Maya realm, as well as their relative numbers, provide ample material for recognizing processes of culture change (see Haviland, this volume). Other models of cultural behaviors, elicited from ethnographic and documentary accounts, may be better at helping us to understand the thoughts, or cognitive processes, operating in the minds of the Maya who created these various PPs. Attempts to understand the Maya through the use of PP studies are slowly developing, and as we enter the new millennium, increasing numbers of young scholars are discovering the predictive values embodied in this approach.

What Do PPs Mean?

PP1 has calendrical-ritual functions, and PP2 commonly relates to a specific type of residential group that includes a shrine used in the veneration of the ancestors. The significance of many other PPs and their variations remains obscure. The assignment of function to any particular architectural group depends on the interpretation of "meaning" in the building plan and associated features. Ritual, domestic, or economic (market) functions must be implied by the analysis of the component architectural and other features within a group. These features, in turn, may offer clues to social and/or ethnic diversity. Some PPs at Tikal may reflect foreign influences. Central Mexican traits are known from Tikal, in ceramics as well as in art and architecture

(C. Jones 1996; Laporte 1989; Sharer, this volume), perhaps reflecting the presence of foreign individuals or emissaries (diplomatic missions, traders). The suggestion that the huge complexes of structure within sites such as Tikal and Calakmul were the residences of exiled or deposed rulers is but one of many possible interpretations. Anthropological data on moieties lead me to suggest that a specific large-building complex may be the residence of an internal affairs leader or of the person ("king") serving as the head of the internal affairs moiety, who regulated basic internal functioning within a complex city (Becker 1983, 1991). An association between a specific PP and "foreigners," through biological or other evidence, remains to be proven, but the possible relationship between PP2 at Tikal and Caracol warrants attention.

Identification of patterning among the residential and other groups at Tikal and surrounding sites is more effective for reconstructing the cultural variations within this part of the Maya realm than has been previously noted. As Héctor Escobedo and Stephen Houston (1997) suggest for Piedras Negras, the orientation of structures may be influenced by terrain in ways that alter the relationship between structure axis and astronomical orientations, but the range of variations at a single site and regional patterns remains to be investigated.

CONCLUSION

1. Synchronic Issues: Social Structure at Tikal

The recognition that structure groups (architectural clusters) are a significant area of research activity has led to the demonstration that their form provides a significant focus for research. Identification of "architectural grammars" or plaza plans (PPs) at Tikal, through surface inspection and excavation, provides us with a useful tool by which we can interpret the archaeology of this urban society. The identification of PPs enables us to predict site composition and Maya concepts of planning, to develop testing strategies at large Maya sites, and to apply sophisticated intersite research strategies, since PPs reflect the heterogenous architecture characteristic of a complex, urban society (compare Pyburn 1997).

2. Economic Structure

Wealth, and possibly social status, may be inferred from the size of Maya architectural groups, but the form of the group is critical in understanding social organization and group membership at Tikal and at other Maya sites. Variations within a single "pattern" of size, as a reflection of wealth, suggest that a review of these data from the perspective of heterarchy will prove useful. The wide range and multiple gradations in the quantity and quality of grave goods associated with burials at Tikal lead to the conclusion that considerable economic and/or social class differentiation existed at Tikal during the Classic period. The recognition of distinctions between class and wealth among the Maya is a task that might best be addressed in terms of studies of medieval Europe. During the medieval period, European sumptuary laws were used to control developing confusion in the expression of wealth among a growing mercantile population. Production and distribution of varied grades of goods reflect a production and distribution system that requires a complex market economy, leading us back to inferences made regarding PP9.

Economic variability can be placed on a relative scale through comparisons of grave goods. PP2 enables us to predict the location of a specific category of burials at Tikal, as well as at many other Maya sites in the Lowlands and beyond—burials believed to be those of lineage leaders. At Quirigua a knowledge of the PP2 grammar enabled an important burial to be located (Becker 1972). Sharer (this volume) suggests that a burial represents the founder of that city, based on the jade inlaid teeth, a jade bead in his mouth, and three vessels placed as offerings. The three-vessel assemblage, often including a small jade bead and small versions of other items, is the same pattern commonly found in association with burials in the shrines on the east of Tikal PP2 groups (see Becker 1999).

3. PPs and Patterning in Time: Diachronic Issues

In addition to working out synchronic relationships in a Classic-period complex state such as Tikal, links between PP2 and the earlier PP10 (E-groups) may reflect the shifts in rituals from the socially homogeneous Maya chiefdoms of the Preclassic to the heterogenous states of the Early Classic period. Diachronic issues also include matters relating to Tikal's expansion beyond its "borders" (conquest, alliance) and to whether Quirigua was a colony or a subordinate of Tikal. As at Quirigua, the "founder" at Copan may have resided in a PP2. The evidence for the impact of outsiders on Tikal (from Teotihuacan?) may be associated with PP1, PP4, or PP10 (E-groups). The evolution of settlement over time at Tikal may be studied by examining the shifts in PPs. Sabloff (pers. comm.) suggests that continuities in these group plans through time may be indicated by patterns found at Late Postclassic–period Mayapan and Tulum and possibly at Cozumel. Other site maps in the Maya area and beyond can be evaluated to see whether the architectural grammars evident at Tikal have a regional distribution or are localized or even unique to Tikal. Specific testing of theories derived from these maps is essential to determining their accuracy and comparability for evaluating the architectural ("grammatical") record.

Plaza plans similar to those described at Tikal are found throughout the Maya area, and aspects of those patterns extend far beyond it. Each of these architectural aggregates may be characteristic of a particular site or period (compare Ashmore 1981:40). These patterns provide a means by which research strategies can be developed for excavations at other Maya cities, as well as offering units for comparing possible interplay between the various ancient inhabitants of the Maya Lowlands and the recognition of change through time.

The devolution of complex Lowland Maya polities, from the Classic-period city-states to the chiefdoms of the Postclassic period, was a slow process that began by the middle of the eighth century (W. R. Coe 1990; Hammond et al. 1998). Some possible exceptions worth noting can be found at sites such as Mayapan, but these also declined through time. "Complex" Maya society in the Lowlands certainly did not end with the imploding bang implied by the term *collapse* but with a slowly diminishing whimper.

DIRECTIONS FOR FUTURE RESEARCH

Excavations to test several theses embedded within the data base noted above include the following:

1. Excavation of Temple VI at Tikal, an excellent and very large example of a PP2 shrine.

2. Wide-area clearing, including taking to bedrock, of an entire architectural group plus its surrounding "houselot" (Becker in prep.) to seek hidden structures and features such as boundary markers that delineate group borders.

3. Wide-area excavation of isolated structures at Tikal to see if another architectural "group" (PP) can be identified or if these "isolates" are parts of groups without building platforms or otherwise undelineated houselots. Candidates are small structures such as Str. 7C-37, 38, 45, and 46 and the isolated structures at the ends of causeways.

4. Axial trenching of the central structure on the east of an E-group (PP10) and deep searches of their lateral buildings to test the thesis that PP2 emerged from PP10.

5. Extensive testing of the central "platforms" of PP4 groups, in addition to a parallel research program demonstrating the absence of small structures or altars in the center of the principal plaza of non-PP4 groups.

6. Excavations of Tikal's Barringer Group that are tied to excavation of Temple V, in a program seeking evidence for dual rulership. Since 1975, I have believed that the Classic-period Maya used moiety divisions in social structure and in political leadership (Becker 1975), and this aspect of their social system may have considerable antiquity. The identification of parallel social hierarchies within each moiety would enable us to answer many questions regarding the social structure at these sites (Becker 1983, 1991) and to interpret the texts in new ways.

Note

I am deeply indebted to Jeremy Sabloff for organizing this conference and inviting me to participate and to Robert Sharer for his important comments on this paper. My sincere thanks are also due to Robert H. Dyson, who directed the field research, and to those directors and staff of the Tikal Project of the University Museum (The University of Pennsylvania) who encouraged and supported this study. Special thanks are due to Diane Z. Chase, Arlen F. Chase, Jon Hageman, Peter Harrison, William A. Haviland, Julia A. Hendon, Elspeth Kursh, Juan Pedro Laporte, Gair Tourtellot, Diane Wayman, Lori Wright, and many others who have shared information on this topic or have commented on earlier versions of this chapter. Many thanks are also due to Wendy Ashmore, Greg Borgstede, Karen Bruhns, Elizabeth M. Brumfiel, William J. Folan,

Stephen D. Houston, Christopher Jones, Ellen Kintz, Mark Metz, Olivier de Montmollin, Deborah L. Nichols, Andy Scherer, John M. Weeks, and many others for their help with earlier versions of the text.

This chapter was completed while I was a Fellow in Anthropology at The University of Pennsylvania. Support for its preparation was provided in part by a grant from the Frank and Mary Ellen Gillon Foundation. Portions of an early version of the chapter were presented at the 1987 Seminar Series of the Centre of Latin-American Studies, The University of Cambridge. The presentation and interpretation of all data and the conclusions offered are my responsibility alone.

10

Thirty Years Later

Some Results of Recent Investigations in Tikal

Juan Pedro Laporte

After the work of the University of Pennsylvania Tikal Project ended, archaeological activity continued at the site, sporadically at first but continuously after 1979. Most of these projects were Guatemalan. At first, they were extensions of the work of the Tikal Project; subsequently, they had independent objectives and research designs. Thirty years and fifteen research projects have clearly added to the information obtained by the Tikal Project (table 10.1).

RESTORATION PROGRAMS AT TIKAL

Some of the research projects were carried out by the conservation and structural restoration programs at Tikal, the results of which can be seen when visiting the site. There are five programs of this type.

Fluted Palace Project

The work on Group 5E-XI between 1972 and 1980 was directed by Miguel Orrego and Rudy Larios (1983). Their report provides important data about architecture, burials, and chronology, as well as graffiti and other painted designs. Group 5E-XI, with its many palaces, began

TABLE 10.1

Tikal Projects between 1972 and 2000

1	Proyecto Palacio de las Acanaladuras	1972–80
2	Proyecto Intersitio: Tikal-Yaxha	1978
3	Proyecto Nacional Tikal: Sección Mundo Perdido	1979–84
4	Proyecto Nacional Tikal: Sección Zonas de Habitación	1982–85
5	Proyecto Nacional Tikal: Sección Apoyo al Parque Tikal	1983–84
6	Proyecto Nacional Tikal: Sección Zona Norte	1984–85
7	Proyecto Cuadrante Noreste (habitacional)	1985
8	Proyecto de Conservación del Templo I	1992–96
9	Proyecto Nacional Tikal: Intersitios	1994–99
10	Proyecto Templo V	1995–2000
11	Proyecto Arqueológico Lacandón	1998
12	Proyecto Templo III	1999
13	Proyecto Bioarqueología en Tikal	1998–2000
14	Proyecto ADN Mitocondrial en Restos Oseos de Tikal	1999–2000
15	Proyecto Nacional Tikal: Sección de Laboratorio	1985–2000

in the Late Classic and continued to develop until the Terminal Classic. Information about the inhabitants in the Postclassic is also found in the ruins of these old palaces.

Tikal National Project: The Program Supporting Tikal National Park

When the Mundo Perdido Project ended in 1982, a program to help Tikal National Park was set up to deal in particular with complexes and buildings with structural problems. This program was headed by Juan Pedro Laporte, Jorge Mario De León, and Vilma Fialko (Laporte 1999a). Four complexes were included in the program: the Five Storied Palace in the Central Acropolis, Group F, Group 6B-II, and the Plaza of the Seven Temples, as well as Structure 5E-38 in the East Plaza, which was handled by Tikal National Park staff.

Tikal National Project: North Zone Section

A new research and restoration project in the North Zone of Tikal, directed by Jorge Mario De León, was begun in 1984–85; however, these explorations were suspended, and the original plan of work was not finished. Restoration efforts were focused on the two largest temples of this architectural complex (3D-40 and 3D-43). Recently, some further work has been carried out, and in 1996 the process of reinforcing these larger structures, which had earlier been halted, resumed (Larios and Orrego 1997).

Six groups of structures in the North Zone of Tikal were chosen for investigation. Three of these groups belong to the ritual center (Groups 3D-XIV, 3D-XV, and 3D-XVI), while the other three plazas belong to the residential area (Groups 3E-XI, 3E-XII, and 3E-XIII). Although few details regarding this project are available, information about the offerings and funerary activity can be summarized (Laporte 2000a). It is clear that the demarcation of the North Zone of Tikal took place in the Early Classic, with occupancy widespread in it both in the Late and the Terminal Classic. It is interesting to note that there were some inhabitants during the Postclassic, as evidenced by the discarded pieces of ceramics inside some of the buildings.

During the exploration of the base of 3D-43, an important tomb that contained a three-dimensional sandstone sculpture known as the *Man of Tikal* was found. This sculpture, although belonging to an earlier phase than the tomb itself, was decapitated and buried, together with several individuals and a generous offering. The *Man of Tikal* is a portrait of Chak Tok Ich'aak I, who ruled between A.D. 360 and 378 (Fahsen 1988; Martin, this volume). The sculpture was later modified by a long text carved on its back, written in the era of Yax Nuun Ayiin I (Curl Nose) (A.D. 378–404). Nevertheless, the history of this sculpture does not end here. The type of ceramics in the offering shows that this burial—perhaps of a historic person or perhaps only of his companions, as some think—dates to the end of the fifth century, nearly a century after the inscription was modified. Temporally, the ceramic content of the offering refers to the final part of the government of K'an Chitam (or Kan Boar, A.D. 458–ca. 486) or even later, to Chak Tok Ich'aak II (or Jaguar Paw Skull, A.D. ca. 486–508). If the principal man in the tomb did head the government, he could be either of the two rulers, but the preferable explanation is that both persons interred were important members of the court of one of those rulers, most likely in the beginning of the sixth century.

Restoration of Temple I Project

Beginning in 1992, the Agencia Española de Cooperación Internacional and Guatemala's Instituto de Antropología e Historia

(IDAEH) began the restoration of Temple I (Muñoz and Quintana 1996). The project's aims were to rebuild areas that had not been rebuilt previously and to assure the preservation of those that had been restored. The only work done on the surroundings was to open the northern corridor separating Temple I from the adjacent buildings of the North Acropolis. Restoration of the southeast corner of Structure 5D-29 led to the discovery of a new monument, Stela 40, which was found covered by the fill and the walls of the last version of this structure, built in the Late Classic. Although the stela was mutilated in antiquity, a large portion of the carving on the four sides can still be seen (Valdés et al. 1997). Three of the sides contain richly dressed personages, and the fourth is a hieroglyphic inscription showing a dedication date of A.D. 468.

Temple V Project

Since 1995 this same team has been working on the restoration of Temple V (Gómez and Vidal 1997; Gómez 1998, 1999), although the Tikal National Project had been interested in protecting the roof comb since 1987. The great staircase of this structure, which includes two balustrades, 2.6 m. wide, extending from beginning to end, is amazing. So far, this decorative element can be seen in three other major Early Classic buildings in Tikal (5D-22, 5D-33, 5C-49). The presence in one of the main temples of this conspicuous and unusual architectural feature for Tikal is an important indicator of continuity because— although appearing sporadically—it is a model used since the Preclassic in the first versions of the Great Pyramid (5C-54) and another smaller structure (5D-77), both belonging to the Mundo Perdido (Laporte 1997, 2000b).

In order to explore the interior of Temple V, a tunnel, starting from the back, was dug along the north-south axis of the base of the pyramid. This investigation showed that Temple V did not contain any other internal structures and thus was built all at once. Analysis of the ceramics gives the beginning of the seventh century A.D. as a tentative date for its construction (Laporte and Gómez 1998). This date, which would place Temple V at an early stage of the building sequence of the main temple of Tikal, is supported by an analysis of the offerings found inside the building.

Temple III Project

Between 1967 and 1969, the Tikal Project's efforts in Temple III were minimal and limited to the upper temple. As recent evaluations (Larios and Orrego 1997) show, some deterioration has occurred in the thirty years since its restoration. The Temple III Project, directed by Francisco De León (1999) and sponsored by Guatemala's Instituto de Antropología e Historia and the Interamerican Development Bank (IDB), was organized to repair the damaged area. Although this was not a research project, an important component was the replacement of the beams of the lintel over the access to Chamber 2 of the Temple and the storing of the original beams in the warehouse at Tikal National Park.

RESEARCH PROGRAMS IN CENTRAL TIKAL

Fifteen Centuries of Development in the Mundo Perdido Group

Mundo Perdido is a major architectural complex, occupying one of the most important places inside Tikal's epicenter (fig. 10.1). The antiquity of the complex, as well as the presence of buildings with unusual architectural characteristics, led to a more systematic exploration. Between 1979 and 1984, the Tikal National Project carried on a large program of investigation and restoration at Mundo Perdido. Because the results of this project have been fully published (Laporte and Fialko 1995), I will only present a synthesis of the cultural history of the complex—mostly derived from the work cited in this chapter—as well as some newer interpretations.

The Establishment of Mundo Perdido in the Preclassic

Two collections from the Mundo Perdido date from the early phase of its settlement and, therefore, represent the initial population of Tikal. Although it is difficult to establish a specific date for the beginning of the Early Eb phase at Tikal, which is of the Pre-Mamom ceramic tradition still in the early Middle Preclassic, it is clearly earlier than 700 B.C. (Laporte and Fialko 1993; Hermes 1993a). These samples were composed of rubbish found in cavities of calcareous stone and not actually part of the buildings. There are similar deposits representing the other phases of the Middle Preclassic: Late Eb (700–600 B.C.) and Tzec (600–350 B.C.).

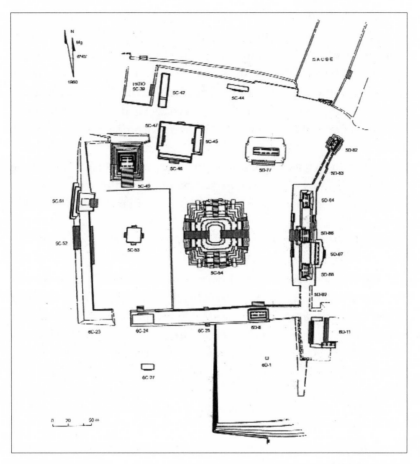

FIGURE 10.1

Plan of Mundo Perdido during the Late Classic, Imix phase.

Two samples from the Chuen complex (350 B.C.–A.D. 1) represent the Late Preclassic. Despite strong evidence of building, no pure deposits belonging to the Cauac phase (A.D. 1–150) of Mundo Perdido were found in the excavations carried out by the Tikal National Project. Accordingly, samples from the tunnels dug into the Great Pyramid (5C-54) were used to study this period.

The typology derived from the analysis indicates a stable period with great ceramic diversity, which supports Culbert's (1977, 1979) proposals. On the one hand, we now have a larger sample of the Pre-Mamom horizon, showing pan-Mesoamerican designs indicating residential stages prior to 700 B.C. (Cheetam 1998). On the other hand, the ceramic stability of the phases associated with the Mamom and Chicanel spheres is indisputable. At that time Tikal's exterior contacts increased, as reflected by the presence of types associated with neighboring areas, including ceramic types manufactured elsewhere, such as Mars Orange.

Even though it seems as if the study of Preclassic ceramics is partially resolved and the possibility of establishing a more definite Pre-Mamom horizon at Tikal appears promising, we need to redefine the typology because the most recent revision is more than ten years old (Laporte and Fialko 1993). The most recent studies of ceramics in Belize (Kosakowsky 1987; Kosakowsky and Pring 1998) and those of the north (Forsyth 1989, 1992) and southeast Petén (Laporte 1995a; Laporte and Alvarado 1999) find some diagnostic types that might expand the reach of Tikal's external relations.

The character, function, and organization of Mundo Perdido began to develop at the end of the Middle Preclassic—that is, about 600 B.C. The building complexes were built gradually on a series of artificial level surfaces, which in some cases are more than 10 m. high. The gradual increase in height developed as the volume of the structures and complexity of the grouping increased.

The pyramid and its counterpart, a long platform that borders the east side (East Platform), structurally and functionally composed what is the oldest architectural unit in Tikal. It has the diagnostic characteristics of those complexes roughly called Group E–type complexes (Ruppert 1940; Rathje et al. 1978; A. F. Chase and Chase 1995): astronomic observatories (Aveni and Hartung 1989), complexes for public ritual (Cohodas 1985; Laporte and Morales 1994), and complexes for astronomic commemoration (Fialko 1988a). The characteristics of the rituals associated with these architectural complexes do not seem to vary significantly either in time or space, if we consider that this plaza pattern continued to be repeated in Tikal and other sites during the entire period of the development of Maya civilization in the Lowlands.

Mundo Perdido had four construction phases during the Preclassic and two more during the Early Classic. Each phase involved a version of the pyramid on the west and the long platform on the east side. All of these and their characteristics, such as balustrades, large masks, building techniques, and discoveries, have been fully described previously (Laporte and Fialko 1995; Laporte 1997). By the Late Preclassic, as a part of the urban planning of the earliest version of Tikal, a monumental causeway, 49 m. wide and 92 m. long, joining the North Acropolis with the Mundo Perdido Group was built.

We can define the monumental architecture of Mundo Perdido on the basis of four plazas surrounding the monumental Great Pyramid (5C-54). Among these, the East Plaza was the largest in antiquity and is associated with the earliest occupation of the Preclassic. The other plazas were built later. The West Plaza Group, which became the largest expansion area in Mundo Perdido, was part of an urban plan intended to create a space such that the Great Pyramid would be in the center of the complex and no longer just at the western end of the plaza where it was first built. This expansion occurred at the beginning of the Early Classic (B.C. 250), and at this time Mundo Perdido achieved its final dimensions of approximately 60,000 m^2. This building expansion was accompanied by a continuous process of filling in the different sectors of the Mundo Perdido Group, which in the beginning did not appear to be closed as it did in later centuries. Each structure in the complex subsequently underwent many remodelings. Each retained its place and function but was remodeled primarily to match the architectural style developing in other complexes in Tikal.

During this expansion, the fifth version of the Great Pyramid (5C-54), which is the version now visible, was built. With a height of approximately 31 m., it was, at the time, the tallest structure in Tikal. The pyramid has more than ten steps and an additional step located below the great *tableros,* with their benches, frames, and inset vertical panels. The *tableros* are forerunners of the architectural formula known as *talud-tablero.* The east and west sides of the pyramid are symmetrical, with central stairs that reach the top, while those on the other sides only reach the eighth step. Other notable features of the building are niches and large masks. Sadly, these are so eroded that it is impossible to determine whether they were anthropomorphic or zoomorphic depictions like those found in other Maya Preclassic structures.

By the Cauac phase, the East Platform of the complex became functionally and structurally more elaborate. The first versions of Temples 5D-84 (north), 5D-86 (central), and 5D-88 (south) were built on top of the four-step platform, foreshadowing the symmetrical pattern that would prevail until the Late Classic. Thus, Temple 5D-86 shares an orienting east-west axis with the corresponding pyramidal version of the Great Pyramid (5D-54). This temple had three longitudinal chambers. The smaller central chamber is notable because of the two great zoomorphic masks flanking its entrance (Laporte and Fialko 1995). The location of these sculptures in the interior of a structure is the only known example of such a placement from all the sculptural corpus of the Late Preclassic. While it is the generally accepted norm for the Late Classic, the predominant practice in the Preclassic was to place architectural sculptures on the exterior (Sanz 1997). It is interesting that these naturalistic masks are the first clear depiction of jaguars in Tikal. Sanz (1997), following a detailed iconographic analysis, says that these great masks could be an early depiction of Nu Balam Chak, one of the protector spirits of Tikal, and were closely associated with warfare.

The Cimi Segment

There has been much discussion concerning the change in ceramics that occurred between the Preclassic and the Classic. The change involved new techniques of manufacture and firing, as well as the appearance of polychromism and the abandonment of techniques of negative decoration. There was also a fundamental change in the shapes of ceramics, the development of supports, and the use of lids at this time.

These new ceramic characteristics appeared during the second and third centuries A.D. (Culbert 1979, 1993; Laporte 1995b). This segment, called Cimi in Tikal, lasted from A.D. 150 to 250, bridging the end of the Late Preclassic and the start of the Early Classic. However, there are no diagnostic architectural styles associated with this ceramic component.

As was the case in the Tikal Project, in Mundo Perdido there were very few objects in Cimi style. Four examples were found, each associated with a different context (Laporte and Fialko 1995). All of them seem to have had uses restricted to elites, as they were associated with burials and votive offerings found primarily in ceremonial areas. These ceramic elements are large, bulbous, mammiform supports on dishes with Usulutan designs. Later on, these supports became smaller and conical and were adapted to dishes, bowls, and vases. This brief development did not last beyond the fourth century A.D. On the other hand, the appearance of polychromy is regarded as a significant development because, in contrast to mammiform supports, it became a long-lasting tradition in the ceramics of the Lowlands. Outside Tikal, examples showing this same Cimi combination (form, support, and decoration) are found in the Topoxte site (Hermes 1993b).

Early Classic Innovations in Mundo Perdido

Even twenty years ago, it was thought that the chronological subdivision of the Early Classic was confusing due to the amazing stability of the types of ceramics, which meant that architectural sequences could not be tied to ceramics from different dates. Furthermore, large samples, which would allow quantitative analyses, were scarce (Culbert 1979). The investigation by the Tikal National Project in Mundo Perdido and its nearby residential areas has turned this around. Dedicatory caches, elite tombs, and different collections of materials (Iglesias 1988, 1996; Laporte 1989) provide an ample analytic spectrum within which to subdivide the three centuries of the Early Classic into the ceramic phases: Manik 1 (A.D. 250–300), Manik 2 (A.D. 300–400), and Manik 3 (A.D. 400–550). Manik 3, in turn, has two subphases (Coggins 1975; Laporte et al. 1992), distinguished by new shapes and decorative motifs in the beginning (Manik 3-A, A.D. 400–480) and by changes in the percentage of their proportions in the later stage (Manik 3-B, A.D. 480–550).

Culbert's (1979) study of the Manik complex, using material from the Tikal Project, found a total of nine ceramic groups and 25 types with their corresponding variations. Classification of the material from the Tikal National Project produced a total of 46 new types, and this typological variety has subsequently been published (Laporte and Fialko 1986; Laporte and Iglesias 1992). This classificatory scheme has no parallel in other sites in the Petén and Belize, except in the nearby Uaxactun, Río Azul, and Yaxha. This is the Tzakol horizon, which is less well defined in other zones and whose absence has led to claims of the abandonment of sites (as in Ceibal and Altar de Sacrificios, among others). Claims have also been made about the predominance of the older Chicanel tradition over the Tzakol, so that the latter is a minor component of the ceramic inventory (as in sites in the Basin of the Mopan and Belize Rivers).

The Early Classic was an era of great growth in Mundo Perdido. A new example of the profusion of architectural sculpture is Structure 5D-82. The first version, built in the fourth century A.D., was a semicircular platform underpinning a longitudinal one-chamber building with a red frieze on the east exterior cornice, elaborately adorned with stucco anthropomorphic personages (Laporte and Fialko 1995; Sanz 1997). The central part of the frieze has a torso and the head of an anthropomorphic figure with chest-high flexed arms. The face has large volutes emanating from the mouth, and it probably once had a beard. There are two large wings over the shoulders, both having a cartouche in the center. Only on the right-hand one can a motif, the symbol for Ahau, be seen. The sides of the frieze have two anthropomorphic faces with a buccal plate; their semisquare pendants are flanked on their upper side by *pop* symbols, and two small zoomorphic heads appear above them. Analyzing these iconographic elements suggests that the central figure of the frieze is a representation of God D, also known as Itzamna, one of the fundamental figures in the Maya religion. The volutes that surround the niches and the central figure possibly represent smoke or blood.

Similarly, the East Platform of the complex was modified several times during the Early Classic. In front of it, at the level of the plaza, a small platform with four staircases stands out. It has a series of holes on the surface that may have been used to hold banners or forked posts. In a large pit under the platform were found 17 bodies of women, men, and children, who were probably sacrificed during an event celebrating the erection of the monument or some other dedicatory ritual. If it were another dedication, it could have been that of Stela 29 (A.D. 292), so far the oldest dated monument in Tikal, which was found on the ground near Temple III. This is a prominent location due to its proximity to the causeway leading to Mundo Perdido.

Stela 39, the next monument erected at Tikal, was found in Temple 5D-86 of the East Platform on the east-west orienting axis of the Mundo Perdido Group (fig. 10.2). It is only the bottom half of the stela, which means that the Maya themselves broke it and placed it inside the building, being interested in saving only this half. The stela is only carved on two sides—the front and the back (Ayala 1987). The front depicts the bottom half of a person, who—as indicated by the remains

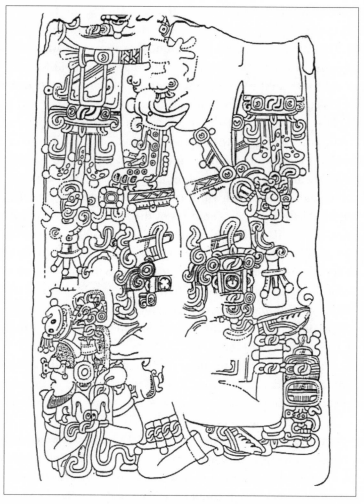

FIGURE 10.2

Mundo Perdido, Structure 5D-86, Stela 39, frontal view.

of the costume—might be a ruler. He is standing atop a captive, who might be a noble because he is not partially naked, as captives are usually represented. The captive also has physical attributes such as a beard that individualize him. The monument celebrates an event that happened in A.D. 376; its presence in Mundo Perdido seems to be related to a parallel funerary event.

In the latter part of the fourth century A.D., the construction of six tombs inside the temples of the East Platform undoubtedly coincided with important changes in the function of the complex. A clear specialization in the manufacture of the ceramic objects in the funerary offerings associated with these tombs is evident in the stylistic similarity found in the different tombs. Effigy vessels shaped like macaws and monkeys also stand out. Considering the high aesthetic and technical quality of the offerings and the location of the tombs, it is clear that the deceased were members of a high-ranking group in Tikal. They might have been members of the ruling dynasty, but perhaps a segment that had lost power and was eliminated during the political changes that occurred at the end of the fourth century A.D.

Thus, it is evident that—at least for a short time and honoring the memory of at least one member of the ruling lineage of the fourth century—Mundo Perdido became a place for ancestors. It later resumed its more general and public role in the complex society of Tikal (Laporte 2000a). Since it is clear that this offering occurred between A.D. 320 and 380—given the definition of the ceramic phase Manik 2—which family could these individuals have belonged to? There is not much choice because only two individuals ruled Tikal in that period: K'inich Muwaan Jol (Bird Skull) between ca. A.D. 330 and 359 and Chak Tok Ich'aak I (Great Jaguar Paw) between A.D. 360 and 378 (Martin, this volume). This same identification may be tied to Stela 39.

Mundo Perdido has other stylistic characteristics that make it conspicuous in Tikal between the fourth and sixth centuries A.D. (fig. 10.3). Architecturally, the presence of the *talud-tablero* style in some buildings in the area of central Tikal, particularly in Mundo Perdido, is notable. *Talud-tablero* architecture is also found in some structures in zones away from the center of the Late Classic city, which are grouped in complexes with specialized functions (Group 6C-XVI; fig. 10.4). This type of grouping has usually been called an "apartment complex." Such structures, which are considered to be dwellings even though they may be very different in size and shape, include platforms, pyramid bases, and palace-type structures that might have had vaulted or flat roofs.

Both the *talud-tablero* and these specialized groups have been used in a facile manner to claim an influence of Teotihuacan on Tikal on the premise that these features were exclusively Central Mexican (R. Millon 1981, 1988). However, this does not take into consideration other crucial

FIGURE 10.3

Mundo Perdido during the Early Classic, Manik 3 phase.

factors that affected architectural and settlement patterns across Mesoamerica, such as influences that were transmitted through the mutual exchange of goods and ideas. In order to explain this model, it was necessary to know in detail the process of insertion of each of these elements into the cultural setting of Tikal (Laporte 1999b). What stands out is the diversity with which these variants were used, demonstrating the eclecticism with which the architectural style was associated.

Other sites in Mesoamerica, even those in the Mexican Highlands, showed this eclecticism in the fourth century A.D. Such eclecticism must have taken place in Teotihuacan itself, whose Preclassic architecture has been poorly defined but which did not generally use the *talud-tablero* until it became predominant in the Early Classic. Once this architectural technique was established, it expanded to sectors and/or zones where Teotihuacan had cultural or political zones of influence.

The late appearance of this architectural feature in Teotihuacan, together with *talud-tablero* use and local development from the third century A.D. in Tikal, shows that, since the late Preclassic, the *talud-tablero,* as a part of a stylistic horizon, was a widely diffused trait across Mesoamerica. This architectural feature was more or less accepted in the various regions, where it was modified to adapt it to the architecture characteristic of each locale. In Tikal (though I do not wish to minimize the presence of outside and multiethnic groups—and not just Teotihuacanos), there was an alternative mechanism that favored

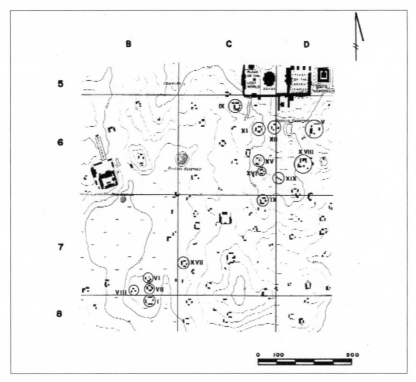

FIGURE 10.4

Position of residential groups explored in the southern section of Mundo Perdido (from Carr and Hazard 1961).

manipulation of architectural styles. This was based on the interaction and interdependence of architectural traits, ceramic styles, and systems of sculpture, which do not in and of themselves directly point to foreign influence.

The best example of the specialized residential complex in the Early Classic in Tikal is Group 6C-XVI. In its most recent version, the Late Classic, it only had a few insignificant dwelling platforms (6C-51/53) (Carr and Hazard 1961) (fig. 10.4 above). Underneath this level we found a group of Early Classic buildings that had been erected and gradually covered up between the third and sixth centuries A.D. There were five patios, around which were grouped numerous small, pyramidal platforms, as well as platforms and palaces with several vaulted chambers, porticoes, and passageways. This monumental

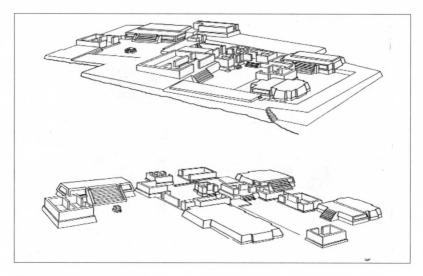

FIGURE 10.5

Group 6C-XVI during stages 3 and 8.

FIGURE 10.6

Group 6C-XVI, plan of the lower levels of occupation.

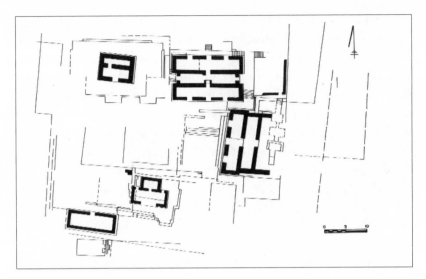

FIGURE 10.7

Group 6C-XVI, plan of the upper levels of occupation.

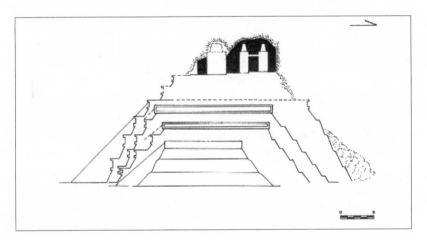

FIGURE 10.8

Mundo Perdido, Structure 5C-49, north-south profile showing several construction stages.

group grew during more than 20 building stages with continuous occupation (Laporte 1989) (figs. 10.5–10.8). They are, therefore, artificial units, which may correspond to reality as they intermix with each other.

Why is 6C-XVI associated with Teotihuacan? Because it fits the easy premises of comparative characteristics: it is composed of multiple

intercommunicating patios; there are *talud-tableros* in a small percentage of its more than 90 structures; and a controversial sculpture, the
so-called "Ball Court Marker of Tikal," was found there. Even if one
uses a simplistic but functional concept of settlement, however, the
surge in residential complexes cannot be attributed to a single center
in Mesoamerica. Despite the apparent structural similarity between the
residential complexes of Teotihuacan and Tikal, there are significant
differences, particularly in their social groupings, the organization of
the complexes, and above all, their functions. The key point is that
6C-XVI is not a dwelling, as can be found in Teotihuacan, because—
after an extensive investigation—no remains such as hearths, middens,
or burials, which would characterize a concentration of inhabitants,
were found.

Since the traces of occupation, kinship, and production inside this
complex are vague, it is necessary to find other attributes that may clarify the function of the complex at least for some part of its lengthy history. The common denominator of the features that stand out in
6C-XVI is their references to the ball game. Although it was not used
for spectators' viewing, the building might have been used for preparations and ritual beginnings, for training on the specifics of the game,
and for the development of a partial or unique aspect of the event.

Why do we propose such a function? To start with, we are not dealing with a ball court and the structures usually associated with it, but
with a series of artistic elements that may refer to ball players: several
murals on the exteriors of the bases of palaces show figures associated
with this type of personage (fig. 10.9). Also, there is the controversial
monument, which could not be a ball-court marker in itself and has a
shape that has previously been found only in Kaminaljuyu and
Teotihuacan. The monument could have been publically exhibited in
the North Patio of the complex and associated with the dynasty (fig.
10.10). Now known as the "Ball Court Marker of Tikal," it has been
described in detail (Fialko 1988b; Laporte and Fialko 1990).

During the Early Classic, as well as before and after it, there were
undoubtedly objects from Teotihuacan and from many other places in
Tikal's inventory. Likewise, there could have been persons who came
from the Mexican Highlands to a metropolis such as Tikal. However, if
we use an interactive model, this should also have taken place in

FIGURE 10.9

Group 6C-XVI, Mural of the Ball Players.

Teotihuacan. But despite aspects of Maya influence on artistic and ceramic levels, which have been widely discussed, evidences of an effective Maya presence in Teotihuacan are difficult to interpret (Linné 1934; C. Millon 1973; Rattray 1987).

It is clear that the two cultures carried on an interchange of ideas and objects for mutual benefit but, at the same time, retained their

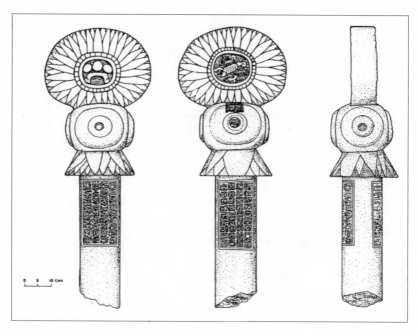

FIGURE 10.10

Group 6C-XVI, the "Ball Court Marker of Tikal."

regional identity (Parsons 1969). This led to a high degree of artistic and architectural innovation, characterized by extremely eclectic styles and the development of an iconographic syncretism (Pazstory 1978). It is most important that we learn when the process began and what happened, after the fall of Teotihuacan, to those concepts that survived because they were part of the cultural tradition of the Early Classic in the Maya Area.

Mundo Perdido in the Late and Terminal Classic

Even though there were changes in manufacturing technology, change in the ceramic sequence between the Early Classic and the Late Classic, which took place between A.D. 550 and 600, was gradual. Eventually, the elements that defined the new ceramic phase—particular decorative modes, ceramic shapes, and color palette—jelled. The kind of technological change that occurred between the Late Preclassic and the Early Classic, however, did not appear between these periods.

There are five collections from Mundo Perdido and, more

recently, from Temple V that represent this transition and the beginning of the Late Classic (Laporte and Gómez 1998). They show that the new technique of using thin clay, mostly in making bowls and pitchers, as shown by the Aduana variety of the Tinaja Group (Adams 1971), began at the end of the Early Classic. The change in polychrome decorations towards the open bowls of the Saxche Group also started at that time. During the Late Classic, new shapes emerged, defining new ceramic phases. The period saw a growing interest in cylindrical vases, the development of bowls with tall vertical sides, and the emergence of barrel-shaped vases with pedestal bases (Holley 1986; Laporte and Gómez 2000). The definition of changes that took place during this period facilitates attribution of the frequent funerary offerings of the Late Classic in Tikal.

The principal modification made at the West Plaza of Mundo Perdido in the Ik phase (A.D. 550–700) was the construction of the fifth version of 5C-49, using the old four-step platform with *talud-tablero* architecture. Its investigation has been published previously (Laporte 1998). This version of 5C-49 involved building a new staircase directly on top of the old one, with a minimum of fill between them, in order to get the angle needed to reach the new temple. It had three rooms and was topped by an elaborate roof comb, now collapsed.

The cyclic ritual associated with the type of complex that Mundo Perdido represented was still being carried out during the seventh century A.D., but it is also evident that these festivities were not accompanied by a complete reconstruction of the complex, as had been the practice in earlier centuries. In contrast with the relatively few changes that took place in the Great Pyramid (5C-54), there were significant changes in the East Platform. The most important of these was the building of a temple on top of the prior version of 5D-87 (Laporte and Fialko 1995) (fig. 10.11). The new temple, which had a single chamber with five doorways facing the Plaza of the Seven Temples, formed the basis for a new orienting axis for the architectural complex. Later, this temple was closed so that it could be used as the base for a new building, erected about A.D. 700. This new temple, which became the third-highest structure of Mundo Perdido, had a four-step platform with moldings. In accordance with the architectural style at the time, the staircase was divided at the first step by a niche or small vaulted

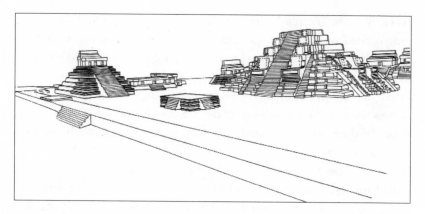

FIGURE 10.11

Mundo Perdido, Structures 5C-54 and 5C-49, during the Late Classic, Imix phase.

chamber. The base was decorated by three stone sculptures of skulls, the central one seen frontally and the two side ones in profile.

The building of 5D-87 was a deliberate action intended to confirm the new orienting axis, which replaced the old one that had been in effect for more than twelve centuries. This action must have been associated with a reorganization, if not the abandonment, of a ritual associated with the complex and tied primarily to the old solar cult. We base this conclusion on the fact that there is no other complex in Tikal at the time with an architectural formula that would have replaced Mundo Perdido in its public role. Nevertheless, it is clear that the late development of a new unit represented by the complexes with Twin Pyramids could have been tied to a move to change the internal organization of the city.

It is also clear that Mundo Perdido continued to be an important burial site during the Imix phase (A.D. 700–850). The current version of 5C-49 had an important collateral funeral role, which can be seen in the fact that at least three adults, two of them male, were buried there (Laporte and Fialko 1995; Laporte 1998, 2000a). The ceramic offering included polychrome vessels with scenes that are important enough to indicate that the deceased must have been high-ranking individuals. A particularly interesting find was a series of extraordinary shell, conch, and nacre objects with anthropomorphic and zoomorphic images. Although we do not have evidence for this, we hypothesize that the individuals buried in 5C-49 belonged to the group ruling Tikal. Their burial in this temple in Mundo Perdido, the extraordinary offering, and their fine garments support the argument that if they were not the rulers themselves, they belonged to groups that supported the rulers politically and economically, and they belonged to the ruling lineage. The buried individuals thus belonged to groups prominent during the second half of the eighth century A.D., when the ruler was Yax Nuun Ayiin II or Ruler C, who ruled over the long and turbulent period between A.D. 769 and 794 (Martin, this volume).

The occupancy and construction of Tikal did not stop near or at the end of the Late Classic, since areas of activity have been found dating well into the ninth century A.D. Between A.D. 800 and 860 there is isolated evidence of habitation and minor remodeling in some buildings or dwelling units in various sectors, but there is no evidence of city-wide activities as there is for previous times. This supports other indications of a general population decline in Tikal.

Some of the most vigorous activity in Mundo Perdido took place during the Terminal Classic, as indicated by collections of lithic and ceramic artifacts, burials, and other ritual elements. The construction was most significant; modes of access were changed and new benches were built in the principal Late Classic structures. Occupancy during the Eznab phase (A.D. 850–950) centered on the northern section, perhaps because it was near the temple's water supply. The largest structure in this sector, 5C-49, was only altered by adjustments in the inside rooms and perhaps by structural reinforcements in the front sections. Although they are partially destroyed and it is not possible to confirm their date, graffiti are very noticeable inside the rooms (Laporte 1998). The Eznab-phase population must have been tied to a lineage that had chosen this temple as its burial site.

The greatest population density in Mundo Perdido during the Eznab phase was not in 5C-49 but rather in a nearby section composed of three vaulted palaces (Laporte 1999d). The information obtained in this complex is very important in relation to the final occupation of Tikal. Construction in 5C-45 involved the addition of some benches, bricking up of old accesses in order to make larger spaces, and building of new sections with several entries, as was usual in the Classic. Late, minor remodeling was also done in other nearby buildings (5C-46,

5C-47, 5D-77, and 5D-82). Generally, such remodeling focused on strengthening areas with structural problems (Laporte 2000b). These were the last changes found in them, because these palaces—like all the other structures in Tikal—were abandoned soon thereafter. Nevertheless, the building activity indicates that there were still elite functions going on in 5C-45. This was no doubt a decadent elite, but one with enough power to maintain the complex building rhythm inherited from previous phases.

The other late activity in Mundo Perdido was ritual. Inside temple 5D-86, located in the center of the platform that dominated the complex in combination with the Great Pyramid, the bottom half of the Early Classic's Stela 39 was worshiped. It was moved from its original position, which might have been associated with the orienting axis I have mentioned (Laporte and Fialko 1995). Ayala (1987) proposed that its transfer inside the temple might have been ordered by the ruler Yax Nuun Ayiin II in order to commemorate the K'atun (9.17.0.0.0, A.D. 771) because, by using a monument from the corresponding K'atun of Cycle 8, he would link his lineage to the mythical Chak Tok Ich'aak I, the fourth-century ruler represented in the monument. There is ample documentation for the movement and relocation of monuments in different parts of Tikal during the Eznab phase (Satterthwaite 1958). Thus, the moving of Stela 39 is just one more example of this late activity. The worship of this stela fragment is shown by the nearby presence of polychrome vessels. It is a clearly an attempt to revive the worship of the old orienting axis of the complex.

The collections of materials from the exterior walls of the cited buildings in Mundo Perdido are the best indicator of population density during the Eznab phase. Burials inside the fallen-down buildings and in casual graves are notable. These are primary and direct burials of individuals of different sexes and ages with few offerings, usually consisting of stone and bone artifacts. The large population of the north sector of Mundo Perdido contrasts with the partial abandonment of the rest of the structures of the complex. A nucleus of population, with some elite fringes, remained there for at least a century after the general abandonment of the other parts of the city, perhaps due to the close proximity of water and to ritual activities that took place near Temple III.

These activities, along with the occupation of Mundo Perdido, ended in the Terminal Classic. There are only a few traces in Tikal in the Postclassic, limited to a few scattered spots inside and outside the site (Culbert 1973; Culbert et al. 1990). With the exception of one locality in Group 6D-XX in the southwest and another in Structure 3D-43 in the North Zone of Mundo Perdido, both composed of surface ceramics, we did not find any occupancy tied to the Postclassic Caban ceramic complex.

Lacandon Archaeological Project

The purpose of the Lacandon project was to study the settlement pattern of this segment of historically known population in the Petén and to determine how contact with other cultures affected their lives (López 1997; Palka 1997a). The Lacandon Archaeological Project, directed by Joel Palka and Claudia Wooley, spent several weeks in Tikal in 1998 looking for traces of occupancies in historic times. Although the reports are not yet available, some remains found in the Campamento and Temple of the Inscriptions quadrants were analyzed, and a few artifacts were recovered. Recent occupations of Tikal have been evaluated (Moholy-Nagy and Palka 1999). Before the brief 1998 season at Tikal, this project's investigations were centered in the area around Sayaxche, in the western part of the Petén.

RESEARCH PROGRAMS IN THE RESIDENTIAL AREA OF TIKAL

After the extensive coverage of different sectors of the residential area by the Tikal Project (Becker 1971; Haviland 1981; Haviland et al. 1985), little was done in this area for several decades. Apart from a brief investigation of some groups in the northeast quadrant of the site in 1985 (Walters et al. 1985), there is only the work of the Tikal National Project, which investigated several (a total of 15) dwelling complexes located south and southeast of Mundo Perdido between 1982 and 1984. On the Tikal map (Carr and Hazard 1961) (fig. 10.4 above), this sector falls into the Corriental and Perdido quadrants, where the Tikal Project had previously done only minor excavations and surveys. We have recently finished the analysis of the information obtained in this exploration (Laporte and Iglesias 2000), which is the source for the following summary.

Groups 6C-XV and 6C-XVI in Southeast Tikal

A unit made up of Groups 6C-XV and 6C-XVI stands out only 300 m. south of Mundo Perdido. We have previously commented on the complexity of their investigation (Iglesias 1987; Laporte 1987, 1998).

Structure 6C-50 stands out in Group 6C-XV because it has a niche dividing the staircase in two. This feature is seldom found in structures in the center of Tikal (5D-82, 5D-87, 5E-38) and is even scarcer in dwelling complexes like this one. The burial in 6C-XV is important because it may be that of a nuclear family including both adults and children. At the beginning of the Imix phase in the Late Classic (A.D. 700), construction in Structure 6C-50 involved two vaulted longitudinal masonry chambers with an access staircase. Six burials with offerings of polychrome ceramics and greenstone and shell ornaments, as well as a secret cache containing a cylindrical incense burner representing a grotesque being, were found in this platform. After the group was abandoned, during the Eznab phase of the Terminal Classic, a new burial was placed in the staircase that led to the superstructure, with an offering consisting of many obsidian and flint artifacts.

During the Late Classic, Group 6C-XVI, only 15 m. from 6C-XV, included three small dwellings (6C-51/53) on a partial base platform, arranged to form a plaza that was open toward the west. Several individual burials dating to the Imix phase (A.D. 700–850) were found. Even though the content of the offerings was very degraded, it is clear that they contained high-quality polychrome ceramics similar to those of the neighboring Group 6C-XV, suggesting a probable kinship.

The most interesting aspect of this group is the presence, from the time of its foundation in the third century A.D., of a strong and (for Tikal) complex building effort during all of the Early Classic. This led us to a long and fruitful exploration (Laporte 1989). Underneath the later occupation, a complex of buildings from the Early Classic, which were built and then covered over between the third and sixth centuries A.D. (figs. 10.5–10.8 above), were found. Multiple small pyramids and platforms and palaces with several vaulted rooms, porticoes, and passageways were grouped around five patios. I discussed above the functions of Group 6C-XVI, its different architectural styles, and some of the artistic and sculptural elements found there.

Another series of decorative motifs found on the walls of the com-

FIGURE 10.12

Group 6C-XVI, Mask in Structure Sub-4.

plex date from the beginning of the construction. A mask made of stone, covered with stucco painted red and black, was found on a fourth-century A.D. platform (fig. 10.12). Its iconography shows that it is a face framed by the paraphernalia typical of headdresses. The lower part has been preserved; it has a zoomorph used as a chin strap and under it three rounded elements forming a version of what usually is called Ahau-bone (Sanz 1997). What appear to be two large bunches of feathers can be seen on the sides of the mask. These could be pennants shown head-on instead of in profile, as is usual. The identity of the figure cannot be determined due to the incomplete state of the mask.

The remains of a scene depicting three personages sitting cross-legged on small jaguar skin were found on an inset *tablero* of a structure built during the fifth century A.D. (Laporte and Fialko 1995). Each of them has on a knee-length skirt and an apron, a belt, and the knot of a breechcloth on the back. It is difficult to interpret much of this scene, but it is surprising that the main character is looking to the right, a pose reserved for deities.

Other buildings, erected later in the Late Classic, have monumental sculpture on their walls. New, large masks and stucco figures adorn the walls of platforms. The large anthropomorphic figures that adorn the four sides of Sub-75 are 1 m. high. Their arms are flexed in front—shoulder high—giving the impression that they are resting on something or supporting something with their shoulders (Laporte and Fialko 1995). The figures wear bracelets, ear flares, necklaces, and a sort of turban on their heads. Five of the ten masks have been mutilated. This assemblage of large masks likely represents the same deity (Sanz 1997). The conical headdresses with two large lateral volutes and many of the figures' physical characteristics allow us to identify the masks in this structure as representations of the Jester God, now known as Sak Hunal, one of the key gods in the expression of Maya political power.

Two of the large masks on the front of the south side of the platform were subsequently covered by two panels containing stucco figures that flank the ends of the staircase. The only surviving panel, located on the eastern side, is locally called "The Lord of the Mirrors" (Laporte and Fialko 1995). It was not placed in front of the platform casually but rather must have been a very important image to have altered the decorative scheme of the structure based on Sak Hunal (Sanz 1997). This stucco figure is a full-length sitting image whose face has been destroyed. His legs are crossed and point west, while his thorax and face point south—that is, towards the front—and one of his hands rests on his stomach. He wears ear flares, a necklace, and bracelets, although his torso, legs, and feet are undecorated. The figure wears a small skirt, with a richly carved belt hanging on the left side. He has ovals identifiable as mirrors inset into his forearms and leg (Sanz 1997). When these appear on the bodies of different personages, they supposedly signify that this is a deity, although not a specific one. The figure is surrounded by small circles, which have been identified as complete shells or their cross sections.

It is impossible to identify the figure iconographically (Sanz 1997). The originality of the Lord of the Mirrors cannot be attributable only to the elements composing it. In the basic aspects of his clothing and the position of his body, the sculpture more closely resembles images in the ceramics of the period than the architectural sculpture of Tikal, either at that time or earlier.

It is clear that the sculptures in Group 6C-XVI, made at the beginning of the Late Classic, carry a clear iconographic message. This message was soon erased, however, when the sculptures were completely covered by a small, insignificant dwelling complex that had no relationship to the group, which had been important for the five previous centuries.

Groups around the Madeira Reservoir

Four groups lie south and southeast of the two largest architectural complexes in Tikal: Mundo Perdido and the Plaza of the Seven Temples. These are Groups 6C-XI, 6C-XII, 6D-V, and 6D-XVIII, which have the Madeira Reservoir in common (Laporte and Iglesias 2000) (fig. 10.4 above). The architecure of these groups is more architecturally complicated than that in other nearby dwelling areas. Except for Group 6D-XVIII, which was constructed during the Late Classic and shows little funerary activity, the other three had significant evolution in construction and include many ritual referents.

Groups 6C-XI and 6C-XII are near the boundary slope of the South Plaza of Mundo Perdido and just west of the Madeira Reservoir. It is interesting to note that there was no connecting path between these groups and the South Plaza because the slope on which the plaza lies is composed solely of tall blocks, sections of which are carved from living rock.

An early occupancy of 6C-XI in the Middle Preclassic was found, restricted to the northern section of the group and to a stucco-covered floor with no associated building. The area began to be populated in the last part of the Early Classic, although a more vigorous building effort did not start until the Late Classic. It is a very dynamic and complex group, both in the remodeling of its four structures and in the presence of burials and caches.

Group 6C-XII has a more formal construction. Although there are ceramic remains, there are hardly any building remains of the Early Classic. Until the end of that phase this space was clear, allowing direct communication between Group 6C-XI and the Madeira Reservoir. The group was completed in the Late Classic, particularly during the Imix phase (A.D. 700–850). The architectural role of the largest building, 6D-14, was perhaps finalized at the beginning of the Late Classic by the erection of a building with two vaulted rooms. Burials were placed inside and outside the building sequentially, with five of these found under the upper rooms. The quality of the materials in the offering and their similarity seem to indicate that they represent a kinship group.

Group 6D-V, which lies a scant 60 m. east of the Madeira Reservoir, has nine structures arranged around a rectangular closed plaza. The most important building in the group is a small palace with six rooms (6D-20) on the west side of the patio. At least six burials and three caches dating to the Late Classic were found in different structures. The chronology of 6D-V began in the Early Classic and was possibly directly related to 6C-XVI, when one of the greatest known occupancies of that period in Tikal, confirmed by numerous burials, caches, and collections of materials, took place (Iglesias 1987, 1988). However, the maximum architectural development of 6C-XVI occurred in the Late Classic, with a slight occupation detectable in both ceramics and caches during the Eznab phase of the Terminal Classic.

The Groups around the Pital Reservoir

Groups 7B-VI, 7B-VII, 7B-VIII, 8B-I, and 7C-XVII are located at the extreme southwest end of the Perdido Quadrant (Carr and Hazard 1961) (fig. 10.4 above) on a limestone rise clearly lower than the rest of the groups I have discussed. The groups included in this sector seem to be more related to the settlement of the Pital Reservoir and the large complex known as the Barringer Group or 6B-II than to Mundo Perdido. Although there are traces of occupancy in these groups since the Early Classic, there is no doubt that the highest occupancy level and construction took place in the Imix phase of the Late Classic. There is little evidence of occupancy in the Terminal Classic and the Postclassic.

The five groups all have the same type of emplacement, with low platforms on each side of a central patio. Only in 8B-I do we see a larger structure—a palacelike building with three crosswise rooms, perhaps vaulted—that takes up the entire north side of the patio. All the rooms resemble each other, and each has a bench along its entire length.

The number of funerals in the group is notable. There are at least 32 individual burials. This large sample, together with those obtained in the other dwelling areas in the south and southeast of Mundo Perdido, shows that the burial pattern during the Late Classic was quite standardized. Adult individuals, often males, were frequently buried inside long, narrow crypts covered by flat flagstones. These were placed inside the core of the structures, usually on the eastern side of the patios or inside their leveling fill. At this time the bodies were usually buried in an extended position, predominantly oriented north-south but also oriented on an east-west axis. They are primary burials, and, with a few exceptions, single individuals. Ceramic offerings are always present, even if they are not large, and include polychrome or two-color vessels. The individuals rarely wear ornaments and in general do not exhibit voluntary cranial deformations or decorative dental work.

This uniformity leads us to believe that the inhabitants of these residential groups belonged to a single nonelite social class, although there were greater offerings for individuals placed in the small temples on the east side of the patio. Perhaps these were the founders of the group and of the family nucleus, as well as male descendants who carried the lineage. Although other investigators in Tikal have been able to document the presence of several social levels within the nonelite category (Haviland and Moholy-Nagy 1992; Haviland 1997), the sample is unclear in this respect. This may be because the groups studied were relatively similar in their social composition and because a clearer differentiation can be seen in the architectural component.

INVESTIGATIONS IN THE PERIPHERY OF TIKAL

In the past 30 years there has been a large increase in the number of studies of settlements in the periphery of Maya cities from the Classic, undertaken in order to understand the political, social, and economic relationships that existed between the urban and secondary centers and between the secondary centers themselves. Although the results of these studies depend to a large degree on the methodology of the transect used to define the population borders and its dispersion from a larger center or nucleus (Fry 1969; Green 1973; MacKinnon 1981; Ford 1982; Fialko 1996), these data have recently been supplemented by archaeological surveys that attempt to study settlements through techniques covering an entire area (Webster 1985; Cowgill 1990; Kowalewski and Fish 1990; Sabloff and Tourtellot 1991). This approach encourages a diachronic regional perspective related to the origin of the archaeological centers and a synchronic focus related to the socioeconomic hierarchy among the various centers.

Intersite Project: Tikal-Yaxha

This project, which was carried out by Anabel Ford (1981a, 1981b,

1982, 1986, 1991) in 1978, focused on obtaining concrete information about the variation in the settlement between the central area and the periphery. In order to do so, a baseline between Tikal and Yaxha was established, and terrain that was potentially habitable was specifically inspected, amounting to an area of 3.2 km. between Tikal and Yaxha. Although at the time this was an ambitious program, subsequent explorations have shown that all areas, even those subject to periodic flooding because they are lowlands, should have been sampled. Nevertheless, these results expanded the concept of Tikal as a dispersed population center like any other center of the Central Lowlands.

Tikal National Project: The Periphery and the Santa Fe Bajo

Since 1994, the Program of Regional Archaeology investigating the areas between major centers has carried out four transects, between Yaxha and Nakum, Yaxha and Naranjo, Nakum and Tikal/Uolantun, and Tikal and El Zotz (Culbert et al. 1996, 1997; Fialko 1996, 1997; Lou 1996, 1997). The only important sites in the latter are Chikin Tikal, mapped by the Tikal Project, and El Palmar, which is intermediate between the two cities. The report on Palmar is still in process.

For this discussion, the important transect is the one between Tikal and Nakum, which is 21 km. long and contains the Santa Fe depression, extending 36 km. between the slope of the Holmul River and the mountain range west of Nakum. Many sites of varying importance were discovered and mapped in this transect. Several of the most complex—El Corozal, Uolantun, and Chalpate—all Tikal dependencies, were investigated. Even though the first two had been reported by the Tikal Project, this investigation drew plans and did drilling in order to determine their age and occupancy history.

The Chalpate site, located in the southeast quadrant of the Tikal National Park, deserves special mention because it is in a class by itself when one compares it to other sites on the periphery of Tikal, such as Uolantun, Chikin, El Corozal, Dos Aguadas, Bobal, Jimbal, and El Ramonal (Fry 1969; D. E. Puleston 1983; Ford 1986; Vidal et al. 1996). Chalpate differs from these other centers in its distance from the urban center of Tikal, its greater size and complexity, and the setting and organization of its structures on the site.

Chalpate is 9 km. southeast of the urban center of Tikal, near

Tikal's supposed defensive earthworks. Although not all its groups have a conventional arrangement, it does have a ball court, a Group E–type complex, a group of Twin Pyramids, twin small temples, palaces, and causeways (Lou 1997). Chalpate's sociopolitical context would have been that of a frontier settlement directly linked to the rural groups that farmed certain areas of the Santa Fe bajo. It would have acted as an intermediate between the rural centers of production and Tikal, where the final redistribution of the material would have been done.

Based on the revised view of Corozal and the Chalpate findings, it is clear that the settlements on Tikal's periphery do not share structural features that would standardize their function and, thus, their relationship to the urban center. For example, sculptured monuments were only found in Jimbal, Uolantun, El Corozal, and El Descanso (Lou 1997). There is no uniformity among them in the presence of ball courts, type-E groups, or complexes with Twin Pyramids. Uolantun and Chikin Tikal are the most complex of the various Tikal secondary sites. Contrary to a prior census (D. E. Puleston 1983), Uolantun was recently found to have Twin Pyramids. Chalpate now constitutes a third site.

To summarize, the investigations of the Santa Fe bajo (Fialko 1995, 1998; Fialko and Culbert, 1999; Lou 1997) have found evidence of additional Preclassic settlements; foremost among them are El Corozal and Chalpate. During the Middle Preclassic, Chalpate must have been an autonomous village cultivating favorable areas of the bajo. Subsequently, in the Late Preclassic, three settlements in addition to Chalpate were found: Escarabajo, about 800 m. from the bajo; Zapote Viejo, about 259 m. from the bajo; and Canti, adjacent to the bajo.

There are clear evidences of building in El Corozal and Zapote Viejo during the Early Classic. The increase in architectural complexity in Chalpate during the Early Classic occurred in the area of the Group E–type complex and in several temples and palaces. It is probable that by that time El Corozal and Uolantun had been absorbed as suburbs of Tikal, which by then had a radius of 5 km. from the center of the city. Considering its distance from the city and the noticeable growth that took place in the Early Classic, Chalpate's assimilation into Tikal's political-territorial sphere must have taken place soon afterward.

Settlements southeast of the bajo increased to 15 during the Late Classic. They were clearly ranked among themselves so that the progression in growth seen in the various settlements based on the formation of new domestic units and the expansion of the volumes of previously existing structures reached a maximum. By that time Chalpate, as the main political entity of the bajo region, would have been assimilated into Tikal's suburbs.

On the other hand, no settlements corresponding to the Preclassic or Early Classic were found in the east basin of the Santa Fe bajo. The first settlements occurred at the beginning of the Late Classic, with a total of nine, also ranked internally. The principal site, Toronjo, is strategically situated between the bajo and the subbasin of the Holmul River. Even though Toronjo never reached the level of urban development achieved by Chalpate, it seems to have developed as a consequence of the expansion of the centers on the west side of the bajo, which by then were probably also suburbs of Tikal.

During the Terminal Classic there was a decrease in building activity in the various settlements on Tikal's periphery, which was limited to the central areas of Chalpate, Uolantun, and El Corozal. The largest quantity of ceramics dating to the Terminal Classic was found in three Minor Centers—Escarabajo, Bejuco de Uva, and Toronjo—where the material was found scattered all over the sites. Lesser amounts were found in even smaller sites such as Canti and Sip (Fialko 1995; Fialko and Culbert 1999). Settlements in the bajo differ from those in larger centers such as Tikal or El Zotz, in that no genuine example of the imported Fine Orange and Fine Grey ceramics found in these larger sites associated with elites has been found in them. When the placement is evaluated, it is clear that all the settlements were located in areas where there was easy access to the water needed for subsistence and agriculture.

RECENT RESEARCH ON ARCHAEOLOGICAL MATERIALS FROM TIKAL

The study of materials recovered in the broad research program of the Tikal National Project in Mundo Perdido and in the residential sites southeast of Tikal and other complexes in the North Zone began at the same time as work in the field and is still ongoing. The material collected includes 685 vessels, 300 greenstone ornaments, 600 objects made from shell and other marine substances (not counting necklace beads as individual units), more than 1,300 bone implements, and more than 1,000 complete stone artifacts. There were also some 34,000 fragmentary objects or chipping debris of obsidian, flint, and other stones. In addition, we retrieved 1,623,513 ceramic sherds. Bernard Hermes (1984b, 1985) was in charge of cataloging the archaeological material and analyzing the many sets of sherds. Later, other special investigations studied the specific ceramics of particular chronological periods. However, much more material in storage in the project's archives is awaiting study.

Osseus Material: Human Bones

Various analyses have been conducted on human-bone remains in the past 20 years. The collection, which is one of the largest assembled in the Lowlands, includes the 231 burials excavated by the Tikal National Project and the skeletons retrieved by the Tikal Project, which are almost as numerous. Additionally, projects in Tikal have retrieved human bones in secondary contexts.

The primary aims of the Tikal National Project's first analyses of the collections (Salas and Pijoan 1982; Pijoan and Salas 1984a, 1984b; Fialko 1987b) were to determine sex, age, and the most noticeable pathologies of the remains. Recently, special studies using new technology have begun.

The Bioarchaeology Project in Tikal has several objectives concerning the biocultural history of the site (Wright 1996; Wright et al. 1999). Possible chronological changes in the diet and health of the inhabitants of Tikal will be examined to determine the amount of difference there was between the diet and health of different social groups. Diet is determined using the stable isotopes of carbon, oxygen, and nitrogen in bones and teeth. The pathologic characteristics of the skeleton will be used to evaluate the consequences of socioeconomic inequality on the health of different groups. One area of research aims to determine whether such possible differences changed over time at the site.

A new research program headed by María Josefa Iglesias and Andrés Ciudad (1999) that was begun in 1999 plans to use mtDNA analysis in the study of the skeletal remains of inhabitants of ancient Tikal. A varied sample of skeletal remains that are clearly contextualized by archaeological excavations, including individuals who belonged to both the middle and lower classes, as well as the elites of Tikal, will facilitate the use of these analyses for new determinations of sex, kinship relations, and possible ethnic variation of the individuals. This may allow us to test existing hypotheses regarding the social and historical development of the city using new approaches that were previously unavailable.

Osseus Material: Bone Artifacts

Bone artifacts from Tikal have been analyzed for their manufacture, the animal species used to make them, and their context, function, and date. The collections from both projects were studied, the Tikal Project collections by Hattula Moholy-Nagy (1994, 1998), while I studied those from the Tikal National Project (1999c).

The collection of the Tikal National Project included 1,387 artifacts made from remains of birds, turtles, human bones, and mammals in general. This series was composed primarily of finished artifacts rather than the residues of various stages in the production of the implements. Because we do not have the broken pieces and trash discarded by craftsmen (Emery 1995, 1997; Moholy-Nagy 1998), there is no evidence that these artifacts come from the place where they were made; rather, they come from domestic middens and other particular finds.

Among the types found, those used as tools (awls, needles, spatulas) predominated; although they were quite different, those used ornamentally (tubes, pendants, beads) were in the minority. The production of bone artifacts was part of the economic activity in Tikal. Even if it did not achieve the level of production of ceramic and stone materials, it was clearly important and should be considered as a definite component of the total economy of Tikal.

Shell and Conch Artifacts

The shell and conch artifacts and ornaments retrieved in the Tikal Project were analyzed from a variety of viewpoints (Moholy-Nagy 1963, 1978, 1985, 1994, 1995), and their social and temporal connections are known. This level of detail is not yet available for the material from the Tikal National Project. The biological-species source and technology of production for some of the shell material has been partially determined in a study (Díaz 1983) that analyzes the collections gathered during the first four years of the Tikal National Project. The shell material totals 3,076 pieces, only half of which are pieces that have been modified.

Stone Artifacts

The artifacts made from flint and obsidian, like the other types of artifacts and ornaments recovered in the Tikal Project, have been fully analyzed (Moholy-Nagy 1976, 1991, 1994; Moholy-Nagy, Asaro, and Stross 1984), and their social and temporal connections are known. The carved and polished stone lithic artifacts from the Tikal National Project have also been studied for their technology of production, the raw material used, and their context and role in the architectural complex. The latter study, however, covers only a portion of the total materials collected (Ruiz 1987, 1989, 1990).

The context—particularly the chronology—of the stone tools recovered in surface surveys of the Mundo Perdido Group was mixed, but it does represent part of the activities at that location for at least two centuries of occupation (Ruiz 1987). A total of 4,933 artifacts were analyzed, of which 4,152 were carved and 781 were polished. It is probable that the artifacts were made in the complex itself; that is, the material was brought in as nodules and preforms to be finished, as can be seen by the presence of debitage from preparing cores, flakes, primary razors, and other tools that were still rough on both sides.

In a second project, Ruiz (1989) studied the tools found in a surface midden in Group 6C-XVI dating to the Terminal Classic. The most common objects found in the 387 items in the collection were obsidian knives, followed by flint chips and bifacial artifacts. There are many projectile points that group into particular types; if each of these types had a specific role in hunting, this might be an indication of the intensity of hunting in a dwelling center.

CONCLUSION

Thirty years have elapsed since the end of the Tikal Project. The vacuum left by its departure was immediately filled by other projects, many of them devoted to conservation of the temples and palaces of the city. There seems to be no end to this need because a constantly growing spiral of people want to visit Tikal, the site is in a precarious state, and damages continually increase. In order to partially solve this problem, a wise decision was made to open new areas to accommodate the crowd of visitors. This provided the impetus behind programs at Mundo Perdido and the North Zone.

The results of these and other research programs did more than simply complement the information produced by the Tikal Project. Both the field studies and the results of analyses of the material gathered have broadened the thirty-year-old image of Tikal. These studies included topics such as architecture; epigraphy; aesthetic concepts; the role and structure of urban complexes; the arrangement of residential complexes; the beginning and final occupancy of the city; the interregional relationships in the Classic; aspects of production in the ceramic, stone, bone, and shell industries; and additional subjects. In all these fields, concepts have been broadened and discussion has been fomented—often, unfortunately, leading to discord and controversy.

An important goal both for this book and for the future is to seek points of agreement between the Tikal Project and the Tikal National Project, while not forgetting other research in Tikal. The result could be a unified view of the political, economic, social, and historical dynamics of this city, which would be fundamental to the study of Maya history. We should consider whether it is possible that a series of analyses carried out individually by each of these programs and little coordinated among themselves can define the importance of Tikal in the Maya area and in Mesoamerica in general. The answer is no. Rather, it is clear that the combined efforts of the two groups of researchers will allow us to place Tikal in the important place it deserves in the Lowlands.

11

Tikal and the Copan Dynastic Founding

Robert J. Sharer

The direction of Maya research was profoundly influenced by the University of Pennsylvania Museum's Tikal Project (W. R. Coe and Haviland 1982; Shook 1967). The comprehensive scope of its research provided numerous breakthroughs in our understanding of Lowland Maya civilization, which continue to foster new research today. One of the most important of these advances stemmed from the combination of archaeological and epigraphic data, which helped transform our understanding of ancient Maya political organization, including the identification of individual kings and the reconstruction of dynastic history (Coggins 1975; Haviland 1977; C. Jones 1977; Harrison 1999). This work is the direct antecedent to the definition and goals of current research in the Copan Acropolis (W. L. Fash and Sharer 1991; Sharer, Traxler et al. 1999).

A broader issue that emerged from the original Tikal Project involves Early Classic interaction and its role in the development of Maya civilization. A variety of evidence for external contacts indicated that Tikal's development was impacted by contacts with other areas of Mesoamerica, especially in the Early Classic (W. R. Coe 1972; Coggins

1975, 1979; D. E. Puleston 1977; Willey and Mathews 1985). This, in turn, reopened discussion of Highland-Lowland contact and its role in the development of Maya civilization (Kidder 1982 [1940]; A. G. Miller 1983; Sharer and Sedat 1987)—especially interaction between Kaminaljuyu and Tikal (Coggins 1975; Ball 1983). Early Classic evidence from Tikal defined a new debate in Maya archaeology: the role of Teotihuacan contacts in the development of Lowland Maya civilization (Sanders and Price 1968; Willey 1974, 1980; Marcus 1983; Sabloff 1990; Culbert 1991a).

Since the close of the original Tikal Project, the amount of both archaeological and epigraphic data from the Early Classic period has increased dramatically, beginning with the subsequent excavations in the Mundo Perdido Group that documented the span of Tikal's contacts with Central Mexico (LaPorte 1988; LaPorte and Fialko 1990). With the critical advances in Maya research in recent years, it is clearer than ever that the Early Classic period saw the emergence of Tikal as a dominant power in the Maya Lowlands (Mathews 1985; Schele and Freidel 1990:131–71; Culbert 1994: Grube, Schele, and Fahsen 1995; S. Martin and Grube 1995). This only reinforces what is perhaps the single most important contribution of the original Tikal research, making clear the pivotal importance of Tikal for understanding the overall development of Lowland Maya civilization.

Recent epigraphic evidence has expanded our understanding of specific events surrounding Tikal's Teotihuacan contacts (Stuart 1997, in press) and the entire issue of the meaning of Early Classic interaction between Central Mexico and the Maya Lowlands (Braswell 2003; Marcus 2003). As a result, research questions posed thirty years ago have been revived, beginning with attempts to understand Teotihuacan-Tikal interaction and the relationship of this connection with Tikal's rise to prominence in the Maya Lowlands. It is apparent that the initial pulse of Tikal's expansionism followed the "arrival of strangers" event in A.D. 378 (Coggins 1975; LaPorte and Fialko 1990; Proskouriakoff 1993), described in the texts as the coming of Siyaj K'ak' or "Smoking Frog" (Fahsen, Schele, and Grube 1995; Stuart 2000). Although there is no known reference to the homeland of Siyaj K'ak', circumstantial evidence suggests that he was from Central

Mexico, or more specifically, perhaps Teotihuacan itself (Stuart 2000). Once in the Maya Lowlands he was given the title "Lord of the West" (Schele, Grube, and Fahsen 1993), which implies the direction of his origin, and Teotihuacan is generally to the west of Tikal. The arrival phrase seems to describe conquest (Stuart in press) and in this case coincided with the death of Tikal's old king Chak Tok 'Ich'aak ("Great Jaguar Paw"), which implies a violent takeover. This was followed by the installation of Yax Nuun Ayiin I, or "Curl Nose," (378–404?) on Tikal's throne (S. Martin and Grube 2000). A Tikal text states that Yax Nuun Ayiin was the son of a ruler named Spearthrower Owl, a name that suggests he was a Teotihuacan king (Stuart 2000). In sum, there is circumstantial evidence for a takeover of Tikal's ruling line by outsiders from Central Mexico (see Martin, this volume).

This apparent intervention at Tikal set in motion a series of events that were recapitulated in the takeover of Copan some 40 years later (S. Martin and Grube 2000:193; Sharer 2003; Stuart 2000:491). In the years following the A.D. 378 takeover, apparently backed by the power and military superiority of Teotihuacan, Tikal embarked on a course of expansion throughout the Maya Lowlands. Although Yax Nuun Ayiin may have been a foreigner, his son and successor, Siyaj Chan K'awiil II, or "Stormy Sky," (411–456) was apparently a thoroughly "Mayanized" king who continued Tikal's expansionist policy. By the end of his reign Tikal achieved a dominant position by military conquest, as at Uaxactun (Schele and Freidel 1990), Río Azul (Adams 1995; Grube, Schele, and Fahsen 1995), and quite likely other centers. Tikal also used royal marriages to create alliances with the ruling houses of other Lowland polities (Marcus 1976, 1992a:249–55). The combination of conquest and royal marriage seems to have been an effective two-stage strategy to gain and maintain domination over its neighbors. Apart from the methods, we know relatively little about the motivations behind this expansion of Tikal's power and influence. Expansion undoubtedly served both political and economic purposes (C. Jones 1979). But Tikal's rise to dominance may also have had an ideological or "millennial" motive driven by the impending 9.0.0.0.0 B'aktun Ending and a desire to reshape the destiny of the new B'aktun that began in our year A.D. 435 (compare D. E. Puleston 1979).

TIKAL'S POSTULATED ROLE IN THE SOUTHEASTERN AREA

This chapter examines one apparent example of Tikal's Early Classic expansionism. Its premise is that in A.D. 426/427 Tikal orchestrated and quite possibly carried out the takeover of Copan's established ruling house. Tikal's expansion into the southeastern Maya periphery was not limited to Copan, for as part of this process, Tikal apparently also oversaw the establishment of the intermediate center of Quirigua as a subsidiary of Copan. At the close of the Quirigua research 20 years ago, an Early Classic colonization from Tikal was proposed at this small lower Motagua Valley center (C. Jones and Sharer 1980; Sharer 1988; see also Proskouriakoff 1993; Schele 1990). This conclusion was based on Early Classic glyphic and sculptural styles (Stela U and Monument 26) with links to Tikal and Uaxactun, Early Classic ceramic affiliations with the Petén, and the citation of an Early Classic ruler recorded on Quirigua Stela C with its 9.1.0.0.0 date (Mathews 1985). Subsequent textual decipherments identified Quirigua's founder and provided evidence that he operated under the authority of Copan's dynastic founder, K'inich Yax K'uk' Mo' (Looper and Schele 1994; S. Martin and Grube 2000).

Morley (1935) originally proposed that Quirigua was settled as a Late Classic colony of Copan. It now seems that Morley was correct insofar as Quirigua's subordinate status is concerned, but wrong in his chronology. The texts of Quirigua Zoomorph P indicate that Quirigua's ruling house was founded in A.D. 426/427 under the authority of Copan (Looper and Schele 1994). This evidence is extremely important for understanding both the strategy of Early Classic Maya dynastic-founding events and the size and organization of Early Classic Maya polities. The inclusion of Quirigua as part of the Copan polity from the time of its founding is consistent with other Mesoamerican states, which often possessed their greatest territorial extent at the beginning of their history (Marcus 1992a). Quirigua's role in the founding process is also important in understanding the motivations for Tikal's postulated colonization of this region. It was proposed that Tikal colonized the southeastern area to control lucrative trade routes and their produce—Quirigua for the Motagua jade route, Copan as the gateway to Central America (Sharer 1988). These postulated economic motives still seem valid today, although additional factors seem equally plausible, such as increased political and ideological power and prestige gained from the expansion of Tikal's sphere of influence into the southeastern Maya area.

We still know very little about the circumstances surrounding Tikal's expansion into the southeastern Maya area. But as we shall see, there is suggestive evidence that the takeover at Copan was a military conquest led by a war leader named K'uk' Mo' who replaced an established ruling lineage at Copan in A.D. 426 or 427. After K'uk' Mo' arrived in Copan and became its new king, he was given the same "Lord of the West" title held by Siyaj K'ak' in Tikal a generation before (Schele and Grube 1992). This suggests a link with Tikal and perhaps specifically a connection to Siyaj K'ak'. If K'uk' Mo' came from Tikal, the timing of the founding dates the takeover to the reign of its 11th ruler, Siyaj Chan K'awiil. Apart from these postulated ties, the takeover of Copan seems to have forged a close and enduring alliance between Tikal and Copan. I also propose that after K'uk' Mo' became Copan's new king, he legitimized his right to rule by marrying a royal woman from Copan's old ruling family. In other words, the Copan takeover was accomplished by the combined strategies of conquest and royal marriage. Of course, the new Copan king became known ever after as K'inich Yax K'uk' Mo' ("He of the Sun, First/Great Quetzal Macaw"). As such, he was proclaimed founder of the Copan dynasty by the 15 kings who succeeded him (Stuart and Schele 1986).

Assuming that the Copan takeover was accomplished by force of arms, and in keeping with what little we know about Early Classic Maya warfare, whatever force K'uk' Mo' brought with him to Copan was probably small and mobile. If a battle for Copan took place, it may have been limited in scope, with the issue settled rather quickly. There is no evidence for fortifications at Copan, so an armed strike aimed specifically at the local ruler and the heart of his capital could have been decisive. Advantages of speed and surprise, along with the same Teotihuacan-inspired militarism that propelled Tikal's expansionism, could have ensured the success of the invaders. There is archaeological evidence at Copan for superior weapons (atlatls) and protection (goggles and shell-platelet armor) derived from Central Mexico immediately after the takeover (Stone 1989). Thus, at a minimum, it seems likely that K'uk' Mo' and his entourage had military advantages due to their Teotihuacan connections (Sharer 2003) like those enjoyed by Tikal.

The remainder of this chapter examines the evidence for Tikal's postulated takeover of Copan's rulership. To do so, the time frame will be limited to the era of the dynastic founder, K'inich Yax K'uk' Mo', and his immediate successor. I will focus on data from recently completed extensive tunneling of the Copan Acropolis.[1] Given its role as the royal center of the Copan polity, the Acropolis seems the most likely place for evidence of Tikal connections. After a review of the textual record for links with Tikal, a summary of the development of the Copan Acropolis during the founding era will set the stage for discussion of Tikal connections seen in Copan's Early Classic architecture, funerary practices, and artifacts. The goal of this chapter is a clearer understanding of Tikal's role in Copan's dynastic founding and the role of other external connections associated with this process. It must be mentioned, however, that the chapter is preliminary. Our research is not yet completed and new data and analyses could well revise the findings presented here.

THE EPIGRAPHIC RECORD
OF COPAN'S FOUNDING ERA

One of the major goals of the Copan Acropolis research is to correlate the archaeological evidence with historical information provided by Maya texts both during and after the founding events (W. L. Fash and Sharer 1991). The rationale behind this objective is a conviction that the most complete picture of the past can be obtained from combining archaeological and historical data. When our research began in 1989, Copan's corpus of inscriptions dated almost entirely from the Late Classic, although these retrospective texts included several key references to the Early Classic founding era. Now, as a result of the Acropolis excavations, this historical record has been enhanced by several newly discovered Early Classic texts—historical inscriptions found directly associated with buildings from the early stages of the Acropolis. These new texts provide crucial information about the individuals and events of Copan's Early Classic era, allowing us to test the validity of later retrospective accounts. They also allow us to directly correlate and

evaluate Early Classic archaeological evidence with historical information dating from the same era (Sharer, Traxler et al. 1999).

The reading of Copan's texts is an on-going process and, of course,
subject to revision based on the availability of new data. This is especially true of the newly discovered Early Classic texts that are not fully
deciphered. Nonetheless, the deciphered portions of these texts provide invaluable information about the founding era, even while being
only fragments of the full story and sometimes subject to differing
interpretations. But when all are taken together, a rather consistent
pattern of information emerges. Part of this pattern suggests that Tikal
played a crucial role in Copan's dynastic founding.

We begin with the textual evidence that K'inich Yax K'uk' Mo' was
foreign to Copan and originally from Tikal. At present, the best indication of this possibility comes from Tikal in two text references to an
individual named K'uk' Mo' on the headless carved-stone statue known
as the Hombre de Tikal (Fahsen 1988) (fig. 11.1a–b). The second mention of K'uk' Mo' in this text appears to name him as the vassal of
another lord, whose name is damaged and thus unreadable (Martin,
this volume). The Hombre de Tikal text is dated at 8.18.10.8.12
(Fahsen 1988), which is during the reign of Tikal ruler Yax Nuun Ayiin
I and 20 years before the Copan founding events (S. Martin and Grube
2000). The name K'uk' Mo' in the Hombre de Tikal text certainly
recalls the initial reference to the founder on Copan Altar Q (K'uk'
Mo' Ajaw; see below). Of course, even with the same name we cannot
be sure that these refer to the same person. However, given the close
proximity in time and the other Tikal connections in the early archaeological record at Copan (discussed below), it seems highly likely that
the Hombre de Tikal text refers to the future Copan founder.

There is a possible reference to Yax K'uk' Mo at Copan that may
actually predate the Hombre de Tikal text by some 30 years. This comes
from the famous carved Peccary Skull (Longyear 1952:fig. 107o), but
the identification of K'inich Yax K'uk' Mo' in this context is by no
means certain. While the date of the carving is not known, it seems to
be a retrospective record of an event dated at 8.17.0.0.0. The event portrayed is a meeting between two figures, shown facing each other on
the carved skull—the Copan ruler on the right and a secondary figure
on the left. Linda Schele, Nikolai Grube, and Federico Fahsen

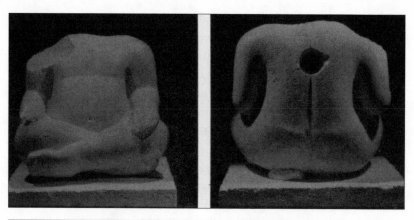

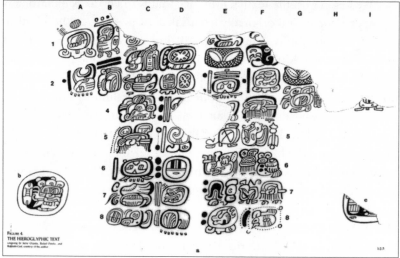

FIGURE 11.1

Hombre de Tikal, (a) *front and back of carved statue and* (b) *drawing of text on the back of the figure.*

(1993:1–2) propose that the secondary figure is none other than K'inich Yax K'uk' Mo'. Their conclusion is based on the Macaw head-dress worn by this figure, which they see as very similar to the *mo'* (macaw) logograph in the Hombre de Tikal text naming K'u Mo'. If so, the Copan Peccary Skull could record a meeting between the future founder and an earlier Copan ruler some 50 years before the founding date, which seems rather unlikely.[2] The purpose of the meeting depicted on the Peccary Skull remains unknown, although the seated facing positions of the two figures is similar to that seen on the Motmot Marker (discussed below), showing the reigning king to the left and his heir to the right. If the Peccary Skull depicts K'uk' Mo' as royal heir, it might actually date later in time and thus be retrospective political propaganda created to help justify the taking of the Copan throne.

There is one other retrospective reference to the Copan founder that associates him with a more feasible predynastic date and also provides evidence for a link with Tikal. A retrospective text on Copan Stela 15 mentions K'inich Yax K'uk' Mo' in connection with an unknown event at 8.19.0.0.0 (Schele, Grube, and Fahsen 1993) that may have something to do with his taking the throne some 10 years later. In another clause the monument's sponsor, Copan ruler Waterlily Jaguar, is referred to as the seventh successor of "the Sun Lord of the West" (Schele, Grube, and Fahsen 1993). This is the earliest of several references at Copan to K'inich Yax K'uk' Mo as "Lord of the West," used by the kings of Tikal who followed Siyaj K'ak', the apparent originator of this title (Schele and Grube 1992).

As has been suggested by the scene on the Peccary Skull, the epigraphic evidence indicates that there were rulers at Copan before the founder, including a mention of a "first ruler" on Stela 24 (Stuart 1989) and a Mak'ina Leaf Ajaw, who was in power at 8.6.0.0.0, on Stela 4 (Stuart 1986) and Stela I (Schele 1987). Thus, the A.D. 426/427 founding date seems clearly to represent a break between an established royal line and a new line imposed by the founder. But the texts do not describe the means used by K'inich Yax K'uk' Mo' to supplant Copan's established royal lineage, although indirect evidence points to military conquest. As mentioned, the "arrival" phrase in Maya texts seems to signify conquest (Stuart in press). The later depiction of Yax K'uk Mo' on Altar Q shows him as a warrior in the Teotihuacan tradition, bearing a "war serpent" shield on his right forearm and goggles over his eyes (fig. 11.2). Schele, Grube, and Fahsen (1993) proposed that a portion of the text on Copan Stela E refers to the conquest of Copan by Yax K'uk' Mo', but this reading has not found total acceptance. In another text, that on the Motmot Marker (discussed below), K'inich Yax K'uk' Mo's name is followed by a title that depicts a burning or smoking temple. This could also be a reference to military takeover, given its similarity to later Mesoamerican burning-temple glyphs to symbolize conquest

FIGURE 11.2

Copan Altar Q (Late Classic). West side with portrait of the dynastic founder, K'inich Yax K'uk'Mo' at center left, facing the monument's sponsor, Yax Pasah. Ruler 2 sits behind (right) *the founder.*

(Marcus 1992b:365,374). Finally, a conquest scenario is at least consistent with the status of the bones in the Hunal Tomb (also discussed below), if we accept that these are the founder's remains. The Hunal bones clearly testify to the kind of injuries suffered by a warrior, all of which healed before death (Buikstra 1997) and which may have resulted from the conquest of Copan, although other causes cannot be ruled out.

Of course, the most well-known retrospective reference to K'inich Yax K'uk' Mo' was carved some 350 years after the founding event on Copan Altar Q (Schele 1989; Schele, Grube, and Fahsen 1993; Stuart in press). Commissioned by Copan's 16th ruler, Yax Pasah, the Altar Q text first records two dates in our year A.D. 426, beginning with 5 Kaban 15 Yaxk'in (8.19.10.10.17) *u ch'am K'awil wi te na K'uk' Mo' Ajaw*, "he took the God K Scepter [at] 'Sprout Tree House' K'uk' Mo' Ajaw," an event signifying his gaining royal status—that is, K'uk' Mo' Ajaw (compare to the K'u Mo' reference in the Hombre de Tikal text) became a Maya king. Then, three days later, on 8 Ajaw 18 Yaxk'in (8.19.10.11.0), *tali wi te na K'inich Yax K'uk' Mo'*, "He came to 'Sprout Tree House'...," his new status as king and founder reflected in his new name, K'inich Yax K'uk' Mo' ("Great Sun, First Quetzal Macaw"). The Altar Q text then refers to a date 152 days later, 5 Ben 11 Muwan (8.19.11.10.13 or February 8, 427), when as "Lord of the West" Yax K'uk' Mo' performed a ceremony and arrived at Ox Witik, a name for Copan. That is, some five months after becoming king, K'inich Yax K'uk' Mo' came to Copan from someplace else—presumably the place where the *wi te na* was located. This place was seemingly 152 days' journey away, but apart from implying a distant location, there is no indication in the Altar Q text to identify this place. The Altar Q account is consistent with, but not definitive for, a proposed Tikal location for both the *wi te na* and the homeland of Yax K'uk' Mo'. This text would also fit a scenario that calls for Yax K'uk' Mo' to be originally from Tikal but then traveling to the *wi te na* at Teotihuacan to gain his royal status, after which he journeyed to Copan to take the throne. The latter scenario would seem to accommodate both the evidence of a Tikal origin for Yax K'uk' Mo' and the use of the "Lord of the West" title, which implies an arrival from Teotihuacan, located to the west of Copan (see S. Martin and Grube 2000:193; Stuart 2000:492–93).

These founding events are repeated on Quirigua Zoomorph P (9.18.5.0.0), although the second event is described as *u tz'apah tun u k'al ox yol tok'*, "he set a stone, he completed three portals (of) flint," *u kabi* "he did it" (title?), *K'uk' Mo' K'inich Kalomte* (Looper and Schele 1994). This Zoomorph P reference to K'inich Yax K'uk' Mo' and the Copan founding dates, along with the naming of an apparent Quirigua underlord, indicates that Quirigua was founded as a subsidiary of Copan.

There are two Early Classic monuments discovered in the Acropolis tunnels that provide important clues to Copan's connections with Tikal. The Motmot Marker was discovered beneath Structure 10L-26 and the Hieroglyphic Stairway (Williamson 1996; W. L. Fash 1998). It portrays both K'inich Yax K'uk' Mo' and his son and successor as Maya-style rulers (fig. 11.3). The Motmot Marker text commemorates the 9.0.0.0.0 Period Ending ceremonies probably associated with the temple located immediately east of the marker (a Petén-style structure given the field designation Motmot). This location could be designated in the Motmot text by the Tikal Emblem Glyph Main Sign, read as "it happened at the 5 mutul house" (Schele, Fahsen, and Grube

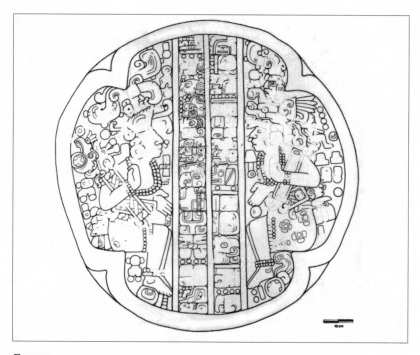

Figure 11.3

Drawing of the Motmot Marker (9.0.0.0.0). The dynastic founder, K'inich Yax K'uk'Mo', is on the left; Ruler 2 is on the right.

1992). However, the Motmot Marker is eroded, and a recent reexamination of the text was unable to verify the presence of the Tikal Main Sign (Stuart in press).

The second inscription is on the Xukpi Stone (fig. 11.4), another recently discovered Early Classic text found in the Acropolis tunnels (Sedat and Sharer 1994), whose context will be discussed later in this chapter. According to the decipherment by Schele, Grube, and Fahsen (1994), the Xucpi text records Ruler 2's dedication of a tomb or funerary temple on November 30, 437. The text closes with the name K'inich Yax K'uk' Mo', followed by a possible relationship glyph and the apparent name Siyaj K'ak', or "Smoking Frog." But there is disagreement among epigraphers as to the reading of this final glyph. If it is a reference to Siyaj K'ak', this text would be a key to understanding the relationship between K'inich Yax K'uk' Mo' and Tikal during the founding era.

Several other bits of epigraphic evidence at Copan hint at close

FIGURE 11.4

The Xukpi Stone (9.0.2.0.0) in situ; reset as base of south wall of the Margarita Tomb
upper chamber.

ties with Tikal (see Fahsen, Schele, and Grube 1995). In addition to
Stela 15 and Altar Q, already mentioned, there are references to
K'inich Yax K'uk' Mo' as "Lord of the West." This title, with its close
associations to Tikal rulers (Schele and Grube 1992:5), also appears
with the founder's name on Stela 10, dedicated by Ruler 10; Stela P,
dedicated by Ruler 11; and Stela 19, dedicated by Ruler 12. Copan Stela
20, dated at 9.1.10.0.0, may refer to a lord from Río Azul who has been
seen as a vassal of Tikal (Grube, Schele, and Fahsen 1995). As pointed
out by Stuart (2000:503–4), the *pu* or "cattail glyph" is part of the name

phrases of both K'inich Yax K'uk' Mo' (on Copan Stela 11) and Yax Nuun Ayiin I (on Tikal Stela 31). Finally, the Early Classic usage of the T168 over a vulture glyph to indicate accession at Tikal and other Petén sites is also found on Copan Stela 24 (Fahsen, Schele, and Grube 1995).

THE FOUNDING-ERA ACROPOLIS

Revealed by tunneling, the sequential levels of Acropolis architecture are dated by associated texts, ceramics, and radiocarbon dates (W. L. Fash 1991; Sharer, Miller, and Traxler 1992). Using this evidence, we can assign the architecture and associated features from the lowest tunnel levels to the general dynastic-founding era (ca. A.D. 400–450). The buildings from this era compose three architectural complexes (Sharer 1996, 1997a; Sharer, Traxler et al. 1999). Each appears to have served somewhat different (but overlapping) functions as part of Copan's original royal center while being integrated over time by floors and platforms, until a single elevated architectural complex, or true Acropolis, emerged. At the very base of the Acropolis, our excavations revealed remnants of demolished structures that predate these three complexes. These earlier structures were apparently small-scale earthen and cobble constructions, and at least some seem to have supported nonelite residential buildings of perishable materials (Sharer, Fash et al. 1999; Traxler 2001). The only large-scale construction in the Copan Main Group that may predate the founding era appears to be beneath Platform 10L-1 (immediately west of the Monument Plaza). Further research may test the hypothesis that Platform 10L-1 was part of the royal center used by the rulers of Copan prior to the arrival of K'inich Yax K'uk' Mo'.

The three complexes provisionally dated to the founding era are designated the Southern Group, the Northeastern Group, and the Northern Group. These complexes represent the first known monumental constructions at the Acropolis locus. The initial monumental structures were of both earthen (or adobe) and masonry construction (Sharer, Fash et al. 1999). The excavations in the Southern Group, supervised by David Sedat, have discovered what appears to have been the original royal center, a series of monumental buildings situated about 100 m. west of the Río Copán, directly beneath Structure 10L-16, near the center of the Acropolis (Sedat 1996). Excavations in the

Northeastern Group, supervised by Loa Traxler and Julia Miller, have revealed several large residential-type structures arranged around central courts, which probably served as the royal palace in the Early Classic period (Traxler 1996, n.d.). In the Northern Group, the tunnels excavated by Bill Fash's program have revealed an early sequence of temples and the initial ball court (now largely beneath Structure 10L-26) that seem to have served rituals dedicated to the 9.0.0.0.0 Period Ending and its association with the Yax K'uk' Mo' dynasty (W. L. Fash et al. 1992; W. L. Fash 1998; Williamson 1996). The following summary emphasizes the development of the Southern Group. The simultaneous growth of the Northeast and Northern groups is presented in several publications (W. L. Fash 1998; Traxler 1996, 2001; Sharer, Fash et al. 1999; Williamson 1996).

Based on the available archaeological evidence, it appears that the three monumental complexes beneath the Acropolis represent a new royal center established by K'inich Yax K'uk' Mo' (Sharer 1996; Traxler 2001). Of these three complexes, the Southern Group was destined to provide the core of the emerging Acropolis. The first monumental buildings of the new Southern Group were placed on a low platform, field-named Yune (Sedat 1997a), constructed on slightly higher ground in the midst of swampy terrain adjacent to the Río Copán (Hall and Viel in press). The central building of Yune Platform, Hunal (fig. 11.5), was apparently unique at Copan for its time—a small masonry platform with a facade in the Central Mexican *talud-tablero* style (Sedat and Sharer 1996; Sedat 1997b). Its final-stage summit building was demolished by later construction, but enough survives to determine that it had a north-facing doorway that opened onto an outset stairway. This building had at least two rooms separated by an east-west interior wall, broken by a doorway offset to the east, equipped with one surviving curtain holder. Debris indicates that its interior walls were probably originally decorated with brilliantly painted murals. Hunal was surrounded by several other structures, some built of adobe, including a sequence of earthen temple-type structures to the northwest that culminated in a monumental terraced substructure named Maravilla (Sedat 1997a; Sharer, Fash et al. 1999). The largest structure on Yune Platform was on its south side, a low platform supporting one or more masonry buildings (Sedat and Lopez in press). Hunal and the other

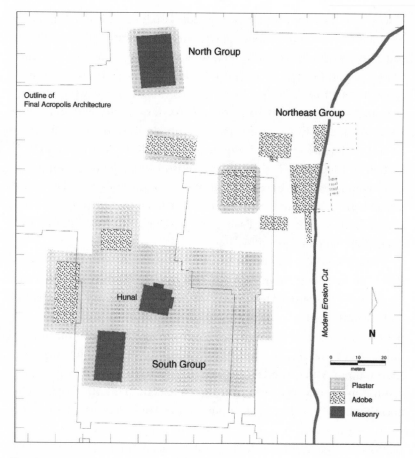

FIGURE 11.5

Preliminary map of founding-era architecture beneath the Copan Acropolis. The Southern Group structures are on Yune Platform. The Northeastern Group has residential-type structures arranged around central courts. The Northern Group comprises an early temple and ball court (computer map by Loa Traxler).

buildings on the Yune platform are interpreted as the royal residential and administrative center constructed for K'inich Yax K'uk' Mo' shortly after the founding in A.D. 427 (Sharer 1996; Sedat 1997a; Traxler 2001).

The new royal center seems to have been laid out on a north-south axis (Sharer 1997a; Traxler 2001). In the Northern Group, directly north of Hunal and Yune Platform, another masonry building, Yax, was constructed during the founding era (W. L. Fash et al. 1992;

Williamson 1996; W. L. Fash 1998). The Northern Group was directly involved with the auspicious Period Ending (9.0.0.0.0), anchoring the new dynasty in Maya time. Associated with its earliest buildings are two texts that commemorate the 9.0.0.0.0 calendrical ceremonies celebrated during the reign of K'inich Yax K'uk' Mo' (Stuart in press). These monuments link the newly founded dynasty with the new B'aktun, seeming to proclaim its destiny to rule for the next four centuries. Yax Structure was soon demolished and succeeded by a larger masonry substructure (Motmot) with a facade decorated by four modeled-stucco sky-band motifs. Its western stairway was served by an extensive plaster floor on its western and southern sides; the former is associated with Copan's earliest-known ball court (Williamson 1996; W. L. Fash 1998). A round tomb chamber in this floor, west of Motmot, was used to bury an adult female accompanied by three male trophy skulls. One suggestion might be that these are trophies of the Copan takeover. Although the pottery offerings from the tomb are probably local in origin, both the interred female and the circular form of the chamber are foreign to Copan, the latter recalling similar features at Teotihuacan (W. L. Fash 1998). The identity of the buried woman remains unknown, but strontium-isotope analyses of her bones show that she was not native to Copan (Buikstra 1997). It is likely that the Motmot Tomb interment was part of the 9.0.0.0.0 Period Ending ceremonies. But there is evidence that the tomb was later reopened for the placement of additional offerings and then sealed by the previously discussed Motmot Marker, a disc-shaped limestone monument (W. L. Fash 1998). The use of limestone is almost unique for Copan monuments and may represent a tangible link to Petén (and Tikal) traditions. As I have already mentioned, the Motmot Marker depicts the founder and his son as orthodox Maya rulers, and its text refers to the 9.0.0.0.0 ceremonies (fig. 11.3 above).

The archaeological evidence indicates that Ruler 2 oversaw the construction of a host of new buildings that first established Copan's Acropolis (Sharer 1996; Sharer, Fash et al. 1999). These included the first in a sequence of temples built over both Yax and Motmot structures, culminating in the Late Classic with Structure 10L-26 and the Hieroglyphic Stairway (W. L. Fash et al. 1992). Ruler 2 also sponsored the first two temples of an even longer sequence of at least seven

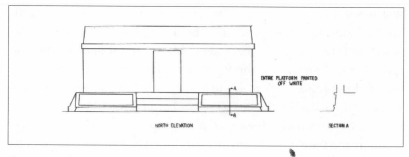

FIGURE 11.6

North side elevation of Hunal Structure (superstructure is conjectural; drawing by David Browning).

FIGURE 11.7

View of the Hunal Tomb, with remains on the burial slab cleared of fallen debris.

temples built directly over Hunal in the Southern Group (Agurcia 1996). The final temple in the southern sequence, Structure 10L-16, together with Altar Q, explicitly commemorates the dynastic founding and K'inich Yax K'uk' Mo' as royal ancestor (Taube in press). Built at the north and south ends of the major axis of Copan's new royal center, these two temple complexes proclaimed the prestige and continuity of power of the new dynasty founded by K'inich Yax K'uk' Mo'.

A vaulted tomb (fig. 11.6) was found at the base of the sequence of temples in the Southern Group, intruded beneath the floor of Hunal (Sedat 1996; Sedat and Sharer 1996). Known as the Hunal Tomb, it is revealed by excavation to contain offerings and the bones of a robust male, a little over 5'6" tall and at least 50 years old at death, according to the analysis by Buikstra (1997). Connections with several important areas of Mesoamerica are apparent in the tomb offerings (fig. 11.7). The forms and decorations of the Hunal vessels closely resemble those from contemporaneous Esperanza-phase tombs at Kaminaljuyu. These, in turn, recall burials from Tikal (Burial 10) and Teotihuacan. Nineteen Hunal tomb vessels were subject to neutron-activation analysis (Reents-Budet et al. in press). This revealed that 11 vessels are of local manufacture, probably made within the Copan Valley. Three vessels are from Central Mexico, and two are from the Tikal region of the central Petén Lowlands (modeled-carved tripod dishes with elaborately decorated lids). A large deer-effigy vessel is likely from the southern Maya Highland center of Kaminaljuyu. In general form, concept, and construction technique, it recalls contemporaneous effigy vessels from Burial 10 at Tikal, identified as that of Yax Nuun Ayiin I. These Tikal effigies are believed to be imports as well (Culbert 1993:figs.14,18). Animal effigy vessels are common at Kaminaljuyu in the Esperanza phase (Kidder, Jennings, and Shook 1946) and probably represent a Highland Maya tradition.

Another possible link to Tikal can be seen in two composite objects made from cut-shell "spangles," one found adjacent to the cranium, the other on the tomb floor (fig. 11.8a, b). These appear to be Teotihuacan-style warrior headdresses similar to those shown in portraits of the Tikal ruler Yax Nuun Ayiin on the sides of Stela 31 (see Stone 1989). Of course, since Yax Nuun Ayiin is dressed as a Teotihuacan warrior in these portraits, these objects may be seen as connections to Central Mexico as well. Another possible link is in a shell pectoral of a type often associated with Central Mexico, manufactured from a species *(Patella mexicana)* from the Pacific Coast of west Mexico (fig. 11.9a) and found in Early Classic burials at Kaminaljuyu (Kidder, Jennings, and Shook 1946:149).

The Hunal Tomb also contains a series of clues that consistently point to its being the burial of K'inich Yax K'uk' Mo' (Sharer 1997b),

FIGURE 11.8

Vessels from the Hunal Tomb sourced by NAA, (a) two vessels from the Tikal region of the Petén and (b) deer effigy vessel from the Kaminaljuyu region (southern Maya Highlands or Pacific Coast).

beginning with the stratigraphic position and dating of the tomb vessels, which are consistent with the presumed death date of the founder in A.D. 437. In addition, the age assessment of over 50 years for the Hunal bones (Buikstra 1997) is a good match with the three-K'atun age (between 40 and 60 years old) attributed to K'inich Yax K'uk' Mo',

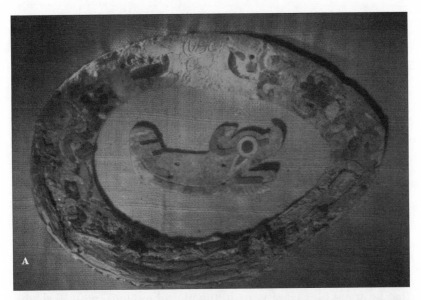

FIGURE 11.9

(a) *Shell pectoral and cut-shell effigy with jade mosaic work from the Hunal Tomb and* (b) *detail of name-tag glyphs on shell pectoral, which may end with a Wi Te phrase (founder's title; photographs by Kenneth Garrett).*

recorded on Copan Stela P (Harris 1998).[2] Several tomb offerings have probable direct links to K'inich Yax K'uk' Mo', including a carved jade with a mat design, a Maya symbol for rulership, and a large jade bar pectoral very similar to the single bar pectoral depicted on the carved

portrait of K'inich Yax K'uk' Mo' on Altar Q (Sharer 1997b). The previously mentioned shell pectoral (fig. 11.9b above) is "name-tagged"
with a short text that may refer to a title used exclusively for the
founder, Wi Te (David Stuart, pers. comm. 1999). The Hunal interment suffered a severe parry fracture of the right forearm (fig. 11.7
above) that is consistent with the depiction of K'inich Yax K'uk' Mo's
portrait on Altar Q, where he holds a small shield on his right forearm,
possibly recalling this injury (fig. 11.2 above). The interment suffered
other combat-style injuries from blows to the left shoulder, chest, and
head. Healing of the bone at the sites of all these injuries indicates that
none were fatal blows, although permanent damage clearly crippled
both his right forearm and left shoulder (Buikstra et al. in press). Also
consistent with later historical accounts of K'inich Yax K'uk' Mo', the
strontium-isotope analysis of the Hunal Tomb bones shows that this
individual was not a Copan native. Rather, the isotope analysis indicates
that he spent his earlier years in the Maya Lowlands, most likely the
Tikal region (Buikstra et al. in press).

The archaeological evidence provides more evidence that identifies the Hunal Tomb with K'inich Yax K'uk' Mo'. Excavation of the
overlying levels reveals that Hunal and its tomb established the symbolic center for the Acropolis that was maintained by the founder's successors during the remainder of Copan's dynastic history (Sharer
1997a). Some seven overlying structures have been identified, and all
appear to have been funerary temples (several are little known due to
near-total demolition). Several of the better-documented examples,
along with an Early Classic text found in the second building above
Hunal (the Xukpi Stone), explicitly refer to K'inich Yax K'uk' Mo' as
royal ancestor (Sharer 1996; Taube in press). The western facade of the
second successor to Hunal (field-named Margarita) was decorated with
polychrome painted–stucco, full-figure emblems of K'inich Yax K'uk'
Mo's name (figs. 11.10, 11.11). The fifth successor to Hunal was the
extraordinarily preserved Rosalila temple built by Ruler 10 (dedicated
in 571, according to its heavily eroded stairway text). The final temple
in the sequence, Structure 10L-16, was built by Ruler 16. Both Rosalila
and Structure 106-16 were decorated with portraits of the founder (B.
Fash 1992; Taube in press), and 10L-16 also had glyphic references to
K'inich Yax K'uk' Mo' (Agurcia 1996).

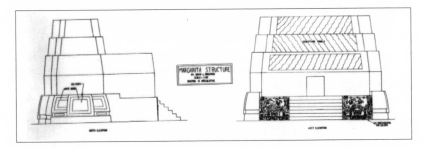

FIGURE 11.10

Reconstructed elevation of Margarita Structure (superstructure is conjectural; drawing of David Browning).

FIGURE 11.11

Modeled stucco full-figure name of the dynastic ruler K'inich Yax K'uk'Mo' on western facade of Margarita Structure (north of stairway).

341

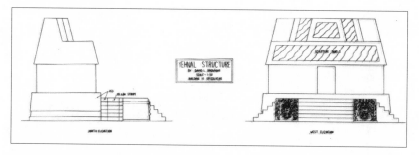

FIGURE 11.12

West side elevation of Yehnal Structure (superstructure is conjectural; drawing by David Browning).

FIGURE 11.13

Modeled stucco sun-god mask on western facade of Yehnal Structure (north of stairway).

The building program sponsored by Ruler 2 expanded all three architectural groups founded by his father and laid the basis for the development of the Acropolis we see today (Sharer 1996; Sharer, Traxler et al. 1999), but the Southern Group was the major focus of this construction effort. After the dedication of the Hunal Tomb, the first two temples built over this locus were constructed within a span of about a decade, along with the beginnings of a larger Acropolis platform that replaced most of the buildings erected by Ruler 2's father (Sedat 1996). The first successor of Hunal, field-named Yehnal, has a Petén-style apron-molded substructure (fig. 11.12) dated to ca. A.D. 437–445, establishing a new westward orientation that was followed by later temples at this location. Yehnal was decorated by painted stucco-relief panels of an aspect of K'inich Ajaw, the Maya sun god, flanking its western staircase (fig. 11.13). These may symbolize the celestial status of the departed founder, K'inich Yax K'uk' Mo'. Inside Yehnal's temple, a masonry stairway led down into a new vaulted chamber that was constructed several meters below its floor (Sedat and Sharer 1996).

Yehnal was replaced by a larger apron-molded structure, Margarita (figs. 11.10, 11.11 above) before the Yehnal chamber was occupied. Dated to ca. A.D. 445–460, an expanded stairway inside the new summit temple allowed continued access to the empty burial chamber (known as the Margarita Tomb) beneath its floor (Sharer, Traxler et al. 1999). The Margarita substructure, like its predecessor, was oriented to the west. An outset stairway on its western facade was flanked by the already mentioned full-figure emblems of the founder's name, clearly identifying it as the second of K'inich Yax K'uk' Mo's funerary temples built at this location (Sharer 1996). Over the years the Margarita substructure was successively buried by platforms built around its perimeter (Sedat 1996). A large western platform ultimately covered the founder's emblems on its west facade. Encased in this western platform was the burial of an apparent sacrificed male, wrapped in a bundle and accompanied by Teotihuacan-warrior paraphernalia, including shell goggles and atlatl darts, along with adornments of shell and jade indicative of his high status (figs. 11.14, 11.15). The strontium-isotope analysis of his bones indicates that this warrior was not native to Copan (Buikstra 1997) but has yet to identify his origins, although the best indication is the northern Maya Lowlands (Buikstra et al. in press).

Margarita's summit temple remained in use even as its substructure disappeared under flanking platforms. Ultimately, however, it was demolished and replaced by Chilan Structure, the third temple to occupy this locus directly above Hunal and its tomb. The event that seems to have triggered the termination of Margarita was the interment of a very important royal lady in the tomb chamber beneath its floor (Sedat and Sharer 1996). Contact with this buried royal woman was

FIGURE 11.14

The warrior burial in the platform west of Margarita Structure.

maintained by a vaulted passageway and stairway leading into the Margarita Tomb. Although there are no texts to identify her, the position and elaborateness of her tomb, together with the huge quantity of offerings of jade and other materials, suggest that she was the widowed queen of K'inich Yax K'uk' Mo' and the mother of Ruler 2 (Sedat and Sharer 1996). Placed on a stone slab in the burial chamber, her body was literally covered with jade and shell adornments. Her postulated status as a local queen is supported by strontium-isotope analysis of her bones (Buikstra et al. in press), indicating that she was from the northern portion of the Copan region.

Offerings of pottery and other materials covered the chamber floor and a chamber above the burial crypt (fig. 11.16 a–c). One of these is an extraordinary lidded, stucco-painted cylindrical tripod (Sedat 1997c). Neutron-activation analysis (Reents-Budet et al. in press) reveals that this vessel was most likely manufactured in Central Mexico. Reents-Budet points out that its proportions are like those of tripods from Kaminaljuyu and Teotihuacan, but its cut-out, hollow slab are like contemporaneous vessels from Uaxactun and Tikal. Its painted design appears to be Teotihuacan in style, but closer examination shows that the building is Maya in style and an iconic rendition of the name Yax K'uk' Mo' is painted at the side of the depicted building. Thus, the evi-

FIGURE 11.15

The Margarita Tomb, view from the northern doorway at the foot on the access staircase.

dence suggests that the vessel was made in Central Mexico using a blend of Teotihuacan, Kaminaljuyu, and central Petén vessel-form modes, while its painter was schooled in Maya pictorial and glyphic systems.

Of the remaining 11 vessels that were sampled from the Margarita tomb upper chamber, six are of local or undetermined manufacture, and five are imports (Reents-Budet et al. in press). The probable local vessels include stucco-painted tripod dishes and ring-base red-orange bowls similar in form and color to Thin Orange pottery from Central Mexico. The imports include two basal-flanged polychrome dishes, one from the central Petén Lowlands and similar to a dish from Tikal Bu. 177 (Culbert 1993:fig.37). While the chemical composition of the second

345

FIGURE 11.16

Vessels from the Margarita Tomb offering chamber, (a) *stucco-painted cylinder tripod from Central Mexico as sourced by NAA,* (b) *polychrome vessel from the Petén as sourced by NAA, and* (c) *polychrome vessel, probably from the Kaminaljuyu region (sourced by style).*

basal-flanged polychrome remains unidentified, it appears to be from Kaminaljuyu based on its form and decoration, which are especially similar to that found on dishes from Tomb A-VI (Kidder, Jennings, and Shook 1946:fig.207). It is also similar to a dish from Tikal Burial 10 (Culbert 1993:fig.18), which may be a Kaminaljuyu import.

A carved, benchlike monument, the Xukpi Stone, was reset into the south wall of the Margarita upper chamber (Sedat and Sharer 1994). As has already been mentioned, its text (Schele, Grube, and Fahsen 1994) records a dedication in A.D. 437, the names Ruler 2 and K'inich Yax K'uk' Mo' and possibly the name of Siyaj K'ak', or "Smoking Frog" (fig. 11.4 above). Unfortunately, since the Xukpi Stone is reset, its original provenience may never be known. Based on the evidence in hand, the most plausible scenarios call for it to have been originally associated with either the Yehnal or Margarita temples, in either case leading to the conclusion that its text refers to the underlying Hunal Tomb and its dedication in 9.0.2.0.0 (A.D. 437). This, in turn, gives us the most plausible death date for K'inich Yax K'uk' Mo' (Sharer, Traxler et al. 1999).

It is clear that after his death K'inich Yax K'uk' Mo' was promoted as Copan's dynastic founder by the efforts of his son and heir to honor his father. These efforts included the sponsorship of a vast building program and the carving of several stone monuments. During his reign, Ruler 2 expanded the royal center his father had founded and began the process that would integrate the three original architectural groups into a single Acropolis (Sharer 1996). It would also seem that Ruler 2 was the first ruler to integrate Platform 10L-1 with the new royal center (Traxler 2001). Overall, Ruler 2 seems to have emphasized Lowland Maya traditions. The architecture of the expanding royal center seems to have increasingly emphasized Lowland architectural canons, as masonry buildings gradually superseded earlier adobe constructions. Part of this process was also the replacement of the *talud-tablero*-style Hunal Structure by a succession of funerary temples constructed with Lowland Maya apron-molded facades (Yehnal and Margarita Structures).

THE SIGNIFICANCE OF TIES WITH TIKAL DURING COPAN'S FOUNDING ERA

Connections to several major areas of Mesoamerica are apparent in the archaeological evidence from the founding era (W. L. Fash 1997; Sharer 1997c). Here we are most concerned with Copan's links to Tikal and, more specifically, to the question of K'inich Yax K'uk' Mo's origins. Obviously, the identification of the remains in the Hunal Tomb as those of K'inich Yax K'uk' Mo' is critical to this question. As I have mentioned, the strontium analyses of the Hunal bones show that this man was not native to Copan and most likely was from the Tikal region (Buikstra et al. in press). Thus, if we accept the Hunal Tomb as the founder's burial, the strontium-isotope results are consistent with the account of his "arrival" at Copan, probably from Tikal, in A.D. 427.

The archaeological evidence indicates that the earliest Acropolis manifested three major architectural traditions. The first is earthen architecture, which probably emerged from a general southeastern Maya tradition, with ties to the great Highland center of Kaminaljuyu (Kidder, Jennings, and Shook 1946; A. L. Smith 1965) and Chalchuapa (Sharer 1978). The second tradition is Central Mexican–style *talud-tablero* architecture, represented by one example—Hunal—in the initial construction phase of the Southern Group. The lack of decoration on the Hunal *tableros* recalls the Kaminaljuyu tradition (Kidder, Jennings, and Shook 1946), in contrast to the decorated *tableros* typical of Teotihuacan and Tikal. On the other hand, rather than being constructed of earth and adobe as at Kaminaljuyu, the masonry and plaster construction of Hunal could well derive from Tikal (Traxler n.d.), where similar *talud-tablero* substructures were well established by this time (LaPorte and Fialko 1990).

The third tradition utilized masonry and was closely allied to the Early Classic architecture of the central Petén (Pollock 1965), providing the closest architectural connections with Tikal (W. R. Coe 1990). The early Copan masonry substructures have apron moldings with inset corners, are often red painted, and are decorated with polychrome stucco masks or panels. The masonry apron-molded substructure of Motmot is dated to the reign of the founder. Two examples of this style, Margarita and its predecessor, Yehnal, seem to date from the reign of Ruler 2. The rear (eastern) apron-molded facade of Margarita's substructure was decorated with panels defined by red, light red, and cream paint. The summits of Copan's early masonry substructures supported both vaulted and unvaulted buildings, judging by wall thickness. The initial-stage building on Hunal was probably vaulted but was later replaced by a larger, unvaulted masonry building (Sedat and Lopez in press). Other early examples of masonry construction—Motmot, Yehnal, and Margarita—were probably temple-type vaulted buildings (figs. 11.11–11.14 above). During the first few decades after the Founding, masonry became more prevalent and was used to construct new buildings that replaced most earthen constructions, including the palace-type structures in the Northeastern Group (Traxler 1996, 2001). These masonry palace-type structures also seem to be in the general Petén tradition, with stucco-decorated upper zones, triple doorways, curtain holders, and multiple rooms.

Similar evidence of external connections during the founding era emerges from the Early Classic Acropolis burials and grave goods. Two royal tombs, Hunal and Margarita, are within the Lowland Maya tradition (Krejci and Culbert 1995). Both are vaulted chambers with single supine interments on stone slabs elevated by stone pedestals. Motmot is the only round masonry funerary chamber at Copan; this and its seated burial position provide a connection to Teotihuacan (W. L. Fash 1998).

On the other hand, unlike the solitary interments in the Hunal and Margarita Tombs, the Motmot lady was accompanied by trophy skulls and animal remains, recalling similar grave goods from both Kaminaljuyu (Kidder, Jennings, and Shook 1946:93) and Tikal (Coggins 1975). The numbers of pottery vessels in the Hunal and Margarita Tombs are about the same, far more than in the more limited space of the Motmot chamber. But both the Hunal and Motmot Tombs have far fewer offerings of jade and other materials than the Margarita lady has. While the vessels in the Motmot Tomb are generally of local traditions (W. L. Fash 1998), those in the two royal tombs signal diverse external connections. Imports from the Tikal, Kaminaljuyu, and Teotihuacan regions have been identified in the Hunal and Margarita Tombs (figs. 11.7, 11.16 above). Both tombs also contain vessels of local manufacture.

The warrior paraphernalia preserved in Early Classic funerary contexts provides clear associations with Teotihuacan warfare traditions and indirect support for the conquest scenario as the means for the Copan takeover. As I have already mentioned, the Hunal Tomb furnishes skeletal evidence for combat-style injuries. Two composite-shell warrior headdresses found in the tomb identify the occupant, presumably K'inich Yax K'uk Mo', as a warrior with likely connections to Tikal and Yax Nuun Ayiin, since this ruler is portrayed twice on Tikal Stela 31 wearing similar shell-platelet helmet headresses. Given the link between this type of headdress and Teotihuacan warriors (Stone 1988), this indicates that the Hunal Tomb occupant was associated with Teotihuacan military traditions (consistent with the founder's later portrait on Copan Altar Q). The burial of an apparent warrior sacrifice west of the Hunal and Margarita Tombs was laden with Teotihuacan military paraphernalia, including cut-shell "goggles" in place on the forehead and a bundle of atlatl darts (fig. 11.14 above).

CONCLUSION

While multiple external ties are reflected in the data from Copan's founding era, strong support for an especially close connection between Tikal and Copan comes from a variety of archaeological, textual, and bioanthropological evidence. More specifically, there is a very plausable case for positing that the origins of the Copan founder,

K'inich Yax K'uk' Mo', were closely associated with Tikal. This association can be traced back to the reign of Tikal's tenth ruler, Yax Nuun Ayiin I (378–411). After Siyaj Chan K'awiil (411–456), the son and successor of Yax Nuun Ayiin, took the throne as Tikal's 11th ruler, it appears that the Copan founder, then an elite warrior named K'uk' Mo', was promoted to carry the banner of Tikal's expansionism into the southeastern Lowlands. His royal status sanctified by rituals in A.D. 426 (possibly after his traveling to Teotihuacan) and renamed K'inich Yax K'uk' Mo', the new king arrived in Copan in A.D. 427 to take the throne, most likely by means of conquest. Whether or not K'inich Yax K'uk' Mo' was ever in Teotihuacan, the close links with Central Mexico seen at Tikal during the reigns of both Rulers 10 and 11 could well explain the Teotihuacan connections apparent in the contemporaneous Copan architecture, tomb vessels, and warfare paraphernalia. In any case, these elements from Central Mexico were likely imported into Copan by the founder to sanction and reinforce his ruling authority. At the same time, traditional Lowland forms, which were especially prevalent in monuments, architecture, and funerary practices, were promoted by both the founder and his son to reinforce the legitimacy of the newly established royal line at Copan. His legitimacy was probably further cemented by a marriage between K'inich Yax K'uk' Mo' and a royal woman from Copan's old ruling lineage.

Overall, this reconstruction describes a foreign conqueror who used military advantages and powerful connections to both Tikal and Teotihuacan to seize and consolidate power at Copan. This conqueror was succeeded by a son who used his father's prestige and success to promote a new dynasty (and reinforce his own authority) by emphasizing orthodox Lowland Maya traditions. Such a scenario certainly echoes an earlier episode that has been reconstructed for Tikal rulers Yax Nuun Ayiin I and his son Siyaj Chan K'awiil (Coggins 1975; Proskouriakoff 1993).

The circumstances surrounding Copan's dynastic founding appear to highlight the expansion of Tikal's power, which seems ultimately to have stemmed from a takeover at Tikal promoted by Teotihuacan in A.D. 378. Copan appears to have been a major component of Tikal's agressive expansionist policy. Although the actual events and motives for the Copan takeover may elude us, military conquest for political, economic, and ideological purposes seems highly likely. It also seems likely that after the Copan takeover, Tikal would have enjoyed increased assess to, and control over, the lucrative resources and trade routes in the southeastern Maya area. Copan is positioned to control the major trade routes connecting the Maya area with Central America to the southeast. The subsidiary center of Quirigua is positioned to control the Motagua route between the Maya Highlands and the Caribbean.

The Copan founding events provide us with an expanded understanding of Early Classic Maya political history and the institution of Maya rulership. The Copan founding tells us how individual rulers lost or gained power, how they reinforced their authority, and how royal authority was maintained over time. Like many historical events, the Copan dynastic founding involved a winner and a loser. The latter was most likely an established Copan ruler who lost power to a foreign conqueror and as a result is all but unknown to history. Conjunctive research at Copan has revealed a great deal more about the winner, apparently a successful conqueror who used his foreign associations to seize and maintain his newly won kingdom. His successors thereafter used their real or fictive connections to him, including symbols derived from Tikal and the Maya Lowlands, to reinforce their power for the remainder of the Classic period. But in a larger sense, the founding era illuminates the origins of the Copan state and its connection to the expansion of Tikal's power in the Early Classic period. These events set the stage for the shattering confrontation with Calakmul a little more than a century later, which both brought a dark age to Tikal and marked the end of the Early Classic era across the Maya Lowlands.

Notes

For twelve seasons the excavations of the Early Copan Acropolis Program were conducted by a team of dedicated archaeologists and other specialists. It is not possible to mention all of these people, but I do wish to acknowledge my field director, David Sedat, who has also supervised most of the day-to-day excavations in the early levels of the Acropolis Southern Group, along with documenting both the Margarita and Hunal Tombs and excavating many of the Margarita Tomb materials. My gratitude is also extended to Loa Traxler, who has supervised the excavations in the early palaces in the Acropolis Northeast

Group, in addition to surveying and compiling the essential record of all areas of Early Classic Acropolis architecture, using an electronic-total station and CAD software. The work done by Christine Carrelli is greatly appreciated; since day one she has cataloged Early Classic Acropolis architecture and has recorded construction methods. Equally appreciated is Eleanor Coates, who has expertly photographed the exposures of Early Classic buildings in the tunnels and the artifacts in the Centro de Investigaciones. Special thanks go to Ellen Bell, our skilled artifact specialist, who has registered the objects from the Margarita Tomb and the other burials mentioned here, as well as excavating many of these offerings. The objects from the Hunal Tomb have been registered and excavated by Loa Traxler, Ellen Bell, and me. Biological anthropologist Jane Buikstra's Acropolis research has given invaluable insights regarding the human remains in the Acropolis burials and tombs. The conservation of the artifacts from these tombs, burials, and other ECAP excavations has been expertly accomplished by Lynn Grant and Harriet Beaubien, ably assisted by Rufino Membraño. Also deserving of mention for their many contributions to ECAP's research are the other recent members of our field staff, Marcello Canuto, Julie Miller, Alfonso Morales, Christopher Powell, Charles Golden, and Edward Barnhart. Last but not least, the contributions of my other PAAC colleagues, William Fash, Barbara Fash, Ricardo Agurcia, Will Andrews, Rudy Larios, and Fernando Lopez, have been vital to all aspects of our research. Finally, I want to pay special tribute to the late Linda Schele, who worked with our ECAP team from the beginning until her final visit to Copan a year before her untimely death in 1998. Her contributions to ECAP's work remain with us, but she will be especially missed for her relentless pursuit of knowledge, her unbridled enthusiasm, and her brilliant insights, all of which were critical to the development of our research.

Over the years, support for ECAP research has been provided by the University of Pennsylvania Museum (Boyer and Shoemaker Chair Research Funds), the University of Pennsylvania Research Foundation, the National Science Foundation, the National Geographic Society, the Foundation for the Advancement of Mesoamerican Studies, the Maya Workshop Foundation, the Kislak Foundation, the Selz Foundation, the Holt Family Foundation, and a series of private donors.

1. The Early Copan Acropolis Program (ECAP) of the University of Pennsylvania Museum operated from 1989 to 1996 as part of a consortium of programs investigating the Copan Acropolis, the Proyecto Arqueológico Acrópolis Copán (PAAC), organized and directed by William I Fash, under the

auspices of the Instituto Hondureño de Antropología e Historia (IHAH). Although the PAAC ended in 1996, ECAP continued its excavations under contact with IHAH from 1997 to 2000. At the close of excavations in 2000, ECAP had excavated some 3 km. of tunnels under the Acropolis, starting from the "corte" created along the eastern edge of the Acropolis by the Río Copán. The ECAP tunnel network was also linked with the tunnels beneath Structure 10L-16 (excavated under the direction of Ricardo Agurcia) and the tunnels beneath Structure 10L-26 (excavated under the direction of William I. Fash). Together, these three programs opened the most extensive system of tunnels ever excavated at a Maya site, covering the estern two-thirds of the Copan Acropolis.

2. If we assume that the Copan founder was a maximum of 60 years old at death, as may be implied by the Stela P text and the Hunal Tomb bone assessments, he would have been about 30 years old at the time he was mentioned on the Homre de Tikal text. This evidence seems to rule out the possibility that the secondary figure on the Copan Peccsary Skull could be an actual historical reference to K'inich Yax K'uk' Mo' (Schele, Grube, and Fahsen 1993), since the date for the purported meeting between K'inich Yax K'uk' Mo' and an earlier Copan ruler depicted on the Peccary Skull (8.17.0.0.0) is some 50 years before the A.D. 426 founding date and more than 60 years before his apparent death in A.D. 437. This would imply that Copan's founder was about 80 years old at death, assuming that he was a young man of 20 years old or so when the 8.17.0.0.0 meeting took place. While possible, this age is clearly beyond the estimated age range for the bones in the Hunal Tomb given by Buikstra and the possible three-K'atun age recorded on Stela P.

References

Adams, R. E. W.

1971   *The Ceramics of Altar de Sacrificios.* Papers of the Peabody Museum of Archaeology and Ethnology, vol. 63, no. 1. Cambridge, Mass.: Peabody Museum of Archaeology and Ethnology, Harvard University.

1982   Rank Site Analysis of Northern Belize Maya Sites. In *Archaeology at Colha, Belize: The 1981 Interim Report,* edited by T. R. Hester, H. J. Shafer, and J. D. Easton, pp. 60–64. San Antonio, Texas, and Venice, Italy: Center for Archaeological Research, University of Texas at San Antonio, and Centro Studi e Ricerche Ligabue.

1995   Early Classic Maya Civilization: A View from Río Azul. In *The Emergence of Lowland Maya Civilization,* edited by N. Grube, Acta Mesoamericana 8. Mockmuhl, Germany: Verlag Anton Saurwein.

1998   *Río Azul: An Ancient Maya City.* Norman: University of Oklahoma Press.

Adams, R. E. W., and R. C. Jones

1981   Spatial Patterns and Regional Growth among Classic Maya Cities. *American Antiquity* 46:301–22.

Adams, R. E. W., and A. S. Trik

1961   *Temple I (Str. 5D-1): Post-Constructional Activities.* Tikal Reports no. 7. Philadelphia: University Museum Publications, University of Pennsylvania.

REFERENCES

Agurcia Fasquelle., R.
1996   Rosalila, el corazón de la Acrópolis: el templo del rey-sol. *Yaxkin* 14:5–18.

Angulo, J.
1987   Nuevas consideraciones sobre los llamados conjuntos departamentales, especialmente Tetitla. In *Teotihuacan: nuevos datos, nuevas síntesis, nuevas problemas*, edited by E. McClung de Tapia and E. Rattray, pp. 275–316. Mexico City: Instituto de Investigaciones Antropológicas, Universidad Autonoma de México.

Arnold, J. E.
1985   The Santa Barbara Channel Islands Bladelet Industry. *Lithic Technology* 14(2):71–80.

Ashmore, W.
1981   Some Issues of Method and Theory in Lowland Maya Settlement Archaeology. In *Lowland Maya Settlement Patterns*, edited by W. Ashmore, pp. 37–69. Albuquerque: University of New Mexico Press.

1987   Research at Quirigua, Guatemala: The Site-Periphery Program. In *The Periphery of the Southeastern Maya Realm*, edited by G. W. Pahl, Los Angeles: Latin American Center Publications, University of California Los Angeles.

1991   Site Planning Principles and Concepts of Directionality among the Ancient Maya. *Latin American Antiquity* 2(3):199–226.

1992   Deciphering Maya Architectural Plans. In *New Theories on the Ancient Maya*, edited by E. C. Danien and R. J. Sharer, pp. 173–84. Philadelphia: University Museum Publications, University of Pennsylvania.

1998   Monumentos Políticos: sitios, asentamiento, y paisaje por Xunantunich, Belice. In *Anatomia de una civilización: apoximaciones interdisciplinarias a la cultura Maya*, edited by A. C. Ruiz, Y. Fernandez Marquínez, J. M. Garcia Campillo, M. J. Iglesias, A. L. Garcia-Gallo, and L. T. Sanz, pp. 161–83. Madrid: Sociedad Española de Estudios Mayas.

Aveni, A. F., and H. Hartung
1982   Precision in the Layout of Maya Architecture. *Annals of the New York Academy of Sciences* 63–80.

1989   Uaxactun, Guatemala, Group E and Similar Assemblages: Archaeoastronomical Reconsideration. In *World Archaeoastronomy*, edited by A. Aveni, pp. 441–61. Cambridge: Cambridge University Press.

Ayala, M.
1987   La Estela 39 de Tikal, Mundo Perdido. In *Memorias del Primer Coloquio Internacional de Mayistas 1995*, pp. 599–654. Mexico City: Centro de Estudios Mayas, Universidad Nacional Autónoma de México.

Ball, J. W.

1983   Teotihuacan, the Maya, and Ceramic Interchange: A Contextual Perspective. In *Highland-Lowland Interaction in Mesoamerica: Interdisciplinary Approaches*, edited by A. G. Miller, pp. 125–45. Washington, D.C.: Dumbarton Oaks.

Barrera Vásquez, A., ed.

1980   *Diccionario Maya Cordemex*. Mérida, Yucatan: Ediciones Cordemex.

Bassie-Sweet, K.

1991   *From the Mouth of the Dark Cave: Commemorative Sculpture of the Late Classic Maya*. Norman: University of Oklahoma Press.

1996   *At The Edge of the World: Caves and Late Classic Maya World View*. Norman: University of Oklahoma Press.

Becker, M. J.

1971   The Identification of a Second Plaza Plan at Tikal, Guatemala, and Its Implications for Ancient Maya Social Complexity. Ph.D. dissertation, Department of Anthropology, University of Pennsylvania.

1972   Plaza Plans at Quirigua, Guatemala: The Use of a Specific Theory Regarding Cultural Behavior in Predicting the Configuration of Group Arrangements and Burial Patterns in a Yet Untested Community Settlement Pattern. *Katunob* 8(2):47–62.

1973a   Archaeological Evidence for Archaeological Specialization among the Classic Period Maya at Tikal. *American Antiquity* 38:396–406.

1973b   The Evidence for Complex Exchange Systems among the Ancient Maya. *American Antiquity* 38:222–23.

1975   Moieties in Ancient Mesoamerica: Inferences on Teotihuacan Social Structure. Parts I and II. *American Indian Quarterly* 2:217–36, 315–30.

1979   Priests, Peasants and Ceremonial Centers: The Intellectual History of a Model. In *Maya Archaeology and Ethnohistory, Papers of the Second Cambridge Symposium on Recent Research in Mesoamerican Archaeology*, edited by N. Hammond and G. R. Willey, pp. 3–20. University of Texas Press: Austin.

1980   The Copan River Cut Project 1979: A Preliminary Report on Goals and Achievements. Report submitted to Dr. C. Baudez, Proyecto Arqueologico Copan (January 30).

1982   Ancient Maya Houses and Their Identification: An Evaluation of Architectural Groups at Tikal and Inferences Regarding Their Functions. *Revista Española de Anthropología Americana* 12:111–29.

1983   Kings and Classicism: Political Change in the Maya Lowlands during the Classic Period. In *Highland-Lowland Interaction in Mesoamerica: Interdisciplinary Approaches*, edited by A. G. Miller, pp. 159–200. Washington, D.C.: Dumbarton Oaks Research Library and Collection.

1986   Household Shrines at Tikal, Guatemala: Size as a Reflection of Economic Status. *Revista Española de Antropología Americana* 16:81–85.

1988   Changing Views of the Changing Maya: Evolution and Devolution in an Ancient Society. *Revista Española de Antropología Americana* 18:21–35.

1991   How the Divine Magic of the King Keeps the Streets Clean. Paper presented at the 1991 Maya Weekend. Philadelphia: University Museum Publications, University of Pennsylvania.

1992   Burials as Caches, Caches as Burials: A New Interpretation of the Meaning of Ritual Deposits among the Classic Period Lowland Maya. In *New Theories on the Ancient Maya*, edited by E. C. Danien and R. J. Sharer, pp. 185–96. University Museum Monograph 77 (Symposium Series Volume 3). Philadelphia: University Museum Publications, University of Pennsylvania.

1996   Medieval Mortuary Customs in Italy: Skull Relocations and Other Unusual Burial Procedures. *Archeologia Medievale* 23:699–714.

1999   *Small Structure Excavations and the Definition of Plaza Plan 2.* Tikal Reports no. 21. University Museum Monograph 104. Philadelphia: University Museum Publications, University of Pennsylvania.

n.d.   Processes of Culture Change in the Lowland Maya Realm: The Emergence and Spread of Plaza Plan 2B as a Variation on Plaza Plan 2 ("Temple on the East"). In prep.

Becker, M. J., with C. Jones

1999   *Excavations in Residential Areas of Tikal: Groups with Shrines.* Tikal Reports no. 21. Philadelphia: University Museum Publications, University of Pennsylvania.

Berjonneau, G., and J. L. Sonnery

1985   *Rediscovered Masterpieces of Mesoamerica.* Boulogne, France: Editions Arts.

Binford, L. R.

1971   Mortuary Practices: Their Study and Their Potential. In *Approaches to the Social Dimensions of Mortuary Practices, Memoir 25*, edited by J. A. Brown, pp. 6–29. Washington, D.C: Society for American Archaeology.

Bishop, R. L.

1994   Pre-Columbian Pottery: Research in the Maya Region. In *Archaeometry of Pre-Columbian Sites and Artifacts*, edited by D. A. Scott and P. Meyers, pp. 15–65. Los Angeles: The Getty Conservation Institute.

Black, S. L., and C. K. Suhler

1986   The 1984 Río Azul Settlement Survey. In *Río Azul Reports no. 2: The 1984 Season*, edited by R. E. W. Adams, pp. 163–92. San Antonio: Center for Archaeological Research, University of Texas.

Blanton, R. E., and G. M. Feinman

1984   The Mesoamerican World-System: A Comparative Perspective. *American Anthropologist* 86:673–82.

Blanton, R. E., S. A. Kowaleski, G. M. Feinman, and J. Appel

1982   Monte Alban's Hinterland. Part 1: Prehispanic Settlement Patterns in the Central and Southern Parts of the Valley of Oaxaca, Mexico. In *Prehistory and Human Ecology of the Valley of Oaxaca*, vol. 7, edited by K. V. Flannery and R. E. Blanton, Memoirs of the University of Michigan, no. 15. Ann Arbor: Museum of Anthropology.

Blom, F.

1924   Report on the Preliminary Work at Uaxactun, Guatemala. *Carnegie Institution of Washington Yearbook* no. 23:217–18.

1932   The Maya Ball-Game Pok-ta-pok. *Middle American Research Institute Publication* 4(13):486–527.

Brady, J. E., J. W. Ball, R. L. Bishop, D. C. Pring, N. Hammond, and R. A. Housley

1998   The Lowland Maya "Protoclassic": A Reconsideration of Its Nature and Significance. *Ancient Mesoamerica* 9:17–38.

Braswell, G., ed.

2003   Teotihuacan and the Maya: Reinterpreting Early Classic Interaction. In *Teotihuacan and the Maya: Reinterpreting Early Classic Interaction*, edited by G. Braswell, Austin: University of Texas Press.

Buikstra, J.

1997   The Bones Speak: High-Tech Approach to the Study of Our Ancestors. Lecture presented to the Loren Eiseley Associates. Philadelphia: University Museum Publications, University of Pennsylvania.

Buikstra, J., D. Price, J. Burton, and L. Wright

n.d.   The Early Classic Royal Burials at Copan: A Bioarchaeological Perspective. In *Understanding Early Classic Copan*, edited by E. Bell, M. Canuto, and R. J. Sharer, Philadelphia: University Museum Publications, University of Pennsylvania. In Press.

Bullard, W. R., Jr.

1960   Maya Settlement Pattern in Northeast Peten, Guatemala. *American Antiquity* 25:355–72.

Carlson, J. B.

1991   *Venus-Regulated Warfare and Ritual Sacrifice in Mesoamerica: Teotihuacan and the Cacaxtla "Star Wars" Connection.* Center for Archaeoastronomy Technical Publications, no. 7. College Park, Md.

Carr, R. E., and J. E. Hazard
1961   *Map of the Ruins of Tikal, El Peten, Guatemala.* Tikal Reports no. 11.
Philadelphia: University Museum Publications, University of Pennsylvania.

Carrasco Vargas, R., S. Boucher, P. A. Gonzalez, V. T. Blos, V. G. Vierna,
R. G. Moreno, and J. V. Negrete
1999   A Dynastic Tomb from Campeche, Mexico: New Evidence on Jaguar Paw, a
Ruler of Calakmul. *Latin American Antiquity* 10(1):47–58.

Chase, A. F.
1994   A Contextual Approach to the Ceramics of Caracol, Belize. In *Studies in the
Archaeology of Caracol, Belize,* edited by D. Chase and A. Chase, pp. 157–82.
San Francisco: Pre-Columbian Art Research Institute.

Chase, A. F., and D. Z. Chase
1987   *Investigations at the Classic Maya City of Caracol, Belize: 1985–1987.*
Pre-Columbian Art Research Institute Monograph 3. San Francisco:
Pre-Columbian Art Research Institute.

1994   Maya Veneration of the Dead at Caracol, Belize. In *Seventh Palenque Round
Table, 1989,* edited by M. G. Robertson and V. M. Fields, pp. 55–62. San
Francisco: Pre-Columbian Art Research Institute.

1995   External Impetus, Internal Synthesis, and Standardization: E Group
Assemblages and the Crystallization of Classic Maya Society in the
Southern Lowlands. In *The Emergence of Lowland Maya Civilization: The
Transition from the Preclassic to the Early Classic,* edited by N. Grube,
pp. 87–101. Acta Mesoamericana, vol. 8. Möckmühl, Germany: Verlag
Anton Saurwein.

1996   More than Kin and King: Centralized Political Organization among the
Late Classic Maya. *Current Anthropology* 37:803–30.

1998   Late Classic Maya Political Structure, Polity Size, and Warfare Arenas. In
*Anatomía de una civilización: approximaciones interdisciplinárias a la cultura
Maya,* edited by A. C. Ruiz et al., pp. 11–29. Madrid: Sociedad Española
de Estudios Mayas.

Chase, D. Z.
1988   Caches and Censerwares: Meaning from Maya Pottery. In *A Pot for All
Reasons: Ceramic Ecology Revisited,* edited by L. Lackey and C. Kolb,
pp. 81–104. Philadelphia: Temple University Press.

Chase, D. Z., and A. F. Chase
1992   *Mesoamerican Elites: An Archaeological Assessment.* Norman: University of
Oklahoma Press.

1998   The Architectural Context of Caches, Burials, and Other Ritual Activities
for the Classic Period Maya (as Reflected at Caracol, Belize). In *Function
and Meaning in Classic Maya Architecture,* edited by S. D. Houston,
pp. 229–332. Washington, D.C.: Dumbarton Oaks.

Chase, D. Z., A. F. Chase, and W. A. Haviland

1990   The Classic Maya City: Reconsidering the Mesoamerican Urban Tradition. *American Anthropologist* 92:499–506.

Cheetham, D.

1998   Interregional Interaction, Symbol Emulation, and the Emergence of Socio-Political Inequality in the Central Maya Lowlands. M.A. thesis, Department of Anthropology, University of British Columbia.

Chinchilla Mazariegos, O.

1990   Observaciones sobre los nombres personales en las inscripciones Mayas del periodo Clásico Temprano, con especial referencia a Tikal. B.A. thesis, School of History, University of San Carlos, Guatemala City.

Clancy, F. S.

1979   A Reconsideration of the Mexican Artistic Traits Found at Tikal, Guatemala. Paper presented at the 43rd International Congress of Americanists, Vancouver, Canada.

Closs, M. P.

1985   The Dynastic History of Naranjo: The Middle Period. In *The Palenque Round Table Series,* vol. 8, edited by M. Greene Robertson and V. M. Fields, pp. 65–78. San Francisco: Pre-Columbian Art Research Institute.

Coe, M. D., and J. Kerr

1982   *Old Gods and Young Heroes: The Pearlman Collection of Maya Ceramics.* Jerusalem: The Israel Museum.

Coe, W. R.

1962   A Summary of Excavation and Research at Tikal, Guatemala: 1956–1961. *American Antiquity* 27:479–507.

1964   Current Research (Tikal). *American Antiquity* 29:411–13.

1965a   Current Research (Tikal). *American Antiquity* 30: 379–83.

1965b   Tikal: Ten Years of Study of a Maya Ruin in the Lowlands of Guatemala. *Expedition* 8(1):5–56.

1967   *Tikal: A Handbook of the Ancient Maya Ruins.* Philadelphia: University Museum Publications, University of Pennsylvania.

1972   Cultural Contact between the Lowland Maya and Teotihuacan as Seen from Tikal, Peten, Guatemala. In *Teotihuacan, XI Mesa Redonda Sociedad Mexicana de Antropología* (México) 2:257–71.

1990   *Excavations in the Great Plaza, North Terrace and North Acropolis of Tikal.* Tikal Reports no. 14. 6 vols. Philadelphia: University Museum Publications, University of Pennsylvania.

References

Coe, W. R., and V. L. Broman
1958   *Excavations in the Stela 23 Group.* Tikal Reports no. 2. Philadelphia: University Museum Publications, University of Pennsylvania.

Coe, W. R., and W. A. Haviland
1982   *Introduction to the Archaeology of Tikal, Guatemala.* Tikal Reports no. 12. Philadelphia: University Museum Publications, University of Pennsylvania.

Coe, W. R., and J. J. McGinn
1963   Tikal: The North Acropolis and an Early Tomb. *Expedition* 5(2):24–32.

Coggins, C. C.
1975   Painting and Drawing Styles at Tikal: A Historical and Iconographic Reconstruction. Ph.D. dissertation, Department of Art History, Harvard University. University Microfilms, Ann Arbor.

1979   A New Order and the Role of the Calendar: Some Characteristics of the Middle Classic Period at Tikal. In *Maya Archaeology and Ethnohistory*, edited by N. Hammond and G. R. Willey, pp. 38–50. Austin: University of Texas Press.

1980   The Shape of Time: Some Political Implications of a Four-Part Figure. *American Antiquity* 45:727–39.

1983   *The Stucco Decoration and Architectural Assemblage of Structure 1-Sub, Dzibilchaltun, Mexico.* Middle American Research Institute Publication 49. New Orleans: Tulane University.

Coggins, C. C., and J. M. Ladd
1992   Wooden Artifacts. In *Artifacts from the Cenote of Sacrifice, Chichen Itza, Yucatan*, edited by C. C. Coggins, pp. 235–344. Memoirs of the Peabody Museum of Archaeology and Ethnology, vol. 10, no. 3. Cambridge, Mass.: Peabody Museum of Archaeology and Ethnology, Harvard University.

Cohodas, M.
1985   Public Architecture of the Maya Lowlands. *Cuadernos de Arquitectura Mesoamericana* (Mexico) 6:51–68.

Cowgill, G. L.
1979   Teotihuacan, Internal Militaristic Competition, and the Fall of the Classic Maya. In *Maya Archaeology and Ethnohistory*, edited by N. Hammond and G. R. Willey, pp. 51–62. Austin: University of Texas Press.

1983   Rulership and the Ciudadela: Political Inferences from Teotihuacan Architecture. In *Civilizations in the Ancient America*, edited by R. Leventhal and A. Kolata, pp. 313–43. Albuquerque: University of New Mexico Press.

1990   Toward Refining Concepts of Full-Coverage Survey. In *The Archaeology of Regions: A Case for Full-Coverage Survey*, edited by S. Fish and S. Kowalewski, pp. 249–60. Washington, D.C.: Smithsonian Institution Press.

Crumley, C. L.

1987   A Dialectical Critique of Hierarchy. In *Power Relations and State Formation*, edited by T. C. Patterson and C. W. Gailey, pp. 155–69. Washington, D.C.: American Anthropological Association.

1995   Heterarchy and the Analysis of Complex Societies. In *Heterarchy and the Analysis of Complex Societies*, edited by R. M. Ehrenreich, C. L. Crumley, and J. E. Levy, pp. 1–6. Archaeological Papers of the American Anthropological Association, no. 6. Washington, D.C.: American Anthropological Association.

Culbert, T. P.

1963   Ceramic Research at Tikal, Guatemala. *Ceramica de Cultural Maya* 1:34–42.

1973   The Maya Downfall at Tikal. In *The Classic Maya Collapse.*, edited by T. P. Culbert, pp. 63–92. Albuquerque: University of New Mexico Press.

1977   Early Maya Development at Tikal, Guatemala. In *The Origins of Maya Civilization.*, edited by R. E. W. Adams, pp. 77–101. Albuquerque: University of New Mexico Press.

1979   The Ceramics of Tikal: Eb, Tzec, Chuen, Cauac, Cimi, and Manik Complexes. Unpublished ms.

—, ed.

1991a   *Classic Maya Political History*. Santa Fe and Cambridge: School of American Research Press and Cambridge University Press.

1991b   Polities in the Northeast Peten, Guatemala. In *Classic Maya Political History*, edited by T. P. Culbert, pp. 128–46. Cambridge: Cambridge University Press.

1993   *The Ceramics of Central Tikal*. Tikal Reports no. 25A. Philadelphia: University Museum Publications, University of Pennsylvania.

1994   Los cambios sociopolíticos en las tierras bajas mayas durante los siglos cuatro y cinco dc. In *VII Simposio de Investigaciones Arqueológicas en Guatemala*, edited by J. LaPorte and H. Escobedo, pp. 391–96. Guatemala City: Instituto Nacional de Antropología e Historia.

Culbert, T. P., V. Fialko, L. Grazioso, G. Martínez, and J. Murphy

1999   Proyecto Comunidades de los Bajos: *Informe 1999*. Guatemala City.

Culbert, T. P., V. Fialko, B. Mckee, L. Grazioso, J. Kunen, and L. Paez

1997   Investigaciones arqueológicas en el bajo La Justa, Petén. In *X Simposio de Investigaciones Arqueológicas en Guatemala (1996)*, pp. 367–72. Guatemala City: Museo Nacional de Arqueología y Etnología.

Culbert, T. P., L. J. Kosakowsky, R. E. Fry, and W. A. Haviland

1990   The Population of Tikal, Guatemala. In *Precolumbian Population History in the Maya Lowlands*, edited by T. P. Culbert and D. S. Rice, pp. 103–21. Albuquerque: University of New Mexico Press.

Culbert, T. P., L. J. Levi, B. Mckee, and J. Kunen

1996   Investigaciones arqueológicas en el bajo La Justa, entre Yaxha y Nakum. In *IX Simposio de Investigaciones Arqueológicas en Guatemala (1995)*, pp. 51–58. Guatemala City: Museo Nacional de Arqueología y Etnología.

Culbert, T. P., and L. A. Schwalbe

1987   X-Ray Fluorescence Survey of Tikal Ceramics. *Journal of Archaeological Science* 14:635–57.

Dahlin, B.

1976   An Anthropologist Looks at the Pyramids: A Late Classic Revitalization Movement at Tikal, Guatemala. Ph.D. dissertation, Department of Anthropology, Temple University.

De León, F.

1999   *Informe final del Proyecto de Restauración Templo III de Tikal.* Guatemala City: Corporación Arqueológica S.A. *(COARSA).*

Demarest, A. A., and R. J. Sharer

1982   The Origins and Evolution of Usulutan Ceramics. *American Antiquity* 47: 810–22.

de Montmollin, O.

1988   Scales of Settlement Study for Complex Societies: Analytical Issues from the Classic Maya Area. *Journal of Field Archaeology* 15:151–68.

Diaz Del Castillo, B.

1963   *The Conquest of New Spain.* J. M. Cohen, transl. Hammondsworth, England, and Baltimore: Penguin Books.

Díaz, B.

1983   La industria de la concha en Mundo Perdido, Tikal. B.A. thesis, Escuela de Historia, Universidad de San Carlos, Guatemala City.

Dunning, N. P.

1992   *Lords of the Hills: Ancient Maya Settlement in the Puuc Region, Yucatan, Mexico.* Madison, Wis.: Prehistory Press.

Ehrenreich, R., C. L. Crumley, and J. E. Levy, eds.

1995   *Heterarchy and the Analysis of Complex Societies.* Archeological Papers of the American Anthropological Association, no. 6. Washington, D.C.: American Anthropological Association.

Eliade, M.

1959   *The Sacred and the Profane.* New York: Harcourt and Brace.

Ellul, J.

1964   *The Technological Society.* J. Wilkinson, transl. New York: Knopf.

Ember, C. R., and M. Ember

1996   What Have We Learned from Cross-Cultural Research? *General Anthropology* 2(2):5.

Emery, K. F.

1995   Manufactura de artefactos de hueso en la región Petexbatun: un taller de producción de herramientas de hueso del sitio Dos Pilas, Petén, Guatemala. In *VIII Simposio de Investigaciones Arqueológicas en Guatemala (1994),* 315–34. Guatemala City: Museo Nacional de Arqueología y Etnología.

1997   The Maya Collapse: A Zooarchaeological Investigation. Ph.D. dissertation, Department of Anthropology, Cornell University.

Escobedo, H. L.

1999   Vasija PNTA-221: una escena ritual del inframundo. Report. Proyecto Arqueológico Piedras Negras, Guatemala.

Escobedo, H. L., and S. D. Houston

1997   Introduccion: la primera temporada de campo del Proyecto Arqueologico Piedras Negras, 1997. In *Proyecto Arquelogico Piedras Negras: Informe Preliminar no. 1, Primera Temporada 1997,* edited by H. L. Escobedo and S. D. Houston, pp. iii–vi. Report to Instituto de Antropologia e Historia de Guatemala.

Fahsen, F.

1987   Los personajes de Tikal en el Clásico Temprano: la evidencia epigráfia. In *Primer Symposio Mundialsobre Epigrafia Maya,* 47–60. Asociación Tikal, Guatemala.

1988   *A New Early Classic Text from Tikal.* Research Reports on Ancient Maya Writing 17. Washington, D.C.: Center for Maya Research.

2002   Rescuing the Origins of Dos Pilas Dynasty: A Salvage of Hieroglyphic Stairway 2, Structure L5-49. Report to the Foundation for the Advancement of Mesoamerican Studies.

Fahsen, F., L. Schele, and N. Grube

1995   *The Tikal-Copan Connection: Shared Features.* Copán Note 123. Copán Acropolis Archaeological Project and the Instituto Hondureño de Antropología e Historia, Austin, Texas.

Fash, B. W.

1992   Late Classic Architectural Sculpture Themes at Copan. *Ancient Mesoamerica* 3:89–102.

Fash, W. L.

1991   *Scribes, Warriors, and Kings: The City of Copan and the Ancient Maya.* New York: Thames and Hudson.

1997   Official Histories and Archaeological Data in the Interpretation of the
         Teotihuacan-Copan Relationship. Paper presented at the Symposium,
         "A Tale of Two Cities: Copan and Teotihuacan," Harvard University,
         Cambridge.

1998   Dynastic Architectural Programs: Intention and Design in Classic Maya
         Buildings at Copan and Other Sites. In *Function and Meaning in Classic
         Maya Architecture*, edited by S. D. Houston, pp. 223–70. Washington, D.C.:
         Dumbarton Oaks.

n.d.   Classic Copan and the Theater State. In *Copan: The Rise and Fall of a Classic
         Maya Kingdom*, edited by E. W. Andrews and W. L. Fash, Santa Fe: School
         of American Research Press. In press.

Fash, W. L., and R. J. Sharer
1991   Sociopolitical Developments and Methodological Issues at Copan,
         Honduras: A Conjunctive Perspective. *Latin American Antiquity* 2:166–87.

Fash, W. L., R. V. Williamson, C. R. Larios, and J. Palka
1992   The Hieroglyphic Stairway and Its Ancestors: Investigations of Copan
         Structure 10L-26. *Ancient Mesoamerica* 3:105–15.

Feinman, G. M.
1982   Patterns in Ceramic Production and Distribution, Periods I through V. In
         *Monte Alban's Hinterland, Part 1: Prehispanic Settlement Patterns of the Central
         and Southern Parts of the Valley of Oaxaca. Prehistory and Human Ecology
         of the Valley of Oaxaca*, vol. 7, edited by K. V. Flannery and R. E. Blanton,
         pp. 181–206. Memoirs of the University of Michigan, no. 15. Ann Arbor:
         Museum of Anthropology.

1995   The Emergence of Inequality: A Focus on Strategies and Processes. In
         Foundations of Social Inequality, edited by T. D. Price and G. M. Feinman,
         pp. 225–79. New York: Plenum Press.

Feinman, G. M., and J. Marcus, eds.
1998   *Archaic States.* Santa Fe: School of American Research Press.

Ferree, L.
1972   The Pottery Censers of Tikal, Guatemala. Ph.D. dissertation, Department
         of Anthropology, Southern Illinois University. Ann Arbor: University
         Microfilms.

Fialko, V.
1987a   El marcador de juego de pelota de Tikal: nuevos referencias epigráficas
         para el Clásico Temprano. In *Primer Symposio Mundial sobre Epigrafía Maya*,
         pp. 61–80. Guatemala City: Asociación Tikal.

1987b   Informe sobre el análisis osteológico de los restos del Proyecto Nacional
         Tikal. Paper presented at the Proyecto Nacional Tikal, Instituto de
         Antropología e Historia (Guatemala), and Escuela de Historia,
         Universidad de San Carlos, Guatemala City.

1988a   Mundo Perdido, Tikal: un ejemplo de complejos de conmemoración astronómica. *Mayab* (Madrid) 4:13–21.

1988b   El marcador de juego de pelota de Tikal: nuevas referencias epigráficas para el Clásico Temprano. *Mesoamérica* (Guatemala) 15:117–35.

1995   Sangre, Sudor y Lágrimas: Reporte 1. Monografía de los sitios arqueológicos descubiertos, mapeados y muestreados en los espacios intersitios entre los centros urbanos Mayas de Tikal y Nakum. Manuscript on file at Archivo PRONAT, Instituto Antropología e Historia, Guatemala City.

1996   Yaxha y Nakum: Jerarquías y patrones de asentamiento en sus espacios intersitios. *Mayab* (Madrid) 10:15–24.

1997   Arqueología regional de intersitios entre los centros urbanos Mayas de Yaxha y Nakum. *Sonderdruck aus Beiträge zur Allgemeinen und Vergleichenden Archäologie* 17:311–24.

1998   Distribución de los asentamientos Preclásicos entre Tikal, Nakum, Yaxha y Naranjo. Presented at *XII Simposio de Investigaciones Arqueológicas en Guatemala,* Museo Nacional de Arqueología y Etnología, Guatemala City.

Fialko, V., and T. P. Culbert
1999   Implications of the Tikal and Yaxha Bajo Communities for Understanding the End of the Classic Period in Peten, Guatemala. Unpublished ms.

Flannery, K. V.
1998   The Ground Plans of Archaic States. In *Archaic States,* edited by G. M. Feinman and J. Marcus, pp. 15–57. Santa Fe: School of American Research Press.

Fletcher, L. A.
1978   Socioeconomic Implications of the Linear Features at Cobá, Quintana Roo, Mexico. Ph.D. dissertation, Department of Anthropology, State University of New York, Stony Brook.

1983   Coba and Mayapan: A Comparison of "Solares" and Household Variation. In *Cobá: A Classical Maya Metropolis,* edited by W. J. Folan, E. Kintz, and L. A. Fletcher, pp. 200–18. New York: Academic Press.

Fletcher, L. A., J. May Hau, L. M. Florey Folan, and W. J. Folan
1987   *Un análisis estadístico preliminar del patro'n de asentamiento de Calakmul.* Campeche, Mexico: Universidad Autónoma del Sudeste.

Florey Folan L. M., W. J. Folan, J. Marcus, S. Pincemin, M. Del Rosario Dominguez Carrasco, L. A. Fletcher, and A. Morales López
1995   Calakmul: New Data from an Ancient Maya Capitol in Campeche, Mexico. *Latin American Antiquity* 6:310–34.

Folan, W. J., J. D. Gunn, and M. Del Rosario Dominguez Carrasco

2001   Triadic Temples, Central Plazas and Dynastic Palaces: A Diachronic
         Analysis of the Royal Court Complex, Calakmul, Campeche, Mexico. In
         Royal Courts of the Ancient Maya, vol. 2, Data and Case Studies, edited by
         T. Inomata and S. D. Houston, pp. 223–65. Boulder, Colo.: Westview Press.

Ford, A.

1981a   Conditions for the Evolution of Complex Societies: The Development of
         the Central Lowland Maya. Ph.D. dissertation, Department of
         Anthropology, University of California, Santa Barbara.

1981b   Patrones de asentamiento maya durante el periodo Clásico Tardío y el
         problema de la complejidad económica y política. *Antropología e Historia*
         (Guatemala) 3:7–23.

1982   Los Mayas en El Petén: distribución de las poblaciones en el periodo
         Clásico. *Mesoamérica* 3 (Guatemala):124–44.

1986   *Population Growth and Social Complexity.* Anthropological Research Papers,
         no. 35. Tempe: Arizona State University.

1991   Problems with Evaluation of Population from Settlement Data:
         Examination of Ancient Maya Residential Patterns in the Tikal-Yaxha
         Intersite Area. *Estudios de Cultura Maya* 18:157–86.

Forsyth, D. W.

1989   *The Ceramics of El Mirador, Petén, Guatemala.* El Mirador Series, Part 4.
         Papers of the New World Archaeological Foundation, no. 63. Provo, Utah:
         Brigham Young University.

1992   Un estudio comparativo de la cerámica temprana de Nakbe. In *IV Simposio
         de Investigaciones Arqueológicas en Guatemala, 1990,* 45–56. Guatemala City:
         Museo Nacional de Arqueología y Etnología.

Frankfort, H., H. A. Frankfort, J. A. Wilson, T. Jacobsen, and W. A. Irwin

1946   *The Intellectual Adventure of Ancient Man.* Chicago: University of Chicago
         Press.

Freidel, D. A.

1981a   Civilization as a State of Mind: The Cultural Evolution of the Lowland
         Maya. In *The Transition to Statehood in the New World,* edited by G. D. Jones
         and R. R. Kautz, pp. 188–227. Cambridge: Cambridge University Press.

1981b   Continuity and Disjunction: Late Postclassic Settlement Patterns in
         Northern Yucatan. In *Lowland Maya Settlement Patterns,* edited by
         W. Ashmore, pp. 311–32. Albuquerque: University of New Mexico Press.

Freidel, D. A., L. Schele, and J. Parker

1993   *Maya Cosmos: Three Thousand Years on the Shaman's Path.* New York:
         William Morrow.

Freidel, D. A., and C. K. Suhler

1995   The Tikal Sky Seat: Maya Wars in Monumental Architectural Context. Paper presented at the 2nd UCLA Maya Weekend, University of California at Los Angeles.

Fry, R. E.

1969   Ceramics and Settlement in the Periphery of Tikal, Guatemala. Ph.D. dissertation, Department of Anthropology, University of Arizona.

1972   Manually Operated Post Hole Diggers as Sampling Instruments. *American Antiquity* 37(4): 259–61.

1979   The Economics of Pottery at Tikal, Guatemala: Models of Exchange for Serving Vessels. *American Antiquity* 44:494–512.

1980   Models of Exchange for Major Shape Classes of Lowland Maya Pottery. In *Models and Methods in Regional Exchange.* Society for American Archaeology Papers 1:3–18.

1981   Pottery Production-Distribution Systems in the Southern Maya Lowlands. In *Production and Distribution: A Ceramic Viewpoint,* edited by H. Howard and E. L. Morris, pp. 145–67. Oxford, England: BAR International Series 120.

1999   Ceramics and Settlement in the Periphery of Tikal, Guatemala. Ph.D. dissertation, Department of Anthropology, University of Arizona. Ann Arbor: University Microfilms.

n.d.   Dating of Defensive Earthworks at Tikal, Guatemala. Department of Sociology and Anthropology, Purdue University.

Fry, R. E., and S. C. Cox

1974   The Structure of Ceramic Exchange at Tikal, Guatemala. *World Archaeology* 6:209–25.

García Campillo, J. M., M. J. Iglesias, A. L. Garcia-Gallo, and L. T. Sanz

1990   Estudios de fragmentos cerámicos con inscripciones glíficas del clássico temprano de Tikal. *Mayab* 1990(6):38–40.

Gendorp, P.

1985   Los remates o coronamientos de techo en la arquitectura mesoamericana. *Cuadernos de Arquitectura Mesoamericana* 4:47–50. Universidad Nacional Autonimo de México.

Gifford, J. C.

1976   Prehistoric Pottery Analysis and the Ceramics of Barton Ramie in the Belize Valley. In *Memoirs of the Peabody Museum of Archaeology and Ethnology,* vol. 18., compiled by C. A. Gifford, Cambridge, Mass.: Peabody Museum of Archaeology and Ethnology, Harvard University.

Gillespie, S. D., and R. A. Joyce

1998   Deity Relationships in Mesoamerican Cosmologies. *Ancient Mesoamerica* 9(2):279–96.

Gómez, O.

1998   Nuevas excavaciones en el Templo V, Tikal. In *XI Simposio de Investigaciones Arqueológicas en Guatemala (1997)*, pp. 55–70. Guatemala City: Museo Nacional de Arqueología y Etnología.

1999   Excavaciones en el interior del Templo V, Tikal. In *XII Simposio de Investigationes Arqueológicas en Guatemala 1998*, edited by J. P. Laporte, H. L. Escobedo, and A. C. Monzón de Suasnávar, pp. 187–94. Guatemala City: Ministerio de Cultura y Deportes, Instituto Antropología e História, and Asociación Tikal.

Gómez, O., and C. Vidal

1997   El Templo V de Tikal: su excavación. In *X Simposio de Investigaciones Arqueológicas en Guatemala 1996*, pp. 309–24. Guatemala City: Museo Nacional de Arqueología y Etnología.

Graham, I.

1975   *Corpus of Maya Hieroglyphic Inscriptions*, vol. 2, part 1, *Naranjo*. Cambridge, Mass.: Peabody Museum of Archaeology and Ethnology, Harvard University.

Graham, I., and E. Von Euw

1977   *Corpus of Maya Hieroglyphic Inscriptions*, vol. 3, part 1: *Yaxchilan*. Cambridge, Mass.: Peabody Museum of Archaeology and Ethnology, Harvard University.

Green, E. L.

1970   The Archaeology of Navajuelal, Tikal, Guatemala and a Test of Interpretive Method. Ph.D. dissertation, Department of Anthropology, University of Pennsylvania.

1973   Locational Analysis of Prehistoric Maya Sites in Northern British Honduras. *American Antiquity* 38:279–93.

Grove, D. C.

1999   Public Monuments and Sacred Mountains: Observations on Three Formative Period Sacred Landscapes. In *Social Patterns in Pre-Classic Mesoamerica*, edited by D. C. Grove and R. A. Joyce, pp. 255–99. Washington, D.C.: Dumbarton Oaks.

Grube, N.

1988   "Städtegründer" und "Erste Herrscher." *Hieroglyphentexten der Klassischen Mayakultur. Archiv für Völkerkunde* 42:69–90.

1994   Epigraphic Research at Caracol, Belize. In *Excavations at Caracol, Belize*, edited by A. Chase and D. Chase, San Francisco: Pre-Columbian Art Research Institute.

1998   Una revision de la secuencia dinastica de Tikal para el Clasico Temprano.
        Paper presented at the 4th Congreso Internacional de Mayistas, Antigua,
        Guatemala.

Grube, N., and L. Schele
1994   Kuy, the Owl of Omen and War. *Mexico* 16(1):10–17.

Grube, N., L. Schele, and F. Fahsen
1995   *The Tikal-Copan Connection: Evidence from External Relations.* Copan Note
        121. Copán Acropolis Archaeological Project and the Instituto Hondureño
        de Antropología e Historia, Austin, Texas.

Guenter, S. P., and M. Zender
1999   Palenque and Yaxchilan's War against Piedras Negras. Unpublished ms.

Hageman, J. B.
1999   Ideology and Intersite Settlement among the Late Classic Maya. Paper
        presented at the 64th Annual Meeting of the Society for American
        Archaeology, Chicago.

Hall, J., and R. Viel
n.d.   The Early Classic Copan Landscape. In *Understanding Early Classic Copan*,
        edited by E. Bell, M. Canuto, and R. J. Sharer, Philadelphia: University
        Museum Publications, University of Pennsylvania. In press.

Hammond, N.
1980   Early Maya Ceremonial at Cuello, Belize. *Antiquity* 54:176–90.

1986   New Light on the Most Ancient Maya. *Man* (new series) 21:399–413.

Hammond, N., ed.
1991   *Cuello, an Early Maya Community in Belize.* Cambridge: Cambridge
        University Press.

Hammond, N., G. Tourtellot III, S. Donaghey, and A. Clark
1998   No Slow Dusk: Maya Urban Development and Decline at La Milpa, Belize.
        Antiquity 72:831–37.

Hansen, R. D., R. L. Bishop, and F. Fahsen
1991   Notes on the Maya Codex-Style Ceramics from Nakbe, Peten, Guatemala.
        Ancient Mesoamerica 2:225–43.

Harris, J.
1998   Yax K'uk' Mo': An Inscriptional Retrospective. *The Codex* 6(2):33–45. The
        PreColumbian Society, Philadelphia.

Harrison, P. D.
1970   The Central Acropolis, Tikal, Guatemala: A Preliminary Study of the
        Functions of Its Structural Component during the Late Classic Period.
        Ph.D. dissertation, Department of Anthropology, University of
        Pennsylvania. University Microfilms, Ann Arbor.

1989 Spatial Geometry and Logic in the Ancient Maya Mind, Part 2: Architecture. In *Seventh Palenque Round Table, 1989*, edited by M. G. Robertson and V. M. Fields, pp. 243–52. San Francisco: The Pre-Columbian Art Research Institute.

1997 Triangles of Love: A Case History from 8th Century Tikal. In *Proceedings of the 1995 and 1996 Latin American Symposia*, edited by A. Cordy-Collins and G. Johnson, pp. 81–89. San Diego Museum Papers, no. 34. San Diego: San Diego Museum.

1999 *The Lords of Tikal: Rulers of an Ancient Maya City*. London: Thames and Hudson.

Hartung, H.

1984 Alignments in Architecture and Sculpture of Maya Centers: Notes on Piedras Negras, Copan and Chichen Itza. *Ibero-Amerikanisches Archiv* 2(10):223–39.

Haviland, W. A.

1963 Excavation of Small Structures in the Northeast Quadrant of Tikal, Guatemala. Ph.D. dissertation, Department of Anthropology, University of Pennsylvania. University Microfilms, Ann Arbor.

1965 Prehistoric Settlement at Tikal, Guatemala. *Expedition* 7(3):14–23.

1966a Maya Settlement Patterns: A Critical Review. Middle American Research Institute, Tulane University Publication 26:21–47.

1966b Social Integration and the Classic Maya. *American Antiquity* 31:625–31.

1967 Stature at Tikal, Guatemala: Implications for Ancient Maya Demography and Social Organization. *American Antiquity* 32:316–25.

1970 Tikal, Guatemala, and Mesoamerican Urbanism. *World Archaeology* 2:186–98.

1972 A New Look at Classic Maya Social Organization at Tikal. *Ceramica de Cultura Maya* 8:1–16.

1977 Dynastic Geneologies from Tikal, Guatemala: Implications for Descent and Political Organization. *American Antiquity* 42:61–67.

1981 Dower Houses and Minor Centers at Tikal, Guatemala: An Investigation into the Identification of Valid Units in Settlement Hierarchies. In *Lowland Maya Settlement Patterns*, edited by W. Ashmore, pp. 89–117. Albuquerque: University of New Mexico Press.

1985 Population and Social Dynamics: The Dynasties and Social Structure of Tikal. *Expedition* 27(3):34–41.

1988 Musical Hammocks at Tikal: Problems of Reconstructing Household Composition. In *House and Household in the Mesoamerican Past*, edited by R. Wilk and W. Ashmore, pp. 121–34. Albuquerque: University of New Mexico Press.

1992a   Status and Power in Classic Maya Society: The View from Tikal. *American Anthropologist* 94:937–40.

1992b   From Double-Bird to Ah Cacao: Dynastic Troubles and the Cycle of the Katuns at Tikal, Guatemala. In *New Theories on the Ancient Maya,* edited by E. C. Danien and R. J. Sharer, pp. 71–80. Philadelphia: University Museum Publications, University of Pennsylvania.

1994   Star Wars at Tikal, or Did Caracol Do What the Glyphs Say They Did? In *Anthropology,* 7th ed., edited by William A. Haviland, pp. 266–70. Fort Worth: Harcourt Brace.

1997   The Rise and Fall of Sexual Inequality: Death and Gender at Tikal, Guatemala. *Ancient Mesoamerica* 8:1–12.

2000   *Anthropology,* 9th ed. Fort Worth: Harcourt, Brace.

n.d. a   *Excavations in Residential Areas of Tikal: Non-Elite Residential Groups without Shrines.* Tikal Reports no. 20. Philadelphia: University Museum Publications, University of Pennsylvania. In press.

n.d. b   *The Skeletal Series of Tikal.* Tikal Reports no. 30. Philadelphia: University Museum Publications, University of Pennsylvania. In press.

n.d. c   *Excavations in Group 7F-1 at Tikal.* Tikal Reports no. 22. Philadelphia: University Museum Publications, University of Pennsylvania. In press.

Haviland, W. A., with M. J. Becker, A. Chowning, K. A. Dixon, and K. Heider
1985   *Excavations in Small Residential Groups of Tikal: Groups 4F-1 and 4F-2.* Tikal Reports no. 19. Philadelphia: University Museum Publications, University of Pennsylvania.

Haviland, W. A., and H. Moholy-Nagy
1992   Distinguishing the High and Mighty from the Hoi Polloi at Tikal, Guatemala. In *Mesoamerican Elites: An Archaeological Assessment,* edited by D. Z. Chase and A. F. Chase, pp. 50–60. Norman: University of Oklahoma Press.

Hayden, B., and A. Cannon
1984   *The Structure of Material Systems: Ethnoarchaeology in the Maya Highlands.* Society for American Archaeology Papers, no. 3. Washington, D.C.: Society for American Archaeology.

Hendon, J. A.
1991   Status and Power in Classic Maya Society: An Archaeological Study. *American Anthropologist* 93:894–918.

1992   Variation in Classic Maya Sociopolitical Organization. *American Anthropologist* 94:940–41.

1999 Multiple Sources of Prestige and the Social Evaluation of Women in Prehispanic Mesoamerica. In *Material Symbols: Culture and Economy in Prehistory*, edited by J. E. Robb, pp. 257–76. Center for Archaeological Investigation, Occasional Paper no. 26. Carbondale: Southern Illinois University Press.

Heredia, V.

1998 Material Possessions as Communicators of Wealth Status in a Rural Lowland Maya Community. M.A. thesis, Department of Anthropology, Purdue University.

Heredia, V., and R. E. Fry

n.d. Material Possessions as Communicators of Wealth Status in a Rural Lowland Maya Community. In *New Horizons for Ancient Maya Ceramics*, edited by H. McKillop and S. Boteler-Mock, Gainesville: University of Florida Press. In press.

Hermes, B.

1984a Adiciones tipológicas a los Complejos Eb, Tzec y Manik de Tikal. Report, Proyecto Nacional Tikal, Guatemala.

1984b La secuencia cerámica de Mundo Perdido, Tikal: una visión preliminar. Paper presented at Simposio "La Plaza de la Gran Pirámide o Mundo Perdido," Instituto de Antropología e Historia, Guatemala.

1985 Informe sobre fechamiento de lotes cerámicos de las exploraciones de Mundo Perdido y Zonas de Habitación, Tikal. Report, Proyecto Nacional Tikal, Guatemala.

1993a Dos reportes del laboratorio cerámico: vasijas miniatura y adiciones tipológicas para la época Preclásica. In *Tikal y Uaxactun en el Preclásico*, edited by J. P. Laporte and J. A. Valdés, pp. 43–52. Mexico City: Instituto de Investigaciones Antropológicas, Universidad Autonoma de México.

1993b La secuencia cerámica de Topoxte: un informe preliminar. *Sonderdruck aus Beiträge zur Allgemeinen und Vergleichenden Archäologie* 13:221–51.

Hirth, K. G.

1998 The Distributional Approach: A New Way to Identify Marketplace Exchange in the Archaeological Record. *Current Anthropology* 39:451–76.

Holley, G. R.

1986 The Ceramic Sequence at Piedras Negras, Guatemala. *Cerámica de Cultura Maya* 14:49–72. Philadelphia: Temple University.

Hopkins, M. R.

1987 An Explication of the Plans of Some Teotihuacan Apartment Compounds. In *Teotihuacan: nuevos datos, nuevas síntesis, nuevos problemas*, edited by E. McClung de Tapia and E. Rattray, pp. 369–88. Mexico City: Instituto de Investigaciones Antropológicas, Universidad Autonoma de México.

Houston, S. D.

1987   Notes on Caracol Epigraphy and Its Significance. In *Investigations at the Classic Maya City of Caracol, Belize: 1985–1987, Appendix 2*, edited by A. Chase and D. Chase, pp. 85–100. Pre-Columbian Art Research Institute Monograph 3. San Francisco: Pre-Columbian Art Research Institute.

1991   Appendix: Caracol Altar 21. In *Sixth Palenque Round Table, 1986*, edited by M. Greene Robertson and V. M. Fields, pp. 38–42. Norman and London: University of Oklahoma Press.

1992   Classic Maya Politics. In *New Theories on the Ancient Maya*, edited by E. C. Danien and Robert J. Sharer, pp. 65–69. Philadelphia: University Museum Publications, University of Pennsylvania.

1993   *Hieroglyphs and History at Dos Pilas: Dynastic Politics of the Classic Maya*. Austin: University of Texas Press.

1998   Classic Maya Depictions of the Built Environment. In *Function and Meaning in Classic Maya Architecture*, edited by S. D. Houston, pp. 333–72. Washington, D.C.: Dumbarton Oaks Research Library and Collection.

Houston, S. D., H. L. Escobedo, and M. Child

1999   Al filo de la navaja: resultados de la segunda temporada del Proyecto Arqueológico Piedras Negras. In *XII Simposio de Investigaciones Arqueológicas en Guatemala (1998)*, pp. 373–92. Guatemala City: Museo Nacional de Arqueología y Etnología.

Houston, S. D., and P. Mathews

1985   *The Dynastic Sequence of Dos Pilas, Guatemala*. Pre-Columbian Art Research Institute Monograph 1. San Francisco: Pre-Columbian Art Research Institute.

Houston, S. D., and D. Stuart

1996   Of Gods, Glyphs and Kings: Divinity and Rulership among the Classic Maya. *Antiquity* 70:289–312.

1998   The Ancient Maya Self: Personhood and Portraiture in the Classic Period. *RES* 33:73–101.

Houston, S. D., D. Stuart, and J. Robertson

1998   Disharmony in Maya Hieroglyphic Writing: Linguistic Change and Continuity in Classic Society. In *Anatomia de una Civilizacion: aproximaciones interdisciplinarias a la cultura Maya*, edited by A. Ciudad et al., pp. 275–96. Madrid: Sociedad Espanola de Estudios Mayas.

Houston, S. D., S. Symonds, D. Stuart, and A. Demarest

1992   A Civil War of the Late Classic Period: Evidence from Hieroglyphic Stairway 4. Unpublished ms.

Houston, S. D., and K. Taube

1987   Name-Tagging in Classic Mayan Script. *Mexico* 9:2.

Iglesias, M. J.

1987 Excavaciones en el Grupo Habitacional 6D-V, Tikal, Guatemala. Ph.D. thesis, Department of Geography and History, Facultad de Geografía e Historia, Universidad Complutense de Madrid.

1988 Análisis de un depósito problemático de Tikal, Guatemala. *Journal de la Societe des Americanistes* 74:25–48.

1996 El hombre depone y la arqueología dispone: formas de deposición en la cultura Maya, el caso de Tikal. *Los Investigadores de la Cultura Maya* 4:187–217. Campeche, Mexico: Universidad Autónoma de Campeche.

Iglesias, M. J., and A. C. Ruiz

1999 Los Mayas prehispánicos ante el siglo 21: aplicación de análisis de ADN mitocondrial al estudio de las clases sociales de la ciudad arqueológica de Tikal, Guatemala. Research proposal to the Instituto de Antropología e Historia, Guatemala.

Iglesias, M. J., and L. T. Sanz

2000 Patrones de replicación iconográfica en materiales del Clásico Temprano de Tikal. In *XII Simposio de Investigationes Arqueológicas en Guatemala 1998*, edited by J. P. Laporte, H. L. Escobedo, and A. C. Monzón de Suasnávar, pp. 169–86. Guatemala City: Ministerio de Cultura y Deportes, Instituto Antropología e História, Asociación Tikal.

Jarquín, A. M.

1987 Arquitectura y sistemas constructivos de la fachada de la Ciudadela. In *Teotihuacan: nuevos datos, nuevas síntesis, nuevos problemas*, edited by E. McClung de Tapia and E. Rattray, pp. 512–15. Mexico City: Instituto de Investigaciones Antropológicas, Universidad Autonoma de México.

Jarquín, A. M., and E. Martínez Vargas

1982 Exploración en el lado este de La Ciudadela (Estructuras 1G, 1R, 1Q y 1P). In *Memoria del Proyecto Arqueológico Teotihuacan 1980–82*, edited by R. Cabrera, I. Rodríguez, and N. Morelos, pp. 19–47. Mexico City: Instituto Nacional de Antropología e Historia.

Jones, C.

1969 The Twin-Pyramid Group Pattern: A Classic Maya Architectural Assemblage at Tikal, Guatemala. Ph.D. dissertation, Department of Anthropology, University of Pennsylvania. University Microfilms, Ann Arbor.

1977 Inauguration Dates of Three Late Classic Rulers of Tikal, Guatemala. *American Antiquity* 42:28–60.

1979 Tikal as a Trading Center. Paper presented at the 43rd International Congress of Americanists, Vancouver.

1985 The Life and Times of Ah Cacau, Ruler of Tikal. Paper presented at the Primer Simposio Mundial de Epigrafia Maya, Guatemala.

1991   Cycles of Growth at Tikal. In *Classic Maya Political History: Hieroglyphic and Archaeological Evidence*, edited by T. P. Culbert, pp. 102–27. Cambridge: Cambridge University Press.

1996   *Excavations in the East Plaza of Tikal.* Tikal Reports no. 16. Philadelphia: University Museum Publications, University of Pennsylvania.

Jones, C., and M. Orrego

1987   Corosal Stela 1 and Tikal Miscellaneous Stone 167: Two New Monuments from the Tikal Vicinity, Guatemala. *Mexico* IX(6):129–32.

Jones, C., and L. Satterthwaite, Jr.

1982   *The Monuments and Inscriptions of Tikal: The Carved Monuments.* Tikal Reports no. 33A. Philadelphia: University Museum Publications, University of Pennsylvania.

Jones, C., and R. J. Sharer

1980   Archaeological Investigations in the Site-Core of Quirigua. *Expedition* 23(1):1–19.

Jones, T.

1996   Polyvalency in the 'Xok' Glyph: Phonetic u and a Morphemic Patronym. In *Eighth Palenque Round Table, 1993*, vol. 10, edited by M. Macri and M. Greene Robertson, pp. 325–42. San Francisco: Pre-Columbian Art Research Institute.

Kaufman, T. S., and W. M. Norman

1984   An Outline of Proto-Cholan Phonology, Morphology and Vocabulary. In *Phoneticism in Mayan Hieroglyphic Writing*, edited by J. S. Justeson and L. Campbell, pp. 77–166. Institute for Mesoamerican Studies Publication 9. Albany: State University of New York at Albany.

Kerr, J.

1989–97   *The Maya Vase Book: A Corpus of Rollout Photographs of Maya Vases.* 5 vols., edited by B. Kerr and J. Kerr, New York: Kerr Associates.

Kidder, A. V.

1943   *Spindle Whorls from Chichen Itza, Yucatan.* Notes on Middle American Archaeology and Ethnology 16. Carnegie Institution of Washington, Division of Historical Research, Washington, D.C.

1982   Archaeological Problems of the Highland Maya. In *The Maya and Their Neighbors*, edited by C. L. Hay, R. L. Linton, S. K. Lothrop, H. L. Shapiro, and G. C. Vaillant, pp. 117–25. Salt Lake City: University of Utah Press.

Kidder, A. V., J. D. Jennings, and E. M. Shook

1946   *Excavations at Kaminaljuyu, Guatemala.* Carnegie Institution of Washington Publication 501. Washington, D.C.

King, E.

1990   Maya Household Organization and the Problem of Isolated Mounds: A Perspective from Colha, Belize. Paper presented at the 55th Annual Meeting of the Society for American Archaeology, Las Vegas.

2000   The Organization of Late Classic Lithic Production at the Prehistoric Maya Site of Colha, Belize: A Study in Complexity and Heterarchy. Ph.D. dissertation, Department of Anthropology, University of Pennsylvania.

King, E., and D. Potter

1994   Small Sites in Prehistoric Maya Socioeconomic Organization: A Perspective from Colha, Belize. In *Archaeological Views from the Countryside: Village Communities in Early Complex Societies*, edited by G. M. Schwartz and S. Falconer, pp. 64–90. Washington, D.C.: Smithsonian Institution Press.

Kosakowsky, L. J.

1987   *Preclassic Maya Pottery at Cuello, Belize.* Anthropological Papers of the University of Arizona 47, Tucson.

Kosakowsky, L. J., and D. C. Pring

1998   The Ceramics of Cuello, Belize: A New Evaluation. *Ancient Mesoamerica* 9-1:55–66.

Kowalewski, S. A., and S. K. Fish

1990   Conclusions: The Archaeology of Regions. In *The Archaeology of Regions: A Case for Full-Coverage Survey*, edited by S. Fish and S. Kowalewski, pp. 261–77. Washington, D.C.: Smithsonian Institution Press.

Krejci, E., and T. P. Culbert

1995   Preclassic and Early Classic Burials and Caches in the Maya Lowlands. In *The Emergence of Lowland Maya Civilization: The Transition from the Preclassic to the Early Classic*, edited by N. Grube, pp. 103–16. Acta Mesoamericana, vol. 8. Mockmuhl, Germany: Verlag Anton Sauerwein.

Kunen, J. L., T. P. Culbert, V. Fialko, B. R. McKee, and L. Grazioso

n.d.   Bajo Communities: A Case Study from the Central Peten. Copy on file, West Chester University of Pennsylvania.

Landa, Friar Diego de

1978   *Yucatan before and after the Conquest.* William Gates, trans., with notes. New York: Dover Publications.

Laporte, J. P.

1987   El Grupo 6C-XVI, Tikal, Petén: un centro habitacional del Clásico Temprano. In *Memorias del Primer Coloquio Internacional de Mayistas*, pp. 221–44. Mexico City: Centro de Estudios Mayas, Universidad Autonoma de México.

1988   El Complejo Manik: dos depósitos sellados, Grupo 6C-XVI, Tikal. In *Ensayos de alfarería prehispánica e histórica de Mesoamérica, Homenaje a Eduardo Noguera,* edited by M. Serra and C. Navarrete, pp. 97–185. Mexico City: Instituto de Investigaciones Antropológicas, Universidad Autónoma de México.

1989   Alternativas del clasico temprano en la relacion Tikal-Teotihuacan; Grupo 6C-XVI, Tikal, Peten, Guatemala. Ph.D. dissertation, Universidad Nacional Autónoma de Mexico.

1993   Architecture and Social Change in Late Classic Maya Society: The Evidence from Mundo Perdido, Tikal. In *Lowland Maya Civilization in the Eighth Century A.D: A Symposium at Dumbarton Oaks (1989),* edited by J. A. Sabloff and J. S. Henderson, pp. 299–320. Washington, D.C.: Dumbarton Oaks Research Library and Collection.

1995a   *Una actualización a la secuencia cerámica del área de Dolores, Petén.* Atlas Arqueológico de Guatemala 3:35–64. Guatemala City: Instituto de Antropología e Historia and Universidad de San Carlos, Guatemala.

1995b   Preclásico a Clásico en Tikal: proceso de transformación en Mundo Perdido. In *The Emergence of Lowland Maya Civilization: The Transition from the Preclassic to the Early Classic,* edited by N. Grube, pp. 17–33. Acta Mesoamericana, vol. 8. Möckmühl, Germany: Verlag Anton Saurwein.

1996   *Organización territorial y política prehispánica en el sureste de Petén.* Atlas Arqueológico de Guatemala, no. 4. Guatemala City: Instituto de Antropología e Historia.

1997   Exploración y restauración en la Gran Pirámide de Mundo Perdido, Tikal (Estructura 5C-54). In *X Simposio de Investigaciones Arqueológicas en Guatemala (1996),* pp. 325–50. Guatemala City: Museo Nacional de Arqueología y Etnología.

1998   Exploración y restauración en el Templo del Talud-Tablero, Mundo Perdido, Tikal (Estructura 5C-49). In *XI Simposio de Investigaciones Arqueológicas en Guatemala (1997),* pp. 21–42. Guatemala City: Museo Nacional de Arqueología y Etnología.

1999a   Trabajos no divulgados del Proyecto Nacional Tikal, Parte 1: Palacio de los Cinco Pisos, Grupo F, Grupo 6B-II, Plaza de los Siete Templos. In *XII Simposio de Investigaciones Arqueológicas en Guatemala (1998),* pp. 159–68. Guatemala City: Museo Nacional de Arqueología y Etnología.

1999b   Una visión de la interacción Tikal-Teotihuacan durante el Clásico Temprano. Paper presented at the 64th annual Meeting of the Society for American Archaeology, Chicago.

1999c   Contexto y función de los artefactos de hueso en Tikal, Guatemala. *Revista Española de Antropología Americana* 29:31–64.

1999d   Exploración y restauración en el conjunto de palacios de Mundo Perdido, Tikal (Estructuras 5C-45/47). In *XII Simposio de Investigaciones Arqueológicas en Guatemala (1998)*, pp. 195–234. Guatemala City: Museo Nacional de Arqueología y Etnología.

2000a   *Ofrenda cerámica y cambio social en Mundo Perdido, Tikal, Guatemala.* Utz'ib. Guatemala City: Asociación Tikal.

2000b   Exploración y restauración en tres estructuras de rango medio en Mundo Perdido, Tikal (Estructuras 5D-77, 5D-82 y 6D-8). In *XIII Simposio Nacional de Arqueología y Etnología (1999)*, pp. 467–94. Guatemala City: Museo Nacional de Arqueología y Etnología.

n.d.   Excavations at Uaxactun, Guatemala: 1974 and 1984 Seasons. In prep.

Laporte, J. P., and M. T. Alvarado
1999   El periodo Preclásico en el sureste de Petén: asentamiento, arquitectura, cerámica. In *XII Simposio de Investigaciones Arqueológicas en Guatemala (1998)*, pp. 79–98. Guatemala City: Museo Nacional de Arqueología y Etnología.

Laporte, J. P., and V. Fialko
1985   *Reporte Arqueológico (1979–1984): Mundo Perdido y zonas de habitación, Tikal, Petén.* Guatemala City: Ministerios de Educación y Comunicaciones, Transporte y Obras Públicas.

1987   La cerámica del Clásico Temprano desde Mundo Perdido, Tikal: una Reevaluación. In *Maya Ceramics: Papers from the 1985 Maya Ceramic Conference,* edited by P. M. Rice and R. J. Sharer, pp. 123–81. Oxford: BAR International Series 345(1).

1990   New Perspectives on Old Problems: Dynastic References for the Early Classic at Tikal. In *Vision and Revision in Maya Studies,* edited by F. Clancy and P. D. Harrison, pp. 33–66. Albuquerque: University of New Mexico Press.

1993   Análisis cerámico de tres depósitos problemáticos de Fase Eb, Mundo Perdido, Tikal. In *Tikal y Uaxactun en el Preclásico,* edited by J. P. Laporte and J. A. Valdés, pp. 53–69. Mexico City: Universidad Nacional Autónoma de México.

1995   Un reencuentro con Mundo Perdido, Tikal, Guatemala. *Ancient Mesoamerica* 6:41–94.

Laporte, J. P., and O. Gómez
1998   Depósitos de material como actividad ritual en Tikal: nueva evidencia del inicio del Clásico Tardío. Paper presented at the Congreso Internacional de Mayistas, Antigua, Guatemala.

1999   Análisis de materiales cerámicos de depósitos especiales de Tikal. Report to the Asociación Tikal, Guatemala.

2000 Una propuesta para la clasificación tipológica de los materiales cerámicos del Clásico Tardío en Tikal. Paper presented at the *XIVth Simposio de Investigaciones Arqueológicas en Guatemala,* Museo Nacional de Arqueología y Etnología, Guatemala City.

Laporte, J. P., B. Hermes, L. V. de Zea, and M. J. Iglesias
1992 Nuevas entierros y escondites de Tikal, Subfaces Manik 3a y 3b. *Ceramica de Cultura Maya* 16:69–101.

Laporte, J. P., and M. J. Iglesias
1992 Unidades cerámicas de la Fase Manik 3, Tikal, Guatemala. *Ceramica de Cultura Maya* 16:69–101.

2000 Más allá de Mundo Perdido: investigación en grupos residenciales de Tikal. *Mayab* 11. Madrid: Sociedad Española de Estudios Mayas.

n.d. Más allá de Mundo Perdido: investigación en Grupos Residenciales de Tikal. Ms. in review.

Laporte, J. P., and P. I. Morales
1994 Definición territorial en centros Clásicos de Tierras Bajas: una aplicación metodológica a la región de Dolores. In *VII Simposio de AAr Arqueología Guatemalteca (1993),* pp. 247–73. Guatemala City: Museo Nacional de Arqueología y Etnología.

Larios, C. R., and M. Orrego (Crisarq-Consult.)
1997 *Términos de referencia para la conservación de Tikal.* Proyecto de Conservación Tikal Etapa 1. Guatemala City: Ministerio de Cultura y Deportes, Instituto de Antropología e Historia, Parque Nacional Tikal.

LeCount, L. J.
1996 Pottery and Power: Feasting, Gifting and Displaying Wealth among the Late and Terminal Classic Lowland Maya. Ph.D. dissertation, Department of Anthropology, University of California, Los Angeles.

Lehner, M.
1997 *The Complete Pyramids: Solving the Ancient Mysteries.* London: Thames and Hudson.

Lewis, R. B., and C. Stout
1998 *Mississippian Towns and Sacred Places: Searching for an Architectural Grammar.* Tuscaloosa and London: University of Alabama Press.

Linné, S.
1934 *Archaeological Researches at Teotihuacan, Mexico,* no. 5, pub. 1. Stockholm: Ethnographic Museum of Sweden.

Lischka, J. J.
1968   An Investigation of Cultural Variability between Tepeu 2 Platform Mounds at Tikal. Paper presented at the Annual Meeting of the Society for American Archaeology, Santa Fe.

1970   The Use of Ceramics in Discovering Prehistoric Cultural Patterns of the Late Classic Lowland Maya at Tikal. Unpublished ms.

Longyear, J. M.
1952   *Copan Ceramics: A Study of Southeastern Maya Pottery.* Carnegie Institution of Washington Publication 597. Washington, D.C.

Looper, M. G., and L. Schele
1994   *The Founder of Quirigua, Tutum Yol K'inich.* Copan Note 119. Copán Acropolis Archaeological Project and the Instituto Hondureño de Antropología e Historia, Austin, Texas.

López Olivares, N. M.
1997   Proyecto Arqueológico Lacandon. In *X Simposio de Investigaciones Arqueológicas en Guatemala (1996)*, pp. 557–62. Guatemala City: Museo Nacional de Arqueología y Etnología.

Lou, B.
1996   Exploraciones arqueológicas en los espacios intersitios entre Yaxha y Nakum. In *IX Simposio de Investigaciones Arqueológicas en Guatemala (1995)*, pp. 37–50. Guatemala City: Museo Nacional de Arqueología y Etnología.

1997   Chalpate, análisis del asentamiento y orientación de un centro satélite de Tikal. In *X Simposio de Investigaciones Arqueológicas en Guatemala (1996)*, pp. 373–80. Guatemala City: Museo Nacional de Arqueología y Etnología.

Lowe, G., and P. Agrinier, eds.
1960   *Excavations at Chiapa de Corzo, Chiapas, Mexico.* New World Archaeological Foundation, Papers 8–11. Provo, Utah: Brigham Young University.

Lundell, C. L.
1933   Archaeological Discoveries in the Maya Area. *Proceedings of the American Philosophical Society* 72(3):147–79.

Lynott, M. J.
1995   Ethical Principles and Archaeological Practice: Development of an Ethics Policy. *American Antiquity* 62:589–99.

Lynott, M. J., and A. Wylie
1995   Stewardship: The Central Principal of Archaeological Ethics. In *Ethics in American Archaeology: Challenges for the 1990s*, edited by M. J. Lynott and A. Wylie, pp. 28–32. Special Report, Society for American Archaeology. Washington, D.C.: Society for American Archaeology.

MacKinnon, J. J.

1981   The Nature of Residential Tikal: A Spatial Analysis. *Estudios de Cultura Maya* 13:223–49.

MacLeod, B.

1990   The God N/Step Set in the Primary Standard Sequence. In *The Maya Vase Book*, vol. 2, *A Corpus of Roll-Out Photographs*, edited by B. Kerr and J. Kerr, pp. 331–47. New York: Kerr Associates.

1991   T135 (The G9 Superfix) and T108 (The "Guardian" Superfix). North Austin Hieroglyphic Hunches no. 6. Unpublished ms.

Maler, T.

1911   *Explorations in the Department of Peten, Guatemala, Tikal.* Memoirs of the Peabody Museum of Archaeology and Ethnology, vol. 5, no. 1. Cambridge, Mass.: Peabody Museum of Archaeology and Ethnology, Harvard University.

Manzanilla, L., and L. Barba

1990   The Study of Activities in Classic Households: Two Case Studies from Cobá and Teotihuacan. *Ancient Mesoamerica* 1:41–49.

Marcus, J.

1976   *Emblem and State in the Classic Maya Lowlands.* Washington, D.C.: Dumbarton Oaks Research Library and Collection.

1983   Lowland Maya Archaeology at the Crossroads. *American Antiquity* 48:454–88.

1989   Zapotec Chiefdoms and the Nature of Formative Religions. In *Regional Perspectives on the Olmec*, edited by R. J. Sharer and D. C. Grove, pp.148–97. Cambridge: Cambridge University Press.

1992a   Political Fluctuations in Mesoamerica. *National Geographic Research and Exploration* 8:392–411.

1992b   *Mesoamerican Writing Systems: Propaganda, Myth, and History in Four Ancient Civilizations.* Princeton: Princeton University Press.

1995   Where Is Lowland Maya Archaeology Headed? *Journal of Archaeological Research* 3:3–53.

2003   Commentary on Teotihuacan and the Maya: Reinterpreting Early Classic Interaction. In *Teotihuacan and the Maya: Reinterpreting Early Classic Interaction*, edited by G. Braswell. Austin: University of Texas Press.

Marcus, J., K. V. Flannery, and R. Spores

1983   The Cultural Legacy of the Oaxacan Preceramic. In *The Cloud People: Evolution of the Zapotec and Mixtec Civilizations of Oaxaca, Mexico*, edited by K. Flannery and J. Marcus, pp. 36–39. Albuquerque: University of New Mexico Press.

Martin, P. S.

1971   The Revolution in Archaeology. *American Antiquity* 36(1):1–8.

Martin, S.

1994   Warfare and Political Organization in the Late Classic Central Southern Highlands. Paper presented at the 10th Texas Symposium on Ancient Maya Writing and Culture, University of Texas at Austin.

1995   New Epigraphic Data on Classic Maya Warfare. Paper presented at the Primera Mesa Redonda de Palenque, Nueva Epoca, Palenque, Chiapas, Mexico.

1996a   Calakmul en el Registro Epigráfico. In *Proyecto Arqueológico de la Biosfera de Calakmul: Temporada 1993–94*, edited by R. Carrasco V. et al. Centro Regional de Yucatán, unpublished report to INAH.

1996b   Tikal's "Star War" against Naranjo. In *Eighth Palenque Round Table, June 1993*, edited by M. Macri and M. Greene Robertson, pp. 223–36. San Francisco: Pre-Columbian Art Research Institute.

1997   The Painted King List: A Commentary on Codex-Style Dynastic Vases. In *The Maya Vase Book*, vol. 5, *A Corpus of Roll-Out Photographs*, edited by B. Kerr and J. Kerr, pp. 846–63. New York: Kerr Associates.

1998a   Middle Classic Tikal: Kings, Queens and Consorts. Paper presented at "Lindafest," a symposium in honor of Linda Schele at the University of Texas at Austin.

1998b   Investigación Epigráfica de Campo: 1995–1998. In *Proyecto arqueológico de la biosfera de Calakmul: Temporada 1995–98*, edited by R. Carrasco V. et al. Centro Regional de Yucatán, unpublished report to INAH.

1998c   At the Periphery: Early Monuments in the Environs of Tikal. Paper presented at the 3rd European Maya Conference, University of Hamburg.

2000a   At the Periphery: The Movement, Modification and Re-Use of Early Monuments in the Environs of Tikal. In *The Sacred and the Profane: Architecture and Identity in the Southern Maya Lowlands*, edited by P. R. Colas, K. Delvendahl, M. Kuhnert, and A. Pieler, pp. 51–62. Acta Mesoamericana 10. Hamburg, Germany: Markt Schwaben.

2000b   Nuevos datos epigráficos sobre la guerra Maya del Clásico. In *La guerra entre los antiguos Mayas, memoria de la Primera Mesa Redondo de Palenque 1995*, edited by Silvia Trejo, pp. 105–24. Mexico City: Instituto Nacional de Antropología e Historia.

2000c   Court and Realm: Architectural Signatures in the Classic Maya Southern Lowlands. In *Royal Courts of the Ancient Maya*, vol. 1, edited by T. Inomata and S. D. Houston, pp. 168–94. Boulder: Westview Press.

2000d   Los señores de Calakmul. *Arqueología Mexicana* 7(42):40–45.

2001a   The Power in the West—The Maya and Teotihuacan. In *Maya: Divine Kings of the Rainforest*, edited by N. Grube, pp. 98–111. Hamburg, Germany: Könemann.

2001b   Unmasking "Double Bird," Ruler of Tikal. *PARI Journal* 2(1):7–12. San Francisco: Pre-Columbian Art Research Institute.

2002   Baby Jaguar: An Exploration of Its Identity and Origins in Maya Art and Writing. In *La organización social entre los Mayas, memoria de la Tercera Mesa Redonda de Palenque*, vol. 1, coord. by Vera Tiesler Blos, Rafael Cobos, and Merle Greene Robertson. Mexico City and Merida: Instituto Nacional de Antropología y Historia and Universidad Autónoma de Yucatán.

n.d.   Thematic Issues in the Epigraphy of Tikal. Changing Perspectives on Tikal and the Development of Ancient Maya Civilization. Paper presented at School of American Research Advanced Seminar, Santa Fe.

Martin, S., and N. Grube
1994   Evidence for Macro-Political Organization amongst Classic Maya Lowland States. Preliminary version, London and Bonn.

1995   Maya Superstates. *Archaeology* 48(6):41–46.

2000   *Chronicle of the Maya Kings and Queens: Deciphering the Dynasties of the Ancient Maya*. London and New York: Thames and Hudson.

Mata Amado, G.
1999   Monumento de piedra en silueta del área de Amatitlán. *Utz'ib* 2–6:24–26. Guatemala: Asociación Tikal.

Mathews, P.
1975   The Lintels of Structure 12, Yaxchilan, Chiapas. Paper presented at the Annual Conference of the Northeastern Anthropological Association, Wesleyan University.

1985   Maya Early Classic Monuments and Inscriptions. In *A Consideration of the Early Classic Period in the Maya Lowlands*, edited by G. R. Willey and P. Mathews, pp. 5–55. Institute for Mesoamerican Studies Publication 10. Albany: State University of New York at Albany.

Maudslay, A. P.
1889–   *Biologia Centrali-Americana: Archaeology*. 5 vols. London: R. H. Porter,
1902   Dulau and Co.

Mayer, K. H.
1978   *Maya Monuments: Sculptures of Unknown Provenance in Europe*. Ramona, Calif.: Acoma Books.

May Hau, J., R. C. Muñoz, R. González, and W. J. Folan
1990   *El Mapa de Calakmul*. Campeche, Mexico: Universidad Autonoma de Campeche.

McAnany, P.

1993   The Economics of Social Power and Wealth among Eighth-Century Maya Households. In *Lowland Maya Civilization in the Eighth Century A.D.: A Symposium at Dumbarton Oaks (1989)*, edited by J. A. Sabloff and J. S. Henderson, pp. 65–89. Washington, D.C.: Dumbarton Oaks Research Library and Collection.

Michelon, O., ed.

1976   *Diccionario de San Francisco.* Bibliotheca Linguistica Americana, vol. 2. Graz, Austria: Akademische Druck-u. Verlagsanstalt.

Miller, A. G., ed.

1983   *Highland-Lowland Interaction in Mesoamerica: Interdisciplinary Approaches.* Washington, D.C.: Dumbarton Oaks.

1986   *Maya Rulers of Time.* Philadelphia: University Museum Publications, University of Pennsylvania.

Miller, J.

1974   Notes on a Stela Pair Probably from Calakmul, Campeche, Mexico. In *Primera Mesa Redonda de Palenque, Part I*, edited by M. Greene Robertson, pp. 149–62. Pebble Beach, Calif.: Robert Louis Stevenson School.

Millon, C.

1973   Painting, Writing and Polity in Teotihuacan, Mexico. *American Antiquity* 38:294–314.

Millon, R.

1981   Teotihuacan: City, State, and Civilization. *Supplement to the Handbook of Middle American Indians. Archaeology*, vol. 1, edited by J. A. Sabloff, pp. 198–243. Austin: University of Texas Press.

1988   The Last Years of Teotihuacan Dominance. In *The Collapse of Ancient States and Civilizations*, edited by N. Yoffee and G. Cowgill, pp. 102–64. Tucson: University of Arizona Press.

Moholy-Nagy, H.

1963   Shells and Other Marine Material from Tikal. *Estudios de Cultura Maya* 3:65–84.

1976   Spatial Distribution of Flint and Obsidian Artifacts at Tikal, Guatemala. In *Maya Lithic Studies*, edited by T. R. Hester and N. Hammond, pp. 91–118. Center for Archaeological Research, Special Report no. 4. San Antonio: University of Texas, San Antonio.

1978   The Utilization of Pomacea Snail at Tikal, Guatemala. *American Antiquity* 43:65–73.

1985   Social and Ceremonial Uses of Marine Molluscs at Tikal. In *Prehistoric*

Lowland Maya Environment and Subsistence Economy, edited by M. Pohl, pp. 147–58. Papers of the Peabody Museum of Archaeology and Ethnology, vol. 77. Cambridge, Mass.: Peabody Museum of Archaeology and Ethnology, Harvard University.

1991   The Flaked Chert Industry of Tikal, Guatemala. In *Maya Stone Tools: Selected Papers from the Second Maya Lithic Conference*, edited by T. R. Hester and H. S. Shafer, pp. 189–202. Madison, Wis.: Prehistory Press.

1994   Tikal Material Culture: Artifacts and Social Structure at a Classic Lowland Maya City. Ph.D. dissertation, Department of Anthropology, University of Michigan.

1995   Shells and Society at Tikal, Guatemala. *Expedition* 37:3–13. Philadephia: University Museum Publications, University of Pennsylvania.

1997   Middens, Construction Fill and Offerings: Evidence for the Organization of Classic Period Craft Production at Tikal, Guatemala. *Journal of Field Archaeology* 24:293–313.

1998   A Preliminary Report on the Use of Vertebrate Animals at Tikal, Guatemala. In *Anatomía de una civilización: aproximaciones interdisciplinarias a la cultura Maya*, edited by A. Ciudad et al., pp. 115–30. Madrid: Sociedad Española de Estudios Mayas.

1999   Mexican Obsidian at Tikal, Guatemala. *Latin American Antiquity* 10(3):300–13.

Moholy-Nagy, H., F. Asaro, and F. H. Stross
1984   Tikal Obsidian: Sources and Typology. *American Antiquity* 49:104–17.

Moholy-Nagy, H., and J. Palka
1999   The Discovery of 19th Century Maya Habitation at the Ruins of Tikal, Guatemala. Paper presented at Midwest Mesoamericanist Meeting, Chicago.

Moore, J. D.
1996   The Archaeology of Plazas and the Proxemics of Ritual: Three Andean Traditions. *American Anthropologist* 98:789–802.

Morley, S. G.
1935   *Guide Book to the Ruins of Quirigua.* Carnegie Institution of Washington Supplemental Publication 16. Washington, D.C.

1937–38 *Inscriptions of the Peten.* Carnegie Institution of Washington Publication 437. 5 vols. Washington, D.C.

Mumford, L.
1961   *The City in History: Its Origins, Its Transformations, and Its Prospects.* New York: Harcourt, Brace, and World.

Muñoz, G., and O. Quintana

1996 Intervenciones de restauración en el Templo I de Tikal, 1992–1994. In *IX Simposio de Investigaciones Arqueológicas en Guatemala (1995)*, pp. 335–42. Guatemala City: Museo Nacional de Arqueología y Etnología.

Murray, P., and L. Murray

1959 *A Dictionary of Art and Artists*. Harmondsworth: Penguin Books.

Olson, G. W., and D. E. Puleston

1972 Soils and the Maya. *Americas* 24:33–39.

Orrego, M., and C. R. Larios

1983 *Tikal, Petén: reporte de las investigaciones arqueológicas en el Grupo 5E–11.* Parque Nacional Tikal, Instituto de Antropología e Historia, Guatemala.

Palka, J. W.

1997a Desarrollo, interacción y cambios en las comunidades y los sistemas agrícolas de los Lacandones del siglo XIX. In *X Simposio de Investigaciones Arqueológicas en Guatemala (1996)*, pp. 563–72. Guatemala City: Museo Nacional de Arqueología y Etnología.

1997b Reconstructing Classic Maya Socioeconomic Differentiation and the Collapse at Dos Pilas, Peten, Guatemala. *Ancient Mesoamerica* 8:293–306.

Parsons, L.

1969 *Bilbao, Guatemala: An Archaeological Study of the Pacific Coast Cotzumalhuapa Region*. Publications in Anthropology no. 11–12. Milwaukee: Milwaukee Public Museum.

Pasztory, E.

1978 Artistic Traditions of the Middle Classic Period. In *Middle Classic Mesoamerica: A.D. 400–700*, edited by E. Pasztory, pp. 108–42. New York: Columbia University Press.

Pendergast, D. M.

1991 And the Loot Goes On: Winning Some Battles, but Not the War. *Journal of Field Archaeology* 18:89–95.

Pijoan, C. M., and M. E. Salas

1984a Costumbres funerarias en Mundo Perdido, Tikal. In *Estudios de Antropología Biológica, II Coloquio de Antropología Física Juan Comas*, edited by R. Ramos and R. Ramos, pp. 237–52. Mexico City: Instituto de Investigaciones Antropológicas, Universidad Autónoma de México.

1984b Dientes esgrafiados en Mundo Perdido, Tikal, Guatemala. Report to the Proyecto Nacional Tikal, Guatemala, and to Departamento de Antropología Física, Instituto Nacional de Antropología e Historia, México.

Plunket, P., and G. Uruñuela

1998   Preclassic Household Patterns Preserved under Volcanic Ash at Tetimpa, Puebla, Mexico. *Latin American Antiquity* 9:287–309.

Pollock, H. E. D.

1965   Architecture of the Maya Lowlands. In *Handbook of Middle American Indians,* vol. 2, edited by R. Wauchope, pp. 378–440. Austin: University of Texas Press.

Ponciano Ortiz, C., and M. Del C. Rodriguez

1998   Olmec Ritual Behaviour at El Manati: A Sacred Space. In *Social Patterns in Pre-Classic Mesoamerica,* edited by D. C. Grove and R. A. Joyce, pp. 225–54. Washington, D.C.: Dumbarton Oaks.

Porter, J. B.

1992   "Estelas celtiformes": un nuevo tipo de esculptura olmeca y sus implicaciones para los epigrafistas. *Arqueología* 8:3–14.

Potter, D., and E. King

1995   A Heterarchical Approach to Lowland Maya Socioeconomics. In *Heterarchy and the Analysis of Complex Societies,* edited by R. M. Ehrenreich, C. L. Crumley, and J. E. Levy, pp. 17–32. Archaeological Papers, no. 6. Arlington, Va.: American Anthropological Association.

Proskouriakoff, T.

1950   *A Study of Classic Maya Sculpture.* Carnegie Institution of Washington Publication 593. Washington, D.C.

1993   *Maya History.* Edited by R. A. Joyce. Austin: University of Texas Press.

Puleston, D. E.

1968   Brosimium alicastrum as a Subsistence Alternative for Classic Maya of the Central Southern Lowlands. M.A. thesis, Department of Anthropology, University of Pennsylvania.

1973   Ancient Maya Settlement Patterns and Environment at Tikal, Guatemala: Implications for Subsistence Models. Ph.D. dissertation, Department of Anthropology, University of Pennsylvania. University Microfilms, Ann Arbor.

1977   The Discovery of Talud-Tablero Architecture at Tikal. In *Los Procesos de Cambio, XV Mesa Redonda.* Sociedad Mexicana de Antropología 2:377–84.

1979   An Epistemological Pathology and the Collapse, or Why the Maya Kept the Short Count. In *Maya Archaeology and Ethnohistory,* edited by N. Hammond and G. R. Willey, pp. 63–71. Austin: University of Texas Press.

1983   *The Settlement Survey of Tikal.* Tikal Reports no. 13, University Museum Publications, University of Pennsylvania.

Puleston, D. E., and D. W. Callender, Jr.

1967   Defensive Earthworks at Tikal. *Expedition* 9(3):40–48.

Puleston, O. S.

1969   Functional Analysis of a Workshop Tool Kit from Tikal. M.A. thesis, Department of Anthropology, University of Pennsylvania.

Pyburn, K. A.

1989   Prehistoric Maya Community and Settlement at Holmul, Belize. BAR International Series 509, Oxford.

1997   The Archaeological Signature of Complexity in the Maya Lowlands. In *The Archaeology of City States*, edited by D. L. Nichols and T. H. Charleton, pp. 155–68. Washington, D.C.: Smithsonian Institution Press.

Quintana, O., and R. Noriega

1992   Intervenciones en el Templo V de Tikal, Petén, Guatemala. *Cuadernos de Arquitectura Mesoamericana* (México) 20:52–76.

Rands, R. L.

1967   Ceramic Technology and Trade in the Palenque Region, Mexico. In *American Historical Anthropology*, edited by C. L. Riley and W. W. Taylor, pp. 137–51. Carbondale: Southern Illinois University Press.

Rathje, W. L., D. A. Gregory, and F. Wiseman

1978   Trade Models and Archaeological Problems: Classic Maya Examples. In *Mesoamerican Communication Routes and Cultural Contacts*, edited by T. Lee and C. Navarrete, pp. 147–75. Provo, Utah: Papers of the New World Archaeological Foundation.

Rattray, E. C.

1987   Introducción. In *Teotihuacan: nuevos datos, nuevas síntesis, nuevos problemas*, edited by E. McClung de Tapia and E. C. Rattray, pp. 9–56. Mexico City: México Instituto de Investigaciones Antropológicas, Universidad Autónoma de México.

Reents-Budet, D., E. E. Bell, and R. Bishop

n.d.   Early Classic Ceramic Offerings at Copán: A Comparison of the Hunal and Margarita Tombs. In *Understanding Early Classic Copan*, edited by E. E. Bell, M. Canuto, and R. J. Sharer. Philadelphia: University Museum Publications, University of Pennsylvania. In press.

Reents-Budet, D., and T. P. Culbert

n.d.   Early Classic Funerary Offerings from Tikal and Kaminaljuyu: Regional and International Relationships. Unpublished ms.

Reents-Budet, D., and V. Fields

1988   Incised Classic Maya Jades and Slate Disks from Costa Rica. Unpublished ms.

Renfrew, C.
1977   Alternative Models for Exchange and Spatial Distribution. In *Exchange Systems in Prehistory*, edited by T. K. Earle and J. E. Ericson, pp. 71–90. New York: Academic Press.

Renfrew, C., and J. F. Cherry, eds.
1986   *Peer Polity Interaction and Socio-Political Change*. Cambridge: Cambridge University Press.

Rice, D. S.
1988   Classic to Postclassic Maya Household Transitions in the Central Petén, Guatemala. In *Household and Community in the Mesoamerican Past*, edited by R. R. Wilk and W. Ashmore, pp. 227–48. Albuquerque: University of New Mexico Press.

Rice, D. S., and D. E. Puleston
1981   Ancient Maya Settlement Patterns in the Petén, Guatemala. In *Lowland Maya Settlement Patterns*, edited by W. Ashmore, pp. 121–56. Albuquerque: University of New Mexico Press.

Rice, D. S., P. M. Rice, and T. Pugh
1998   Settlement Continuity and Change in the Central Petén Lakes Region: The Case of Zacpeten. In *Anatomía de una civilización*, edited by A. Ciudad et al., pp. 207–52. Madrid: Sociedad Española de Estudios Mayas.

Rice, P. M.
1979a   Ceramic and Nonceramic Artifacts of Lakes Yaxha-Sacnab, El Petén, Guatemala. Part I, The Ceramics. Section A, Introduction and the Middle Preclassic Ceramics of Yaxha-Sacnab, Guatemala. *Ceramica de Cultura Maya* 10:1–36.

1979b   Ceramic and Non-Ceramic Artifacts of Lakes Yaxha-Sacnab, El Petén, Guatemala. Part I, The Ceramics. Section B, Postclassic Pottery. *Ceramica de Cultura Maya* 11:1–85.

Ricketson, O. G., Jr., and E. B. Ricketson
1937   *Uaxactun, Guatemala. Group E 1926–31*. Carnegie Institution of Washington Publication 477. Washington, D.C.

Riese, B.
1984   Hel Hieroglyphs. In *Phoneticism in Mayan Hieroglyphic Writing*, edited by J. S. Justeson and L. Campbell, pp. 263–86. Institute for Mesoamerican Studies Publication 9. Albany: State University of New York at Albany.

Ringle, W. M.
1993   Preclassic Cityscapes: Ritual Politics among the Early Lowland Maya. Paper presented at the Dumbarton Oaks Symposium on Ritual Behavior, Social Identity, and Cosmology in Pre-Classic Mesoamerica, Washington, D.C.

1999   Pre-Classic Cityscapes: Ritual Politics among the Early Lowland Maya. In
            Social Patterns in Pre-Classic Mesoamerica, edited by D. C. Grove and
            R. A. Joyce, pp. 183–223. Washington: Dumbarton Oaks.

Rivera Grijalba, V.
1984   Tepepulco. *Cuadernos de Arquitectura Mesoamericana* (México) 2:41–46.

Robiscek, F., and D. M. Hales
1981   *The Maya Book of the Dead, The Ceramic Codex: The Corpus of Codex-Style
            Ceramics of the Late Classic Period.* Charlottesville: University of Virginia Art
            Museum.

Ruiz, M. E.
1987   Análisis preliminar de la lítica de Mundo Perdido, Tikal. In *Memorias del
            Primer Coloquio Internacional de Mayistas*, pp. 331–60. Mexico City: Centro
            de Estudios Mayas, Universidad Autónoma de México.

1989   Instrumentos líticos procedentes de un basurero, Tikal, Petén. In *Memorias
            del II Coloquio Internacional de Mayistas 1*, pp. 569–602. Mexico City: Centro
            de Estudios Mayas, Universidad Autónoma de México.

1990   Comparación de instrumentos líticos en diferentes áreas de actividad:
            Mundo Perdido, Tikal. In *Etnoarqueología: Primer Coloquio Bosch-Gimpera*,
            edited by Y. Sugiura and M. Serra, pp. 527–54. Mexico City: Instituto de
            Investigaciones Antropológicas, Universidad Autónoma de México.

Ruppert, K.
1940   Special Assemblage of Maya Structures. In *The Maya and Their Neighbors*,
            edited by C. Hay et al., pp. 222–31. New York: Appleton Century Crofts.

Ruppert, K., and J. H. Denison, Jr.
1943   *Archaeological Reconnaissence in Campeche, Quintana Roo and Petén.* Carnegie
            Institution of Washington Publication 543. Washington, D.C.

Sabloff, J. A.
1975   *Excavations at Seibal, Department of the Petén, Guatemala: The Ceramics.*
            Memoirs of the Peabody Museum of Archaeology and Ethnology, vol. 13,
            no. 2. Cambridge, Mass.: Peabody Museum of Archaeology and Ethnology,
            Harvard University.

1990   *The New Archaeology and the Ancient Maya.* New York: W. H. Freeman.

Sabloff, J. A., and G. Tourtellot
1991   *The Ancient Maya City of Sayil: The Mapping of a Puuc Region Center.* Middle
            American Research Institute Publication 60. New Orleans: Tulane University.

Sagebiel, K.
2000   Análisis espacial y funcional de cerámicas en contextos funerarios del
            Clásico Temprano Maya. In *XIV Simposio de Investigaciones Arqueológicas en
            Guatemala*, pp. 277–90. Guatemala City: Instituto Nacional de
            Antropología e Historia.

Salas, M. E., and C. M. Pijoan

1982   Informe sobre los restos óseos de Mundo Perdido, Tikal. Report to the
         Proyecto Nacional Tikal, Guatemala, and Departamento de Antropología
         Física, Instituto Nacional de Antropología e Historia, México.

Sanders, W. T., J. R. Parsons, and R. S. Santley

1979   *The Basin of Mexico: Ecological Processes in the Evolution of a Civilization.* New
         York: Academic Press.

Sanders, W. T., and B. J. Price

1968   *Mesoamerica: The Evolution of a Civilization.* New York: Random House.

Sanz, L. T.

1997   Espacios rituales, imágenes sagradas: estudios sobre la escultura arquitec-
         tónica de Tikal, Guatemala (100 AC–500 DC). Ph.D. dissertation,
         Department of Anthropology, Universidad Complutense, Madrid.

Satterthwaite, L.

1958   *The Problem of Abnormal Stela Placements at Tikal and Elsewhere.* Museum
         Monographs, Tikal Reports no. 3. Philadelphia: University Museum
         Publications, University of Pennsylvania.

Scarborough, V. L.

1991   Courting in the Southern Maya Lowlands: A Study in Pre-Hispanic
         Ballgame Architecture. In *The Mesoamerican Ballgame,* edited by
         V. L. Scarborough and D. Wilcox, pp. 129–44. Tucson: University of
         Arizona Press.

Scarborough, V. L., and D. R. Wilcox, eds.

1991   *The Mesoamerican Ballgame.* Tucson: University of Arizona Press.

Schele, L.

1986   The Founders of Lineages at Copan and other Maya Sites. Copán Note 8.
         Unpublished ms.

1987   *Stela I and the Founding of the City of Copan.* Copán Note 30. Copán Mosaics
         Project and the Instituto Hondureño de Antropología e Historia, Austin,
         Texas.

1989   *A Brief Commentary on the Top of Altar Q.* Copán Note 66. Copán Mosaics
         Project and the Instituto Hondureño de Antropología e Historia, Austin,
         Texas.

1990   *Early Quirigua and the Kings of Copan.* Copan Note 75. Copan Mosaics
         Project and the Instituto Hondureño de Antropología e Historia, Austin,
         Texas.

1992   The Founders of Lineages at Copan and other Maya Sites. *Ancient
         Mesoamerica* 3(1):135–44.

1994a   Some Thoughts on the Inscriptions of House C. In *Seventh Palenque Round Table*, 1989, vol. 9, edited by M. Greene Robertson and V. M. Fields, pp. 1–10. San Francisco: Pre-Columbian Art Research Institute.

1994b   The Iconography of Maya Architectural Facades. In *Function and Meaning in Classic Maya Architecture*, edited by S. D. Houston, pp. 479–517. Washington, D.C.: Dumbarton Oaks.

Schele, L., F. Fahsen, and N. Grube

1992   *The Floor Marker from Motmot*. Copán Note 117. Copán Acropolis Archaeological Project and the Instituto Hondureño de Antropología e Historia, Austin, Texas.

Schele, L., and D. Freidel

1990   *A Forest of Kings*. New York: William Morrow.

Schele, L., and N. Grube

1992   *The Founding Events at Copan*. Copán Note 107. Copán Acropolis Archaeological Project and the Instituto Hondureño de Antropología e Historia, Austin, Texas.

1994a   Some Revisions to Tikal's Dynasty of Kings. Texas Notes on Pre-Columbian Art, Writing, and Culture 67. University of Texas at Austin. Unpublished ms.

1994b   Notebook for the XVIIIth Maya Hieroglyphic Workshop at Texas, March 12–13, 1994, edited by T. Albright. Austin: University of Texas at Austin.

Schele, L., N. Grube, and F. Fahsen

1993   *The Tikal-Copan Connection: The Copan Evidence*. Copán Note 122. Copán Acropolis Archaeological Prohject and the Instituto Hondureño de Antropología e Historia, Austin, Texas.

1994   *The Xukpi Stone: A Newly Discovered Early Classic Inscription from the Copan Acropolis. Part II, Commentary of the Text*. Copán Note 114. Copán Acropolis Archaeological Project and the Instituto Hondureño de Antropología e Historia, Austin, Texas.

Schele, L., and P. Mathews

1979   *The Bodega of Palenque*. Washington, D.C.: Dumbarton Oaks Research Library and Collection.

1998   *The Code of Kings: The Language of Seven Sacred Maya Temples and Tombs*. New York: Simon and Shuster.

Schele, L., and M. E. Miller

1986   *Blood of Kings*. Fort Worth, Tex.: Kimbell Art Museum.

Schortman, E. M.

1993   *Archaeological Investigations in the Lower Motagua Valley, Izabal, Guatemala*. University Museum Monograph 80. Philadelphia: University Museum Publications, University of Pennsylvania.

Schwalbe, L. A., and T. P. Culbert

1988   Analytical Measures of Variability and Group Differences in X-Ray
Fluorescence Data. *Journal of Archaeological Science* 15: 669–81.

Sedat, D. W.

1996   Etapas tempranas en la evolución de la Acrópolis de Copán. *Yaxkin*
14:19–27.

1997a   *The Founding Stage of the Copan Acropolis.* ECAP Papers no. 2. Instituto
Hondureño de Antropología e Historia and the Early Copan Acropolis
Program, Philadelphia.

1997b   *The Earliest Ancestor to Copan Str. 10L-16.* ECAP Papers no. 3. Instituto
Hondureño de Antropología e Historia and the Early Copan Acropolis
Program, Philadelphia.

1997c   *Vessel 1 from the Margarita Tomb.* ECAP Papers no. 7. Instituto Hondureño
de Antropología e Historia and the Early Copan Acropolis Program,
Philadelphia.

Sedat, D. W., and F. Lopez

n.d.   The Initial Stages in the Formation of the Copan Acropolis. In
Understanding Early Classic Copan, edited by E. E. Bell, M. Canuto, and
R. J. Sharer. Philadelphia: University Museum Publications, University of
Pennsylvania. In press.

Sedat, D. W., and R. J. Sharer

1994   *The Xukpi Stone: A Newly Discovered Early Classic Inscription from the Copan
Acropolis. Part I, The Archaeology.* Copan Note 113. Copan Acropolis
Archaeological Project and Instituto Hondureño de Antropología e
Historia, Austin, Texas.

1996   Evolución de la Acrópolis de Copán durante el Clásico Temprano. Paper
presented at the 6th Encuentro de los Investigadores de la Cultura Maya,
Universidad Autonoma de Campeche, México.

Sempowski, M. L.

1987   Differential Mortuary Treatment: Its Implications for Social Status at
Three Residential Compounds in Teotihuacan, Mexico. In *Teotihuacan:
nuevos datos, nuevas síntesis, nuevos problemas,* edited by E. McClung de
Tapia and E. C. Rattray, pp.115–32. Mexico City: Instituto de
Investigaciones Antropológicas, Universidad Autónoma de México.

Shafer, H. J., and T. R. Hester

1983   Ancient Maya Chert Workshops in Northern Belize. *American Antiquity*
48:519–48.

Sharer, R. J., ed.

1978   *The Prehistory of Chalchuapa, El Salvador.* 3 vols. University Museum
Monograph 36. Philadelphia: University Museum Publications, University
of Pennsylvania.

1988   Quirigua as a Classic Maya Center. In *The Southeast Maya Zone*, edited by
            E. H. Boone and G. R. Willey, pp. 31–65. Washington, D.C.: Dumbarton
            Oaks.

1996   Los patrones del desarrollo arquitectónico en la Acrópolis de Copán del
            Clásico Temprano. *Yaxkin* 14:28–34.

1997a   *Formation of Sacred Space by the First Kings of Copan*. ECAP Papers, no. 10.
            Instituto Hondureño de Antropología e Historia and the Early Copan
            Acropolis Program, Philadelphia.

1997b   *Initial Research and Preliminary Findings from the Hunal Tomb*. ECAP Papers,
            no. 5. Instituto Hondureño de Antropología e Historia and the Early
            Copan Acropolis Program, Philadelphia.

1997c   K'inich Yax K'uk' Mo' and the Genesis of the Copan Acropolis. Paper pre-
            sented at the symposium, "A Tale of Two Cities: Copan and Teotihuacan,"
            Harvard University, Cambridge, Mass.

2003   Founding Events and External Interaction at Copan, Honduras. In
            Teotihuacan and the Maya: Reinterpreting Early Classic Interaction, edited by
            G. Braswell. Austin: University of Texas Press.

Sharer, R. J., W. L. Fash, D. W. Sedat, L. P. Traxler, and R. V. Williamson
1999   Continuities and Contrasts in Early Classic Architecture of Central Copan.
            In *Mesoamerican Architecture as a Cultural Symbol*, edited by J. K. Kowlaski,
            pp. 220–49. New York: Oxford University Press.

Sharer, R. J., J. M. Miller, and L. P. Traxler
1992   Evolution of Classic Period Architecture in the Eastern Acropolis, Copan,
            Honduras. *Ancient Mesoamerica* 3:145–59.

Sharer, R. J., and D. W. Sedat
1987   *Archaeological Investigations in the Northern Maya Highlands: Interaction and
            the Development of Maya Civilization*. University Museum Monograph 59.
            Philadelphia: University Museum Publications, University of Pennsylvania.

Sharer, R. J., L. P. Traxler, D. Sedat, E. E. Bell, M. A. Canuto, and C. Powell
1999   Early Classic Architecture beneath the Copan Acropolis: A Research
            Update. *Ancient Mesoamerica* 10(1):3–23.

Shaw, L. C., E. M. King, and B. K. Moses
1999   Constructed Landscape as Ideology: Archaeology and Mapping at Ma'ax
            Na in the Three Rivers Region of Belize. Paper presented at the 65th
            Annual Meeting of the Society for American Archaeology.

Shook, E. M.
1957   *The Tikal Project*. University Museum Bulletin 21(3). Philadelphia:
            University Museum Publications, University of Pennsylvania.

1967   Descubrimiento, exploración, e investigación de Tikal, Guatemala. *Revista
            de Antropología e Historia de Guatemala* 19(2):3–7.

Shook, E. M., and William R. Coe

1961   *Tikal: Numeration, Terminology, and Objectives.* In Tikal Reports no. 5–10.
        Philadelphia: University Museum Publications, University of Pennsylvania.

Siemens, A. H., and D. E. Puleston

1972   Ridged Fields and Associated Features in Southern Campeche: New
        Perspectives on the Lowland Maya. *American Antiquity* 37:228–39.

Smith, A. L.

1950   *Uaxactun, Guatemala: Excavations of 1931–1937.* Carnegie Institution of
        Washington Publication 594. Washington, D.C.

1965   Architecture of the Maya Highlands. In *Handbook of Middle American
        Indians,* vol. 2, edited by R. Wauchope, pp. 76–94. Austin: University of
        Texas Press.

1982   Major Architecture and Caches. In *Excavations at Seibal, Department of Peten,
        Guatemala,* edited by G. R. Willey, Memoirs of the Peabody Museum of
        Archaeology and Ethnology, vol. 15, no. 1. Cambridge, Mass.: Peabody
        Museum of Archaeology and Ethnology, Harvard University.

Smith, C. A.

1976   Exchange Systems and the Spatial Distribution of Elites: The Organization
        of Stratification in Agrarian Societies. In *Regional Analysis,* vol. 2, *Systems,*
        edited by C. A. Smith, pp. 309–74. New York: Academic Press.

Smith, R. E.

1955   *Ceramic Sequence at Uaxactun, Guatemala.* Middle American Research
        Institute Publication 20. New Orleans.

Smith, R. E., G. R. Willey, and J. C. Gifford

1960   Type-Variety Analysis of Maya Pottery. *American Antiquity* 23:330–40.

Stark, B. L., and P. J. Arnold III, eds.

1997   *Olmec to Aztec: Settlement Patterns in the Ancient Gulf Lowlands.* Tucson:
        University of Arizona Press.

Stone, A.

1989   Disconnection, Foreign Insignia, and Political Expansion: Teotihuacan
        and the Warrior Stelae of Piedras Negras. In *Mesoamerica after the Decline of
        Teotihuacan, A.D. 700–900,* edited by R. A. Diehl and J. C. Berlo,
        pp. 153–72. Washington, D.C.: Dumbarton Oaks.

Storey, R.

1987   A First Look at the Paleodemography of the Ancient City of Teotihuacan.
        In *Teotihuacan: nuevos datos, nuevas síntesis, nuevos problemas,* edited by
        E. McClung de Tapia and E. C. Rattray, pp. 91–114. Mexico City: Instituto
        de Investigaciones Antropológicas, Universidad Autónoma de México.

Strömsvik, G.

1952   The Ball Courts at Copan with Notes on Courts at La Union, Quiriguá, San Pedro Pinula and Asuncion Mita. *Carnegie Institution of Washington Contributions to American Anthropology and History* 11(55):182–214.

Stuart, D.

1986   *The Chronology of Stela 4 at Copan.* Copán Note 12, Copan Mosaics Project and the Instituto Hondureño de Antropología e Historia. Austin, Texas.

1988   Blood symbolism in Maya Iconography. In *Maya Iconography*, edited by E. P. Benson and G. G. Griffin, pp.175–221. Princeton: Princeton University Press.

1989   *The "First Ruler" on Stela 24.* Copán Note 7, Copan Mosaics Project and the Instituto Hondureño de Antropología e Historia. Austin, Texas.

1997   Smoking Frog, K'inich Yax K'uk' Mo', and the Epigraphic Evidence for Ties between Teotihuacan and the Classic Maya. Paper presented at the symposium, "A Tale of Two Cities: Copan and Teotihuacan," Harvard University.

1998   "Fire Enters His House": Architecture and Ritual in Classic Maya Texts. In *Function and Meaning in Classic Maya Architecture*, edited by Stephen D. Houston, pp. 373–425. Washington, D.C.: Dumbarton Oaks Research Library and Collection.

1999   The Name of the Tikal Founder. Unpublished ms.

2000   "The Arrival of Strangers": Teotihuacan and Tollan in Classic Maya History. In *Mesoamerica's Classic Heritage*, edited by D. Carrasco, L. Jones, and S. Sessions, pp. 465–513. Boulder: Westview Press.

n.d.   K'inich Yax K'uk' Mo' and the Early History of Copan. In *Understanding Early Classic Copan*, edited by E. E. Bell, M. Canuto, and R. J. Sharer. Philadelphia: University Museum Publications, University of Pennsylvania. In press.

Stuart, D., and S. D. Houston

1994   *Classic Maya Place Names.* Studies in Pre-Columbian Art and Archaeology no. 33. Washington, D.C.: Dumbarton Oaks.

Stuart, D., S. D. Houston, and J. Robertson

1999   Recovering the Past: Classic Maya Language and Classic Mayan Gods. Notebook to the 23rd Linda Schele Forum on Maya Hieroglyphic Writing, March 13–14, 1999, University of Texas at Austin.

Stuart, D., and L. Schele

1986   Yax K'uk' Mo', the Founder of the Lineage of Copán. Copán Note 6. Unpublished ms.

Sugiyama, S.

1993   Worldview Materialized in Teotihuacan, Mexico. *Latin American Antiquity* 4(2):103–29.

1995   Mass Human Sacrifice and Symbolism of the Feathered Serpent Pyramid in Teotihuacan, Mexico. Ph.D. dissertation, Department of Anthropology, Arizona State University.

Taladoire, E.

1981   *Les terrains de jeu de balle (Mesoamerique et sud-ouest des Etat-Unis).* Etudes Mesoamericaines, Series II:4. Mission Archeologique et Ethnologique Française au Mexique.

Taschek, J. T.

1994   *The Artifacts of Dzibilchaltun, Yucatan, Mexico: Shell, Polished Stone, Bone, Wood, and Ceramics.* Middle American Research Institute Publication 50. New Orleans: Tulane University.

Tate, C. E.

1999   Patrons of Shamanic Power. *Ancient Mesomerica* 10(2):169–88.

Taube, K.

1992a   *The Major Gods of Ancient Yucatan.* Washington, D.C.: Dumbarton Oaks.

1992b   The Temple of Quetzalcoatl and the Cult of Sacred War at Teotihuacan. In *RES: Anthropology and Aesthetics* 21:53–87.

n.d.   The Early Classic Antecedents to Structure 10L-16, Copan, Honduras: Fire and the Evocation and Resurrection of K'inich Yax K'uk' Mo'. In *Understanding Early Classic Copan,* edited by E. E. Bell, M. Canuto, and R. J. Sharer, Philadelphia: University Museum Publications, University of Pennsylvania. In press.

Tedlock, D.

1985   *Popol Vuh: The Mayan Book of the Dawn of Life.* New York: Simon and Schuster.

Thompson, J. E. S.

1934   *Sky Bearers, Colors and Directions in Maya and Mexican Religion.* Carnegie Institution of Washington Publication 436:209–42.

1960   *Maya Hieroglyphic Writing: An Introduction.* Norman: University of Oklahoma Press.

1962   *A Catalog of Maya Hieroglyphs.* Norman: University of Oklahoma Press.

Thompson, R. H.

1958   *Modern Yucatecan Maya Pottery Making.* Memoirs of the Society for American Archaeology no. 15.

Tourtellot, G., III

1988   *Excavations at Seibal, Department of Petén, Guatemala: Peripheral Survey and Excavation, Settlement and Community Patterns.* Memoirs of the Peabody Museum of Archaeology and Ethnology, vol. 16. Cambridge, Mass.: Peabody Museum of Archaeology and Ethnology, Harvard University.

1990   Burials: A Cultural Analysis. In *Excavations at Seibal, Department of Petén, Guatemala,* edited by G. R. Willey, Memoirs of the Peabody Museum of Archaeology and Ethnology, vol. 17, no. 2. Cambridge, Mass.: Peabody Museum of Archaeology and Ethnology, Harvard University.

Tourtellot, G., III, and J. A. Sabloff

1994   Community and Structure at Sayil: A Case Study of Puuc Settlement. In *Hidden among the Hills: Maya Archaeology of the Northwest Yucatan Peninsula,* edited by H. J. Prem, pp. 71–92. Mockmuhl, Germany: Verlag von Flemming.

Townsend, R. F.

1979   *State and Cosmos in the Art of Tenochtitlan.* Studies in Pre-Columbian Art and Archaeology no. 20. Washington, D.C.: Dumbarton Oaks.

Traxler, L. P.

1996   Los grupos de patios tempranos de la Acrópolis de Copán. *Yaxkin* 14:35–54.

2001   The Royal Court of Early Classic Copan. In *Royal Courts of the Ancient Maya,* vol. 12, edited by T. Inomata and S. D. Houston, pp. 46–73. Boulder: Westview Press.

n.d.   At Court in Copan: Palace Groups of the Early Classic. Prepared for a projected volume of Maya palaces, edited by J. Christie.

Traxler, L. P., and R. J. Sharer

2001   Early Classic Organization at Copan: Prelude to the Late Classic Kingdom. Paper presented at the Annual Meeting of the Society for American Archaeology, New Orleans.

Trigger, B. G.

1990   A Thermodynamic Explanation of Symbolic Behaviour. *World Archaeology* 22(2):119–32.

Trik, A. S.

1963   The Splendid Tomb of Temple I at Tikal, Guatemala. *Expedition* 6(1):2–18.

Valdés, J. A., F. Fahsen, and G. Muñoz

1997   *Estela 40 de Tikal: Hallazgo y Lectura.* Instituto de Antropología e Historia (IDAEH) y Agencia Española de Cooperación Internacional, Guatemala.

Valenzuela, J.

1945   Las exploraciones efectuadas en Los Tuxtlas, Veracruz. *Anales del Museo de Arqueología, Historia y Etnografía (México)* 3:83–105.

Vidal, C., S. Teufel, and V. Fialko

1998 Exploraciones Arqueologicas en El Corozal, Centro Periferico de Tikal. In *IX Simposio de Investigaciones Arquológicas en Guatemala (1995)*, pp. 59–68. Guatemala City: Museo Nacional de Arqueología y Etnología.

Vogt, E. Z.

1969 *Zinacantan: A Maya Community in the Highlands of Chiapas.* Cambridge: Belknap Press of Harvard University Press.

Von Euw, E.

1985 *Corpus of Maya Hieroglyphic Inscriptions,* vol. 5, part 1, *Xultun.* Cambridge, Mass.: Peabody Museum of Archaeology and Ethnology, Harvard University.

Walker, W. H.

1995 Ceremonial Trash? In *Expanding Archaeology,* edited by J. M. Skibo, W. H. Walker, and A. E. Nielsen, pp. 67–79. Salt Lake City: University of Utah Press.

Walters, G. R., R. Torres Arce, W. Clary, F. Frost, and R. Chable

1985 Resultados preliminares de la Temporada 1985 en Tikal, Guatemala. Earthwatch and Triad Research Services, Columbia, Mo. Report to the Instituto de Antropología e Historia, Guatemala.

Wauchope, R.

1938 *Modern Maya Houses: A Study of Their Archaeological Significance.* Carnegie Institution of Washington Publication 502. Washington, D.C.

Webster, D. L.

1976 *Defensive Earthworks at Becan, Campeche, Mexico: Implications of Maya Warfare.* Middle American Research Institute Publication 41. Tulane University, New Orleans.

1985 Recent Settlement Survey in the Copan Valley, Honduras. *Journal of New World Archaeology* 5–4:39–50.

1998 Classic Maya Architecture: Implications and Comparisons. In *Function and Meaning in Classic Maya Architecture,* edited by S. D. Houston, pp. 5–47. Washington, D.C.: Dumbarton Oaks.

Webster, D. L., and N. Gonlin

1981 Household Remains of the Humblest Maya. *Journal of Field Archaeology* 15:169–90.

Whalen, M. E., and P. E. Minnis

1996 Ball Courts and Political Centralization in the Casas Grandes Region. *American Antiquity* 61: 732–46.

Wilk, R. R., and W. L. Rathje, eds.

1982   Archaeology of the Household: Building a Prehistory of Domestic Life. *American Behavioral Scientist* 26(6). Beverly Hills, Calif.: Sage Press.

Willey, G. R.

1974   The Classic Maya Hiatus: A Rehearsal for the Collapse? In *Mesoamerican Archaeology: New Approaches,* edited by N. Hammond, pp. 417–30. Austin: University of Texas Press.

1980   Towards a Holistic View of Ancient Maya Civilization. *Man* 15:249–66.

1982   Maya Archaeology. *Science* 215:260–67.

1991   Horizontal Integration and Regional Diversity: An Alternating Process in the Rise of Civilizations. *American Antiquity* 56:197–215.

Willey, G. R., W. R. Bullard, Jr., J. B. Glass, and J. C. Gifford

1965   *Prehistoric Maya Settlements in the Belize Valley.* Peabody Museum Paper no. 54. Cambridge, Mass.: Peabody Museum of Archaeology and Ethnology, Harvard University.

Willey, G. R., T. P. Culbert, and R. E. W. Adams

1967   Maya Lowland Ceramics: A Report from the 1965 Guatemala City Conference. *American Antiquity* 32: 289–315.

Willey, G. R., and P. Mathews, eds.

1985   *A Consideration of the Early Classic Period in the Maya Lowlands.* Institute for Mesoamerican Studies Publication 10. Albany: State University of New York at Albany.

Williamson, R. V.

1996   Excavations, Interpretations, and Implications of the Earliest Structures beneath Structure 10L-26 at Copan, Honduras. In *Eighth Palenque Round Table,* edited by M. G. Robertson, M. J. Macri, and J. McHargue, pp. 169–75. San Francisco: The Pre-Columbian Art Research Institute.

Wright, L. E.

1996   The Inhabitants of Tikal: A Bioarchaeological Pilot Project. Final Report to the Foundation for the Advancement of Mesoamerican Studies, Department of Anthropology, Texas A&M University.

Wright, L. E., M. Vásquez, M. A. Morales, and M. Valdizón

1999   La bioarqueología en Tikal: resultados del primer año del Proyecto Osteológico Tikal. Paper presented at the 13th Simposio de Investigaciones Arqueológicas en Guatemala, Museo de Arqueología y Etnología, Guatemala.

Zender, M., R. Armijo, and M. J. Gallegos-Gomora

2000   Vida y obra de Aj Pakal Tahn, un sacerdote del siglo VIII en Comalcalco, Tabasco. Paper presented at the 10th Encuentro Internacional, "Los investigadores de la cultura Maya," University of Campeche, Mexico.

Index

Abandonment: ceramic deposits and natural processes after, 49; of residential structures, 126–27, 140–41

aesthetics, of Central Acropolis, 205

Agencia Española de Cooperación Internacional, 283

agriculture: elites and land management for, 133; periphery and basic tools of, 157. *See also* diet; food; maize

Aguila Orange ceramics, 58

alignments, and architecture of Central Acropolis, 198–200

"altars," and plaza plans, 262–64

ambilocality, and settlement patterns, 129

ancestors: dynastic politics and carvings of names from Early Dynasty, 7; kinship groups and veneration of, 131–32

Animal Skull: and ceramics from burials, 73; and dynastic chronology, 25, 26, 29, 39n11, 43–44n40–41

archaeology: epigraphy and correlation of textual data with evidence from, 36; and research programs on materials from Tikal, 314–17; studies of periphery and fieldwork, 168–70. *See also specific sites and topics*

architecture: of Central Acropolis, 172, 182–84, 196–204; and founding-era acropolis in Copan, 332–47; Minor Centers and public, 109; and Mundo Perdido, 287–88, 291–92; of North Acropolis, 233–51; social differentiation and peripheries, 155–56; *talud-tablero* style of, 293–95, 347–48; Tikal and monumentality in Maya, 228–33, 237, 238, 240, 246, 249–50. See *also* plazas; temples

astronomy: and alignments in Central Acropolis, 200; and plaza plans, 266–67

Baby Jaguar, and dynastic iconography, 9, 15

B'aktun (Copan), 335

in burials, 78–79; and dynastic iconography, 12, 13; monuments and dynastic events, 34; and political power, 105

Ucanal, 16

Umbra period (A.D. 562–692), 24–30

University of Pennsylvania Museum, and influence of Tikal Project on direction of Maya research, 319

Uolantun: and ceramics, 87, 88, 91, 100–101, 147–48; and complexity of secondary sites, 313; and plaza plans, 258

Usulutan Style and Usulutan Ware, 56, 57, 71

utilitarian artifacts: and Cauac complex, 89–90; and Chuen complex, 87–88; and Eb complex, 85; and Eznab complex, 101–102; and Ik complex, 96; and Imix complex, 99; and Manik complex, 92–93; and Tzec complex, 86. *See also* lithic artifacts

Venus, and East Plaza Ball Court, 223, 224

vessel shapes, and classification of ceramics, 52

Vierra, Carlos, 172

visual deception, and architecture of Central Acropolis, 182–84

Wak Chan K'awiil (Double Bird): and construction of earthworks, 141; and dynastic chronology, 23–34, 42–43n33–34, 43n36

Wak Kab'nal (Naranjo capital), 31

warfare: and analysis of artifacts, 105–106; and ball-game rituals, 224; and construction boom in Late Classic, 31; and contacts between Copan and Teotihuacan, 349; and death of Chak Tok 'Ich'aak, 321; New Order and earliest description of in Maya text, 16–17; and earthworks, 141; and expansionism in Early Classic, 322–24; and settlement patterns, 129; and "star war" attack of Calakmul against Dos Pilas, 28; "star war" and defeat of Tikal, 23; and takeover of Copan, 321, 323–24

water-carrying jars, and prestige value, 164

West Plaza, of Mundo Perdido, 301

wheels, and Ik complex, 98

Wi Te (Copan), 340

witz, and *k'u* power in landscape features, 231

women, social rank and political power of elite in Classic period, 104. *See also* gender

woodworking, and specialized occupations in periphery, 167

worldview, and monumentality in Maya architecture, 230, 231–33

Xbalanque (god), 221–23

Xnuc complex, and censers, 103

X-Ray fluorescence, and ceramic pastes, 64–66

Xukpi Stone, 330, 346

School of American Research
Advanced Seminar Series

PUBLISHED BY SAR PRESS

CHACO & HOHOKAM: PREHISTORIC
REGIONAL SYSTEMS IN THE AMERICAN
SOUTHWEST
Patricia L. Crown &
W. James Judge, eds.

RECAPTURING ANTHROPOLOGY:
WORKING IN THE PRESENT
Richard G. Fox, ed.

WAR IN THE TRIBAL ZONE: EXPANDING
STATES AND INDIGENOUS WARFARE
R. Brian Ferguson &
Neil L. Whitehead, eds.

IDEOLOGY AND PRE-COLUMBIAN
CIVILIZATIONS
Arthur A. Demarest &
Geoffrey W. Conrad, eds.

DREAMING: ANTHROPOLOGICAL AND
PSYCHOLOGICAL INTERPRETATIONS
Barbara Tedlock, ed.

HISTORICAL ECOLOGY: CULTURAL
KNOWLEDGE AND CHANGING
LANDSCAPES
Carole L. Crumley, ed.

THEMES IN SOUTHWEST PREHISTORY
George J. Gumerman, ed.

MEMORY, HISTORY, AND OPPOSITION
UNDER STATE SOCIALISM
Rubie S. Watson, ed.

OTHER INTENTIONS: CULTURAL
CONTEXTS AND THE ATTRIBUTION
OF INNER STATES
Lawrence Rosen, ed.

LAST HUNTERS–FIRST FARMERS: NEW
PERSPECTIVES ON THE PREHISTORIC
TRANSITION TO AGRICULTURE
T. Douglas Price &
Anne Birgitte Gebauer, eds.

MAKING ALTERNATIVE HISTORIES:
THE PRACTICE OF ARCHAEOLOGY AND
HISTORY IN NON-WESTERN SETTINGS
Peter R. Schmidt &
Thomas C. Patterson, eds.

SENSES OF PLACE
Steven Feld & Keith H. Basso, eds.

CYBORGS & CITADELS:
ANTHROPOLOGICAL INTERVENTIONS IN
EMERGING SCIENCES AND TECHNOLOGIES
Gary Lee Downey & Joseph Dumit, eds.

ARCHAIC STATES
Gary M. Feinman & Joyce Marcus, eds.

CRITICAL ANTHROPOLOGY NOW:
UNEXPECTED CONTEXTS, SHIFTING
CONSTITUENCIES, CHANGING AGENDAS
George E. Marcus, ed.

THE ORIGINS OF LANGUAGE: WHAT
NONHUMAN PRIMATES CAN TELL US
Barbara J. King, ed.

REGIMES OF LANGUAGE: IDEOLOGIES,
POLITIES, AND IDENTITIES
Paul V. Kroskrity, ed.

BIOLOGY, BRAINS, AND BEHAVIOR: THE
EVOLUTION OF HUMAN DEVELOPMENT
Sue Taylor Parker, Jonas Langer, &
Michael L. McKinney, eds.

WOMEN & MEN IN THE PREHISPANIC
SOUTHWEST: LABOR, POWER, & PRESTIGE
Patricia L. Crown, ed.

HISTORY IN PERSON: ENDURING
STRUGGLES, CONTENTIOUS PRACTICE,
INTIMATE IDENTITIES
Dorothy Holland & Jean Lave, eds.

RECONSTRUCTING PREHISTORIC PUEBLO
SOCIETIES
William A. Longacre, ed.

NEW PERSPECTIVES ON THE PUEBLOS
Alfonso Ortiz, ed.

STRUCTURE AND PROCESS IN LATIN
AMERICA
Arnold Strickon &
Sidney M. Greenfield, eds.

THE CLASSIC MAYA COLLAPSE
T. Patrick Culbert, ed.

METHODS AND THEORIES OF
ANTHROPOLOGICAL GENETICS
M. H. Crawford & P. L. Workman, eds.

SIXTEENTH-CENTURY MEXICO:
THE WORK OF SAHAGUN
Munro S. Edmonson, ed.

ANCIENT CIVILIZATION AND TRADE
Jeremy A. Sabloff &
C. C. Lamberg-Karlovsky, eds.

PHOTOGRAPHY IN ARCHAEOLOGICAL
RESEARCH
Elmer Harp, Jr. ed.

MEANING IN ANTHROPOLOGY
Keith H. Basso & Henry A. Selby, eds.

THE VALLEY OF MEXICO: STUDIES IN
PRE-HISPANIC ECOLOGY AND SOCIETY
Eric R. Wolf, ed.

DEMOGRAPHIC ANTHROPOLOGY:
QUANTITATIVE APPROACHES
Ezra B. W. Zubrow, ed.

THE ORIGINS OF MAYA CIVILIZATION
Richard E. W. Adams, ed.

EXPLANATION OF PREHISTORIC CHANGE
James N. Hill, ed.

EXPLORATIONS IN ETHNOARCHAEOLOGY
Richard A. Gould, ed.

ENTREPRENEURS IN CULTURAL CONTEXT
Sidney M. Greenfield, Arnold Strickon,
& Robert T. Aubey, eds.

THE DYING COMMUNITY
Art Gallaher, Jr., &
Harlan Padfield, eds.

SOUTHWESTERN INDIAN RITUAL DRAMA
Charlotte J. Frisbie, ed.

LOWLAND MAYA SETTLEMENT PATTERNS
Wendy Ashmore, ed.

SIMULATIONS IN ARCHAEOLOGY
Jeremy A. Sabloff, ed.

CHAN CHAN: ANDEAN DESERT CITY
Michael E. Moseley & Kent C. Day, eds.

SHIPWRECK ANTHROPOLOGY
Richard A. Gould, ed.

ELITES: ETHNOGRAPHIC ISSUES
George E. Marcus, ed.

THE ARCHAEOLOGY OF LOWER CENTRAL
AMERICA
Frederick W. Lange &
Doris Z. Stone, eds.

LATE LOWLAND MAYA CIVILIZATION:
CLASSIC TO POSTCLASSIC
Jeremy A. Sabloff &
E. Wyllys Andrews V, eds.

Participants in the School of American Research advanced seminar
"Changing Perspectives on Tikal and the Development of Ancient
Maya Civilization," Santa Fe, New Mexico, September 1999.
Front row from left: William A. Haviland, Jeremy A. Sabloff,
Marshall Joseph Becker, and Christopher Jones. Standing from
left: Juan Pedro Laporte, Simon Martin, T. Patrick Culbert,
H. Stanley Loten, Hattula Moholy-Nagy, Robert J. Sharer,
Robert E. Fry, and Peter D. Harrison.